EX LIBRIS

VINTAGE CLASSICS

# THE LETTERS OF JOHN CHEEVER

John Cheever was born in Quincy, Massachusetts, in 1912, and went to school at Thayer Academy in South Braintree. He is the author of seven collections of stories and five novels. His first novel, *The Wapshot Chronicle*, won the 1958 National Book Award. In 1965 he received the Howells Medal for Fiction from the National Academy of Arts and Letters and in 1978 he won the National Book Critics Circle Award and the Pulitzer Prize. Shortly before his death in 1982 he was awarded the National Medal for Literature.

ALSO BY JOHN CHEEVER

Novels

*The Wapshot Chronicle*
*The Wapshot Scandal*
*Bullet Park*
*Falconer*
*Oh What a Paradise It Seems*

Short Stories

*The Way Some People Live*
*The Enormous Radio*
*The Housebreaker of Shady Hill*
*Some People, Places and Things*
*That Will Not Appear in My Next Novel*
*The Brigadier and the Golf Widow*
*The World of Apples*
*The Stories of John Cheever*

Journals

*The Journals*

JOHN CHEEVER

# The Letters of John Cheever

EDITED BY
Benjamin Cheever

WITH AN INTRODUCTION BY
Jay McInerney

**VINTAGE BOOKS**
London

Published by Vintage 2009

1  3  5  7  9  10  8  6  4  2

Copyright © Benjamin Cheever 1988
Introduction © Jay McInerney 2009

First published in Great Britain by Jonathan Cape in 1989
First published by Vintage in 1992

Vintage
Random House, 20 Vauxhall Bridge Road,
London SW1V 2SA

www.vintage-classics.info

Addresses for companies within The Random House Group Limited
can be found at: www.randomhouse.co.uk/offices.htm

The Random House Group Limited Reg. No. 954009

A CIP catalogue record for this book
is available from the British Library

ISBN 9780099529644

The Random House Group Limited supports The Forest
Stewardship Council (FSC), the leading international forest
certification organisation. All our titles that are printed on
Greenpeace approved FSC certified paper carry the FSC logo.
Our paper procurement policy can be found at:
www.rbooks.co.uk/environment

Printed and bound in Great Britain by
CPI Cox & Wyman, Reading, RG1 8EX

# Introduction

When I was a graduate student in the early eighties, there were few living writers more fervently admired by aspiring young fictionists than John Cheever. My teacher, Raymond Carver, was perhaps one of those few, and he himself was a great admirer, inevitably including Cheever in his class 'Form and Theory of the Short Story', along with Chekhov, Babel, Hemingway and Flannery O'Connor. *The Stories of John Cheever* had been published in 1979 to an avalanche of critical praise and spent months on the *New York Times* bestseller list – a virtually unprecedented feat for a collection of stories. And yet, he has never been widely read in the UK, while in the two plus decades since his death, several generations of American readers seem to have failed to make his acquaintance, in part perhaps because his work hasn't really managed to lodge itself in the curriculum of the academy.

This isn't the first time Cheever's reputation has been in danger of extinction. When I first heard his name during my undergraduate years Cheever was a byword for a kind of outdated domestic realism. His ostensibly realistic tales of suburban life were judged to be quaint and irrelevant by many commentators in the midst of the social and aesthetic upheavals of the sixties and the seventies. The appearance of the arch postmodern stories of Donald Barthelme in the pages of the *New Yorker*, where since the 1930s Cheever had published the majority of his stories, seemed to signal the end of the kind of traditional domestic narrative in which

Cheever supposedly specialised, even as fellow realists like John Updike, Norman Mailer and Phillip Roth outflanked him with their sexual frankness.

His letters from this period reflect a certain sense of feeling left behind. 'While all my friends are describing orgasims (sic) I still dwell on the beauty of the evening star.' (p. 263) And later, discussing the critical failure of his book *Bullet Park*, he writes, 'I may have made a mistake in using a suburb as a social metaphor. One would sooner read about fornicating in mountain passes and storms at sea.' (p. 277) In this he was no doubt echoing some of his critics. For much of his career Cheever came up against a longstanding historical bias in American literary criticism against any treatment of the middle and upper middle classes that wasn't overtly hostile or at least satirical. The classism inherent in some of the negative criticism of Cheever's work recalls the contemporary response to Fitzgerald's fiction, particularly the withering reviews of *Tender is the Night*, with its well-born, fashionable protagonists, published in the depths of the depression.

Even Malcolm Cowley, whose 1951 edition of Fitzgerald's stories helped revive his dormant reputation and who was a supporter of Cheever's career from the moment he published his first story, was always urging Cheever to get the hell out of the suburbs, implying that his work was in danger of becoming provincial. (One wonders if Cowley reconsidered after reading the few twee stories which came out of Cheever's year in Rome.) Cheever wrote memorably about Manhattan, where he spent nearly a decade, perhaps never so memorably as when he later described 'a long-lost world when the city of New York was still filled with a river light, when you heard the Benny Goodman quartets from a radio in the corner stationery store, and when almost everybody wore a hat.' (Preface to *Collected Stories*, p. vii)

But his best work is set in a small patch of Westchester County an hour or so out north of the city, and his name inevitably evokes the suburbs, that in-between kingdom which became emblematic of postwar American life, for better and for worse, and the vicissitudes of his critical reputation sometimes reflected the ambivalent if not downright hostile attitude of the urban intelligentsia towards his subject matter.

As of 1950, the year before Cheever moved to Scarborough New York, more than half of Americans dwelt in the suburbs. As Blake Bailey points out in his superb new biography, 'the suburbs of the Northeast were still an experiment of sorts – "an improvised way of life", as Cheever liked to say – and he was quite curious about things: given the cultural vacuum, what sort of traditions would be established by such a diverse group of educated, affluent people.' (Bailey, p.183) Like some of his New York friends, Cheever feared he might find the landscape too sterile for art, but Westchester proved to be his Yoknapatawpha County, and over the next fifteen years or so his talent blossomed as he produced a series of brilliant stories set in the fictional suburbs of Shady Hill and Bullet Park, and perfected the narrative sensibility which would infuse prosaic domestic scenes with a sense of cosmic wonder.

Cheever remained ambivalent about his adoptive home for the rest of his life; in an early letter he speaks of 'the mental emptiness of my friends and neighbors.' To Malcolm Cowley he writes: 'I have come to agree with you on the relative unimportance of Northern Westchester. I was delighted when we first came here to be asked to so many parties (I have always been afraid of being left alone) – delighted to find myself in the thick of such a rich, powerful and unselfconscious community. But . . . I seem to have been wrong in assuming that because they are rich – because they give an illusion of timeliness – their deterioration is significant.' (p.174) Already the rap against the suburbs was a cliche. In his classic 'The Housebreaker of Shady Hill', his suburban narrator tells us, 'Shady Hill, as I say, a *banlieue* and open to criticism by city planners, adventurers and lyric poets, but if you work in the city and have children to raise I can't think of a better place.' Cheever knew this was an unfashionable sentiment, and he can be an acute critic of the suburban idea. Francis Weed, the troubled protagonist of 'The Country Husband', recognises the maid passing canapés at a suburban party as the same woman he saw stripped and jeered as a Nazi collaborator shortly after the war in a little town in Normandy. He wonders if he should tell someone but realises the story would be entirely out of place in his community. Only days earlier, his family and friends had trouble accepting the fact that he'd been in a plane crash. 'The people in the Farquarsons living room seemed united in their tacit claim that there had been no past, no war – that there was no danger or trouble in the world.' Francis begins to scorn this artificial society and its conventions, only to find himself facing the void.

Cheever's most luminous fiction ultimately celebrates the world around him in spite of its banality, and occasionally portrays his chosen land as a kind of Arcadia. In the closing lines of 'The Country Husband', having survived the plane crash and a torrid passion for his babysitter, Francis Weed carves wood in his basement while outside his neighbour plays the Moonlight Sonata and his wife trims the roses in her garden. 'A door on the Babcock's terrace flies open, and out comes Mrs. Babcock without any clothes on, pursued by a naked husband. (Their children are away at boarding school, and their terrace is screened by a hedge.) Over the terrace they go and in the kitchen door, as passionate and handsome a nymph and satyr as you will find on any wall in Venice.' (*Collected Stories*, p.446) The story closes with a soaring, improbable image: 'Then it is dark; it is a night where kings in golden suits ride elephants over the mountains.' There may be a touch of Fitzgerald here, but it's hard to imagine Richard Yates or John Updike or almost anyone else writing this line, and it reflects the whimsical, romantic, fantastical strain of his imaginative world. In fact, for all his reputation as a domestic realist, some of his most successful stories employ elements of what would later be known as magic realism, although they have their precedents in Hawthorne and Washington Irving. In 'The Enormous Radio', an apartment dwelling couple are made privy to the secrets of their neighbours via the agency of a new radio with supernatural powers; in 'The Swimmer' a middle-aged man who decides to swim through every pool between a garden party and his own home returns to find it abandoned – his family long gone – having aged along the way like an amphibious Rip Van Winkle.

For all the emotional wisdom of his fictive voice and his scrupulous observation of the manners and mores of a generation that prized the ideal of adulthood more than our own, Cheever maintained a childlike sense of wonder at the simple pleasures of nature and the fellowship of humans. In a 1964 interview with *Time* magazine in which his picture graced the cover, Cheever said, 'My sense of literature is a sense of giving, not diminishment. I know of almost no pleasure greater than having a piece of fiction draw together disparate incidents so that they relate to one another and confirm that feeling that life itself is a creative process, that one thing is put purposefully up on another, that what is lost in one encounter is replenished in the next, and that we possess some power to make sense of what takes place.' (*Letters*, p. 240) It would be many years before Cheever's readers realised how hard he struggled to make sense, and to maintain his sense of giving and of wonder.

The *Time* cover story solidified Cheever's persona as the bard of Westchester and anatomist of monogamy, but the posthumous publication of his letters and journals revealed the bitter struggles and conflicts of Cheever's psychic life. In the letters we see the semi-public Cheever, wry and whimsical, the suburban squire documenting his domestic life and the ups and downs of his career. His references to drinking become more ominous over the years: 'I try not to drink until noon but I am not always successful', he confides to his Russian translator.

And yet he can tell that same correspondent, 'I would like to live in a world in which there are no homosexuals but I suppose Paradise is thronged with them.' (p. 264). But within a year a series of letter to the novelist Allan Gurganus, then an openly homosexual graduate student at the University of Iowa, clearly expresses his desire for his student. 'Dearest Allan, My sexual and epistolary importunities are well-known. I do wish you had been more yielding about the former.' (p. 304) Later in life, Cheever's struggle with alcoholism became public and he finally went into treatment. He began dropping hints about his homosexual urges, and his 1978 novel *Falconer* shocked some of his readers with its portrait of a middle class convict who falls in love with a fellow prisoner.

The publication of the letters gave strong hints of Cheever's conflicts but it was only with the posthumous publication of his journals in 1991 that we became aware of the extent to which he had been tormented by his lifelong recognition of his own bisexuality, and the degree to which his persona as a suburban monogamist and 'a celebrant of light', had been constructed in part as a defense against his sense of his own dark and sinful nature. Even as he celebrated the joys of domestic carnality, the Ovid of Ossining was lusting after the paperboy and trying desperately to make it through the morning without a drink. There were those who felt that the journals somehow invalidated or at least called into question his accomplishment. Even Bob Gottlieb, who edited the *Journals*, had his doubts about the enterprise, and the reviews tended to convey a sense of sadness and even disgust. John Updike, who confessed that he was shocked by the book, wrote that 'Cheever's confessions posthumously administer a Christian lesson in the dark gulf between outward appearance and inward condition . . .' (Bailey, p.671) It is a lesson that shouldn't shock sophisticated readers and yet the disparity between Cheever's public persona during his lifetime and the posthumous revelations may help in part to explain why his place in the canon seems at present so uncertain. Some misguided notion of authenticity seems to be at stake here, an unexamined notion of art as an unmediated transcript of personal experience. A persona, once acquired, is difficult to modify and fine tune. After the publication of the journals Cheever had two diametrically opposed personae, one of which made him a punch line on an episode of *Seinfeld* when a supposed cache of his homosexual love letters turns up to embarrass one of the characters.

What is clear from reading the journals and the letters is that Cheever's was a divided nature and he chose to struggle toward what he perceived to be the light. In fact, Cheever's *Journals* contain some of his finest and most luminous prose, alongside the sordid personal revelations. And the fiction, the short fiction in particular, seems even more miraculous against the backdrop of the journals. Cheever's celebration of nature, of the gossamer bonds of friendship and community, and even the joys of heterosexual union, seem to me all the more powerful for being hard earned. There have been thousands of sexually conflicted alcoholics, but only one of them wrote 'The Housebreaker of Shady Hill' and 'The Sorrows of Gin'.

The reissue of his letters along with publication of Blake Bailey's *Cheever: A Life*, should be the occasion to reconsider the life and the work. The letters provide us with a fascinating record of the man and the writer. Indeed the earliest letters are artless enough to make us marvel that the author would go on to become one of the great stylists of the language. It's fascinating to watch Cheever grope his way toward mastery as he attempts to use his increasing eloquence to disguise his fears and his desires. Ultimately, it is the stories which make the case for Cheever as a great American writer, one who continues to deserve our attention and admiration.

Jay McInerney, 2009

# ACKNOWLEDGMENTS

This book itself is an acknowledgment: first it's an acknowledgment of my father's talent, then of the affection he felt for the people to whom he wrote. Finally, this collection acknowledges the love that they, in their turn, felt for him. He kept no carbons, and urged people to throw away his letters. Had it not been for the prescience of his correspondents, no letters would have been saved, and no book would have been possible.

First I want to thank William Maxwell. He took the time to talk with me at length about my father, and to add substantially to my knowledge of the man I knew so well. He's been my Father Confessor and my friend. And when all else was said and done he read over the manuscript and made suggestions that were both delicate and brilliant.

Tanya Litvinov provided me with a batch of magnificent letters. Many of these had been lost for a time, and she unearthed them and sent me copies. She also wrote me kind and thoughtful letters about my father. Her support and goodwill meant more to me than I can say.

Josephine Herbst was dead when I began this project, but I don't believe people like Josie die, and often felt her at my elbow.

I hardly knew Eleanor Clark when I began to work on this book, but she too has been a great help. Her recollections of my father's youth were as helpful to me as were the letters she provided.

Ned Rorem took the time to shed light on the riddle of my father's complex sexual nature. He told me, among other things, that for my father, orgasm was always accompanied by a vision of sunshine, or flowers.

John Updike was a good and loyal friend to my father. His notes to me and my father's letters to and about him seem to illustrate that even in the most competitive situation, friendship between good men will not only survive, it will triumph.

Saul Bellow too has been generous with letters and with support. His friendship was also of great importance to my father during his lifetime.

I must also thank his son, Adam Bellow. The long walks we took together taught me a good deal about what it means to be the son of a well-known writer, and what it doesn't mean.

Philip Schultz didn't have a lot of letters, but he is a great listener, and if he had been my psychiatrist instead of my friend, he would now be a wealthy man.

Raymond Bonner gave consistent and brilliant advice. When we ran together in the afternoon, he told me over and over that writing a book is just like running a marathon, "except that every time you cross the finish line, they move it."

Because this book is about my father the line between work and life is often arbitrary, and this is particularly true when it comes to family. It was my wife Janet's narrow back that most often bore the weight of my doubt and self-loathing. It's a cliché for a man finishing a book to thank his wife for having withstood his abuse, but it doesn't seem like a cliché when it's your own kitchen, and you've got your back up against the sink, and you can hear yourself shouting. It seems then like the first fight in the world between the first man and the first woman. Janet has known this work in its every phase, but she will not learn until she reads this, that during one of my rages I shattered the leg of the old wooden rocking chair. Later, in a fit of remorse, I repaired the break with glue and the chair still works, as does the marriage.

It was my sister, Susan, who first urged me to put this collection together, and I'm still not sure if I should be thankful for that. But since then she has been consistently supportive. Parts of this book must be painful for my mother, but she has shared my commitment to the whole truth, and for this courage I am extremely thankful. My brother Fred has also been generous and enthusiastic.

John Weaver has come to seem almost a member of the family. He has been in on the project from the beginning. His vast, secret store of letters has been a joy, and his support has been unstinting. To me his entire personal and professional life seems to have been a brilliant demonstration of loyalty and charity.

Elizabeth Logan Collins provided helpful background and a fat envelope of great letters. She also manages to make sure that my mother and I go with her to the Metropolitan Museum of Art at least once a year.

Joe Hotchkiss, Michael Bessie and Arthur Spear have all three been friendly and forthcoming. Each of them provided information, and each of them bought me at least one lunch. I brought my own lunch when I saw Hope Lange, but I think she would have fed me if I'd let her, and her recollections of my father were both vivid and thoughtful. Frederick Exley also accompanied his packet of letters with a note to me, and followed this note up with phone conversations.

Thanks also to Peter Canning and Jeremy Dole for encouragement, and to Martin Garbus for legal guidance.

Jane Cheever Carr wasn't able to turn up any new material, but I believe she did make some unsuccessful trips to the attic, and for this I am thankful. I am now acutely aware of how hard it can be to go into attics.

I first met Andrew Wylie years ago. Despite his carefully nurtured reputation for toughness, I have known him only as a good and gentle friend. In this and in other projects his enthusiasm and support have been a great comfort.

Allen H. Peacock has been my editor at Simon and Schuster, and he's been a gentleman in this most ungentlemanly of worlds. I think he knew how painful this project would be for me, and he has guarded me scrupulously against any hells that were not of my own making. It has also been a pleasure to work with Sophie Sorkin on the copy desk at Simon and Schuster.

I want to thank the Yaddo Corporation and the American Academy and Institute and Arts and Letters. I was also helped by the staff at the Beinecke Rare Book and Manuscript Library at Yale University and by Robert Rosenthal, the Curator of Special Collections at the University of Chicago Library. Thanks also to John Leggett, the Director of the Program in Creative Writing at the University of Iowa, and to Elizabeth A. Falsey of the Houghton Library at Harvard University. The University of Delaware Library provided material, as did the Newberry Library in Chicago and the Brandeis University Library.

I have been the undeserving recipient of an enormous reservoir of good feeling that still exists toward my father. Every letter in this book seems to attest to that good feeling. Among those who wrote me and sent me copies of letters are Stephen Becker, Peter and Ebbie Blume, Mimi and Philip Boyer, Frances Lindley, Bev Chaney, Jr., Malcolm Cowley, John and Mary Dirks, Don and Katrina Ettlinger, Christopher Lehmann-Haupt, Natalie Robins and Philip Roth. Helen Puner, Esse Lee and Allan Gurganus also provided letters. Tom Glazer gave me a letter and lunch. Candida Donadio and I had one meeting which I enjoyed enormously. She didn't give me any letters, but she did tell my fortune. Robert Cowley and I have had lunch every six months or so, but I think this has been more in the spirit of friendship than research. It's been hard in every case to separate my desire for information from the extreme pleasure I have found in the company of my father's old friends.

If immortality can be found in the memories of those people we loved, then my father is as alive today as he was when he came squalling into the world on May 27, 1912.

# CONTENTS

*The Letters of*

# JOHN CHEEVER

# THE MAN
# I THOUGHT I KNEW

* * *

When my father stopped breathing, I tried to start his lungs again by blowing air through his lips. Then I put my arms around him. My mother and sister joined in the embrace. I could hear my sister and my mother crying and then I could hear myself.

We were standing at the end of the bed when the man from the funeral home arrived. All three faces were wet with tears.

My father was naked except for a fresh white cast on one leg. He had taken a bad fall earlier in the week. His skin was pale and luminous, like parchment, and I remember thinking that it looked as if it still had many years of wear in it.

The undertaker carried a folding stretcher with wheels and a green body bag. He was a burly man in a dark pin-striped suit, which he wore in precisely the way a workman might wear a pair of coveralls. The formality of his dress seemed not to indicate respect. First he assembled his contraption, then he asked us to leave the room. We refused. "I don't think you want to see this," he said. "He's got a catheter on." We said we knew. We said we had put the catheter on. The undertaker shrugged and went to work. He breathed heavily as he moved. He handled the body the way one would handle a five-foot-six-inch sack of potatoes. He got it onto the gurney and zippered it into the green plastic shroud.

Then he rolled the stretcher out of the room and began to yank and force it down the stairs to the driveway. "Can I help?" I asked. "No," he said, jouncing the gurney down another flight of stairs. I followed the stretcher out onto the driveway.

"Better treat him well, or he'll bite you," I said.

"That's all right," the man said. "I handled Rockefeller."

"Yes," I said, "but Rockefeller was dead."

It's still difficult to understand that my father is dead. I've been working ever since that afternoon toward two apparently contradictory goals. The first is to acknowledge this death; the second is to defeat it.

My father died at about 4 P.M. in the master bedroom of his house in Ossining, New York. That was on June 18, 1982. Since then I've found a lot of moderately successful ways of bringing him back, of making him close and real. I wear his watch, reread his books, speak with his friends. I read his letters.

He used to urge me to throw them away. "Saving a letter is like trying to preserve a kiss," he said. I was an obedient son, but in this case I didn't listen. I treasured his correspondence, and so did a lot of other people. And the reason these letters are so powerful, the reason they bring him so vividly to mind, is that the writer honestly thought that they were going to be thrown away.

My father was extremely, almost compulsively candid with his children. I knew when he had had too much gin, I knew when he embarrassed himself, I knew when he committed adultery. I even knew what shade of lipstick she was wearing. I often heard more than I wanted to. But I was still shocked by some of what I found in the letters.

The most difficult revelation for me, as a son, was the extent of my father's homosexuality. It's impossible for me to be objective about this, or to separate his fears from my own, but he was certainly troubled by the issue. In one of the papers found on his desk after he died he had written: " 'You are afraid of skating on transparent ice, aren't you,' said my daughter. 'I noticed that you and Ben are afraid of skating where you can see the bottom.' That I'm afraid is quite true. I was for years and years afraid of the fact that I might be a homosexual. I can't think of a more legitimate source of fear. I had homosexual instincts and the only homosexuals I knew corresponded in no way to what I hoped to make of myself. . . ." This was one of the ways in which he seems to have failed to meet his own standards.

I was surprised by the fact that he was sometimes capable of cold-blooded hypocrisy. I knew he told stories, and I knew that he would change them at will, but I always thought he did this for the sake of the story, and in order to increase the pleasure it gave. I still think that this was most often the case, but there are also instances in which he can be seen flattering a writer, then savaging that same writer when corresponding with a mutual colleague.

But these grievances, and the far more common complaints of the child of an alcoholic, are not the subject of this book. These letters were written by an extraordinary man, and what was extraordinary about my father was not his cruelty or his failings. What was extraordinary was his joy and the talent he had for passing that joy on to the people around him.

The upbeat is often associated with the simplistic, with an unwillingness to see the dark side of things or to recognize its temptations. This was not the case with my father. After he was treated rather grandly in a *Time* cover story titled "Ovid in Ossining," the novelist Josephine Herbst wrote him to say that the celebration of life trumpeted in the *Time* story didn't come out of nothing, but rather out of a deep pessimism. The more I learn about him, the more this rings true.

In that same *Time* story, which ran on March 27, 1964, my father said, "I know almost no pleasure greater than having a piece of fiction draw together disparate incidents so that they relate to one another and confirm that feeling that life itself is a creative process, that one thing is put purposefully upon another, that what is lost in one encounter is replenished in the next, and that we possess some power to make sense of what takes place."

The attempt to bring life together into a galaxy that was interconnected and that made a moral sense did not stop when he stepped away from the typewriter. Everything he saw and touched was alive and had a meaning, a positive or negative charge. We used to play a game in which we would pick out a stranger on the street and imagine the rest of his life for him, the silvered wallpaper in his bathroom, the burned muffins he preferred for breakfast, his mortal allergy to egg yolks.

When I was living at home he used to wait up for me at night in a yellow armchair, which stood by the fireplace in the dining room. He usually had a glass of gin on the table and a cigarette in his hand. He'd want to talk. Sometimes he wanted to hear about my troubles, sometimes he wanted to speak about his own. He used to say that I must wish I had a father who didn't drink so much, and I'd always say no. I suppose this makes me what Alcoholics Anonymous would call an enabler, somebody who makes it all right for the alcoholic to destroy himself. Maybe so, but I thought then and think now that you have to take the people you love pretty much the way you find them. Their worst qualities are often linked with their very best ones.

When we were done talking, we'd take all the pillows off the upholstered chairs and sofas so that the dogs would not sleep on them, and we'd head up to bed. His later troubles with booze have colored my recollections of his drinking, and it is certainly true that our relationship had its ups and downs. He liked to say that he remembered quarreling with me only once, but his memory was much more selective than my own. And I have sometimes thought of him with bitterness, but it remains that while I am not a heavy drinker myself, or a smoker, I still find the smell of gin and tobacco a delicious combination.

My father was a man of massive and fundamental contradictions. He was an adulterer who wrote eloquently in praise of monogamy. He was a bisexual who detested any sign of sexual ambiguity. Growing up, I didn't know what the word "homophobic" meant, but I knew what the word "faggot" meant, and I heard it used. My father once said his epitaph should read: "Here lies John Cheever/He never disappointed a hostess/Or took it up the ass." This sounds today like a classic case of denial. It seems everybody should have known that John Cheever was bisexual, but I didn't even suspect it until he was in his sixties. Some of his friends and neighbors deny it to this day. And yet his wasn't a case of simple closet homosexuality. It seems to me now that the deception was an essential part of his character. Besides, his homosexual impulses never eclipsed his heterosexual ones. While in his late sixties, when he was writing wickedly obscene love letters to more than one young man, he was also getting up at seven in the morning to fix a tray for my mother. This would include an English muffin, an egg, fresh orange juice and a bud vase with a rose. He would take it to her in bed, and then he'd try to get in after it.

But he was quite well aware of his contradictions, and of the simple and ridiculously inadequate explanations that could be made for them. From a letter in 1966 to his friend the writer John Weaver: "I went to a shrink named Hayes who said that I had developed a tragic veneer of amiability in order to conceal my basic sense of alienation and hostility and I was brooding about this an hour ago when the phone rang and it was ESQUIRE saying that they were doing a spread of Janet Landgard and that Janet had asked if dear Mister Shiffers (a common mispronunciation of Cheever) would please write her captions because she didn't want her captions written by anyone but Shiffers and I said that

I would write the captions and that's where things stand." Janet Land-gard was an actress whom he'd met on the set of *The Swimmer*, and had described in another letter to Weaver as "this terrific 18-year-old dish. She has natural, honey-colored hair and enormous pale blue eyes and slightly crooked teeth and beautiful helpless-looking legs."

Despite, or perhaps because of, these contradictions, John Cheever was successful, not just as a writer of fiction but as a father, a husband, friend and lover. And he was great fun. Here, for example, are excerpts from two letters written in 1965 to Frederick Exley, author of *A Fan's Notes* (1968). My father had recently been to a dinner at the White House.

... Coming in late last night I opened the ice-box and grabbed at a piece of cold meat, swallowing a false tooth which included a plastic backside and two sharp hooks. Neither the doctor nor the dentist (a Watertown boy) are expected in their offices until tomorrow, but noon is approaching and I seem to be experiencing no more than the customary anguish of an overcast Monday. I keep telling myself that I am rich, beloved by many passionate and exceptionally beautiful women, the owner of an 18th century stone house and a brace of faithful Labrador retrievers, the father of three comely and brilliant children and a frequent guest at the White House. How could such a paragon be felled by a false tooth?

And a week later:

Dear Mr. Exley,

It was the Watertown-born dentist who, in the end, seemed to suffer most. Having got me bibbed and tuckered he asked what part of the bridge had I swallowed. When I said that I had swallowed it all he got white. I said cheerfully that I thought I had passed it. He said, in a hoarse voice, that I couldn't have passed it without medical assistance. "Not" he said, "with those hooks." I wished to hell he would shutup; but he seems to have been wrong. It is true that when I fart these days it sounds like a police whistle but I suffer little pain and it's very easy for me to get cabs.

I remember the night my father thought he had swallowed his false teeth. We had been swimming at a neighbor's pool, and after the discovery we returned with a flashlight, which he held while I dived for the bridgework. We didn't find it. The false teeth were ultimately recovered from the pool's filter system, and I seem to remember that the gardener was looking for a diamond ring that had been lost by some other, more prosperous bather. There was in any case no significant alteration in the tone or volume of my father's farts. I make these points because it is important to know from the outset that my father's interest in telling a good story was greater than his interest in what we might consider the facts. He touched on this in a letter he sent to John Updike in 1980, when he was writing *Oh What a Paradise It Seems* (Knopf, 1982): "I'm working on a novel but I find it very difficult to say so. I wonder if you have this difficulty. At the end of the evening people sometimes ask: 'Are you still writing?' 'Oh yes,' I say, 'I'm writing the definitive biography of Booth Tarkington.' It works but it isn't the truth."

What worked often wasn't true. These distortions, however, are frequently entertaining, and sometimes revealing. In this book, I've included excerpts from his journals and his fiction, so that one can see the life—sometimes the same incident—reflected differently through the prism of his prose.

This will not be a collection of letters in the conventional sense, but rather, I hope, a picture of the man as revealed through his correspondence. No significant episode in my father's life passed without being recounted in letters. He wrote between ten and thirty a week, and he wrote them under all sorts of circumstances. He wrote them to his wife and his children, to his mistresses, to his editors, and to the men with whom he was sexually involved. He wrote when he was at home and nothing much was happening, but he also wrote from Rome, from hospital beds and dry-out tanks. He wrote from army camps in Georgia and from the Beverly Wilshire. And he wrote well. His *New Yorker* editor William Maxwell, with whom he corresponded for more than forty years, said, "John Cheever never wrote a bad letter. When he wrote to me it was always precisely as if he were on the high wire."

He wasn't much good on the phone. "I sent you a letter," he'd say, and then there'd be a long, painful pause. What he had to say—exactly what he had to say—was in the mail. And often his letters communicated that which he had not, or would not have otherwise, made clear. For instance, during my first months at college, I was arrested in Cincinnati, Ohio, while protesting against the war in Vietnam. It was not until some months afterward that I discovered that my father approved of my action, or at the very least approved of me in spite of it. He wrote that he had been invited to Cincinnati to make a speech. He wrote me that he had turned the offer down: "I told them I would not make a potholder in the city that had arrested my eldest son."

One of the points my sister made in her memoir *Home Before Dark* (Houghton Mifflin, 1984) was that our father didn't have a star-studded social life. He knew many of the outstanding writers and editors of his time, but he didn't see them often. He did, however, have an exalted correspondence. He wrote to Saul Bellow, Malcolm Cowley, William Maxwell, Eleanor Clark, John Updike, Josie Herbst, John Weaver, E. E. Cummings, and the actress Hope Lange. The bulk of his correspondence has been lost. He kept no carbons and destroyed most of what he got in return. There are, however, still thousands of letters that were saved by the people to whom they were sent, letters that reveal the parallel development of the writer and the man.

The connection between his life and his work was intimate, but it was also mysterious. My father was fond of saying that fiction was not "crypto-autobiography." One obvious reason for this statement is that it protected him from the attacks of friends and family who felt that they'd been libeled in his prose. But his oft-repeated argument was that good writing so transcended the life it came from that an examination of the life could lead to gross misunderstandings. He was right, of course; but these are his letters, not his dental records. His correspondence will not provide a concrete explanation of his life or his fiction, but it should shed light on both. It has for me.

In putting together this book I was surprised and impressed by the difficulties my father had faced in making his living as a writer. He was thirty-five when I was born, in 1948, and by the time I became aware of the world around me, his professional and financial positions seemed secure. It was not until I read these letters that I fully realized how hard won that security had been, and how fragile it remained. I had not known, for instance, that he had been trying to write a novel since he was in his teens. I had assumed that being a short-story writer for *The New Yorker* was sufficient, but this was not the way he himself looked at it. In 1947 he wrote to John Weaver that financial necessities had forced him to back off on the novel once again and work on short stories, and that "I want to write short stories like I want to fuck a chicken."

Malcolm Cowley encouraged him early on to try to get an advance for a novel, so he showed chapters of one of the early versions to Malcolm and threw them away after his mentor expressed reservations. Another version, titled *The Holly Tree*, was rejected by Simon and Schuster in the 1930s. Houghton Mifflin turned down a manuscript, or at least an outline, after that. He came back with another book in 1952, which Random House didn't want to publish. *The Wapshot Chronicle* was finally published by Harper & Row in 1957.

Reviews of his early collections of short stories condemned him for excessive control. He wrote beautiful, polite little pieces, they said. He was a great middlebrow writer. He wrote stories that were liked by the wrong people, for the wrong reasons. The curse of being condemned as the skilled craftsman of the suburban short story was only momentarily broken by the success of *The Wapshot Chronicle*, and although *The Wapshot Scandal*, published by Harper & Row in 1964, was well reviewed, the praise was not universal. Stanley Edgar Hyman had this reaction: "When a highly esteemed short-story writer tries a novel and fails at it, in this amazing country, he is rewarded just as though he had succeeded. . . . John Cheever's 'The Wapshot Chronicle' won a National Book Award. In 'The Wapshot Scandal,' Cheever has again tried, and again failed, to make short-story material jell as a novel. As a two-time loser, he can probably expect the Pulitzer Prize." When my father moved away from the more traditional novel in 1969 with *Bullet Park* (Knopf) the reaction was more intensely negative.

This was a hard time, and as his alcoholism grew more acute and the diseases that accompanied it more pronounced, there was a good deal of unhappiness in the family. This period, however, was the exception and not the rule. It is a cliché in this age to picture the artist as a tortured soul, and it is certainly true that my father knew great depths of unhappiness and uncertainty; at the same time it is important to recall that he could also be, and often was, deliriously happy. Speaking about this with Bill Maxwell, I said it would be inaccurate to see my father as an unhappy man.

"It would not only be inaccurate," said Bill, "it would be impertinent."

I talked with Bill about how much I'd enjoyed my father's company in the summers when my mother went off to the family place in New Hampshire and I stayed home to work, he to write. "It was like there were no adults in the house. We used to eat Stouffer's Frozen Roast Beef Hash. We'd sit on the slate stones of the porch at the house in Ossining, and we'd put the aluminum container down between us. We'd each have a fork, we'd eat toward the middle, and whoever ate fastest got the most. I remember the dogs would sit around us in a circle and watch this with great interest. We were always laughing, and he was in his fifties then."

"Yes," said Bill, "he lived like a child."

"Except a child can't ever do what he wants. Someone would make a child eat at the table."

"That's right," said Bill. "He lived as a child would live if a child were able."

It would be a mistake to think that these childlike qualities made him either pitiful or helpless. It would also be the kind of mistake that is all too frequently made. In the writing of biography, a lesser man can convincingly drag down his betters, seizing one genuinely vile or ridiculous characteristic and using this to color our perception of the entire man. It doesn't seem to occur to the chronicler that a certain degree of wickedness may be as essential in the unusual man as it is common in the common man.

The theory of evolution teaches us that once in a long while there is born a fish that can walk on land, and that this fish survives and prospers. I've always had trouble with this concept, because it seems to me that when one fish learns to walk, the others respond by cutting him dead at cocktail parties, firing him from his job at the firm and foreclosing on his mortgage. The chances of such a fish prospering seem infinitesimal. But my father was such a fish, and he did prosper, but deception was part of the trick. He showed the world what he thought it wanted to see. The picture he presented was sharp, witty, cogent, and often false.

Discovering that I was one of the deceived has been a painful process. Here, as in many places where I've had difficulty understanding his life, his fiction is instructive. I think of the opening pages of *The Wapshot Scandal*. It is Christmas Eve and old Mr. Jowett, the station-master, is looking out onto his beloved St. Botolphs. A heavy snow is falling. "It was one place in a million, Mr. Jowett thought. Even with his pass, he had never wanted much to travel. The village, he knew, had, like any other, its brutes and its shrews, its thieves and its perverts, but like any other it meant to conceal these facts under a shine of decorum that was not hypocrisy but a guise or mode of hope."

So perhaps his decorum was not bald hypocrisy but a guise or mode of hope.

Knowing what I now know, I could not present a sanitized image of the man, nor would he want me to. One has to have an almost total commitment to the recognition of the brutish aspects of life to write as he did. Some people were deeply offended by his fiction for this reason. He often said that he wrote out of an impulse to "bring glad tidings." He would not, however, diminish the world in order to make it a more cheerful place. He loved life too much for this, and had too much respect for his readers.

The man who comes alive again in these letters is more complete than the man I thought I knew and knew I loved. He is not, however, a stranger to me, any more than he would be a stranger to any of the many other people who cared about him or admired his work. He is intensely himself, and he gives the world a blessed wholeness, a wholeness that I always felt in his company, and that I sorely miss.

\* \* \*

## A NOTE ON THE EDITING

My father often said that "interest is the first canon of aesthetics," and I've tried in selecting and editing these letters to make interest my overriding concern.

*New Yorker* editor Robert Gottlieb told me that when he put together *The Stories of John Cheever* (Knopf, 1978) he found that the earlier sketches were just not as good as the later work. I remember doubting this judgment. I thought of my father's talent as a constant. I know now that Gottlieb was right, and that the stories and the letters my father wrote improved as he went on. The early letters had wide margins and frequently ran to two pages, and sometimes even three or four. By 1950 the style was crisper, the margins narrower, and a letter rarely went more than three paragraphs. I am, however, reproducing some of the earlier and sometimes weaker correspondence at a greater length than quality demands, so that these letters can act as a foil to the better, later writing and because the man stands revealed in a different light. Besides, I find it fascinating to watch him learning how to write. The process is clearly visible in his letters. I don't believe he ever rewrote a letter, and in some cases he appears not to have even reread them.

Where parts of paragraphs have been cut I have indicated this with three dots. The name of one correspondent has been omitted for reasons of discretion, and I have also taken the liberty of changing full names to initials in the cases of people who do not play an important part in the exposition, but who get a nasty glancing blow. The letters are just as amusing without the proper names, and less damage is done. In other cases identities cannot be hidden, and I thank all those whose exposure has helped make this book possible.

Errors in spelling and grammar have not been corrected except in those cases in which a correction seemed essential for understanding. This is not because it's fun for me to find my father out in a mistake, although it is fun, but because I want to let the reader in on the spontaneity with which the letters were written.

My father almost never dated his correspondence. "Tuesday," he'd write at the top of the page, and sometimes "Tuesday, I think." I recall him telling me once that he had written half a dozen letters and dated them July 15, and then realized that it was August. This seemed funnier then than it does now.

The chronology I've worked out is accurate in its larger features, and for this I owe a great deal to the help I've gotten from the friends who saved his letters and sometimes even the envelopes they came in. The brackets—[——]—indicate dates I have added, or other small notes of time and place. Otherwise the letter headings included are reproduced exactly.

Whatever my father would have felt about this project, it is certainly accurate to say that he never prepared for it. The sort of vanity that such preparations might imply would have seemed repellent to him. In late 1959 his old friend the novelist Josephine Herbst wrote him that she was saving his correspondence. The Joe Schrank referred to in his reply was a mutual acquaintance, and was not held to be particularly discerning.

Scarborough

Friday

Dear Josie,

I'm tickled to know that the letters still serve, although I always throw the damned things away myself. Yesterday's roses, yesterday's kisses, yesteryear's snows. I'm embarrassed to find out that Joe Schrank thinks I'm on the way to getting famous but I think that's what it amounts to: Joe Schrank. If I am famous why should I have a hole in the seat of my pants and not enough money for last month's bills. . . .

---

# *JOHN WILLIAM CHEEVER*

\* \* \*

John William Cheever was born in Quincy, Massachusetts, on May 27, 1912. He was the second son of Frederick Lincoln Cheever (1863–1946), a shoe salesman.\* My father's mother, Mary Deveraux Liley Cheever (1873–1956), was born in England. He told us years later that he was an unwanted child, that his father suggested the pregnancy be terminated, and even invited an abortionist for dinner.

His family was prosperous at the time of his birth, but they ran into financial difficulties as he grew up. Frederick Lincoln Cheever got out of the shoe business in the 1920s and bought stocks that became worthless after the Crash. Then the elder Cheevers began borrowing

---

\*Late in his own life my father would describe his father as the owner of a shoe manufacturing firm. He said that on holidays his father would take him to the plant and hold him up so that he could blow the luncheon whistle. I assumed this was true, although I did notice early on in this project that the characters in my father's fiction were almost always shoe salesmen, and not shoe manufacturers. In the 1964 *Time* cover story Frederick Lincoln Cheever is described as a salesman. I assume the factory had not yet been invented.

against their large Victorian house at 123 Winthrop Avenue. They lost it in 1933 to foreclosure. After the loss of the house my father's parents lived for three years with family and in rentals. They separated, but were later reconciled and moved back in together, although my grandfather remained unemployed while my grandmother ran gift shops and a tearoom. The gift shop operation involved the sale of some of the family's own possessions. My father told me that his mother sold the bed he had slept in.

In a page of notes my grandfather sent my father years later, he described his ruin: "The bank, after handling my money for 24 years, foreclosed my home. . . . Cashed two life insurance policies at sixty cents on the dollar. At end of 53 years labor am washed up completely. . . . "

During this difficult time my father's most significant relationship was with his older brother, Frederick (1905–76). He and Fred went on a walking tour of Germany in 1931. After this they lived together, but my father used to tell me that he realized at that point that their friendship was too intense, and he fled to New York City. The high regard shared by the brothers survived this rupture. Fred used to send the young writer $10 a week. The troubled love for a brother—part myth and part reality—appears again and again in the fiction. One sibling gets hit on the back of the head with a piece of driftwood in "Goodbye, My Brother" (*The New Yorker*, 1951). Another is murdered in *Falconer*. There are indications that Fred may have been my father's first homosexual partner, although it's also entirely possible that their love was platonic, and that his allusions to its carnality made later in life were just an attempt to create the sort of synthesis for which he is properly famous. My father dated Iris Gladwin, whom Fred later married.

Malcolm Cowley was the first magazine editor to publish a Cheever story. "Expelled" ran in *The New Republic* in October of 1930. It was written after its author had been "fired out of Thayer Academy at 17 for smoking," or that's how he told it.

In 1979, at a dinner given by the Newberry Library in Chicago in Malcolm's honor, my father recalled a party he had been to at Malcolm's in New York.

Malcolm's first wife, Peggy, met me at the door and exclaimed, "You must be John Cheever, everyone else is here." Things were never like this in Massachusetts. I was offered two kinds of drinks. One was greenish. The other was brown. I was told that one was a Manhattan, and the other Pernod. My only intent was to appear terribly sophisticated and I ordered a Manhattan. Malcolm very kindly introduced me to his guests. I went on drinking Manhattans lest anyone think I came from a small town like Quincy, Massachusetts. Presently, after four or five Manhattans, I realized that I was going to vomit. I rushed to Mrs. Cowley, thanked her for the party, and reached the apartment-house hallway, where I vomited all over the wallpaper. Malcolm never mentioned the damages beginning a long friendship in which his kindness and generosity have never been lacking.

# THE
# 1930s:
# STARTING OUT

* * *

This letter was written from my grandparents' home in Quincy, Massachusetts. My father had recently been at a party at the Cowleys', a party that included many celebrities, one of whom may or may not have been Mae West. Curtis Glover was never mentioned again, and Malcolm has no recollection of the name. Fritz is a diminutive for Fred. I'm running this letter exactly as I found it, so the ellipses are his own and do not indicate deletions. The spelling errors are also his. This is by far the worst piece of writing by my father that I have ever seen, but do not be discouraged, it is no indication of things to come.

malcolm cowley:

yesterday afternoon curtis glover came out to the house "to talk educational problems over". if you remember (I had never heard of him before) he ran away from high school several years ago and he ran away from dartmouth the year before last. we met with the common bond of being radical . . . "to be radical in modern america is to be lonely. it is to feel that you are an outcast, and because so many people hold you in contempt, a little inferior . . ."

I have not had so much fun in a very long time.

He was tall, blonde,with a pink and white complexion,wide hips and a loose mouth. He laughed through his nose,ate his toast with a knife and fork and read the "new republic" faithfully. he had no enthusiasim, no passion and no chin. We parted with promises to corresspond.

he is going to teach math in high school next year.

however it was a great deal of fun. obviously he ran away from college because of associations rather than educational troubles. he is now at harvard. he thinks spengler is a bit to disagreable and joyce a bit to pornographic. I played "sacre du printemps" on the gramaphone and he did'nt even jump. he is going to finish harvard this year and "throw what weight I have into gradually modifying the present system."

if you can possibly find the university of syracuse letter (it was on the floor under mae west the last time I saw it) would you mail it to me. I would like to answer them.

as soon as I can get enough money together I am going away for a week or two and continue thesketches. the family make it quite unbearable by asking me "have you been writing to-day . . . isn't that nice. . . . and what have you been writing today . . . "and telling everyone from the char to the president of the woman's club that I'm going to write a book. will I be paid for the new republic article and if the forum takes one will they pay for it? As soon as the music season starts again I will go back to the newspaper for a week or two. prescot townsend will very nearly give me his house in provincetown for a month and fritz is going to pay for my meals.

after having seen harte crane I went home and read the bridge. I do not like it very well. After one was pushed through the contrapuntal fretwork of superimposed imagery one does not seem to find a corresponding depth of matter. in the face of "ash wendesday" it seems probable that his obscurity is on the wrong side of his poetry. his force, his passion, his grand eyesight are all swell but the nervous tendencies of his poetry mark him (almost) as a man who has been broken by a civilization whose force no sensitive person could comprehend and remain normal . . . . a man who has contracted aesthetic st. vitus from hearing continually the sound of taxi horns and machinery.

however I am lousy with adolescence and I do not know. I have never yet fallen in love.

but eliot does seem to write with more important internal obscurity placing our broken megalopolitan existance on the plane upon which it belongs.

they are both perhaps two antithetical species of maniac brought about by our cement our hammers our coffee cups and our cigarets.

but crane might belong to the middle or the climax of the decline whereas eliot is perhaps the last of the species.

John Cheever

thanks for a swell tuesday night.

One of the first pieces my father published, "Late Gathering," ran in *Pagany; A Native Quarterly* in 1931. *Pagany* was edited by Richard Johns, to whom the following two notes were written. At this time my father was signing his name Jon.

thanks also for the h in my name. something i've been wanting to get back for a long time

richard johns:

thanks a lot for announcing my story for future publication.

it does get tiresome as hell to sit at the typewriter for a long time and to get nothing in the mail but polite notes telling one that after second thought and on the advice of several hundred advisory editors the editor and his advisory editors have decided not to publish this particular poem or story but that issue four is in preperation and that the editor would be glad to see other poems or stories.

i am not very sure what late gathering was about but if it was about a farm and if the names,mani,rachel,or jean are used could you change them.

and thanks a lot again

john cheever

this is a very bad story but because
you are an editor it is your
duty to read it —

Iam very sorry that it is so
bad but I couldn't help it —
— It is a horrible condition
to be in.

Yours Cheever

I hope all this is not bothering you
— It is not bothering me —

Yours Cheever

Yaddo is the artist colony in Saratoga Springs, New York. Elizabeth Ames was the executive director. Years later my father would describe it thus in a letter to a young protégé: "Yaddo is a few hundred acres—a castle and out-buildings—that was opened in the late twenties as a place where writers, painters and composers could work."

It's interesting to note the scholarly approach to literature taken below by someone who had been expelled from high school. The man I knew read literary criticism, but he almost never discussed it in any depth. I remember him being amused during the filming of his short story "The Swimmer" in 1966 by the fact that Burt Lancaster was impressed with his credentials as an intellectual and academic. "He's trying to place me on an island that I've spent most of my adult life trying to get a boat off of," he told me.

[1933]
Six Pinckney Street

Wednesday

Dear Malcolm,

Thanks for recommending me to Mrs. Ames. I wrote to her but evidently Yaddo is full right now. But she said that there might be a vacancy later on in the summer or in the fall, which would be more fun. My case is not very urgent for I have a roof over my head and a great deal of food which is, I imagine, more than a lot of people have.

I'm glad that the things you returned on rereading them were not published. They wouldn't have given anyone else pleasure, they would have caused me a great deal of displeasure and I probably would have mispent the money. I don't expect to do anything worth publishing for five years or so. There is a lot of time. I don't even know what I want to do but I have discovered that knowing what you want to do has very little effect on getting the work in hand actually done. The presence of t.s. eliot in Cambridge this winter has been equally sterilizing and stimulating. The shadow of discipline that he has cast over criticisism is splendid (not that criticisisim has improved any but there is probably less of it); but it is not so splendid when applied to poetry or prose. There is some discrepancy apparent when you speculate on what would happen to his critical machinery if it were applied to crane or cummings. . . .

as ever
John Cheever

Composer and writer Ned Rorem, another Yaddo guest, remembers seeing my father at the common dinner table with Elizabeth Ames in the early 1960s. Elizabeth was hard of hearing, and Ned recalls that my father—already a minor celebrity—was willing to shout at her in order to be heard, and that his affection for the old woman clearly overrode any embarrassment. My father moved around a good deal during the 1930s, staying with his brother, his parents, at Yaddo, and in various apartments and rooming houses in Manhattan, Massachusetts, and Washington, D.C.

[1934 Boston]

Dear Mrs. Ames,

Last year at about this same time I wrote you, at Malcolm Cowley's suggestion, asking about coming to Yaddo. The letter was pretty late in the season and there was no room, and Mr. Cowley suggested that I write again this year.

He wrote you, I think, about my work. What or how much he said I don't know. The facts in the case are simple enough. I am twenty-two years old and have been writing for a number of years although I haven't published anything since 1932. I can vouch for the quantity if not for the quality and promise of the work I would do if there were a vacancy at Yaddo.

Everyone is, I imagine, reluctant to refer to the work in hand. I have lived all of my life within view of, and nearly every day of the last two years within, Boston. The city is old, out of step with the century, but age only seems to have quickened its elements. The Communists are clubbed in front of a staid, Georgian facade. Relics from the past continually pierce the present. Some dream of love survives the sandstone apartment houses. A paranoid ruins the Public Library. And within a half an hour's ride is the New England country where occasionally an abandoned house or a view surviving the hoardings and hot-dog stands gives the memory an unexpected twist. The work in hand I think would deal with the horror and glory of this particular brick horizon.

The idea of leaving the city for a short while, after two uninterrupted years, has never been so distant or so desirable.

Sincerely yours,
John Cheever

He'd been to Yaddo for a long stay in 1934. In New York he read and synopsized books for M-G-M and was paid $5 a shot. Higher-ups would use these when deliberating about which books would become movies.

633 Hudson Street
New York City

Dear Mrs. Ames,

Hudson Street is a far cry from anything in Boston and so far the difference stands in favor of Hudson Street. I arrived here on Wednesday and found some work at once. The income is still pretty precarious, the landlady worries and worries but I think it will hold out for another couple of weeks at least. I'm reading novels for M-G-M and some book reviewing may turn up next week. The income is barely enough to live on but enough if you go carefully. My only objection is that staying here and doing this work precludes any chances of doing work of my own. The work in itself doesn't take a great deal of time but during the hot weather Mrs. Lewton, the woman who rations out the work, keeps irregular and unpredictable hours and you spend more time waiting around for books and worrying about the next day's finances than you do in actual work. So it goes.

Giving up my own work, even temporarily, makes me impatient and discouraged. I still have the bundle of stories from Yaddo that are not completed and I would like to try a novel. I get tired of my own ways, tired of refinement, discretion, excessive detail, lack of action. Even while working there is a certain amount of impatience and when the work is suspended altogether the impatience increases. And it is almost impossible, after working over other people's books all day in this small room, to start up after supper and write a book of your own. If there should be a vacancy in Yaddo during September or October I would deeply appreciate it.

As ever,
John Cheever

*The New Yorker* bought its first two Cheever works of fiction in the spring of 1935, paying $90 for "The Brooklyn Rooming House" and $45 for "Buffalo." My father's tendency to make things up because they sounded right convinced me that the title of the piece he sold to *STORY*, "Homage to Shakespeare," was pure invention, but my father-in-law, Paul Maslin, discovered it in the library of a cruise ship. It may not have tempted anyone taking a train to Baltimore, but it did make *The Oxford Collection of Short Stories*. Triuna is the name for a clump of islands in Lake George also owned and operated by the Corporation of Yaddo.

733 Commercial Street
East Weymouth, Massachusetts

April 22, 1935

Dear Mrs. Ames,

For the first time since a rainy day last October when I left Yaddo, I'm in the country again. For a couple of days anyrate. Its not the same country. Its southern Massachusetts at the begining of the cape. There aren't any mountains. The ground is flat, stony or sandy and all the trees were cut down about ninety years ago to be shoveled, apparently into the maws of steam engines. But its all right and I like it although, for all of its celebration the beauties of this part of Massachusetts seem to be summed up in a tract of scrub-maple and a heap of rusted mill-machinery. I'm living in what was once a farm (my mother runs it as a restaurant in the summer) with my seventy-one year old father. I'm only staying a few days. Its pleasant enough but once out of the city my income stops and so back to New York pretty soon.

The winter hasn't exactly held any conquests, any literary conquests anyrate. I've sold stories to the New Republic and the New Yorker. Story magazine has evidently decided to postpone publication of my thing indefinitely. They are losing money and anxious to get newstand circulation and the title ("Homage to Shakespeare") won't tempt any-one, taking a train to Baltimore, to buy a copy. I get worried sometimes about my inability to sell. Its about time I did. I got an agent a few days ago and this may help but I think the fault so far is mostly my own. When an editor hits an extrodinary story they know it and so far my stories haven't been good enough to jolt them. And in the meantime I've started a book which, I'm confident, will be very good. I've kept off a sustained thing for a long time feeling that the novel (and its only definition seems to be negative) was created largely by and for the growth and decline of a middle-class that men of my generation are strangers to. Our lives have not been sustained or constant or ordered. Our characters don't die in bed. The powerful sense of passed and passing time that seems to be the one definable and commendable quality of the novel is not our property. Our lives are not long and well-told stories. But then these are not limitations. They seem in the course of work to be exciting discoveries.

In this connection, in connection with sustained work, I'm still anxious to hear from you about Yaddo or Triuna. There seems to be a lot to do, everything to do in my case and I would be very grateful for a chance to write during the summer and I know that there is no better place. If it would make it more possible I would be glad to work for the chance. I can drive, swim, well enough to be intrusted with a boat, handle an axe; nothing spectacular but generally useful. And a job could probably be fitted in with working hours.

As ever,

John Cheever

P.S. Remembering your interest in "miracles" I noted in the local evening paper that a silver crown, "Property of the Holy Ghost Society Inc., of Bridgewater, Mass." has been credited with four small cures. The crown, which is placed in the custody of the Society's President during his term of office, is loaned for the use of anyone "who gives a qualified reason for wanting it."

J.C.

The individuality of my father's experience makes it easy to forget that unemployment was at crisis level. When FDR was inaugurated in 1933 the fear of unrest was so high, that machine guns were mounted along the parade route.

Elizabeth had suggested my father find a job.

Assinippi, Massachusetts

May 4, 1935

Dear Mrs. Ames,

I was very glad to hear your advice about putting in time at some other occupation besides writing. I have thought about it a lot and worried about it a lot. And also your remarks about the expenditure of energy in protection instead of adjustment. I can't help but view the thing in an intensely personal light. I have thought about it continually during the past winter and during the time I have been in Massachusetts. The problem is not, I think, the evasion of occupation and the enforced lack of adjustment. It is not a problem peculiar to writers but the problem of an entire generation of younger men.

From the time when I took a job as a stock-boy in an abandoned subway tube when I was about 15, I have almost always worked. I have held the average run of jobs, driving a truck, working on a small newspaper etc. But about two years ago the possibility of holding these jobs stopped. I have no trade, no degree, no special training. Straightforward application for any kind of work from a bus-boy to an advertising copy-writer has been completely ineffectual. During the winter of '33 I held a part time job. In the winter of '34 I held a political job. I have supported myself this winter by writing synopses for M-G-M, not because I like to but because I can't find work as a loom-fixer or anything else. By pulling every possible wire I may be able to get a job in a ship-building plant this fall. I would much prefer it to any other opening; an editorial position.

The matter of adjustment seems to be a matter of personal courage and talent. Some people can have a great many lovers and take airplanes and trains from state to state and country to country and still remain cowards and children. Other people remain in one town and remain faithful to one wife and grow into mature and convincing men. There is a small number of scholars and artists who, through the illusion of research and work, fail to make any but the earliest adjustments and who you find at the ages of thirty and forty, sitting in the same rooms, weighing the same, unimportant decisions with their correspondence unmailed and dust settling on their youths. But financial and emotional independence seems to make such a condition impossible. When you have no money you live, at least, in continual anxiety.

I've gone into this at length, I'm afraid, more to ease my own conscience than anything else, and I hope it hasn't been too confusing or dull. I hope to hear from you soon.

As ever<br>John Cheever

He was twenty-three when he wrote the letter below. The $3-a-week room on Hudson Street was sufficiently barren to be the subject of a Walker Evans photograph that hangs in the Museum of Modern Art. Muriel is Malcolm's second wife, the woman to whom he has been married since 1932.

633 Hudson Street
New York City

October 23, 1935

Dear Malcolm,

I ran into Muriel on a rainy night on Banks Street about a week ago. For a little while she thought I was a drunk but then she recognized me. . . .

Right now, New York looks about the same as it did last winter. I can't get a WPA job because I can't get on relief because I can't establish residence. And there don't seem to be any other jobs. . . . Meanwhile I'm doing a lot of waiting and wondering.

And if there's anything I can do, don't hesitate to ask me because I've got all kinds of time.

As ever
John Cheever

Malcolm had suggested that my father try to get an advance for a novel. Harrison Smith seems to have requested an outline.

Thursday
633 Hudson Street

Dear Malcolm,

Smith's objection to giving me an advance was that a story writer and a novelist are two different birds and that no amount of stories I write will convince him that I'm a novelist. So I'll do what he wants in Massachusetts. I'm perfectly confident that I can do the book, that it will be a good book and that it might even sell. But there's no reason why anyone should believe in me until they've seen it.

He seemed to have an idea, gathering in his mind about me. He asked how long I'd been writing. Ten years-I said; true enough. He looked at me dubiously, nearly sadly-And this is all you've done? And this is as far as you've gone? Ten years.

My regards to Muriel
As ever,
John

He had found part-time work as an assistant to Walker Evans.

c/o Walker Evans
20 Bethune Street
New York City

Tuesday

Dear Mrs. Ames,

It was good to hear from you again. And this is a maelstrom. My relations with this city are various and intricate. My main reason for liking it and for remaing here is because it does not, in any way, remind me of a small American city. Two days in Boston were two days too many. It was pretty and the weather was clear and the crowds around Dock Square and Fanueil Hall were allright but the minute you go towards Pemberton Square and the Barrister's offices and Ashburton Place you begin to run into those pale, contrite faces. And after having lived with them for several years, in indifference and in intense hate, I was glad to take the boat. And I did take the boat out. It was a clear night and the pleasant trip and it was good watching the Custom House get smaller and smaller and lower and lower. But that was a long time ago.

For the last couple of weeks I've been working as a photographer's assistant. And the New Republic and Story both took other stories so that was a little money. And I may be able to get a department store job for Christmas.

And as ever,
John

He was at his parents' house and it's indicative of his modesty, false or otherwise, that he didn't tell Elizabeth that the second letter was being written on his twenty-fourth birthday. He was going to Bolton Landing because that is where the boats for Triuna docked. He was going to work as a boatman for Yaddo. The novel was rejected.

60 Spear Street
Quincy, Massachusetts

May 25, 1936

Dear Elizabeth,

We drove directly from Saratoga to here and I've been here ever since, living with my parents, finishing the novel, drinking, bowling and seeing people I used to know and its been very good. Its a town of about sixty thousand, settled in the early seventeenth century. It grew wealthy on leather and granite and has since grown very poor on leather and granite. Henry Adams used to spend his summers in a house down the street. Everyone has an antique name. The Unitarian Church is very beautiful and Richardson built the Public Library and in the middle of the square is a fourteen storied sky-scraper, built by Delcevare King whose wife won't bear him a son because she doesn't think any man should have to carry the name of Delcevare. Its the town I know best and although I wouldn't want to live here, its always good to come back.

My plans are still up in the air and dependent entirely upon money. The only definite thing is that I will be in Bolton on June first, and I look forward to it. The novel is finished and in the mail. I celebrated by driving down to Orleans and eating a whole chicken and drinking a bottle of Burgundy on the beach. We also went swimming and wrestled. I had not been on Cape Cod for a couple of years and it was a good experience. Crossing the canal at Sagamore or Bourne is like coming into another world and always will be for me. Even the clapboarding on the gas-stations is different and the marshes around Barnstable are different and the dunes looked good and familiar and the sea was running high, white, mighty, cold, and smelling strong. If I don't get to New York I won't feel any great loss. Simon and Schuster won't have read the novel by this time and to talk with them is my only real reason for going there.

And I'll see you in Bolton.
As ever,
John

60 Spear Street
Quincy, Massachusetts

May 27, 1936

Dear Elizabeth,
My father keeps telling me, and asking me not to forget, that one whistle means a starboard passing, two, a port passing, three a salute and four means astern. I've also been studying Marine engine instruction books.

As ever,
John Cheever

Yaddo
Saratoga Springs
New York

December 16, 1936

Dear Malcolm,

I received the check and I'm very grateful. My financial condition has been worse in the last two months than it has been at any time during the last two years. It makes me sad. I hope I'll be able to repay you in a week or so. The Atlantic is holding a long story and they may kick through.

Meanwhile the novel is gathering dust and it makes me very sore. Sometimes I get it out at night and look at it and get excited about it but then I have to put it away in the morning and go back to my short stories. I've had to take most of my notes for long work and convert them into short things and it seems like wanton destruction.

It's winter up here now. we've had about thirty inches of snow at one time or another. The rains took most of it and spoiled what skiing there was. Its a good place for work but after a month of it my heart gets heavy and I wake up in the morning thinking in big images like armies and banners and municiple monuments. . . .

As ever,
John

At Yaddo my father met Josephine Herbst. The last time I saw Josie was at the reception that followed my sister's marriage to Robert Cowley, Malcolm's son, in 1967. I thought of her not as a distinguished writer, but as a small woman in an orange serape who smoked heavily and kept saying, "For Heaven's sakes." Josie had visited us often when I was a child, and when I was very young we spent some time at her house in Erwinna, Pennsylvania. This property was a rural refuge for my father, and then for my father and mother, and then for the family. That house was one of Josie's few possessions, but she had a Marxist's sense of the responsibilities of ownership, and shared the place freely with other people, both when she was there and when she was not.

Josie was a single woman throughout the time I knew her, and childless. In fact she may have lost the ability to bear children because of an abortion she had during an affair with the playwright Maxwell Anderson. She might have been expected not to understand the particular sensitivities of the young, but this was not the case. My sister, Susan, and I disagreed on just about every issue, but we were unanimous in our admiration for Josephine Herbst. Josie had a rich, husky voice, doubtless at least partly the result of all those cigarettes. She would read to us for hours, filling a rainy afternoon with vivid colors and events. Whatever the moral significance of kindness to children, and the New Testament is quite explicit on this point, Josie was wonderful to us. If God is a three-year-old—and Jesus is often depicted as a child—I'm certain that she sits at His right hand. But Josie was Marxist and would probably have nothing to do with Him.

It was not until I began work on this book that I read Elinor Langer's superb 1984 biography, *Josephine Herbst* (Little, Brown), and became aware of the many accomplishments of the woman who had been so kind to children. My father had told me when, as a teenager, I read *The Sun Also Rises* that Josie had been a friend of the author's, and that on one occasion Hemingway had taken her and some others out in his boat during a hurricane. The sea grew high, and all the passengers were frightened and begged Hemingway to turn for port. When he would not do this, Josie went below and got the rifle that was kept aboard to shoot sharks. She brought it up on deck and trained it on the man who defined masculine courage for a generation. She told him that they would start for land immediately. They did. I don't know if this story is accurate, but it does express some of the admiration my father had for his old friend. It is also supported by what is known of Josie's courage as a correspondent during the Spanish Civil War.

Josie was kindly, and affectionate, but she was also hard as nails. The friendship between my father and Josie lasted until she died, in 1969, although there was a period of several years during which they didn't write or speak to each other. This had to do with a cat named Delmore Schwartz.

P.O. Box 1
Bolton, New York

Monday Night

Herbst:

I ran the boat all summer. That was allright. A lot of scotch got consumed one way or another and there was a lot of scenery and a lot of nice girls from places like William and Mary and Beaver and Syracuse and some aquaplaningThen I woke one morning with a hangover and not a red cent and God only knows how I'll get out of this place. I have a car but the steering gear is broken.

It's windy as hell, cold as hell, scenic as hell, lonely as hell, but I'll probably get some work done. I've got to go over the whole novel again, word for word. But why should I have to live in the backwoods, or on islands, to write a book about Boston and New York is something I can't get straight.

As ever,
John


Yaddo

February 1, 1937

Dear Elizabeth,

. . . My editors finally came through with a small sum of money and I returned to work on Thursday. Returning was very pleasant. There's nothing I'd rather do than work on the book. And no place where I'd rather work. The air is fine. The grounds are quiet. A man couldn't ask for more.

Before returning I went over to New York for a week and saw a few people I've been wanting to see. Then my brother appeared in town on Friday morning and I took the four o'clock train to Boston with him. It was a crowded week and I came up the Main Street of Quincy Friday night, while the iron bell in the church where John and John Quincy and Henry Adams worshipped was ringing nine.

. . . My father's memory is very acute and colorful and his story is exciting. He remembers the Typhoid after the Civil War that laid an already impoverished and disillusioned Newburyport, even lower. He remembers his mother's delirium and his Aunt Juliana who used to sit among the manderine coats and ivory junks that her husband brought back from the east, and talk with an Indian "medium". His uncle Ebenezer was an abolitionist. he ran a biscuit factory that turned out hard-tack for the sailing vessels. When the war between the States was declared he was offered a contract by the government to make hard-tack for the soldiers. He rejected the offer because he felt that his hard tack wasn't good enough for the Union Soldiers. A competitor named Pierce, then accepted the contract and made a fortune and founded a dynasty on the procedes. Uncle Ebenezer had no regrets. He played the flute. The Pierce bakery has since grown into the National Biscuit Company while the wind whistles through Uncle Ebenezer's abandoned flour mill.

As ever,
John

Back at his parents' home in Quincy again. Malcolm and Muriel lived then as they do now in a house in Sherman, Connecticut. It's interesting to note that my father said he was not going to write about his grandmother. Honora Wapshot, while not precisely modeled on any one individual, certainly had a lot in common with the women in his family, and she was a central character in his first two novels.

60 Spear Street
Quincy, Massachusetts

May 25, 1937

Dear Malcolm and Muriel,

The ride down was fine and I saw a double rainbow a little north of Hartford. That makes three in a row. The thunder storm that I waited to avoid, followed right along behind me and caught up with me in Hartford but it wasn't bad and the wiring didn't get wet. The country you live in seems to be the best along the road. It gets very flat around Providence and although there are hills around here, you don't get that impression. Everything seems to be four-way turnpikes, leading to Hyannis and everybody has the heirlooms up for sale along the road. I like it but I wouldn't want to live here and hard as I try I can't work here. I feel very strongly that this part of the country has nothing to do with the rest of the world and I'm more interested in the world than I am in my grandmothers. It would be all right if I were writing about my grandmothers but I'm not.

The circus was in town last night but it wasn't a very good circus. It smelled of elephant shit and crushed grass which is like the smell of home to me but it was a shocking racket and they charged one price to get in and another to sit down and another to remain. There was a girl in the Scotch band whom I've seen before in some of the Sparks shows. You may have seen her. She's very beautiful but she only has one eye. But she's very beautiful.

As ever,
John

In 1938 he got a writing job with the WPA. At the time this letter was written, he was living in a boarding house in Washington, D. C., with the writer Nathan Asch, son of the writer Sholem Asch (d. 1957). The "old

Ford" was a Model A, and when I was a grown man he still spoke fondly
of its reliability and simplicity. Apparently he owed Yaddo money.

2308 20th Street,N.W.
Washington, D.C.

Saturday morning

Dear Elizabeth,

Without too much difficulty I arrived here yesterday morning in the
footsteps of John Adams. I had a flat tire in Yonkers and an enflamed
eye in Hyattsville and it probably would have been more intelligent
and economical to take the train. But I wouldn't have seen the country
I saw or the people, and although its never exactly a pleasure it always
is an experience to go rattling over a strange road in an old Ford with
not much money in your pockets through country that isn't your
country. . . .

Nathan took me sight seeing yesterday and this afternoon I hope to
meet some of the people I'm going to work with. Nathan is in fine
fettle. I have Josie's old room with a porch and a lot of trees around it
and it seems to be a good and inexpensive place to live in. I hope I can
save enough money to finance a novel and that's all I ask.

Love,
John

2308 20th Street, N.W.
Washington, D.C.

Dear Elizabeth;

. . . The boarding house we live in is a little alcoholic as boarding house
go and for table mates we have two secretaries from the Russian em-
bassey, two librarians, a man from the tarrif commission, a government
clerk and another man from my office. There is also an old lady who
sits at the head of the table and says all W.P.A. workers are lazy and
good-for-nothing and she's finding it harder and harder to get me to
pass her the lima beans.

One of the distinguishing features of this city is the rapid passage
and the singular nature of its gossip. . . . In one evening you can pick
up the news that a mouse was found in the National Archives last
week, that the commercial secretary of the Cuban Embassy has been

given a mysterious dismissal, that George Abel's wife is having a child by Drew Pearson, this his Majesties Government has asked His Majesties Ambassador to drive around in an automobile less conspicuous than his Cord, and that Count P—— pays the Italian Embassy for the pleasure of sitting at a desk four hours a day, cutting pictures out of the newspaper, etc. A few days ago the widow of a General of the Regular Army took me into a corner and gave me a sure-fire solution for my success in Washington. "Now John L. Lewis has a daughter," she said. "She's rather stout and she's not awfully pretty but if you rush her, you're made."

I neglected to send you any money on my debt last pay day because of another increase in my obligations. I'm buying my father a set of teeth. That inexhaustible man went swimming a month ago. A wave picked him up, knocked him down, lifted out his teeth and swept them off into the bowels of the Atlantic.

Love,
John

### WORKS PROGRESS ADMINISTRATION
Walker-Johnson Building
1734 New York Avenue NW.
Washington, D.C.

Harry L. Hopkins
Administrator
2308 20th St. N.W.

Thursday

Dear Jo

. . . I don't know whether to try and crack Colliers again or not. I rather think not. I'm going to wait until this last story comes out and see how the movies feel about it and if the movies are indifferent well then I'll try something else. I do want a house in that part of the country; a house a wife a bottle of whiskey and a chance to work. I don't want another bloody thing.

Love,
John

1603 19th NW until the 1st

Dear Jo,

About the only cheery note is a couple of days I spent on a horse. Its turned out to be cheaper than drinking and you do see the country. I drove into Maryland Saturday afternoon and rode in the woods outside of Fort Belvoir until dark. It was good. The wooden bridges thunder when you ride over them. The corn was up in bundles, there was a haze over the fields, and the beech trees have changed color. This is Maryland, said I to myself, this is Maryland you sonofabitch and you're on a horse. . . .

Love,
John

He worked on the final edit of the WPA's *New York City Guide*. This letter was written on stationery from the Hotel Chelsea at "West Twenty-Third Street at Seventh Avenue under Knott Management." At the bottom of the stationery there's a note that reads: "Plan to visit New York World's Fair 1939." By "suburb of the Nation," he meant Washington, D.C.

Dear Jo,

. . . I've been spending my time twisting into order the sentences written by some incredibly lazy bastards. The weather, above what every sentence in the guide book describes as a 'canyon', seems to be fine. . . .

New York has seemed fine after that suburb of the Nation. The part I like best about it is the presence of the waterfront. There were some noon sailings today and the whole godamned westside shook under the blasts. The clerks don't speak in southern accents and the street isn't full of snot-nosed Government clerks. You can stand up at bars and drink on Sunday.

Love,
John

From another letter on Hotel Chelsea stationery.

Dear Elizabeth,

I'm working day and night in order to get the copy to Washington by the fifteenth and I've seen no one and done nothing for a week. Nathan was in town for the New Year, very natty; and I met him in a penthouse on 57th street. His job seems to be good until July anyhow and I feel that he has all the requirements of a Washington success if he wants one. . . . If you stay in the north-west of Washington its very difficult to remember or imagine insecurity. Every time I saw a beggar in the streets there, I used to wonder why anyone would chose that way of making a living; why didn't they go to work for the goverment.

Love,
John

The Eleanor here referred to is Eleanor Clark, novelist, short-story writer, and the wife of Robert Penn Warren. My father met her at Yaddo in the winter of 1936. Eleanor and Josie were friends at the time, but their relationship was cooled and finally vitiated by political differences. Josie was a Stalinist, while Eleanor was a Trotskyite. Eleanor actually went to Mexico and spent some time with Trotsky. The 1936 Moscow trials made it difficult for a Stalinist and a Trotsky supporter to get along. My father never fully acknowledged the lessening of affection between his two friends.

The Lake

Wednesday night
[1939]

Dear Jo,

The news has sort of got me down, the news, a howling wind that shakes the island, and a violent change in the whole atmosphere and coloring of this place. Bolton Landing is empty. "If Mrs. Ormsby wants me to," I heard the butcher in the A&P telling a woman today, "I'll take this meat up to her in time for supper." There's hardly a boat left on the lake. It's been very cold. The light is grey and the sun is weak and any afternoon now I expect to see a crowd of Indians come raging down Buck Mountain, hot for the British. I can't believe that this is autumn and that they're bringing the wounded back into Paris. The morning Times looks like a 1917 copy of the ragpaper edition someone swiped from a library.

My father has taken the whole crisis as a springboard for his memories of the post-civil war period. I'm quite anxious to hear from my brother, New England is so incredibly slow to react to anything like a European war. I'm working, without a great deal of zest, but I can't blame the war for that. I'm quite anxious to get to New York, to see how the girls look in their Mainboucher corsets and to make some arrangements for holing in during the winter. . . .

The lighter side of life is largely water-skiing. A little while after we put Eleanor on the bus Monday, Comstock came snoring over in his Gar-Wood and we skiied until dark. The Gar-Wood is a great improvement over our boat and you get a hell of a ride once you're out of the wake. You also get a good substantial jump leaving the wake; a matter of two or three feet. And now that the Comstocks have departed we go pooping up and down these reaches of abandoned water behind our own locomotive. But even, and I hate to say it, but even water skiing can get damned dull.

Don't get the impression that the scenery isn't impressive. Every so often I get up from my typewriter and take a gander at the sky and mountains. Phew. You wouldn't know the place for the change a week of north-east winds and an absence of tourists can make. And when are you leaving and where are you leaving for; in any case I'll see you soon.

My best to Eleanor.

Love,<br>John

"Blind alley" was the term Eleanor used to describe the realistic style in which he wrote at this time. When I asked Eleanor recently about this she said that she'd disagreed with him on his early commitment to realism in fiction, and had said that "frivolous realism" was a blind alley. Loyd (Pete) Collins, another writer, was a longtime friend. His first novel, *Call Me Ishmael*, was published by Dodd, Mead & Co. in 1935. His second novel was never published. His first wife was Frances Lindley, who would later be one of my father's editors at Harper's. His second wife, Lib Logan Collins, is an artist and continues to be a friend of the family.

Triuna Island
Bolton
New York
Sunday

Dear Jo,

. . . I saw Eleanor Clark yesterday. I'm trying to bully her into coming up here; she's still sick and covered with a rash. She's working on a story. I asked where she expected to print it, since that seems of some importance, and she said either in the Partisan Revue, the Southern Review, or New Letters. It's the vision of those three sheets lined up on a book-shelf with their air of profound compromise, unjustifiable snobbishness, and phoney calm, that makes me so happy in my rank, blind alley.

Pete's up here and he spends a lot of time trolling for a seven pound lake trout he thinks is lurking in the bottom of the lake. I've been out with him and it's pleasant, sculling along, waiting for a strike, watching it get dark; and then just at dark all the other fishing boats leave the banks, zooming off like flies off a garbage pail. We play darts for drinks with the bartender in town. I went down to Yaddo for dinner one night to find that that was a part of my life way the hell beyond recall. I can't think of anything, except possibly the toys I played with in my childhood, that has become as strange to me as the hall, the carpets exhaling must, some composer tripping down the stairs in his tennis sneakers, and the obscure, harmonious chiming of the dinnergong drifting through hushed corridors and libraries to tell thirty anxious ears that another day has ended and the drinking can set in Oh, Jesus.

John

Much later in life he wrote a letter at Malcolm's request recalling the 1930s. My father had gone on a walking tour of Germany with his brother, Fred. Bruce Bliven was then editor of The New Republic. Niles Spencer was a painter and drinking companion. Mary is Mary Winternitz, the woman he would marry in 1941.

Dear Malcolm,

In going over my notes on the thirties I don't seem to find much that would be useful. The decade doesn't have any reality for me as a segment of time; no particular flavor, music, nothing much but the grainy darkness of an approaching war. There appears to be an edge of light at the begining of the decade but the rest of it all seems dark. I spent the summer of 31 in Germany with Fred. Everything I saw meant war although no one, especially Bruce Bliven seemed interested in my accounts of the National Socialist Party. In 32 Kruger and Toll went bankrupt, my father lost the last of his money, the bank foreclosed the mortgage on our house in Quincy and my Mother opened a gift shop and restaurant in the farm in Hanover. There wasn't anything there for me and so I moved to New York.

I was poor, cold when it was cold and sometimes hungry. Shorty Quirt said: "Someday I'm going to get some money and what I'm going to do is to shave with a fresh razor blade every morning, every single morning and put on clean socks. I'm going to wear clean socks every day." In my notes I find many accounts of loosely organized cocktail parties where the talk was all down-hill. "Isn't it true that life ended for all of us at twenty-one," a man asked me. Walker Evans said: "I feel confident that we are going to be involved in a war and that I will be killed." That glass of fashion. Birth control equipment had made great advances and the ceremony of abortion was on it's way out although I remember going up to the Murray Hill Hotel for a drink with C after she had aborted. There was a sad little party and it seemed to me that I saw a page in history being turned. I have an undated entry, probably '37, of a drunken woman on 11th Street screaming at 3 A.M.:"I am the United States of America I am the United States of America." The skyline of course was all different, even in the village, different to look at and when you went to the window you heard phonographs and radios, a soft sound, never gunfire from tv and of course there were no antenae, no air-conditioners. I have an undated entry describing a crowd gathered around a 1910 Pierce Arrow parked in front of Rikers. Niles Spencer, fairly drunk, is standing on the running-board saying: "Don't you laugh at this car, don't you dare laugh at this car. The world in 1910 was a much better place than you have ever known."

Mary spent the summer of '36 barn-storming New England with a Peace group. "Each breath you draw," she said, "brings you nearer to organized slaughter. You face conscription. Every man, woman and child among you will be called upon to give your labor, your lives and your loved ones to the juggernaut of war." She spoke from band-stands on summer nights. The people were amiable but listless and used to fan themselves with the literature.

There was Washington of course, but my notes are mostly of going out to Griffith Stadiium, going to parties, goosing a waitress, riding at Fort Belvoir (fireflies, etc.) and the personality of the President reflected in those cards who used to impersonate his accent at parties. Before I left Hanover for the last time I spaded the vegetable garden and planted a potato patch. It was Memorial Day. I could hear the band in the village. I thought that I would never return to eat the potatoes I had planted (I don't like potatoes) and that in the years ahead the approach of war would trim and color most of my impulses; and in fact, pretty much from the time we sailed from Antwerp in August 31 until the day when I joined the army this turned out to be true.

As ever,
John

# WAR
# AND MARRIAGE

* * *

My father had just come back from Yaddo and was on his way to see his agent, Maxim Lieber, when he first saw my mother. They were both in the elevator of the building that housed Lieber's office at 545 Fifth Avenue. It was 1939. My father was twenty-seven. My mother was twenty-one. She had graduated from Sarah Lawrence in the spring and was working in Lieber's office. My father used to say that he was struck by her beauty, and knew immediately that he wanted to marry her.

My mother recalls that my father was wearing a brown tweed coat and that the sleeves came down over his hands. "I'll never forget that coat. We used to use it as a blanket on cold nights."

"How did he look?" I asked.

"He didn't look too great," she said.

They both went into Lieber's office, and she went to work, while he went into a back office for a conference with whoever was handling him at the time. My mother remembers clearly that Lieber didn't handle him personally. When he came out of the back office he had something to read and he sat down beside my mother's typewriter to read it. He then struck up a conversation with her.

"And you went on dates?"

"I guess so. All I really remember about that time was how the Scotch and soda tasted."

"How did it taste?"

"It tasted good."

At that point my mother was living in a furnished room on 67th Street. It had a bathroom of its own but no kitchen, and she once cooked my father dinner there. "Lamb chops and fresh peas. I made the peas in the percolator." When she had trouble keeping this room, my father helped her find another one in Rhinelander Gardens, and he moved into a room down the hall.

"Was he handsome?" I asked. "Other people say he was handsome."

"He was very good-looking in his way, but he was kind of slumped over and he was little. He was very little."

After leaving the job with Lieber, my mother went to work for a firm that taught creative writing through the mails. From there she took a job with a publisher, G. P. Putnam's Sons. At first she was a secretary but that didn't work out.

"I can type, but I had a terrible telephone voice, I still do, and I was indiscreet. The wife of the man I worked for called up one day and asked where he was, and I said he was at the bank because he was overdrawn. It never occurred to me that I shouldn't have done that."

My mother stayed at the publishing house, but they moved her into a back room where she worked on manuscripts. "I was pretty good at that, except for that one terrible mistake I made. I was working on a naval history, and there was an admiral of the fleet in it, but the l was missing and I didn't catch it, so where it was supposed to say 'admiral of the fleet,' it said 'admiral of the feet' instead."

There's no mention of my mother in this letter, although she'd already tasted that Scotch. Peg Worthington was a woman with whom my father had had a romance at Yaddo before he met my mother, and Marshall Best was an editor at Viking. The Worden was an establishment in Saratoga with a bar, which is mentioned frequently in the letters, and beds, which are hardly ever mentioned. He was visiting his parents.

67 Spear Street
Quincy, Massachusetts

December 26, 1939

Dear Elizabeth,

Here I am again in what grandmother used to call the house of plenty, sniffing the conflicting aromas of roast duck, Yardley's bath soap and the fir balsalm pillows maiden ladies distribute at Christmas. All in all it's been a rousing holiday. A class-mate of mine had a party on Christmas eve and we sat around a kitchen in Norwell and drank egg-nog out of tennis trophies until two. Many of the kids I had been to Thayer with were there, wearing eye-glasses and escorting pregnant wives. Then back here, a horse-back riding Monday morning in the blue hills, dinner with mother and dad and in the late afternoon we went down to Norwell again and collected a lot of plaid socks, spotted ties, and bright yellow gloves. The house was full of people, there was a lot of champagne, three small children kept circling the living room, breaking the springs in mechanical toys and hollering at the top of their lungs, and a cable came from blacked-out Southampton announcing that auntie Dess (one of the south african aunts) had arrived safely on the blacked-out Scythia. The children played store, played house, played tea-party, the women played bridge, the men played darts, everyone stood knee deep in wrapping paper and outside the windows you could see a light in the sky that is unlike anything I've seen at the foot of New York's cross-town streets. The local squire showed up with a jar of aspic, the children began to destroy the tree ornaments, and driving home the moon was as bright as day and people were skating on every pond. So we remember the Prince of Peace, may it please Him.

I return to New York on the 30th to see Peg Worthington marry Marshall Best and sail for Guatamala. They want to go to Yucatan but "there is a great deal of unrest among the lower classes in Yucatan," they said. The fact that I've been able to do more work in my three days down here than I did in three weeks in New York is proof I guess of how quickly I respond to rural, or at least semi-rural surroundings and I don't look forward to returning to the musty interiors of the

Hotel Chelsea. I may even come up to the Worden for a week. The work I did in the city is no good, the amount of money I spent was crazy, and I haven't even got any memories. There's a lot to be learned by me about living.

Love,
John

My father and mother had gotten to know each other well when the letter below was written in 1940. She was at the family summer camp in Bristol, New Hampshire. The place is called Treetops, and we still go there in the summers. He was staying in the Greenwich Village apartment of the poet Muriel Rukeyser.

Bank Street
Darling,
The book is a pain in the neck. I start it and stop it about six times a day, revile and abuse myself, leer at the novels in the book-case and write long descriptions of my problem. It seems very likely now that I won't have anything to submit. The idea I've taken notes on for the last two years is pretty lame. It seems wrong to start out on anything that I'm not absolutely sure of, to write about anything that I'm not devoted to and familiar with. I don't feel strongly enough about an experience to give it a sustained and realistic account and and I can't seem to conceive a fantasy that will hold up for ninety thousand words. And yet any conventional story or narrative seems to elminate the qualities of modern life that interest me. Haste seems to be the most apparent weakness in everything I attempt. The desk is covered with notes reading: "a realistic piece populated with grotesques, a grotesque populated with familiar characters, etc. Blah, blah, blah.

The lady who studies the viola who continues to eat her dinner out of a paper bag is sawing away unmercifully. She doesn't seem to get any better.

Love,
John

Over
This is another day and the work is going along nicely. (I'm out of envelopes so I had to swipe one of Muriel's at home cards) I've been banging away at the machine which is a pretty good sign. I'll see you

sometime next week. If I can scrape up the money I'll phone you
Tuesday night.

Love, love
John

The man who played boogie-woogie was William Shawn. H&M was
Houghton Mifflin and the outline was for a novel.

Bank Street

Darling,

I . . . went up to the Bests for dinner (You were invited and they kept
asking for you) . . . A little, drooping, small voiced man who played
boogie woogie on the piano, turned out to be the managing editor of
The New Yorker. We played games. (My name begins with S, etc.)
Marshall was it and he chose to represent Captain Simpson, Wallis
Warfield's second husband.

I hope to work straight through this week and see almost no one.
I'm going to give H&M an outline (I should like to write a book about
the people I have known in the last four years) and one long chapter.

John

George Davis was then fiction editor at Harper's Bazaar. N.R. was The
New Republic. Pete and Lib are Pete Collins and Lib Logan Collins.

Darling,

It won't be this week-end, but I'm sure it will be next week. I don't
want to move until I finish the H&M thing; which I'm having some
trouble over. And I'm still waiting on a check. Davis, who bought me
dinner last night, said it left his hands ten days ago so it ought to be at
Lieber's soon. Also Davis said that Carleton Brown (who got the job at
the N.R. I wanted) was taken off to the booby-hatch the day before
yesterday so I'm going to try for that job again. . . .

Yesterday was terrible; muggy and depressing. The old man with the
violin parked himself on my doorstep for a long time and then the
viola player across the way took up the strain and then when she
finished the man with the cornet began to practice. Pete and Lib came

over, not very happily, late in the afternoon and then in the evening
Davis said a lot of things about how people who write for the New
Yorker aren't much good for anything else, etc.

But today is sunny and cool, the viola and cornet are stilled, the
fiddler is covering another beat and,

Love,<br>John

Mme. was *Mademoiselle*.

Darling,

I tore up to the New Republic this morning after writing you, saw
Malcolm and made an appointment with Bliven; but I was already too
late. Some other ghoul has been given Brown's job. But Bliven was
interested and friendly and said that the man they have now is only
temporary and that there's a chance of my being taken on in the fall.
It's apparently an unlucky job. Brown isn't the first one to be taken out
of the office feet first.

This is late at night. I've been working on the book. . . . I'm going to
see Malcolm again tomorrow. He is in a position to know about jobs I
might be able to handle and if I keep pestering him maybe he'll think
of something. Free-lancing, even for the mass magazines, isn't enough
of a living to get married on, and I ought to have some kind of a job.
Mme. wrote today asking me to write them a Christmas story, Ding-
dong, ding-dong. A merry Christmas to you one and all.

Love, love,<br>John

The bb's were bedbugs. Fritz was his brother, Fred; Iris was Fred's wife.

67 Spear<br>Quincy

Darling,

The bb's turned out to be too damned much and I ended up last
night trying to sleep in the bath-tub with the shower dripping on me
and my legs tied up in knots. I stuck it out until it began to get light

when I started for here. I was bleary-eyed and groggy as the devil but the Hudson and the city were beautiful in the early morning. I pulled into a gas station in New Haven and fell sound asleep over the wheel and the gas-station attendant let me sleep for three quarters of an hour. I suppose the fact that I was sleepy and depressed made returning to New England more pleasant and sentimental than usual. The country looked like Gods own and I loved all the homely people.

We sat on the porch after dinner, sniffing the suburban smells and carrying on the kind of aimless conversation that sometimes sounds like music. A long discussion of bloater paste, smoked salmon, the news in the papers, west-side hotels, what children should eat for lunch, cute sayings, the peril of the elm beetle, the rise in real-estate values, the color of the clouds, the cob-webs on the hedge, the smell of the sea, etc. Fritz and Iris were here.

I'm still too sleepy to know exactly what my plans are. I'm particularly worried about the novel. George Davis bought a short story yesterday and asked me why I didn't write them a long one, thirty thousand words or so. boy I'd love to.

All my love,
John

"Lobranao" was Gus Lobrano, an editor at *The New Yorker*. Lobrano became fiction editor after Katharine White. Porter was Katherine Anne Porter. She had been a close friend of Josie Herbst's, but their friendship cooled, and my father often referred to her in later letters to Josie as a figure of fun; a successful, impressive figure of fun, but a figure of fun nevertheless. Flannery Lewis was another writer. Nathan was Nathan Asch. Joan is the housekeeper at Yaddo.

Yaddo
Wednesday

Darling,

The New Yorker turned down a story; which makes the morning look hot, dull and oppressive. I did and typed the revisions of the two Collier's stories yesterday and I guess I'll devote the rest of the week to Lobranao. I worked for an hour in the garden late yesterday afternoon and went down to dinner without a drink. Very dull. People are still intimidated by the atmosphere of the house and the experience of being thrown in with twenty total strangers. The conversation over coffee was conducted in squeaks and grunts. Someone went into the music room and played the sacre du p. A playwright sat on a hornet and got nipped in the rump. One by one they went up to their rooms and sat there with the doors ajar, twiddling their thumbs. At ten o'clock the house was dark. This, of course, is just the lull before the storm breaks. It will be a strange storm and unlike anything that ever happened outside these gates.

At breakfast a number named Ekstrand turned to Porter and asked: What do you do? Are you a writer or what? Porter, dressed in white and smelling faintly of eau de cologne, said why yes, I write. What do you write? Ekstrand asks, leering. Oh, not very much, Porter says, very little really, almost nothing. I mean do you write books or what, Ekstrand asks leering. I've written two books, Porter said sweetly. Oh, Ekstrand said. Porter is wonderful. And while it's none of my business, I can't think of a better place for her particular powers of observation. These bleak and sensitive faces, the ugly house, should be her world.

It looks like rain. All the birds are gabbling. Flannery Lewis is an amiable guy with red eyes. Nathan and Carole are taking an apartment in Saratoga. They seem very happily married and this is a new part for Nathan. She's a good girl. I just heard Joan greeting a new arrival under my window. he looks like a poet; tortoise-shell glasses, black suit, blue shirt and tie. A spider who has fixed a web in the wood-box just caught a fly.

Love,
John



Yaddo

Thursday

Dear Miss Winternitz,
    Why don't you write me, you bum.
    Katherine Anne P. isn't so wonderful. I guess I expected too much. La Porter and Joffee and Flannery and I went down to the Worden last night and the great conversational style was an awful disappointment. Jimmy, the Worden waiter has left and opened a place of his own so

we moved over there. Porter's conversation began with Auden, George Davis, etc. She was side-tracked for a few minutes into talking about her experiences with aviators in the last world war, but then she went back again to Auden, Davis, MacAlmon, Escott. . .

Flannery and I left the others at Jimmys and went over to Charly's which is now called the Ambassador. "On account of the war," Charly said, "we changed the name of the place on account of the war." He thinks I write lyrics and I introduced Flannery as a song-writer and we told him we had just completed the Ghost of Molly Malone. He thought that was a wonderful name for a song and he asked us to notify him when it was going to be released and he'd feature it in his juke box. "I'm featuring the Tales from Vienna Woods now," he said, "I'm trying to educate the public to good music." Then he dropped his voice and asked "Did you ever see a lesbian when you was in Greenwich Village?" We sketched sex life in Greenwich village for him. He took it all without a question and we left him, brooding.

And write me.

Love,<br>John

Don Elder was a writer and an intimate of Katherine Anne Porter's. Daniel Fuchs is a novelist, short-story writer and screenwriter whom my father knew and admired. Fuchs, Jean Stafford, Bill Maxwell and my father collaborated in 1956 on a collection of stories. Marion Greenwood was an artist, and a lover of Josie's.

Sunday night

Darling

Yesterday morning Don Elder shouted up to my window that he was driving to Saratoga to take Katherine-Anne to the races and did I want to come. I didn't particularly deserve a holiday but I agreed and we drove up yesterday morning and returned last night. He and Katherine-Anne went to the races and I tore around saying hello to everybody, shaking hands, grinning and cadging drinks. I had a wonderful time. We spent the evening in Katherine-Anne's rather barren bed-room drinking bourbon. Everyone at Yaddo has been jumping on the poor woman and she's had a nervous breakdown since I saw her in June.

She seemed thoroughly chastened, quite haggard, a much more genuine and attractive person. She sat on the edge of her bed at two in the morning, her make-up worn off, her face lined and weathered, talking about lonelyness and for a moment or two I thought I saw a person through the artificiality and conceit. We left Yaddo at about two. Elder slept all the way back and the drive down was worth the whole business. It was a moonlit night and it smelled good and there wasn't any traffic and it was dawn when we came down the Henry Hudson parkway and into the city; and I get a big kick out of the city and the river at that hour. I went to bed at seven and got up at noon; I do feel kind of washed out now.

. . . Dan and Suzy Fuchs are taking a house in Saratoga for the winter. That town will probably end up as an artist's colony. I saw Nathan and Carole who seemed very happy, having sold a story to Red Book. . . . Marion Greenwood is swooping through the corridors, snatching off the guests. The woods were full of melancholy playwrights, wearing smoked glasses.

It's very muggy here today. Everything sticks to everything else. I see Malcolm tomorrow to continue discussing my employable qualities. We will have a good life darling, a wonderful and beautiful life.

Love,
John


N.Y. is *The New Yorker*.


Spear Street

Saturday

[Sept. Back with his parents]

Darling,

We're just about to saddle and ride off into the quainte countree where everything is over one hundred years old including the fruit salad. It's wonderful September weather and I hope New York will be having some of it when I return on Tuesday. I haven't done much work but I spent yesterday reading passages of the first novel, trying to define my weak spots. There's a story in the N.Y. this week, one of the better kind.

Quincy is a ship-yard town having a boom. I drove down to Fore River yesterday and then along the south shore. The plant was going full blast and it's an exciting damned thing to see. The various establishments that follow a migration of workers (a whore-house, evangelical mission, chain dry-goods store, etc.) have begun to crop up along the main street of Quincy Point. You see the workers in the early evening, cruising along the boulevard in their underwear, admiring the ocean, the beautiful ocean with it's headlands and islands.

And so off to Leftenant Pissamire's for a jot of haddock and a tottle of Johnny Cake in the candlelight.

Love, love, love,
John

Mrs. C. was his mother.

Spear Street

Saturday

Darling,

We drove down to the qaiuntee countree and had some lobsters on a porch, over-looking the ocean. The ocean was a beautiful; green and a lighter green where the shoals are and the lobster boats, bearing the names of homely women, coasting around the traps and the lame and the halt sitting on the beaches and the breakwaters watching the Atlantic with the absent-minded look of someone being read to. I hadn't seen a cranberry bog for a long time; or the irridescent light in those small towns and the low wooden buildings setting on their sills and the large, out-of-state cars inching through the narrow streets and the smell of sea-food. I love it; but until it seems less whimsey I'll go on living inland and love it from a distance. We stopped at one auction but I raced past another so that Mrs. C. didn't have a chance.

The novel worries me all the time. Lobrano will be back on the tenth and I want to have something for him on his return; and there's also the long piece for Davis. I dunno.

John

MLLe. is *Mademoiselle*. I. was Iris, and F. was Fred.

Sunday

Darling,

The paper says a hurricane may strike here tonight so I'm sitting on a tack, waiting for the wind to start howling and the ragged, funereal clouds to come over. I hope it doesn't wash away Fire Island where all the New Yorker staff will be spending the week-end.

I finished the Xmas piece for MLLe. last night and drove down to Norwell and spent the evening with I. and F. and a guest of their's named Bullfinch who had drunk too many cocktails at the charity Bazaar. I. had charge of the raffles at the bazaar and won herself a good english sweater and a large assortment of perrenials. Everybody in Norwell thinks she cheated and so do I. . . .

Love,
John

Eleanor is Eleanor Clark.

114 West 11th [1941]

Tuesday

Dear Eleanor,

Mary and I are going to be married on the twenty second. Mary is going to hang onto her job for obvious reasons, so it means that we will have to stick in the city until fall. . . .

. . . Stop around when you're in town. The doorbell doesn't work but you can force the front door easily. It's top floor front.

John

Doctor and Mrs. Milton Charles Winternitz
Announce the marriage of their daughter
Mary Watson
to
John William Cheever
on Saturday the twenty-second of March
Nineteen Hundred and forty-one
Two hundred ten Prospect Street
New Haven, Connecticut

The "salary" *The New Yorker* paid was for a first-look agreement. This guaranteed a certain number of cents per word when the magazine bought a story, and committed him to show anything he wrote to *The New Yorker* before trying to sell it elsewhere. Although Bill Maxwell says that my father was never paid less than the highest fiction rate, his "salary" never exceeded $1,000 a year.

19 East 8th Street
New York City, New York

January 3, 1942

Dear Malcolm,

I haven't lost much time between finding that you have a job in Washington and between writing to ask you to keep me in mind if there should be any openings. I remember writing similar letters from Saratoga Springs and Georgetown. The New Yorker still pays me a salary but if nothing better shows up, and Mary willing, I think I will try to enlist.

We've been expecting you and Muriel to visit us in this bower since spring. Nathan was in town a week ago, talking about Pre-Catalan. Pete Collins writes from Fort Ethan Allen that he drove through Saratoga Springs a little while ago, behind the shield of a 75.

As ever
John

New Haven was where my mother's parents lived.

January 1942
19 East 8th

Monday

Dear Jo,

. . . Pete has a rating and is filing enemy information in Vermont. Lib is just the same—the nervous army widow—a type of woman that will, I expect, get more and more common around here as time passes. Life at the Cheevers is very happy, very tranquil, and for me altogether vestigial. There might not be any war for us, except that match-papers seem to be getting smaller. I expect to be taken by the army very soon—along with everybody else who shaves—and this puts our happiness in a queer light. We've slipped out of the heavy-drinking set, but everybody else is about the same. We play Badminton on Tuesday nights and eat in a restaurant on Saturdays, but I feel like one of those mental-shock cases where the patient is imprisoned in the habits of his past. Mary is afraid of being incarcerated in New Haven for the so-called duration of what looks to me like a catastrophic war.

John

"Mary's wonderful father," Milton Charles Winternitz, will be referred to in future letters as he was in life: as Winter, Gram, and Guts. He was a man of extraordinary accomplishments. He entered college when he was fourteen years old, and was teaching medicine by the time he was twenty-one. He was dean of the Yale Medical School for fifteen years, during which time he substantially improved the reputation of that institution. He was one of the first Jews to hold an important post at Yale. He was extremely selective in the admission of students to medical school, and has been charged with anti-Semitism. He could be as nasty as he was brilliant, and my father admired him on both counts. He put together a book on the wartime uses of poison gas that is still used as a reference today. He was famous in the family for verbal savagery. One of the great techniques he shared with Polly, his second wife (and my mother's stepmother), was that of saying something wounding when he knew he would be overheard.

A story my father loved to tell was that of how Gram would invite a young doctor up to Treetops, the family summer camp, when he was dean and the man could not refuse. Gram would hint that it was of professional importance. The unfortunate young man would have to borrow a car and take time out for what then must have been at least a six-hour drive. Gram would have flattered his invitee, and insisted that he and his young bride spend the night. When the guests finally found the main house, which lay some way up an unpaved and unmarked road) they would get out of the car, and Binny, having spotted them, would say in a loud voice, clearly sufficient to be overheard, "Oh my God, they've come." This would be the first salvo of a barrage that would last for the entire weekend and would involve every conceivable slight, including the absence of toilet paper in the visitors' cabin.

Family legend has it that when one of Gram's sons brought the girl he intended to marry to New Haven for dinner with his father, Gram heard their approaching footsteps and said, again in a voice that could be overheard, "I don't know what he sees in her. My least competent lab assistant could construct something more attractive out of a dead crow and two wooden laths." But Gram could also be extraordinarily kind and generous, and he and my father were close friends for years.

My mother's mother—Gram's first wife—died young. She was also a doctor. Her name was Helen Watson, and she was the daughter of Thomas Watson, the man who helped Alexander Graham Bell invent the telephone, the man who came when Bell said, "Mr. Watson, please come here, I need you." Gram married Polly after Helen died. Polly was a socialite, and had been married to Stephen Whitney, which counted for a good deal in those days.

[Early 1942]
19 East 8th

Monday

Dear Jo,

I haven't written sooner, because I've been waiting around here for something to happen. Nothing happens. I've had one physical examination for the army. Are you subject to fits or convulsions—they asked —and do you wet the bed? . . .

We spent a week-end in New Haven and Mary's wonderful father took us over to his laboratory and showed us some of his experiments (secret) on the chemistry of courage. He would like to reduce personality to terms of salt and potassium, being a man who has always been overwhelmed by the mysterious forces of his own temperament. Actually the experiments deal with aviation ceilings and shock treatment. The houseman in New Haven puts up blackout curtains every night and Mary's step sister is learning how to make an omlette. . . . I love Mary so much I think we can come through this, one way or another, but I don't think we can circumnavigate it. And what in hell can an able-bodied man in his twenties write about in a time like this, and who would read it if he could write.

John

Dear Jo,

There's been nothing but an ominous silence from the draft board for the last two weeks. The titanic inefficiency that seems about to engulf our world, may begin there. A few more people I know have gone, armed with some eye-wash by Saint Eupery. "There is no despair in defeat . . . the vast brotherhood of death, etc." All I know about war is what I saw in the movies ten years ago, and I still believe all of it; the screams, the amputated hand on the barbed wire fence, and the trench rats. The old guard is still rumbling around the Lafayette and Niles said last night that he was going to Africa and drive an ambulance. In having missed the last war, they seem to have missed a great deal.

John

# BASIC TRAINING

* * *

The Army inducted my father on May 7 of 1942. This was his first extended period of time away from my mother and a typewriter. He suffered mightily on both counts. He continued, however, to write stories and letters in longhand.

His army career was ultimately a success—he was transferred to the Signal Corps, where he attained the rank of sergeant—but the physical hardship of early training was coupled with the embarrassing fact that he did so poorly on the IQ test that he was denied admission to Officer Candidate School. He thus remained a private after most of his friends from the civilian world had been commissioned. This galled him, and he studied up on his math and took the test again; he passed. But his early letters do not completely disguise the bitterness he must have felt. Ultimately, his failure to demonstrate an understanding of simple mathematics may have saved his life, because his original battalion, one that he might have stayed with had he been promoted, faced murderous resistance at the Normandy landing. He used to tell me that the casualty rate was more than 150 percent, which "meant that everybody was wounded, and most of them were killed." This may have been another demonstration of his intuitive approach to mathematics.

Acknowledgments of a low IQ score appear more than once in his fiction. In *Falconer* the protagonist, Ezekiel Farragut, was a professor in civilian life, "but had never tested over 119 and had once gone as low as 101. In the army this had kept him from any position of command and had saved his life."

Army life was a rich source of material for fiction, and there are themes and incidents first described in these letters that appear again and again in his writing, picking up depth and resonance as time goes on. I can remember him telling me about his first sergeant. This officer was extremely cruel, and well hated by the men under him. He ran into some of these men in town and one of them challenged him to a fistfight. Knocked to the ground, the sergeant crawled over to the private and bit him on the leg. The private looked down at his commanding officer. "You're chicken shit," he said. The first fictional variation on this fight appeared in *The New Yorker* story titled "Sergeant Limeburner."

The Sergeant went out of the place first and walked across the street. Brown and Pluzynski and then the other men of the platoon followed. As soon as the Sergeant stopped and Brown caught up with him, the men formed a circle around the two. The Sergeant led nervously with a right and missed. Brown clipped him easily with a left and then cracked him with a right on the jaw that could be heard down the street. The Sergeant landed on his rump in the dirt and put one hand to his jaw.

"You're easy," Brown said. The Sergeant got to his knees and tackled Brown suddenly around the legs, sinking his teeth into Brown's right hand. Brown yelled and kicked him in the stomach. The Sergeant fell on his back. "You're lousy," Brown said.

I guess "chicken shit" was strong for *The New Yorker* in 1943.

There's a similar fight in *The Wapshot Scandal* between Coverly Wapshot and Pete Murphy, a gantry-crew man.

"Listen," Murphy said. "You're trespassing. You're on my land. Get off my land or you'll go home a cripple for life. I'll gouge out your eyes. I'll break your nose. I'll tear off your ears."

Coverly swung a right from the hip, and Murphy, a big man and a coward, it seemed, went down. Coverly stood there, a little bewildered. Then Murphy came forward on his hands and knees and sank his teeth into Coverly's shin.

Still no "chicken shit," but the teeth are going into the leg instead of the hand.

Many of the letters my father wrote in the Army were in longhand, and one of the more legible ones is reproduced. His handwriting was extremely difficult to read. One is reminded of Miss Dent in his short story "The Five-Forty-Eight": "Her writing gave him the feeling that she had been the victim of some inner—some emotional—conflict that had in its violence broken the continuity of the lines she was able to make on paper."

[Longhand]

                                        Wednesday

Darling,

I've just bought a new, two dollar fountain-pen which the man at the Post-exchange said will write by itself so I don't suppose you'll have anymore trouble reading my letters. He had some eight dollar pens which he said would write much better which is undoubtedly true because this one obviously presents some difficulties. I saw a man with a typewriter today. he was on his way to the recreation hall and I'm sure he's a writer. He had glasses and a great, big arse, and an ill-fitting fatigue suit and what else could he have been?

After entering the Army at Fort Dix, he was sent to Camp Croft, just outside Spartanburg, South Carolina. "We will be here for eight to thirteen weeks, taking an intensive course in infantry," he wrote. My mother remembers seeing him on furlough. She said he was painfully thin. She woke in the middle of the night to find him nervously counting time in his sleep. The central figure in the nightmare of basic training was Sergeant Durham who became the basis for a story about the fight mentioned earlier. The piece began:

The surest sign of a green soldier in a unit of the Regular Army is his desire to talk about the severity of the sergeant who instructed him during the first months of his training. After any division has absorbed a group of new men, you hear these stories in the post exchange, in the company street, and in the barracks. This is a story about one of these sergeants, a man named William Limeburner.

The real-life martinet is first mentioned in this letter to my mother.

[Longhand]

Our sergeant is a strange and interesting man. He comes I think from the back-woods of Tennessee or Mississippi, from an unsocial, hard-working people. He has no friends and his one idea is to make his platoon the best in the company. He has an hysterical temper. When he confines us to barracks he goes down to the Post Exchange and has several beers. Then he comes back and explains to us that we are confined for our own good.

Lieber was Maxim Lieber, his agent

[Longhand]

May 28 [1942]

Darling,

The pupils at camp Croft Military School today had a lecture on The Battle of Britain and then began their rifle marksmanship courses. This opened with something called "Triangulation" and Private Cheever didn't do so well. I'm beginning to feel old both on my feet and my eyes. Yesterday I felt every day of thirty. My eyes are funny so when I aim a gun I have to do it with both my eyes open.

Lieber sent down the story today and I'll be able to revise it on Sunday. I'll print the revision in my crabbed little hand, mail it to you, and you can type it and send it to Lieber.

The men were talking last night and it seems that most of them try to stay awake for an hour or so after "lights-out" in order to remember the happy lives they've had. This has become my practice and I was surprised to find that all the jail-birds and steam-fitters had memories; but of course they have.

Love,
John

Darling,

When I wrote last night I forgot to ask you a favor which is will you send me a large box of cookies — . Assorted and tasty. I've been eating so many cookies that belong to other people that I feel guilty. Send them parcel post. Registered mail is a nuisance here.

You have enough money, haven't you darling? Do the New Yorker checks still come though? This is lunch so I'd better quit.

love,

John

[Longhand]

Darling,

. . . We ran through clouds of five poisonous gases without our masks. They are supposed to have various romantic smells like geraniums and garlic but this is true only when they are very diluted. In full strength they all smell like hell. Then we went into a chamber full of gas, etc, etc. The course was conducted by a small, vigorous major who kept throwing smoke-bombs at us to see how quickly we could get into our masks. Then we marched a couple of miles with our gas-masks on. We finished off the morning with close-order drill. This afternoon we had to run and run and fall down and run and bayonet dummies and it was hot as hell. The sergeant was not satisfied with our performance so we had to work after dinner. Then we all went down and had a beer and I bought a fountain-pen and here I am.

. . . The fountain pen isn't going to solve everything but I'm too tired tonight to try very hard. Tomorrow night my penmanship will be a credit to my teachers. Goodnight my love.

John

P.S.

Also I was able to get some stamps and I mailed the story off today. Tell me when you receive it. Also there was a letter from Pete that read not unlike a letter from a sergeant to a private.

Goodnight again.

[Longhand]

. . . Durham was shrieking at us at 5:30 this morning. We carried our beds out of doors because there has been a plague of lice in the barracks. Then we marched way the hell off and gone into the woods and spent the morning digging fox-holes under simulated fire. It began to look like rain at about half-past eleven so we started back at a very fast pace, in order to get our beds in before they got wet. Then we were ordered to run and we ran and ran and ran. It was bedlam. The high point came when Meat Ball's pack came apart. Then his pants fell down. We got back here just as the rain got heavy and we got our beds in without they're getting very wet.

[Longhand]

Wednesday

Darling,

We marched out into the woods and filled in the holes we had dug yesterday. Then we had more rifle-marksmanship exercises and spent the afternoon taking Browning Automatic Rifles apart and putting them together again. Not hard. I forgot to snap the trigger on my rifle so I was gigged along with a dozen other men and we spent the early part of the evening scrubbing baseboards.

This is a recreation hall letter which is to be distinguished from a barracks letter. The noise in both places is about equal but in the recreation hall you have a table to write on and in the barracks you have to write with the pages on your knees. This gives me delusions about the legibility of my penmanship. I also try to write in time to the music.

Goodnight my love,
John

Darling,

The temperature has been around a hundred. One of the men has been fainting pretty regularly and when he felt dizzy yesterday the corporal told him to sit down in the shade for a while. He did. The company marched off and forgot about him. Then he fainted. This all got back to the medical corps and Durham caught hell. "I don't care if you faint," he told us this morning, "but if you're going to faint, tell me about it! You might die of sunstroke and I'd get the blame."

Goodnight, my love,
John

[Longhand]

Monday

Darling

I'm sorry and surprised to find that my letters have such a melancholy sound. I think it must be the handwriting. When I wrote about the lunch hour letters I meant my lunch hour letters. The word was not "loud" or "low" but "LAME." It must be my handwriting, for I am neither low or lonely and I sometimes feel that I love the army

[Longhand]

Camp Croft
Camp Croft, S.C.
July 28

Darling,

This is another letter written on my shaky knees in the barracks. The radio of the first-class machinist—who is a great snob—is playing reflections from the Zeigfield Follies. About half the men are in and it's very hot. Cookie, the half-witted and toothless bus-boy from Childs 59th Street restaurant, is telling about all the rich and beautiful women he has known. On every pay day he goes to Greenville. They serve him a mickey finn, empty his pockets and put him in jail. He always insists that the people who robbed him were nice people.

Goodnight, darling.

Eddie Newhouse is a short-story writer and novelist who remained a friend throughout my father's life. Bill Maxwell was my father's editor at *The New Yorker* for nearly forty years. Ross was Harold Ross, *The New Yorker*'s founding editor. I was surprised to find that my father had been trying to get out of the infantry, because he used to tell me that he'd been reluctant to leave his outfit.

It's interesting to note the sharp dismissal of the letters from my grandfather. Some later letters from Frederick Lincoln Cheever have survived. These are doting and kind, and give no clue as to the inspiration for the stern, unforgiving man who appears in such stories as "The National Pastime."

Spartanburg
Sunday

Darling,

Yesterday was a fairly easy one. We were all churned up for inspection and then the officer didn't come to inspect us. Inspection involves shifting your rifle from hand to hand, staring straight ahead, opening the bolt, etc. The thought of doing this in front of an officer threw so many men into a panic that it would have been a terrible fracas anyhow and might have undermined the officer caste.

I'll be interested to know how Eddie makes out with his commission. The officers here are a very stern and upright lot. They begin the day with drilling four hundred men in calisthenics; something I don't think I'll ever be able to do and something I can't see Eddie doing either.

Dad has started to write me and writes that he has begun to write you. Don't bother to answer them and don't bother to open them unless they interest you.

There was a letter from Gus and Bill today. They bought one of the stories I wrote at Treetops and also the one I wrote on the Monday before I returned to Dix. Also Ross has written to Colonel White about "Yank." They can't do anything until I finish basic training; but Dear Jesus I hope and pray that they will be able to do something then. Two months will go by very quickly and perhaps I can be back in N.Y. with you then. But in the meantime you must come down here for a week-end if it's practical as far as time is involved. I'm ahead in my accounts with The New Yorker and maybe I can stay that way, which will pay for the trip.

Love,
John

I'm greatly moved by the intensity and purity of the passion my parents felt for each other at this stage in their lives. It wasn't always so. It is common practice to end books and movies with a marriage or a death. One presumes the writers stop because they don't know what happens after death, and don't want to know what happens after marriage. When he was an older man, my father would like to refer to the vows of Holy Matrimony as a preposterous but extremely useful lie.

Thursday

Darling

Of course I didn't mean that I'd forgotten our marriage when I said that I felt out of touch. I'll never forget that and its the one big, fine thing that keeps me going down here. What I meant is that I'm getting awfully impatient to see you and that I miss you more and more. The only idea of life I have is life with you. . . .

Love,
John

[Printed by hand]
Darling,

I'm enclosing a story. Would you type it out and send it to The New
Yorker as soon as possible. They might be able to put it into some
shape and use it. I spelled it out carefully like an idiot child, sitting on
the edge of my bunk.

Love, love, love,love,<br>John

# REGULAR ARMY:
## He Was Transferred
## From Camp Croft,
## at Spartanburg,
## South Carolina,
## to Camp Gordon,
## Outside Augusta, Georgia.

* * *

Camp Gordon, Augusta, Ga.<br>Co. E. 22nd Infantry<br>Sunday

Darling,

I got up this morning before dawn to telephone you but all of the
Recreation Halls were locked. I sat on the front steps until eight o'clock

when a man came and unlocked them. By that time the telephone lines were loaded and by the time my call came through you had probably gone to the beach.

We came down here on Friday, of course, arguing all the time about where we were going. We rode in coaches and we had sandwiches for lunch so we figured on a short trip, which it was; but we had to keep waiting at sidings for other trains to go by so it took all day. We were alternatively depressed and excited. When we arrived we hung onto one another like sheep, but they separated us quickly, dividing us up among so many platoons, companies and regiments that none of us are in the same barracks. After we had put our things in order we all met by pre-arrangement at the Post Exhange where everyone admitted that they were homesick for Camp Croft and Sergeant Durham.

Wednesday

Darling,

This is another noon letter. There was a letter in today's mail from a Doctor at the Neurological Institute asking me why I had given up writing. Looking for a patient, I suppose.

Bill Maxwell met my father before the war. "Your father was so young then—he must have been in his twenties—and so handsome. He lived at Rhinelander Gardens, and then suddenly he was married." Bill was my father's editor, advocate and friend at *The New Yorker* from 1936 to 1976, and *The Wapshot Scandal*, published in 1964 was dedicated to W.M. On August 16, 1942, my father wrote Bill from Camp Gordon, Georgia. The story, which is not included in *The Stories of John Cheever*, was almost certainly "Problem No. 4." *The New Yorker* paid $250 for this, and it ran in the October 17, 1942 issue.

Sunday

Dear Bill,

I'm very glad you liked the story. Writing it was a lot of fun; so much so that I spend much time mooning over literary ideas while I should be chasing a training stick with a bayonet. Sometimes it seems as though I should stop writing altogether and then I think: fuck that, as they say around here.

Last Saturday night was the first Saturday night I've spent at Camp Gordon and it wasn't bad. The week-end drinking in town got monotonous. There is one hotel bar that used to be a commercial hotel bar before we came, and that I like to lean on. there is also one ex-resort hotel that will not withstand more than another four months of military treatment. The palms are all dead, the ceilings are cracked and hanging in some places, and most of the furniture has been broken or stolen. There is one stock Hofbrau called the Heidelberg where we drink beer and sing Dei Lorelei and Mein Hertz in Heidelberg, etc. There is one pseudo-westchester joint called the Red Lion where they serve a Sunday night buffet supper; very bad and very pathetic like the English eating bottled peas in Chandrapore. And then there are the soldiers places that come with us and that will go when we leave: juke boxes, spilled beer and an overall policy of the micky finn and the short change, and if you don't like us we'll call the military police.

And today is the first day that we've had anything like eastern weather. Its cold, overcast, and rainy. Its just like a noreaster and it makes me very happy. I can see my old man tapping the barometer, dragging in the porch furniture, and closing up all the windows for three days.

Best,
John

Gus Lobrano used to take my father fishing at a wilderness camp he had on Cranberry Lake in upstate New York. Y--k is *Yank*. Here's the tough sergeant again. In "Sergeant Limeburner" he doesn't come back to camp after the private beats him up in town. I guess the real sergeant had more sand than the fictional one.

Camp Gordon Georgia                                    Co. "E" 22nd Inf.
Dear Gus,

I think of you every time I stumble along a compass azimuth because I remember your telling me about doing this at Cranberry Lake of your own free will. And every time I think of you I hope you haven't enlisted in the Army or the Navy. . . . I was offered a job with a corporal's rating today but it was only the job of secretary to the chaplain and the captain offered it to me with a leer, so I said no. I'm going to steer clear of any non-field jobs until I hear from Y--k. This is a large camp and they seem to give ratings to everyone, including those men who pick up the most cigaret butts in the morning.

There is a very interesting difference between a training camp and the regular army. It is like the Convent and Life. You can always tell a rookie from a training camp because he gets up in the middle of the night and shines his shoes, shaves, dresses, rolls a full field pack, and then sits on the edge of his bunk, trembling. They also begin every conversation with a story of the brutality of their last sergeant. I still do; but then I've only been here three weeks. It looked for a while as though we had our sergeant at Croft beaten. We had driven him so far into drink that he wasn't any use to anyone. One of the privates beat him up severely but he was back in a day or so with his face sewed up and a pair of dark glasses to cover his eyes. it was raining. A few nights before we left he came into the latrine, very drunk, and told us that his girl—the one in Texas—had lost two fingers in a sawmill. On the morning of the day we left he tried to make us fall out of the barracks in fifteen seconds. After nine or ten attempts this turned out to be a physical impossiblity and after several men had hurt themselves falling downstairs he settled for eighteen seconds. My sergeant here is an amiable, beer-drinking fellow . . . , but I miss Durham.

[Longhand]

                                                        Tuesday Night
Darling,

This will probably be proceeded by a frantic wire for money: but I think I am being given a seven and possibly a ten day furlough. . . . I'll wire for sure as soon as I get out of the garrison with a furlough in my pocket. When I arrive in New York depends on the train connections. It will probably be Saturday night. . . . Oh Boy, oh Boy, oh Boy!

                                                        Love,
                                                        John

My sister was conceived on this furlough.

                                                        Wednesday Night
Hello Darling,

And so the letter-writing and the struggle to find time to write letters begins all over again. you're a sweet-heart and boy it was good to spend seven days with you and all the way down on the train I kept thinking about the next reunion. There was plenty of time for this because the ride took twenty-four hours, so I thought it out very carefully. We had forty minutes in Washington so Daly and Levine and I went out to a saloon for a beer. The stories about the women in Washington are evidently true, because the place was crowded with intoxicated women, frightening each other with an artificial mouse. We had the good luck to get into a coach that had a broken-down lighting system so it was dark and I had a pretty good sleep from Washington until some town in the Carolinas when we stopped again. This trip was the first time I've gone from Florence to Augusta in the daylight and I had a good look at the country which was nothing again but varieties of poverty and soil-erosion. These towns must mean home to someone— I keep thinking—when we stop at a dirt-road crossing with a few shantys, a gas-staton, and some razor-back hogs stirring up the dust on the main street. There are also poisonous bogs, dead trees over-weighted with Spanish moss, hungry-looking people, and for hundreds of miles almost all the buildings are the same size and shape: a two-room single story building with a sloping porch roof built on a pile of rocks to keep it off the ground. They have yards of raked or swept clay or dirt and the only green thing is an occasional rusty palmetto or a Daphne bush and why they grow I don't know.

We got into Augusta fairly early in the afternoon shaved and took a shower at the Y and then went out to break the shock of return. There were no soldiers in town, of course, the streets were full of women which only goes to show that they really do keep them in purdah . . . we got into some low company and ended up waltzing a couple of Pineapples around the bon-air bar room. I got to bed at ten o'clock and woke up on a rainy morning, feeling very low. But I'll get used to the place in a couple of days.

All my love sweet-heart.<br>John

My father met E.E. Cummings in the thirties and was a passionate admirer of his writing and his "immense personal style."

[Longhand]

Oct. 8 '42

Co. "E"
22nd Infantry
Camp Gordon, Georgia

Dear Marion and Cummings,

There's not much sense in writing to you in long-hand because no one has ever been able to read my long-hand. There is a typewriter in camp but I haven't been able to use it for the last couple of weeks and when I do get to use it a lot of people gather around me and watch each word as it comes out of the machine. There's a lot to write about and I'll write later; but this is to thank you for the letter, the red leaf, and the five. And many many thanks.

This camp has barracks of white clap-boarding, with small-paned windows and red brick chimnies and sometimes it reminds me of Harvard. The life hasn't been at all rough and of course we haven't seen anything resembling war. Many of the men have gained so much weight that they're bursting the seams of their uniforms and when we go on the rifle range our blouses are always stuffed with fresh fruit.

The army gave me a furlough and I went to New York of course and I don't think I have ever been so happy. What a beautiful, beautiful city. But I'll write about that and all the rest of it when I get a type-writer.

And thanks again.

John

This time he had a typewriter. *The Enormous Room* is the Cummings book about his time in a French prisoner-of-war camp during the First World War. It was one of my father's favorite books.

Camp Gordon
Augusta, Georgia

Dear Cummings and Marion

Someone is reading over my shoulder, of course, so I'll have to cut down on military secrets and tenderness. It was so good to hear from both of you. The army isn't bad at all and from what I've seen in my six months it seems that the American soldier is in greater danger of being killed by kindness and indigestion that he is of being killed by the Germans. There's a good deal of homesickness, of course; homesickness and sex-starvation and an inability to understand why we should have to spend any part of our lives in Georgia. This part of Georgia, Cummings, is terrible. The women are skinny, many of them wear sunbonnets, no alcoholic beverages are sold on Sunday, and soil erosion has advanced to a point where the surrounding countryside looks like the begining of another Yosemite National Park; gutted beds of red and yellow clay, no vegetation to speak of, and a monotonous climate. The faces and the buildings are the faces and buildings Walker Evans and Margert Bourke-White did such a brisk business in; and every time I wave to a share-cropper and his barefoot children from my lightly armored vehicle I thank God that neither curiosity or social service brought me down here.

The people are wonderful. My platoon is made up almost entirely of southerners who believe in the headless people and take off their shoes after retreat. At the training camp in South Carolina we had an ex-smoke eater named Smoko, a clerk from the Chase National Bank, a waiter from the Hotel Westbury, two night club M.Cs, the wine steward from the Pierre, and a dozen or so longshoremen, steam-fitters, elevator operators. Also one sad, sad Jewish fellow who had never done anything. Anything at all.

I think about the Enormous Room whenever I stand prison guard. It's a neat, clean prison full of gay southern boys who run around the yard like a pack of dogs; but it is a prison and they are confined there under armed guard, some of them for as long as two years. Their offense is usually desertion. They stay away three or four months and then return to the barracks some morning, sit on the edge of the bed, bum a cigaret and ask:"What do you know?" They are usually under arrest of quarters for a week before their court martial and then they disappear.

Letters are solid gold down here if you should find time to write again.

Affectionately,
John


My father liked to tell stories about Cummings, and had fond memories of having tea with the poet and his wife, Marion, at Patchin Place in

Greenwich Village. The letter Cummings sent him in the Army passed into family legend, but I'll let my father tell it himself in a note he sent to Marion in 1962, after the poet's death. You'll notice that the five dollars has become ten.

Wednesday [Sept. 5, 1962]

Dear Marion,

I don't like to add to what must be an intolerable burden of correspondence but I can't let this day pass without saying how much I loved Cummings. I do remember, of his boundless kindnesses, a note he wrote me in the army. He wrote:"I too have slept with someone else's boot in the corner of my smile." He enclosed an autumn leaf and a ten dollar bill. I'm not especially pious but I think he was an angel and I expect he still is. The world will be grateful to you for your part in this.

As ever,
John

Camp Gordon
Augusta,Georgia

Darling,

Since talking with you on the telephone I've discovered that they don't make second lieutenants of men approaching or over thirty. They have to get to be first lieutenants or nothing at all. I think that's the way it works. Don't count on a commission for your husband, by the way.

Love,
John

Camp Gordon
Augusta, Georgia

Darling,

Tonight is pay night and the town will be like Carson City. Last night everybody was broke but me, the restaurants were empty, and it was like Augusta must have been before we came. I went into town with an OCS boy who was flunked out five days before he would have been given his commission. . . .

We drank in a place called the Tropical Spot which is an old bank coverted into an imitation New York nitery with a lot of imitation leather and a hot number in an evening gown singing "White Christmas." There were also a couple of other women there, very drunk and they happened to be in the latrine when the singer went in there between numbers to powder her nose, I guess. Anyhow the singer came shooting out, very angry and indignant, and pretty soon the other babies came out, also angry and all three began to call one another trash and slut, etc. and the men all sat around and said: "I wouldn't let anyone call me trash, would you?" trying to egg the babies into a fight but they finally split up and went their various ways without any fight and everybody was disappointed.

Love, sweet,
John

The X signature below seems to have been a demonstration of mock solidarity with his hillbilly colleagues.

Monday

Darling,

We will probably reach one another before this reaches you; mais, ca put, as e.e. cummings wrote in his last hyroglyph, and he even put on the circonflex. I ran from prison guard to the telephone and from the telephone to here. The prison is very interesting, from the outside, anyhow. The prisoners are the finest looking group of men I have ever seen in the army. Their eyes are bright and clear, their teeth are white, their fatigue uniforms are spotless and faded with scrubbing and the stigma of confinement has given them a kind of fire and dash you don't find in the ordinary enlisted man. Their lives are not easy; I imagine their lives are very hard but when they come out of the gates they come out with all their teeth showing and their heads up and the guard mount looks very drab indeed.

My job was to take two men sentenced to hard labor to the wood pile and then stand over them with a loaded gun while they playfully split kindling, ribbed one another, and talked about what they would do when they were released. They are allowed to mail only one letter a week. They are also carefully searched before they leave the stockade and when they return. So as soon as they are out of sight of their gaol they sit down, take off their shoes, and remove a voluminous corre-spondence which a gullible guard like me will mail for them. Both the prisoner and the guard would be punished if this were discovered, but it wasn't discovered. Most of the prisoners are from the south and they will never learn the law.

Also the clerical job isn't coming my way as simply as I had expected. Kenyon called me into his room last night and asked me not to take it, promising to do everything he could for me if I remained with the platoon. Its not easy to disregard the advice of your platoon sergeant. Anyhow, I'm not worrying.

See you soon, Baby

X

The story mentioned below was run in the November 21, 1942, issue of *The New Yorker* under the title "The Man Who Was Very Homesick for New York." He got $365 for it. I asked my mother if she had changed the title when she typed the story for him. She said she didn't remember, but she thought it possible.

Monday

Darling,

There was a letter from Gus. I guess they really did like the story. Where did you get the idea that the title was "The Lonesome man." The title is "The Man Who was Very Homesick for New York." did you make your own title up, or has the New Yorker changed it.

I drilled the platoon for the first time today and got to shout:"Right shoulder HARMS Left shoulder HARMS forward HARCH, etc. It was great fun. That's about all. Its cold as a son of a bitch, down here, tonight. . . .

Love,

John

Friday

Darling,

The package from Macy's came today, the cheese and sardines, etc. and it was fine and not at all silly. I am now sucking hard candies and if I go on a problem next week the fish will be very handy.

Thanksgiving was a cloudy day, something like I remember Thanksgiving down east. No one was noticably depressed. I worked here in the morning and then had a couple of stiff drinks in the boiler-room before dinner. We stood in line in front of the mess hall as usual and the mess-sergeant came out—obviously afraid that our conduct was going to be short of punctilious—and told us to file in quietly and take places at the tables. The tables were covered with sheets and in the center of each was a platter of fruit and nuts, a bowl of olives, cranberry sauce, etc. The first thing the man beside me said: "Jesus Christ. Now we don't get no clean sheets for three weeks." . . . One of the cooks mumbled a prayer ending with the exclamation:"For Christ's sake!"

Love, sweetheart, John

The jacket photograph was being taken for his first book, a collection of short stories titled *The Way Some People Live*, which Bennett Cerf at Random House brought out in March of 1943. Tom is my mother's brother, and Elizabeth is his wife.

December 14

Hello Darling,

Your very fine father wrote me a letter today and sent me a Christmas present which was a ten dollar check. This is unusually good of him. If it's not too late now I'll go in town and have the photographs mailed to you, and Bennet Cerf. . . .

There was a fine spice-cake from Josie in the mail today, packed in a tin box and a lot of waxed paper and moist and smelling of Erwinna when I opened it. Also a small, heavy package from Tom and Elizabeth with a don't open until, etc. on it which I have a fair chance of observing. Mothers are writing to company commanders every day now letters that begin: "My Randolph has always bin home for exmas. We have a big mitting then and i would bless you if you wid give my Randolph a 5 day furlow." Also today I saw a letter which said: "Go to yr Company officer and ask him for a 5 dy leave becas i am 5½ months gone and you had better come home and marry me, etc." Of course this is confidential.

Darling,

. . . I feel like a dope with everybody being made Corporal and Sergeant, etc. and me with my one stripe. I think I can take my IQ over again this week for OCs and maybe I can raise myself out of the moron class. If I can't you'll have to swing along with a moron.

A couple of weeks ago one of the southern boys exclaimed:"Jesus Christ." The rest of the pack were on him in a minute. "What yawl mean by usin' them there northern cuss-words." "Yawl talkin like a damn Yankee,"etc. It was all in fun, but it was the first time it had ever occured to me that taking the name of The Lord (or The Holy Ghost or of His Son) was a Yankee trick. I guess it is.

I had charge of signing the pay roll; one formation at which all the men appear. They filed into the Day Room tonight, one by one, and wrote down their plain and fancy names on the roll while the band in the quadrangle was playing "I'm Dreaming Of A White Christmas" and the regimental guard mount was having their guns inspected. This event—the rigid military demeanor of everyone involved—and the sentimental music always strike me as being funny and moving. Now I see that I've mixed up the payroll and regimental guard mount, which have nothing to do with one another. And I am very tired, sweet,so I'll stop.

Love,
John

It would be an exhaustive and not particularly illuminating exercise to draw attention to every place where the image from a letter echoes in the fiction. What's interesting about the last paragraph of the letter above is the fact that it comes back again and again, with the writing getting more and more beautiful and complex. Perhaps there's no connection beyond the fact that Christmas carols contrast brilliantly with regimentation and even squalor, but when I read this letter, I thought immediately of that dreadful afternoon in *Falconer*. These are prisoners, not soldiers. They've been herded into the prison's education building to fill out forms and have their pictures taken beside a plastic Christmas tree. This is a cynical attempt on the part of the prison administration to keep them from rioting, and the forms they have filled out are ripped up and thrown into the air. But as they file out through this shower of shredded forms, they begin to sing. It's August, remember, and they know what the administration is up to, but as they head away from the artificial Christmas tree, they begin to sing "Silent Night."

... The Cuckold picked up a good bass, and considering the distance they had all come from caroling, they formed a small, strong choir, singing enthusiastically about the Virgin. The old carol and the scraps of paper falling softly through the air onto their heads and shoulders was not at all a bitter recollection on that suffocating rainy day, but a light-hearted memory of some foolishness, linked to a fall of snow.

Polly was also referred to as Binny.

Sunday

Darling,

You can't stop loving me all of a sudden because I'm not photogenic. Anyone but Robert Taylor would look like hell if they sat on a piano stool in Augusta and were snapped and maybe Robert Taylor would look like hell. I guess you'd better call Cerf and tell him to disregard the photograph. I don't mind being ugly but I'd hate to have a sappy smile broadcast around the country.

Both the package from Tom and Eliz and the one from Polly were labeled "Not to be Opened, etc.," but there wasn't any room in my foot locker for anything else so I opened them both. The sweater is beautiful and it also exhaled a beautiful Polly-smell which is something you don't find in an Army camp or even in Georgia. In Georgia the women use perfume that smells a greal deal like fly-killer. Two knives is just about the right amount of knives. I carve up my desk, pare my fingernails, remove staples from Service Records, slice fruit-cake, sharpen tent-pegs, and open cans with one or the other. I'll write Tom and Eliz and Polly.

Love, Sweet,
John

Dear Bill,

This is Christmas eve and I have a terrible hangover. All furloughs have been cancelled and only ten percent of the men will be allowed to leave for the week-end so there is a lot of griping. "This is a hell of a place to spend Christmas," we say to one another, looking out of the windows gloomily. . . .

The Dickens was a wonderful idea, Bill, and many thanks. Pickwick Papers is something I have never read, I have the time to read now, and I've been looking around for something to read. The library here has almost nothing but recent fiction and all of this seems to have been written by ladies. For some reason the periodical department is dominated by a complete collection of alumni bulletins: Harvard, Yale, Williams, Rutgers, etc. Books have turned out to be much better than movies when you get barracks crazy.

One of the southern boys came in yesterday for an emergency furlough. His brother is being electrocuted for the murder of a federal officer and he wanted to go home to say goodbye. Another southern boy came in yesterday for an insurance policy. His name is Calib Muse and his brothers names are Plato and Andy Jackson Muse and they live in Pioneer Tennessee. Calib is thin, old-looking, and spinsterish and when he comes into the barracks another southerner named Bearden always shouts: "Here comes Calib Muse. Stinks like a billy-goat. Naaah, naaaah." . . .


Tootsie refers to my still unborn sister.


December 31, 1942

Darling,

This is New Year's Eve and for the first time in what must be nearly fifteen years there is nothing but a little 3.2 beer running through these old veins. There was some agitation about going into town, but it didn't seem worth while so I went instead to a movie called It happened on a Honeymoon or something like that, with Ginger Rogers and Cary Grant, which all pointed out that the fall of Europe was engineered by a grade B character actor whose name escapes me and who married Ginger Rogers.

This letter has been held up between paragraphs because the charge of quarters has been telling me about his business which was the slot-machine business. He has $7,000 worth of slot machines in a Pittsburgh garage and he's paid $3,000 dollars in license fees on them and now slot-machines have been declared illegal in Pennsylvania and his wife writes him: "You shouldn't have tied up all your money in those slot machines. Can I eat them?"

Today the entire division went off into the woods (cooks, MPs, Clerks and all) and 40 machine guns fired over our heads, four batteries of field artillery also fired over our heads, Mustangs machine-gunned the territory in front of us, glide-bombers sprayed us with tear-gas, and heavy bombers dropped five hundred pound bombs all around. The most impressive were the Mustangs and they come in on target in the same way that a hawk or a gull hunts, only much faster and much more deadly. They start at about 3,500 feet and come down to within 15 feet of the target. Very pretty.

I won't wish you a happy New Year, but I will wish that you and I and tootsie can be together this time next year and I don't see why we shouldn't be.

Love,
John

Fred worked for a firm that manufactured sheets.

Camp Gordon
Augusta, Georgia

Friday night

Hello sweet,

Big day in the field, I hear. General Barton was down this morning and that always throws everyone into a furor. Then this afternoon there was a six mile run which I did not make. This is about the tenth time the men have made the course and naturally they're beginning to discover little short-cuts through the bushes and other various labor-saving devices. Well, the company commander caught all the miscreants, restricted them for a week, and they will run the course every night this week.

There was a grouchy letter from Fred in which he said the government has just bought eleven million sheets. He doesn't see how Pepperell can be expected to manufacture so many sheets on a 40 hour week. He also mentioned your delicate condition and what a fine girl you are, as do both mother and dad whenever they write. And you certainly are a fine girl and I hope you don't get too sick. I don't see why you should have to give up smoking. Iris smoked all the time. She wasn't able to drink much toward the end, but even then she could drink beer and wine.

Love, sweet,
John

Monday

Darling,

It's still cold here, as it was when I wrote you eight or nine hours ago. The people who live in cabins around here, black and white, must have a hell of a time. Last night I read some of Look Homeward Angel and it seemed very good to me. The Oh, lost, oh lost passages seemed inoffensive and the rest of it seemed garrulous, witty, and a lot like an old-fashioned English novel. I only read a couple of chapters. Tonight I'll try to write Polly and your father, thanking them for their presents.

That's all honey.

Love,
John

My father was fascinated by the "southern boys" he met in the Army. I remember him telling me that he'd gone into the shower once and found that Calib had painted his toenails and fingernails passion pink. "Ain't that pretty?" he asked my father, with absolutely no awareness of the strict sexual mores he was violating. "Tootsie" was a name for my unborn sister. My mother was looking for a larger apartment.

Monday

Hello Sweet,

Farewell to Arms [is] a wonderful book, but it doesn't have anything in it about spending a year or two in the Carolinas or Georgia. And there are no beautiful English nurses here. Sometimes the camp, when you're coming back from a march, looks like an Italian city on the hill because of the pines and the sand and the white, red-roofed buildings. But we don't drink kummel in hospitals and champagne in barns and Strega in cafes. And I guess you don't either, honey. Time mag said that beef liver cost $1.15 a pound in N.Y. Is this true. I hope you and tootsie get enough lean meat.

I don't dream about apartments but I do dream continually about the day when the war will be over. It's always in the country somewhere, always in the east where there is grass and where there are elm trees, and you're always wearing a sweater. . . . But army life, like any other kind of life, depends upon your own resourcefulness, and I hope to get to be more resourceful and make this more of a life.

Love from your very gloomy husband, sweet.
John

Cheever was and is an unusual name. My mother's family lived in New Haven.

Wednesday night

Darling,

... Lieutenant Alcorn is now in charge. He is not a rebel which is something. His voice is pleasant and he has an up-turned nose with a small wart on it. He walks with his head way up, moving a little as though the arches of his feet had been broken. I keep trying to estimate these men by imagining the clothes they would have worn in civilian life. This is a grave limitation on my part, of course, but dressed in khakis, with a sub-machine gun slung over one shoulder and a kettle-shaped helmet on their heads you often wonder what in hell they were in the past. In six months a first lieutenant can develop the temperament of a Prima Donna, a very stagey manner, an exaggerated walk, and a touch of gastric ulcers; luxuries none of them would be entitled to in civilian life. . . .

In the noon mail was a letter from Josie . . . and a letter from a Mary Ann Cheever in Springfield, Illinios who writes: "I am 19 years old and work for the state. I have 4 older sisters, 1 older brother, & 1 younger brother. How old are you? Am I impertinent?" She saw my name in Colliers and wants to know if its really, truly my name.

. . . Getting mail from you every day in the week, and sometimes twice a day, makes me very happy. If the Sundays are grim I should think a junket to New Haven now and then would be nice. I wish I could be with you on Sundays. On Mondays too. There was a news story in the Atlanta Constitution about a couple who kept their romance burning for thirty years through the United States mails.

Love, honey,
John

The story about an entire company being restricted to barracks because of a theft of cash is so common to literature that taken by itself it makes a considerable argument for the existence of a preordained order in the universe. It happened to my father's company in Augusta. Herman Nelson's misfortune was probably the inspiration for a *New Yorker* story run in August of 1943 and titled "The Invisible Ship." Nelson becomes Algot Larssen, who loses sixty dollars. The fictional theft was less than the sixty-six dollars and change that was taken in real life, proving—for those who need proof—that fiction need not exaggerate in order to be effective. It is true that the criminal in the short story is caught and punished, while the real-life thief is never even identified, but that's an entirely different matter.

                                                                          Thursday
Darling,

Someone stole some money out of Herman Nelson's pocket the night before last so the company is restricted indefinitely. Herman Nelson, a nice fellow from North Dakota, is being discharged today. They can't find the thief of course and suspicion rests on everyone, and poor old Herman has to go back to North Dakota without any money. "I" company is restricted because of mumps so CAPTAIN Alcorn called us into the day room last night and said that theft was worse than mumps and that we would be restricted until further notice.

The restriction may mean that I won't get a chance to write you; but the captain may lift it tonight or tomorrow.

                                                                    All my love, sweet,
                                                                          John


Geoffrey was another name my father used in referring to my unborn sister.

                                                                          Friday Night
Hellow Sweet,

Alcorn lifted the restriction last night. The thief was not discovered and I imagine that the affair will be forgotten in a few days. Nelson was a very nice fellow who bunked beside me. He was thirty-eight years old and a wheat farmer from North Dakota, which is why they discharged him. He had been saving his money against this time and had managed to scrape up sixty-six dollars and some change, which is what the thief took. We made up a collection of twenty-five dollars and I guess he'll get along allright. We are losing all our men of thirty-eight or over and their places are being taken by the eighteen and nineteen year olds.

There was a letter from Noel Hemendinger today who has just been commissioned. He will teach law to other officers. Nat Goldstein was also commissioned and is out in Little Rock, complaining about the price of uniforms. This is all the news from the commisioned department, except that Seabiscuit is trying for a direct commission as a laundry officer. The enlisted men are still as fine as ever. Last night one of them, named Hardwick, showed me a letter written by one of his girls. It was a masterpiece of misspelling. He had sent his photograph to one girl, and this other girl was asking for his photograph and asking why he had forgotten her. "Doan you remember what you done to me," she asked, "on the floor under the stove at Uncle Joe's that night. Didn't you mean it?"

I hope you get some good-looking clothes to fit you and Geoffrey, honey. It seems like they should have something at Saks or Mary Lewis. And would you send me the book on easy ways to get a high I.Q. Love, sweetheart, and I wish I were with you.

John

Tuesday night

Hello Sweet,

I've been eating meals at the Service Club, the result of which is that I need some money. Could you send me some money airmail. A check is as good as a money order. A check is even better, and easier to cash, now that Captain Brill will endorse them. Captain Leeb called me up about an hour ago, and said that an order for my being editor of the regimental paper was going through and would be out tomorrow or the day after. This has been hanging fire for so long that I'm not very enthusiastic about it. Linn Streeter is going to do the cartoons and we ought to be able to bring out a good paper. It also means that I may have some time to study long division and fractions, which I don't have around here. I've looked at the math book and it's wonderful and thanks a lot for sending it darling. I wish I were with you and could tell you about integers and regimental newspapers and Special Service captains and improper fractions.

Love, darling
John

Monday

Darling,

One of the members of the band went out with a girl who turned out to have spinal menengitis so we don't have a band anymore and we don't have close order drill in the morning, retreat parade, or formal guard mount and I guess we won't have until the band comes out of quarantine. . . .

There is an inspection at eight-thirty tomorrow morning; and another on Wednesday. All this scrubbing and polishing has got the men talking again and the most likely story seems to be that General (Yoo Hoo) Lear is cruising around the neighborhood and will inspect the camp. He is supposed to be a hell raiser and naturally the officers would be embarrassed if he should find any dust around. A rumor that was circulated yesterday brought out a characteristic side of the army. In the army there are a number of men who used to be Pennsylvania coal miners. They talk all the time about how they would rather (sooner) be in the most dangerous mine, working for dirt pay, than be in the army. Yesterday the rumor went that coal miners would be withdrawn from service and sent back to the mines. The coal miners were shy on the whole proposition. It's easy to see that they'll go back to the mines only under great pressure, and that the army life will look very carefree and happy from a mine shaft.

Love, my brave blood donor. This private first class would have fainted dead away.

John

Wednesday

Hello Darling,

A week-end pass was out of the question because I have to take rifle marksmanship on Friday and Saturday, in preparation for the range again. This will be the third time that I've prepared. The great paper is all stenciled and will be run off the mimeograph machine sometime tomorrow and stapled sometime tomorrow and then we'll start getting ready for the next issue. Streeter and I had some fun in this issue writing a burlesque of the Division paper's Inquiring Reporter. I'll send a copy of it along. I don't know how the Major will take it, but I'm sure the men will like it. Tonight I went to the movies and saw Ann Southern as a great violinist. I hope you wait for me and don't go chasing off after a very classy composer and a very snotty music critic like Ann Southern did, the minute Melvin Douglas went to Lisbon. Christ almight, what tripe.

Goodnight, sweet-heart,
John

The DD is the *Double Deucer*, the regimental paper my father and Linn
Streeter collaborated on.

Thursday

Hello Honey,

This morning I went over to the Rec Hall at about seven. It was
about zero and the furnace was out, so I started to build a fire. I
couldn't get the thing started. Then O'Keefe came along and we tried
together, without any luck. Then Lt. Jackson came along with the
determined air officers learn at OCS and said: "We will build a fire in
the correct manner." We did too. The fire got started and the building
began to warm up so I went into my office, which is at the back of the
building and started cutting the stencils for this week's DD. Goldie and
Streeter came in about ten o'clock. Then we heard Lt. Jackson shouting: "Leave the building immediately." I picked up the typewriter with
the stencil on it and ran out the back door, which fortunately was
open. Smoke and flames followed us out the door and in about twenty
minutes the building was a ninety percent loss. Boards have been
convening all day and since the furnace was operated automatically the
blame falls on no one. There was apparently some defective wiring in
the system.

It was a first rate fire with fire-engines, geysers of water, collapsing
chimneys, the General with his crop and about ten Colonels. Poor
captain Leeb, who was in charge of the building will probably be
investigated. He's a very unlucky man. Last fall he organized a swimming party and one of the soldiers drowned. Now his office is a smoking ruin. We were able to get all of our stuff out and tomorrow we
bring out a special fire issue of the DD.

Saturday

Honey,

You're a sweet-heart with your fig newtons and tootsie and I hope
you get a nice place to live in. Your letters are very sweet and make me
happy.

Last night I went in town with O'Keefe and had dinner in a southern
cafeteria. The place was well-lighted and extremely clean and an old
character sits by the window playing sad music on an organ. She wears
a bandana around her head and gold earrings. The food is good—

about the automat caliber—and after you've filled up your tray a neatly uniformed waitress takes it away from you and carrys it to a table to save you the embarrassment of being seen with a tray in your hands. She sets the table and then on every table there is an electric candle and when you want some ketchup or another cup of tea you just turn on the candle and down comes one of the neatly uniformed waitresses to cater to your every whim. Which just goes to show that this part of the country is so accustomed to slave labor that the operation of a cafeteria has to be modified.

I'm sending you three copies of the DD and also a copy of the Ivy Leaf which is O'Keefe's baby. The only copy of the first issue I could find has it's front page printed upside down. We took copies of the third issue, which came out the day after the fire, stacked them and ran a blow torch over the edges so it looked as though they were salvaged. The damage to the second issue is genuine.

Love, sweetie,
John

The matter-of-fact reference to the "falsification of my tax" came as something of a shock, not because of its planned dishonesty but because of the implied cupidity. My father was often quite poor, but he was rarely tight. He must have been one of the only men in Westchester who always paid the sticker price for a new car. Shopping made him nervous, and he never bargained. On one occasion he went to a jewelry store in search of a gift for my mother. He pointed through a glass case at a bracelet. The clerk reached into the case and pulled out the wrong bracelet. My father, embarrassed by the man's incompetence, nodded his head in agreement, and paid the list price for the bracelet that had been displayed next to the one he'd wanted to buy. The clerk tried to lower the price, but my father hadn't let him get in a word.

[February of 1943]

Darling,

In a way I'm glad the New Yorker sent the voucher because it will be a good basis for a falsification of my tax. I'll just add my army salary to that, make some deductions, and let it go. I'm pretty sure Collier's won't send a voucher. It's too late now. I may go over to personnel tonight and have Jaffee work it out for me there. he loves to work out other people's income taxes and he's very good at deductions.

I spent the morning looking through rifle sights and this afternoon we went out and fired the grenade-launcher. Then I skipped retreat, took a shower, ate a bar of candy and now I feel dandy. But the Georgia weather today is something I wouldn't want to send you any of. A medium-sized dust-storm has been blowing since noon. The dust gets into everything and goes everywhere. Even with all the windows and doors closed, it gets into the barracks and the mess hall, it gets into your teeth and your eyes. This afternoon you could hardly see the targets, and figures were continually appearing and disappearing in clouds of dust. All of which reminded me of the Biblical scenes we used to have on the range at Croft when the dust blew up and suddenly out of the dust would appear a hundred or more men, staggering under the weight of the range officer's tower.

> Love, sweetheart, and goodnight.
> John

*The Way Some People Live* was published by Random House in the spring of 1943. This, his first collection of stories, came to the attention of an officer who had him pulled out of the infantry and put into the Signal Corps.

Sunday

Hello Sweet,

I don't count on the rumors for anything, but we've been told that we can write our families to tell them that we're moving to Fort Dix sometime in April, and that we are making a permanent change of station which means that we are not going overseas. I wouldn't be surprised if we ended up in Wyoming, but I've got my fingers crossed.

I distributed the book carefully among a few officers. I've got to give the Colonel a copy and I sold my copy last night to my gravedigger friend from Croft. We drank beer together and he was in fine form, telling me about how they planted Samuel Untermyer. "Planted" is the word he uses. He also pronounces mausoleum like linoleum and he says that the rich people who have plots at Woodlawn are the most unreliable of them all. If you don't watch them they'll steal one another's azaleas or swipe the iron benches. He talks very intimately about

the Vanderbilts and the Morgans and Tex Rickard, all of them interred,
of course. And there's nothing goulish about him at all. He liked his
job because it didn't change very much during the depression.

I'll get to work on a story now honey. It's a good day here; warm and
pleasant. I was glad to see the stories in a book because they give me
an idea of how much I have to learn and what not to do.

Love,
John

Sunday [March 1943]

Hello Sweet,

Streeter and I came in on an ammunition carrier Friday. The camp
was deserted and the barracks had an attic-smell and the cockroaches
were sporting with one another. It was a beautiful spring evening, sad
and clear and warm, and it felt like coming here for the first time. . . .
. . . Give Tootsie a little calsimine for me, and all my love, honey.

John

I read the Rose Feld review and she sure didn't think much of the
book. The review seemed allright, but she hasn't any idea of what I'm
writing about.

Rose Feld's review appeared in the March 14, 1943, *Book Review* and said
in part:

> To the extent that in the writing world any material—sketch, article,
> newspaper report, fiction—is called a story, John Cheever's book, *The Way
> Some People Live*, may be called a collection of stories. But in the conven-
> tional sense, only a few of the thirty pieces that make up the volume fulfill
> the ordinary requirements of the short-fiction form. The rest are moments
> or moods caught in the lives of his characters, pointed in quality, but
> inconclusive in effect.

Tuesday [March 1943]

Hello Darling,

A couple of underworld characters that might interest you crossed
my path recently. One of them blew in today, a fellow named —— , a

former Flatbush Master of Ceremonies who was recently tried and acquitted for pimping for young girls in Augusta. He has the morals of a depraved tom-cat and if he wasn't guilty I'd like to know why. . . .

Then he went on to talk about Fort Sill, Oklahoma, where his outfit was recently stationed. I asked him if it wasn't a small town. "No, no," he said with a perfectly straight face, "My Gawd no it was no small town. Why it had side streets!" He gave a long account of an affair he had with a tap-dancer in Fort Sill. She was married to a saxaphone player in a band there but, "because I'm a comedian she figures she'll be more happy with me than she is with a saxaphone player because a comedian is good for a lot of laughs and a saxaphone player has to work all night. I call her parrot because she has a big nose and she's no whore. I swear to God she's no whore, she's more the woman type which is more pleasurable for me." He recounted the affair up to the climax where the husband turns —— out of the house saying, "Please go away from here because you broke my house."

The second joker is a man named ——, the judo and wrestling instructor for the regiment. He went out with us on the maneuvers and I had a good chance to watch him. He calls everybody chicken. "I used to work for the loan sharks in New York, chicken," he told me. "I know names chicken. I know the four hundred." He's very muscular, very lazy, and very vain. He used to get up in the morning and worry about his face and his clothes like a woman. he used to work in carnivals as the Masked Marvel fighting yokels against a time limit and a purse. His nose is badly broken and I think he's punchy. At anyrate he is capable of grasping only the most rudimentary facts, and he always has the bewildered and simple look of a man who is deaf or stupid. He once acted as a body guard in New York and from his associations with the cafe society one third of his speech is along the lines of a Schrafft's hostess: "I'll have a drop more of coffee tew, plueeze," he says, crooking his little finger. From this dialect he goes into a you-all, we-all, sho-nuff strata of speech which he's picked up in Augusta. And from this talk he reverts to the tough, obscene language he learned on the east side where he was brought up. And so much for the underworld.

Tomorrow I'm going to run the course with the live machine gun fire. Every one very considerately left my named off the lists so I went into the orderly room tonight and volunteered. Dollard looked at me as though I were out of my head. "This is one I'm going to put in my book," he said. I may as well see what it's like.

John

Random House printed 2,750 copies of *The Way Some People Live* and sold just under 2,000.

[March 1943]

Hello, baby.

I didn't get into town to send you any flowers for your anniversary; and I think Churchill's exaggerating when he says it's going to take another two years to win the war. I'll try and write another story before I leave here, and if I do I want you to buy something for yourself; a good watch or some present from me that's substantial and useful. The book reviews didn't bother me at all. I only hope they don't squelch the sales altogether.

Goodbye, sweet, and goodnight,
John

Friday night

Hello Honey,

I got the clips today and I think the one from the Times is very funny. But all in all—even though they don't like me—the reviewers seem to be very diligent and earnest people, anxious to help a gloomy young writer onto the right path, and to safeguard the investments of their readers.

Did I tell you there is supposed to be a rave review in the Sat Review. Well anyhow Cerf said there was going to be one.

Goodnight, sweetie,
John

Wednesday

Hello Sweet,

. . . This afternoon we got into holes and let tanks run over us. It's something I've heard about for a long time, and something I never believed in but it worked allright. I imagine the first man must have been nervous but the tanks had run over so many before they came to me that it was nothing at all. Then after that went out and crawled around under machine-gun fire. The only tough part of it was the exertion of crawling and you know what I whizz I am at crawling so it didn't bother me. . . .

Camp Gordon [May 1943]
August, GA.

Thursday

Hello Honey,

This is a post-reveille letter; it's just getting light here and I'm not very wide awake. You were sweet to draw the picture of the apartment and it looks fine. I wish I were there to spade the garden and paint the fence and put up shelves and etcetera and maybe I can on a three-day pass. I'm afraid I've forgotten your birthday sweet; but if I had remembered it I wouldn't have been able to send you anything but a card. We go off the training schedule today and spend the rest of our time getting ready for the trip; and if someone doesn't find out about me and make me wash windows I'll be able to finish a story in the next few days and you can buy a birthday present with that. Also I need some money myself for the trip and I may wire you this afternoon for ten dollars.

It seems to have occured to the colonel that I should be made a corporal, but I'm afraid the rating may depend upon a transfer to Service Company, which is a very lousy outfit. Also yesterday I took the I.Q. test over again and passed into group two, which is OCS material. I don't see how I ever flunked it the first time. It's a very simple test and a very good one and if you know basic mathmatics you ought to be able to make a spectacular score. I still don't know mathematics in spite of all the literature you sent me. I'll stay with Special Service until we go up to Dix and see what the score is there, and then if we continue the training schedule I'll go back into the field and try and distinguish myself there.

Friday

Hello Honey,

The Rangers, as you probably know, correspond to the commandos and there is intensive two-weeks ranger course here which is given to one commissioned officer and one sergeant of each company. It's quite rough. Then there is the diluted Ranger course which we took in two days. We got out into the woods about dawn on Wednesday and took some instruction in firing from the hip with a rifle at surprise targets concealed in foxholes. . . .

Then we were given a lecture by a shavetail from the engineers on the properties of certain explosives. He was very wise and kept throwing packages of TNT and dynamite at us, two explosives that do not go off without a detonator. He showed us how to blow a crater with 25 pounds of dynamite. There were a number of craters around the site he picked and a few nosey privates like myself got into the crater nearest the charge. There was a big boom, no concussion because we were below the charge, and then all of a sudden the sky was black and tons of dirt began to rain down onto your head and shoulders. It was only a minute, but it seemed like five and there was the uncomfortable and helpless sensation of being buried alive. . . . Then when it got dark we marched out into the woods and fired into the dark at various sounds, to give you a sense of how accurate or inaccurate your sight-hearing, and sense of direction are in the dark. Then back to the bivouac and to bed. No one slept much but we were allowed to build fires and it was a mild night with a lot of stars.

Then in the morning we went back to the demolition department. . . . A stick of dynamite, a tetro cap and a time fuse was given to each group of four men. We made grenades and lighted the fuses. Then the man who was holding the lighted stick of dynamite, and he was very anxious to get rid of it, was told to hand it to his best friend. A man in our group that I've never seen before and will probably never see again handed me the lighted stick. Then we were told to hand the stick of dynamite to the man standing next to us, but of course by that time there wasn't anyone standing within two hundred yards of us so I chased a clerk from first battalion headquarters across the lot, waving my stick of dynamite at him. I finally pressed it into his hands. "I'm not from your squad," he kept saying, "I'm not even in your battalion." But he had to take it and then the order came to throw the grenades, which he did, and they all went off and kicked up a lot of dirt.

Then we went into a mine-laying department, also run by the engineers, which was very dull. Everybody fell asleep, since there were no explosives involved. Then we assaulted a position and were subjected to a light attack of mustard gas which smells as you know, like garlic. By that time I was so exhausted and hungry that the gas smelled like supper, got my gastric juices working and acted generally as a stimulant. Then we went home in the half-tracks, very dirty and very tired. . . .

We are coming to Dix honey. The order was official today. We're leaving sometime in the middle of April, and who knows, maybe I'll see you in a couple of weeks.

Love, honey,
John

Back at Fort Dix.

[Longhand]
Darling:

I've just bought a $25 fountain pen and I'm trying it out. We worked yesterday until one in the morning loading 150 pound bags of oats. I got up at 4:30 for K.P. and we finished off at eight tonight. I've just had a shower and a glass of beer and I feel completely at peace with the world. It's a clear, still evening around here and it looks like an army post should. There are a lot of lonely men sitting on fence posts looking at nothing and someone is playing "My Melancholy Baby" on an untuned piano. . . .

Love,
John

# MOVIE WAR

**\* \* \***

From Fort Dix my father was assigned to the Signal Corps in Astoria, Queens. Here he put together films about why soldiers should brush their teeth and what to do with a hammer. Among those he worked with and whose company he enjoyed were John Weaver, Irwin Shaw, Don Ettlinger, Leonard Field, E. J. Kahn, Jr., and William Saroyan. This letter was written from the apartment my mother had moved into in Chelsea. After the move to Astoria my father saw my mother so much that letters to her tailed off until 1945 when he went to Los Angeles and the Pacific.

329 West 22nd Street
New York City, New York

August 9, 1943

Dear Jo,

On July 31st about three in the morning, Mary had an eight pound daughter whose name is Susan Liley Cheever. She was in labor for a long time, but that seems to be normal with a first child and Winter, her father, said, that with the exception of illegitimate children, he had never seen such a normal pregnancy and accouchment. She's also feeding the kid and has more milk than the baby needs. She's very proud of herself and makes noises like a female bear when anyone comes near the child. She's due home from the hospital tomorrow.

Eight pounds isn't exactly a delicate little girl which is all for the good because she seems to be able to digest anything, sleep anywhere, and will probably be able to support herself soon. She has a fairly thin face for so young a baby, light blue eyes, light hair, and she's already too big to wear the dear little booties and scratchy bonnets mailed in by her fond relatives. Mary's been wonderful through the whole thing. She liked being pregnant—although she only gained twenty pounds— she didn't mind the delivery, and now she likes nursing. And Thank God I was here for the whole thing. Mental attitudes make a big difference. There was a woman in the same room with Mary whose husband was in Africa. And she didn't have an easy time of it.

My position is still in the dark. I won't care what happens as soon as Mary gets on her feet again. I don't expect to remain here for long but I've been here nearly three months. My venerable division—the "roughest, toughest, fightenest division in the world"—is still garrisoned in southern New Jersey going into their fourth year of pre-battle training.

Love from all of us,
John


Pete was Pete Collins. Elizabeth was Elizabeth Ames.


Friday

Dear Jo,

Pete is back from a trip to England. His stories of the war this time were almost all culinary. He traveled on a Dutch Ship and they drank

Holland Gin and ate Dutch East Indian dishes all the time. He went fishing once and caught a shark, but he's homesick for the speckled trout on the Beaver Kill. I received yesterday a sad, quiet note from Elizabeth who speaks of herself as being in need of a rest, of the mansion as being in need of rejuvenation after its twenty arduous years. . . . If there is anything in my memory that could be called pre-war it is Yaddo. Oh those fountains, oh those box lunches, oh that stained glass at the head of the stairs.

. . . There's a great stir in Chelsea because two negro whores have moved into a house a few doors down the street from us and all the white whores are up in arms . . . and Eddie Newhouse is not yet a major.

Susan has grown a lot since you last saw her, she now has one solitary, sharp little tooth, and she spends a lot of time talking to herself and occasionally to us. She says bottle (bopple) patticake, ball, bye-bye and Mary thinks she says a lot more. She's very happy in Chelsea; particularly in the grocery store where she meets lots of people. Mary will take her to New Hampshire sometime in July.

Best,
John

From Chelsea my parents moved to a town house on 92nd Street, which they shared with two other families. It was these living quarters that gave my father inspiration for the Town House stories. These were later rewritten as a play and produced briefly in Boston and New York.

8 East 92nd Street,

The day before Roosevelt was reelected

Dear Jo,

I am not in Europe. I am here. And here is the story about my trip abroad. In the spring, as you know, it was agreed that I should transfer to Yank and that I would be in France a few weeks after the invasion. Then, since someone else was after me, my colonel decided that he could not let me go. He used to be president of paramount and he decided that Yank was RKO or 20th Century Fox and that he was not going to let them have one of his writers. So a few days before I was to leave he destroyed the request for transfer and all my fond farewells went sour. But he assured me that he would send me overseas under much better circumstances and so in the last of July I prepared for a second trip. This fell through. Then there was a third. Then there was a fourth. I have now been given injections for everything but bubonic plague and I have been waiting to leave the country any minute for four months. I'm still waiting.

Naturally Mary is kind of bored. She planned to live without me and came uptown to share a house with two other families. Now we're all in one another's hair. Come and see us. We have a library, a morning room, eight flush toilets, and our telephone number is Atwater 9-6118. When you telephone us wait a long time because the phone is in our bedroom and Mary is apt to be in the library, for instance, or in the morning room doing a little needle point and it takes her about twenty minutes to climb up to our personal bedchamber. And I hope we see you soon.

> Love from Susan and Mary,
> John

He spent some time in Los Angeles, then went on to the Pacific, returned to Los Angeles, and then to New York. These few letters are from California and from islands in the Pacific.

Wednesday

Hello Darling,

Today I had lunch at one of the Brown Derbies with Carl Foreman. The restuarant looked like one of Howard Johnson's only it was a brown derby instead of a colonial manor. For lunch Carl had something called a Monte Christo sandwich. This is made of three slices of French toast, turkery meat between the toast, the top sprinkled with powdered sugar and the whole cut into three sections, each looking like a Napoleon. This is eaten with a knife and fork. And this is my only life in Hollywood note for today.

SERVICE MEN'S TELEPHONE CENTER
THE PACIFIC TELEPHONE AND TELEGRAPH COMPANY

Tuesday

Hello Sweet,

The delays continue and there's still nothing in the way of news. I've finished Adam Bede and am halfway through The Mill on the Floss and maybe I'll be able to finish Romola and Silas before I leave the ground. George Eliot is a very good choice for this kind of a trip and I'm enjoying the novels. The only thing about the novels that seems dated are the pious and long-suffering women who appear in most english literature of the time and who finally developed into pious little Esther Summerson of Bleak House. The motivations behind the conduct of the heroines seems considerably simplified—a reflection of the position of women in the 19th century I suppose—and as I noticed in Hardy the Freudian categories that we take for granted are as far into the future as electricity. All of which goes to-show that I will hit the keys of a typewriter, even if my head is as empty as a peashell.

The weather I can talk about, and the weather has been magnificent. The sun is hot, the shadow is cold, the skies are cloudless and in the evening the afterglow is a much deeper and more intense blue than we have in the east. The life in the barracks here is not as noisey or drunken or bloody as it was in Georgia but there are plenty of types. Last night two fuckups were discussing their disatisfactions with the army and the type runs so true to form that you could almost jump their lines. One was a Mexican who didn't like the army because the army doesn't serve Mexican food. he was very bitter and thought he might starve to death if they didn't put some peppers into his dehydrated eggs. The other was a Texan who wanted to see action. "If they'd only let me soldier I'd be allright," he kept saying. This is always the refrain of the true fuckup.

I miss not hearing from you and I keep rereading an old letter of yours about walking down Fifth Avenue with Sue on Easter. But still no address.

Love,
John

April 23rd

Somewhere in the Phillipines

Hello Sweet,

Those questionable pictures of you and Sue that Sonami took a year ago are giving me a great deal of pleasure. I know that neither of you look very much like the photographs but I spend a lot of time looking at them.

It seems quite hot here. At least very close. For lunch we had creamed turkey, cold-slaw, peas, bread pudding, and some cold drink. This morning a native came into our tent, selling bananas. A monkey, sitting on the edge of my bunk, bit the native. The native thought the monkey was mine and blamed me. I'm not crazy; but you can see that our life is not simple.

That's about all, love,Goodnight,
John

May 2, 1945

Hello Sweet,

I've finally bought you a rice-paddy hat which I expect you to wear to the back room at the Plaza on the day when I return; a day I've spent a lot of time planning.

In this part of the world you can buy a monkey for a pet or a small dove with clipped wings to carry in your hand. The dove is worth a package of cigarets. You can buy a piece of meat that has hung in the sun all day or a dried fish strong enough to smell up a city block. You can pick Japanese money off the street. You can buy a lei of small white flowers to wear around your neck to check the famous smells of the far east or you can buy a bottle of Chanel #5 with a broken seal for $75. You can buy bolo knives, hemp cloth, roosters, can alcohol, seashells, commenorative stamp issues, pineapples and a scoop of ice cream as big as a ping-pong ball for twenty-five cents.

In every city large enough to have a Dome there is a plaza crowded with stands selling rosaries, prayer books, toys, hot food from braziers, and a thin stock of cheap novelties. Boney old women sell candles and white-eyed blind men kneel with a rosary in one hand and the other hand open for Centavos. Both central doors of the church stand open and the brisk life of the plaza reachs halfway across the nave. It would be like Italy if it weren't for the sweet, half-dead smell of the east.

He's back in the states. My mother was visiting Josie.

Wednesday

Hello Darling,

You must be in Bucks now and I hope you're getting hot sun, Pennsylvania Dutch meat-loaf, and baths in the brook. I do wish I could be down there with you. The world-famous sun of California never comes out until four in the afternoon and I'm never out of the office until it starts to set. When I came back from the islands I had a black south Pacific tan but now the face I shave in the morning is white with red eyes.

I've been working on the picture during the day, the story nights and Sundays and they both checkmate one another and progress slowly. I go out three nights a week, but nothing much happens, and I'll regale you with my brilliant nightlife when I return. I did go to Chasen's one night for dinner, which is something like 21. There was some trouble about getting a table so I asked for Mr. Chasen and told him I was a friend of Harold Ross's and zowie the place was mine. "Everything I have I owe to Harold Ross," Chasen said. It was the best food I've had out there and the building didn't seem to have been put up ten minutes ago.

That's about all, sweet.

Love,
John

Tuesday

Hello Sweet,

I'm begining to get used enough to Hollywood to feel that critical observations are boorish but there are a couple of details I may as well give you. On Sunday I saw a thin, middle-aged woman and her daughter: a child of about five. The child's yellow hair had been forced into ringlets and the mother was carrying the child's wardrobe over her arm; tutus, a spangled evening dress, and some tights. And one night I had dinner at the Roosevelt. The waiter put a crab-meat cocktail in front of me, pointed to the silver at the left of my plate and said: "Use a fork."

Love,
John

Back in New York waiting for discharge.

Saturday [1945]

Dear Josie,

We've both wanted to write you before this to thank you for the books, and Susie to thank you for her doll, but life seems to have reached an impasse here where writing anything, including short stories for the New Yorker, is a chore. Part of this, I think, is my army post; the post is disintegrating with the same long, deathly, struggle of a government agency that has lost its appropriation. Men from the surplus property board come through every day to copy the numbers off our desks and while we go through the motions of production we know that everything we do will be burned or lost. I ought to be out by Thanksgiving.

The books are wonderful to read as well as ornamental. . . . Since seeing you we spent a week-end in the country near Nyack; a place owned by some wealthy liberals named Mayer. There is a swimming pool at the bottom of the garden and a copy of the New Masses on the spinet and our hostess told a long story about a single tax colony she and her husband invested in one summer near Amherst. The disciple of George who ran the colony turned out to be cruel to animals. He beat a horse to death one day, she said, and that was the end of her interest in the single tax.

A little boy in the park yesterday tried to take Susie's doll-carriage away from her and she bit him.

Love,
John

The letter below was written by my mother. I include it because it gives a glimpse of her very different sensibility, and a description of the apartment at 59th Street, which we lived in until the spring of 1951. The saga of the town house was never sung to the lyre, but it was performed on the stage.

Mrs. John Cheever

July 22nd, 1945

Dearest Jo,

Wonderful news (at last): we have an apartment, and a fine one, and will move into it this week. It is now being all freshly painted and polished. You have to walk down six steps to the living room and Sue has her own room, painted yellow, and her own bathroom. She isn't going to like it, of course, when she finds her own room is a trap and she is no longer able to dog our footsteps and attend our every function, but I think we'll like it. Our getting the place was a stroke of the sheerest luck and was preceded by black despair. Almost from the moment we returned from Erwinna everything went bad and wrong and out of order. In the house there has been constant disorder, hysteria, and vermin. But I won't try to write it because it would depress us both and anyway it's a saga which should be sung to the lyre. Our new address is 400 East 59th Street.

If I hadn't had the wonderful ten days at your house I doubt I could have borne up, and I'm ashamed not to have written and hope it doesn't matter. Did you get the book and cigarettes? There are a lot more cigarettes available here now. . . .

We will probably go to New Hampshire for two weeks after we move, for John's long delayed furlough. Lots of love from us both.

Mary

# MUSTERED OUT,
# NOVEMBER 21, 1945

• • •

Thursday

Dear Jo,

I got out of the army at three thirty on Tuesday. They played some organ music and gave us a very sensible address about our responsibilities as civilians and citizens and set us free. Everybody went running out of the chapel, shouting, like the last day of school, and now it's over. This at Fort Monmouth, New Jersey. Considering how comfortable my army life has been and how dismal the news in the Times still is, there is a fine, wonderful sense of liberation on getting out from under military jurisdiction.

New York isn't much these days. At least I don't think so. We seem to drink a lot of martinis, but the people are the people we've seen too much of and everybody's heard the jokes before. At night I read your copy of "The Ten Days that Shook etcetera and it makes very pleasant reading.

Best,
John

Josie had been married to a member of the American Communist Party who—according to Elinor Langer's book *Josephine Herbst* was involved with Whittaker Chambers. In fact, the book reports convincingly that John Herrmann, Josie's husband, introduced Chambers to Alger Hiss at a Chinese restaurant near Dupont Circle in 1934. My father was as uninvolved with politics as it is possible for a literate man to be. The apolitical writer in America was something of an anomaly in the 1930s. He used to say that when he was in his twenties he had been singled out in *The New Masses* as the last voice of the decadent bourgeoisie. In any case, he was not above ragging Josie about her beliefs.

Friday [January '46]
Dear Josie,
The doll arrived today and Susie was delighted. The doll also completes a representation of the social structure that we've been building up in the nursery. She has a negro doll, a worker-type doll, a rag doll (lumpen), a good assortment of middle-class dolls and now the party with the silk dress and the waved hair completes the picture.

I hope your own picture is as broad as Susie's or at least better than mine. I got out of the army in November and the work I've done since then you could put into a pea-shell. Hollywood has been nibbling fitfully at the Town House series but nothing has happened on that yet and it's very possible that nothing will happen. I want to start on a book but I still have to write three stories and God knows when I'll get those done.

We had a political discussion with Bill Maxwell last week and he said that governmental checks on the inflationary spiral were abortive because roses were fifteen dollars a dozen. A lot of fairly conservative people (and the inflation has made a lot of people fairly conservative) speak continually of Communism; but I'm going all out for some form of sun worship.

John

In 1946 Eleanor Clark published *The Bitter Box* (Doubleday). Carson is Carson McCullers. Bowen is Elizabeth Bowen.

400 East 59th,

Tuesday

Dear Jo,

I've read Eleanor's book and I'd mail it to you if this seemed urgent but you can pick it up in May and I don't think you'll want it until then. (But if you should want any of the books that ornament our shelves drop me a card and I'll shoot them out.) I thought the Bitter B-x very bad. My sympathies lie with Eleanor's enemies rather than her friends, in the first place. Her central character is that chestnut of all time, the prudent solitary with blocked bowels and a domineering mother who lives alone in a furnished room and holds the smallest possible claim on anyone's interest. I remember Eleanor's reference to realism as a "Blind Alley" but I know of no alley so blind and circuitous as the one she finds herself in. I like Eleanor and I admire her devotion to her work, I admire it a great deal, but I'm in another team.

. . . I've also read the Bowen collection of short stories and she can describe a peony, an empty room, a change of light better than any of them, dead or alive; but again and again I kept coming to phrases like this:"She inclined her head toward the flowers, not so much to catch his remark, as to catch the instant," and it seems as though the language had overtaken the subject matter. And having boned up on all the best books I'm leaving for Yaddo tomorrow morning. My excuse is to get some manuscript I left there; my reasons are to get out of town for a day and have a drink at the Worden. I'll stay at the Worden Wednesday night and come down on Thursday; and I'll give your regards to the gloomy firs and the sour lakes, the bust of Brutus and the complete file of Punch, the gilt ceiling in the reception room and the iron bedsteads, to Carson and Katherine Anne.

Best,
John

Edmund Wilson and Mary McCarthy had been married to each other and then divorced.

400 East 59th Street
New York City, New York

March 19, 1946.

Dear Jo,

We have false spring two days out of every week and its wonderful. It gets very hot and the women with fur coats and high shoes go limping along Fifth Avenue; and then it gets cold again. Susie thinks she has a lion in her room and Mary wants new furniture in hers. . . . Houghton Mifflin gave Carson McCullers a cocktail party at the Saint Regis to which I was not invited. Edmund Wilson has printed a collection of questionable short stories and in one there is a long description of carnal copulation which would have done carnal copulation irreperable damage if it hadn't been quite as deeply rooted. Mary McCarthy came to New York to see if she was in the story. "Well is the face recognizable," she asked the publisher, "would you know the woman's face." "No, Mrs. Wilson," he said, "I wouldn't know the woman's face but I could tell her vulva anywhere."

Forgive me and tell us where you are.

John

The family was planning to visit the house in Pennsylvania. Apparently Josie was also kind to the Hemingway children. Eddie is Eddie Newhouse.

June

Dear Josie,

. . . Sue, I'm sorry to say, does nothing but talk about her spring vacation and about how she's going to spend all the nights of it with you, out among the indians, catching trouts and turtles and frogs and moving with a cat-like tread over the dead leaves in order to surprise the game and unfriendly indians. She hasn't forgotten a word you said and I'm afraid you're stuck with a couple of sleepless nights. She's not like those Hemingway boys.

. . . In the last ten or twenty years there has been a rush on the part of many writers, to insinuate themselves into the middle class, to live like bank clerks and to eschew any outward sign of disorder; a splendid manoeuvre, it seems to me, as long as the writer realizes that this is an act of espionage, that this is intended to put him in a position to observe the mores of his natural enemies, but I think Eddie has taken his disguise seriously and that he has forgotten what his reasons were when he began to talk about Groton and wear expensive clothes. Eddie came across the room to tell me, one night this winter, that the Saltanstall family was the only family in the United States who could legitimately use a crest.

I have a hangover; bone up on deer-stalking; come over and see us.

John


This letter was written from Treetops. My mother's stepmother, Polly, had a good deal of class. My mother remembers arriving with her by train in Franklin, New Hampshire. The family party was on the way to Treetops. It was snowing heavily, and it was remembered that the supply of gin at the summer place was low. The liquor store in Franklin was closed. My mother was holding a small child in her arms; she can no longer recall whether it was me or Susan. Polly grabbed the infant out of my mother's arms and marched up to the door of the house behind the liquor store. She banged until it was opened. Polly then said that she would like to make a purchase. The store owner told her that the store was closed, and to open it would be a violation of the law. At this point Polly held the child up to the light. "I have a tiny baby," she said in a tone that must have been both imperious and aggrieved. The man sold her a quart of gin.

Don and Katrina are Don and Katrina Ettlinger. Don Ettlinger is a writer with whom my father worked in the Signal Corps.

[August '46]
Thursday

Dear Josie,

Susie had a modest and a good birthday party. The cook made a cake with White Mountain frosting and Polly decorated the cake with cut flowers. Susie blew out the candles and ate the cut flowers. Mary's unstable sister ate a good deal of the cake and this made me so nervous that I drank too many old fashioneds. Sue was given a wheel-barrow, a rake, hoe and shovel, a doll, a folding chair for funerals and political rallies, and three night gowns and two dresses.

We came up here, as you know on the 18th of June and I planned then to stay three weeks or a month. Then I went back to New York on the 15th of July. I got drunk in a few saloons to celebrate my return and then Don and Katrina, who had just been married in Colorado Springs, came into town on their way to Berne (Suisse) where they are going to live. It was hot and we drank gin and champagne at the Plaza. One night after a big party I stumbled down to Grand Central and took a train back here. The decision to return still troubles me a little—I spend a lot of time describing sunsets and wildflowers—but I like the country, I feel good in the country, and what the hell.

Now and then I'm reminded of Triuna. I work from nine until one when I despatch a big lunch and then I cut and cart wood rake hay, make ice-cream and in the late afternoon I go swimming, which I love. Then we go down to Polly's house and drink martinis and admire the view and after dinner we return there and drink coffee and admire the sunset. The country is beautiful. Most country is, of course, but this is New England, the pastures are stony, the mountains are leonine, the natives are taciturn and venal, the sunsets are red, and in the early evenings you can hear, from the shores of the lake, the brave and innocent voices of little children, singing some gibberish song about what a wonderful time they're having at Camp Wonk-a-tonk.

The cast of characters is varied and colorful. The farmer is a communist and loans me copies of a paper called Action which is printed in Norwalk, Ohio. The cook's little girl is sickly and thin-lipped and passes out religious tracts. Mary's sister is as crazy as a bed-bug. Mary's father lectures us on the chemistry of temperament and Mary's stepmother recalls the evening she was dancing the Castle Walk with Hamilton Fish and tripped on a panier and cracked her skull open. We do a lot of pleasant drinking and you should see Susie's grandmother, after her sixth martini, playing:"This is the way the farmer rides; bumbety-bumb, bumbety-bump . . . "

Naturally I haven't done much reading. I read the first chapters of Eudora Welty's novel and stopped when somebody broke a night-light. I think she is a very minor novelist. I loaned my copy of the Wilson book to Irwin Shaw whose egotism is so immense that he offered, a few days later, to loan the book to me. I'll never see it again. And anyhow it's the kind of a book that is so poorly felt that you can't look at your typewriter for a week after you've put it down. I don't even look at the book news. It's all shit and I know it. The sale of the dramatic rights to Town House has netted me so far one hundred and seventy-three dollars but a drunkard on the west coast named H _____ M _____ is making a play out of the stories. I don't know whether he'll ever finish the play or not but he sounds like a good man to me. Mary and Susie are brown and fair and happy and Susie is going to school in the fall.

John

The Ettlingers lived on Sutton Place. They had just left for Europe. Freddy was Polly's unmarried son by her first marriage. He was devoted to his mother, and dealt in antiques.

Tree Tops,<br>Bristol, N.H.,<br>August 17th

Dear Don and Katrina,

When I said goodbye to you . . . I didn't think you'd make it . Then I got the gold pencil and I thought: They've sent everyone presents and gone into hiding on Sutton Place. We were delighted to get the letter from Paris, although I don't see how you got there in your condition. And I was delighted with the pencil although I'm not going to use it for the novel; I'm going to use it to mark up menus at Sardi's. Susie talks a good deal about Paris and that is where all her imaginary boats and vehicles are taking her.

We went to Massachusetts for a week. . . . I don't suppose that's very impressive for people who fly the Atlantic. Susie had lunch at the Ritz in Boston and we drove back here with Freddy in the most preposterous car I've ever seen. The windows go up and down by machinery, the seats go backwards and forwards with machinery, the top, naturally, goes up and down by machinery, the motor is supposed to go one hundred and twenty miles an hour and there is one machine that sprays little jets of water over the windshield just like Versailles only smaller.

The thing that has absorbed most of my time for the last couple of weeks is a family of coons that has moved into the woods behind the chicken house. They eat the corn and they can eat five or six dozen ears a night. I began to hunt by finding an old rifle in the cellar here, cleaning it picturesquely by the fire one night while I drank my toddy, and giving an astonishing display of marksmanship to the cook's little boy. Then I went into the fields one night after dark but it was so dark that I couldn't see anything and all I hit was some corn. This went on every night for a week until one of the natives suggested that I try traps. Then I bought four traps. The first night I put them out it rained, the springs rusted and the coons left muddy foot-prints on the bait plates. Then I filed the traps down and have gotten them so sensitive that if I put them out before dusk they trap sparrows. This isn't much good so today I went into town and bought four more traps. Mr. Follansbee at the hardware store told me to hang little pieces of mirror above the traps. "That gits their attention," Mr. Follansbee said. I don't know whether he was fooling or not; but I've got my mirrors and I've got my thread and here I go.

Best,
John

Frank, or Fronk, is now a bishop in Chicago.

Tree Tops

August 19th

Dear Don and Katrina,

I've written you before but I forgot to send it par avion and it probably won't get there before Christmas. It wasn't much of a letter anyhow. It was mostly about coons. . . . The gold pencil is splendid and I take it to the village whenever I go there and flash it.

. . . Polly went down to a wedding in Madison and then over to Mason's Island. She came back with her young grandson who is eight years old and who has the most fantastic Brooks-type wardrobe I've ever seen. He comes to the table in little blazers and crooked bow ties and Peale shoes. His manner is a broad imitation of Katherine Hepburn in the Philadelphia Story. "Do let's go swimming after lunch," he exclaims, all blue eyes and crew cut. I get so nervous that I call him Fronk instead of Frank, which is his name, and say things like "Pardon Me." The wind is strong, the leaves are beginning to turn, the lake is black, the fields are full of golden-rod and when you receive the letter that didn't go par avion you'll read about what a terrible time I've had with coons.

Love,
John

The Ettlingers were continuing their tour abroad; Juan-les-Pins is on the coast of France. The novel was one more of many efforts.

400 East 59th
September 9 [1946]

Dear Don and Katrina,

Today is one of those overcast mornings when everything smells of drains and the air is like a piece of dirty grey felt . . . the cost of living is up nearly thirty percent since June and how were things in Juan Les Pins.

We had a wonderful summer. There was just enough violence to keep things from getting dull. I finally trapped a coon and shot a porcupine and the 1928 Studebaker station-wagon burst into flame one afternoon when I was driving it through Bristol village. Before we left the weather got brilliant and wonderful and Polly went through the woods with her hatchet, cutting the colored leaves for her flower arrangments. It got very cold right after dark, the east wind kept blowing down the yellow leaves, the wood-smoke smelled wonderful, the martinis tasted wonderful and the swimming was very cold and exhilerating.

Susie had about the best time of all. The help made a picnic every Thursday and Sunday and they always took Susie with them. Then the cook left a week before we did and for this week Marie—the 72-year-old retainer—took care of Susie. They made a very funny couple. They took one another with a deadly seriousness, called one another sweet-love and other sugary nothings, and took a walk every evening after they had eaten their boiled eggs by the fire. I used to see them start off on these excursions, hand in hand, both of them equally afraid of the dark and the cold, each of them sweet-loving the other. For these junkets Marie wore her best black and Susie wore her night-gown, her party shoes, Marie's pearls, Marie's pocket-book, and an old sweater of Marie's that trailed in the dead grass. They used to start out a little before dark with the cold wind whipping the dead leaves around their tiny feet, they used to walk a good two miles through the woods every night, and when they left you could hear them asking after one another's condition. "Are you warm enough, sweet-love, etcetera.

The novel went well towards the end, but I'm afraid it won't be finished by spring. H ———— M ———— sent on the first act of the adaptation he was doing of Town House. It was very broad and full of funny jokes. Hart telephoned him and told him he didn't like it and M ———— said Hart was crazy, that the play was going to be terrific and that Carol was going to have a miscarriage in the second act. M ———— isn't with the firm anymore and Hart is trying to get Paul Osborn. One of the worst things about M's first act was the influence of Hollywood. All the people came out of a bad picture. There was a woman interior decorator who wore black, drank like a soldier and kept making dry, funny jokes. Then there was a football bore, an old gentlemen with a tough, wise-cracking cutie.

It's a gloomy picture but from where I sit I can see, as I could see all last winter, the interminable funeral procession moving across the Queensboro Bridge to the enormous graveyards in Long Island. Things will look better, I'm sure, as soon as the sun comes out and the truck strike ends and I'll write you a cheery note about Fifth Avenue in the autumn sun, one of these days.

Best,
John

John Cheever
400 East Fifty-Nine Street
New York City

October 2nd

Dear Don and Katrina,

Your letter came on a wet, black morning here and filled our gloomy apartment with the faint and lovely music of cowbells and shaken ice, the latest German tangos and the laughter of youth. I read the letter first, then Mary, then the maid. I can hardly bring myself to write about the photographs, the one of you two dancing at Juan Les Pins moved me so profoundly. Susie got nearly sick with nerves, trying to see over our shoulders so she has been loaned the picture of you at the beach bar to mark the place in her Mother Goose. We all think it was the best letter we have ever received. I keep telling Mary that we should go to Albany or some place so that I can enliven my correspondence with some scenery and a little historical interest; but she doesn't want to go to Albany. She's decided that she has the temperament of an expatriate and that it is now only a question of time before we leave these harsh shores.

Susie is now in her second week at the Walt Whitman School. She boards a station wagon every morning with a good deal of forced poise. Mary watches in her night gown from the 9th floor and I walk up and downthe sidewalk and wring my hands. Sending a child off to nursery school is like sending your bottom drawer off to the board of health. When she returns in the afternoon we corner her like a pair of Gestapo agents and try to wring some information from her about the school day. "What did you have for lunch. What did you do. Where did you go. did you take a nap?" She has not answered one of our questions and for all we know she may be spending her time at a flea-circus. In the meantime Mary is taking up needlepoint.

The city looks about the same. I went to the Central Park Zoo late Sunday afternoon. The foliage was vague and colorless like an industrial overcast and the walks were crowded, the lions roaring, baloons were exploding and I saw a chic woman blow her nose in her white gloves. The hotels are booked until spring, there is no soap or meat for sale in the markets, the cost of living has risen so that people like us make a dinner of canned fish-balls, and the weather is cold enough for mink. At night I read the Divine Comedy and the speeches of Franklin Roosevelt.

It may be because of your being in Switzerland that I think continually of the early twenties and of all the things the Paris crowd used to say about the United States; but in the last few years the emphasis on money in this country has overtaken nearly everything else. Even among our friends there are people who will spend an evening talking about money: How much the Y's pay for their apartment, how much P paid for her fur coat, are J's pearls real, etcetera. This would not have been true six years ago.

I still think I may have the first draft of the novel finished by November, by the last of November. I like the story but I keep asking myself: Is there a character in this book you would enjoy meeting? Then I ask myself: Is there a character in this book you would not avoid meeting if you could? It troubles me. I love a great many people and the color of the sky, but this doesn't describe my work.

> Love from Sue and Mary and
> John

My father would put on his suit in the morning and take the elevator down with the other men heading out to work, but he wouldn't get off at the first floor. He'd go on down to the basement and to a maid's room, which is mentioned below. Here he'd take off his suit, hang it up, and type in his underwear. Thus he was able to keep up appearances and save on dry-cleaning bills. Binny was another name for Polly.

[Received Nov. 6, 1946]

> John Cheever
> 400 East Fifty-ninth Street
> New York City
>
> Sunday

Dear Polly and Winter,

. . . Our only problem has been Susie vs the Walt Whitman School. Having paid out my five hundred dollars I'm bound that she'll go to school, even if she has to be dragged up to 79th Street. She enjoys herself tremendously when she gets there but she has decided that she does not like to leave the nest in the mornings. We've discovered that if the departure is handled gently it goes very well so that now when she is dressed in the mornings—between seven and eight—our anxiety to strike nothing but notes of felicty and sweetness makes this the most painful hour of the day. Our smiles are never relaxed, our voices are never raised until she's stuffed into the taxi.

Excepting to go to the ballet once I don't think we've been out for a month. Mary is studying the administrations of Madison and Jefferson and I spend most of my time in a chamber-maid's cell in the basement, trying to write the novel. Katrina's mother, Mrs. Wallingford, came up for cocktails one day, bringing pictures of the wedding which Mary accepted with dreadful malice, thinking only of the day when she could show them to Binney. Mrs. Wallingford was in her usual humor. "My bones are begining to soften," she told us, "and I've been to two doctors, unknown to one another; that is neither of the doctors knew that I had been to the other. Well both of them told me that I had the lowest blood pressure and the lowest pulse and the lowest everything else of anyone they had ever examined! Anyone living, that is."

We hope we'll see you soon.

As ever,
John

February 24th [1947]

Dear Josie,

. . . We are, as you left us, quite comfortable, vaguely bored and frequently tight. Susie asked for you frequently during the holidays because she got the crazy idea that you were the husband of Mary; La Mary. When people asked her who the figures in the crèche were she would say: "That's Mary and that's Jesus and that's Josie Herbst."

About a month ago Mary took a job teaching English at Sarah Lawrence two days a week and so she journeys out to Bronxville on Tuesdays and Fridays and comes home with a briefcase full of themes written by young ladies named Nooky and Pussy; but these nicknames would give you no indication of what these themes are about. Otherwise things are about the same. Now and then I get enough money to work on the novel for three or four days; but the cost of this comfortable life is fantastic. We went to Vermont with the Shaws for a week's skiing last month and had a wonderful time drinking martinis and playing parchesi. I'll have my memories.

Best,
John

John Weaver is a writer my father met in the Signal Corps. When my father went to Hollywood to work he frequently stayed with John and his wife, Harriet. Leonard Field, another Signal Corps friend, produced *Virginia Reel* by John and Harriet Weaver on April 13 of 1947.

February 24 [1947]

Dear John,

We're very excited about your play here and I'm very envious to hear that you'll have the book done by spring. Envious and glad. My book won't make the April first dead-line and if you don't get them in by then they won't print them until 1950. I got back to work on the book about a month ago, but was dealt some crushing financial blows three weeks later and now I'm back in the short story business. I want to write short stories like I want to fuck a chicken.

John

April 2nd

Dear Pete and Lib,

. . . The Weavers returned hurriedly from California about a month ago because John's play is going to be produced by an experimental theatre group here. Its a good group and all the producers and agents and other shits go to see the plays with an eye towards movie sales or commercial production in the fall so John and Harriet are very excited. John has also finished the first draft of his novel so the Weavers are in fine shape.

Our friends the Ettlingers leave New York on Friday for Spring Valley (near Nyack) where they've rented a house from Waldo Pierce. Katrina will come back to New York in July to have her baby but otherwise they intend to remain in the country. Our friends the Shaws have moved to a place called El Rancho Yucca Loma which is in Southern California; and I think the last party we went to was the one to speed Irwin's departure. Irwin's father was there, a wonderful and vigirous old man from the millinery business who talked about the wonderful family orchestra they used to have. Irwin used to play the cornet. It was the kind of party where everybody thought they were famous. Alan Dunn went up to Stella Adler and said: "You're an extravert." Then he turned to Bill Maxwell and asked: "Do you use your hands. If you use your hands you're saved." I talked with Dunn's wife, Mary Petty, and she may have a heart of gold but she has a rather pasty complexion. Madge Evans was there and she looked at herself in a mirror and said rather bitterly? "I look ten years older than I did when I came here." She went right home after that. The invitation read from nine until twelve and at twelve most of the people gathered their robes, kissed the Shaws and left although there was a lot of scotch and champagne around. I wanted to stay until the bottles were empty but Mary said no. Things have changed.

Mary's step-sister Mrs. Joseph Hotchkiss (the former Hanna Eugenia Lawrence Whitney) had a baby yesterday which is named Noah Webster Hotchkiss. Little Noah has two cousins. One of them is Dudley Lang Whitney and the other is named Whitney Tracey Griswold and I think they're overdoing a good thing. Our relationships with the Ettlingers have cooled considerably since Mary suggested that they name their child either Max or Rubin. Susan Liley Cheever is fine and her teacher at school sent us a little note saying that Sue keeps them all entertained with her fascinating anecdotes. I can imagine what these are about. Mary is fine, or as fine as anybody else at Sarah Lawrence and she sends you her love. I hope we see you soon.

John

Susan was not quite four years old.

John Cheever
400 East Fifty-Nine Street
New York City

June 6th [1947]

Dear Josie,

Susie has nothing on her mind but thirty dollar shoes and mink coats. She has the tastes and dispositions of a Child's hostess and would be as happy as a clam if she could put on a rope of false pearls each morning and spend the day leading people to their tables. Mary had a good time teaching and apparently intends to make a profession out of it. I continue to write stories with one hand and hew at the novel with the other in order to keep Susie in hair-nets and myself in gin.

... Write us in New Hampshire so that when we run to the mail-box each day we won't always find it empty.

Best,<br>John

[Postmarked June 7, 1947, 6:30 P.M.]

John Cheever<br>400 East Fifty-Nine Street<br>New York City<br><br>June 6th

Dear Pete and Lib,

We have very little news excepting Chicken pox. Sue was in quarantine for two weeks and then she was sick for two weeks. Then two weeks later I came down with the pox for a fair. I was and am sores from top to bottom and look like Hogarth's rake in Bedlam. I'm not sick anymore but I can't go out on the street until the sores come off my face. We plan to go to New Haven on Friday and to New Hampshire on Saturday and if I don't get better quick I'll have to go to the train in a veil.

That's about all. Our address in New Hampshire is: Tree Tops, Bristol, and write us when you have the time.

Best,<br>John

This was John Weaver.

[17 July 1947]<br>Thursday

Dear John,

I have my troubles. Mrs. Fitch French, who does my wash, has a middle-aged and crippled cat she wants Susie to have. Susie wants the cat. I don't want Susie to have the cat so on Sunday I bought three rabbits; one for Susie and one each for Irene and Jackie, the cook's children. This cost four dollars. Then I brought the rabbits home. I put them in an old duck pen where I thought they would be comfortable. Irene went around behind the duck pen to take a piss. She sat down on a hornet's nest. The hornets waited until she got to her feet, which is typical of New Hampshire, and then attacked all of us with vigor. We weren't able to go near the duck pen again again until after dark. I then moved the rabbits from an old duck pen to an old turkey pen where there were fewer hornets. The next evening when Susie went to the turkey pen to feed her bunny she found that he was dead. She screamed. She cried. She was inconsolable. I buried the rabbit at the head of the garden while the gardener stood beside me and told me I was wasting my time. I should throw the rabbit into the woods for the skunks, he said. He is a communist and is so steeled against bourgeois sentimentality that he hasn't even given his horse a name. I then went to the duck pen to investigate the causes of the bunny's death and found some poison there, left for the rats by "Guts" Winternitz, my father-in-law. This poison was manufactured by the Chemical Warfare Branch of the United States Army to be fed, presumably to Russians. All of the rabbits tasted the poison but only one of them died. Do you think this is a threat to our national security? Do you think there ought to be a shake-up in chemical warfare? . . . there's a lot of talking about filling the void in Susie's life with Mrs. Fitch French's crippled cat.

As ever,
John

Maxwell Perkins was Josie's editor at Scribner's. Robert Linscott was my father's editor at Random House, and a man for whom he would later develop a hearty dislike.

Tree Tops,
Bristol, N.H., [1947]

Tuesday

Dear Josie,

As soon as we saw about Perkins death in the paper we thought of you. Its a rotten break but it seems as though Perkins must have had someone in the office or at least someone in mind to continue his work. As soon as you get into Scribners and find what the situation is, drop us a line. There are still some good men around. Bob Linscott at Random House is one of them.

John

Fred worked for a company that manufactured sheets. Max Gordon and George Kaufman were working on the adaptation of the Town House stories.

400 East 59th Street,

Sunday

Dear Polly,

My brother is coming here on Wednesday and I'll ask him for sheets then. There is nothing awkward about this. Sheets are easy for him to get and if I can't ask my own brother, my only brother, for sheets, who can I ask?

I'm stage struck. I spend my afternoons in the air-conditioned Lyceum Theatre with Max Gordon and George Kaufman saying No thank you very much to hundreds of women with strawberry hair. I've certainly been wasting my time, trying to write short stories.

As ever,
John

*The New Yorker* had turned the story down. Maxim Lieber had been my father's agent. Russell Lynes was managing editor of Harper's.

May 18th [1947]

Dear Josie,

Harpers Magazine bought Vega, the story I showed you, and I went up there one afternoon last week to take a look at the editors. It's been years since I've been in a magazine office other than the NY'er and the reception room was gloomy and windowless with carved bookshelves and murals and in the corner was a literary tableau that is as familiar, I suppose, as Rogers groups used to be in farmhouse windows a century ago. There was a lady editor, nervous, determined, running her fingers through her thin hair and saying:"Well we feel that if you put less emphasis on the love story and made the problem itself, etc." There was an author in his best suit, and there, blowing on a pipe was Maxim Lieber himself. I met Russel Lynes and told him you'd told me about him because you're the only person who ever has told me about him. He kept answering the telephone and saying: "Love to. Fiveish? Love to. Nineish?" It's a little like a theatrical atmosphere it seems to me after all these years. While I was waiting for the elevator an editor came out, holding an author by the arm. "Well thanks very much for having given us a look at it," the editor said. "Well thanks very much for having read it so carefully," the author said, but you could tell that his heart was broken. I went down with the author. He had on his best suit. When he stepped out onto 33rd Street you could tell that he didn't know where to go. Authors leaving editors offices never know where to go. I went to 34th street and had a drink.

Both Mary and Sue look forward to getting out to your place and I hope the 29th will be allright for you.

John

[Postmarked Oct. 2, 1947, 2 A.M.]

John Cheever<br>400 East Fifty-Nine Street<br>New York City

Dear Pete and Lib,

I got some work done and with some luck and application I ought to finish my celebrated novel by snow-time. Josie came in one night. She had a tough time with her book, as you may have heard. She finished it in the early summer, rushed it to Max Perkins, who took it home and dropped dead. She seems happy with his successor, however and Scribners will bring it out this month.

John

He had to become a member of the Dramatists Guild in order to get paid for the production of the Town House stories. My mother says he never owned a Norfolk jacket. She says he wouldn't have been caught dead in a Norfolk jacket.

December 16, 1947

Dear John

I stuffed the pockets of my Norfolk jacket with manuscripts and went down to the Algonquin last week to have lunch with Ross, Dorothy Parker, the Duke of Windsor, et al. In the middle of lunch a raggle-taggle bunch of hoodlums appeared in the dining-room door. "Sardi's must be on fire," Ross said; and he was right. They had to close it for a week and naturally this has upset a lot of people, including me because Mary is giving me a membership in the Dramatist's Guild for Christmas.

[Mailed Dec. 17, 1947. P.M.]

John Cheever
400 East Fifty-Nine Street
New York City

Dear Pete and Lib,

We don't seem to have much social life although we did go to a party in Tarrytown where Mary talked with John Rockefeller about the elm-blight and I talked with a lady named Mrs. Henderson about the lamentable lack of medical education among the Burmese missionaries. I have an idea that Mrs. Henderson wanted to talk this over with Mr. Rockefeller but she couldn't get to him because Mary was so deep in the elm-blight. Josie steamed in last week. Nathan is living in the Napa Valley where the grapes come from, writing a beautiful, beautiful novel, she says. The tapestry show at the Metropolitan is wonderful.

Best,
John

Wednesday [Feb. 1948]

Dear Polly and Winter,

Sue went up to Brearley for her vivas. She was on her best behavior; scrubbed, plaited, and wearing her knitted Tree Tops dress. Mary left her there, claimed her a few hours later and when she got home we had an inquisition. Sue seems to feel that she satisfied them; but we're not so sure. "They asked me," she said, "to draw with a pencil how a little boy could get from his house to his school without crossing the street but it was very easy because all the little boy had to do was to jump over the hole in the street!" Somehow this doesn't sound like a winning answer.

As ever,
John

Miss Hemingway was a friend of Polly's who had some connection with the Brearley School. My mother was pregnant with me. Soakers are short pants that used to be worn over cloth diapers.

[March 23, 1948]

Dear Polly and Winter,

God Bless Miss Hemingway and God Bless you one and all. Sue was accepted by the Brearley School on Saturday morning and the scotch came on Saturday afternoon. . . . The Brearley acceptance came after a month of anxious waiting. They not only accepted Sue but they wrote a charming letter, all about Sue's independence and extraordinary maturity. These terms must refer to Miss Hemingway since they obviously can't describe our fat and wayward daughter. . . . We celebrated our anniversary by drinking some scotch before dinner last night and going to bed at ten. The scotch is delicious and tastes—as Mary said—like the scotch you used to get before Pearl Harbor.

Elizabeth, Tom's wife, has written Mary several pleasant letters and sent us in the mail yesterday some soakers for the baby. As soon as we turned our backs, Sue had the soakers on her teddy-bear, but we got them away from her and put them with the growing collection of boots and blankets that await the unborn. Sue still thinks she's the Queen of Egypt, but she gets down off her throne on Sundays long enough to go over to Central Park with me for a ride on the carrousel. She likes the flying horses nearly as much as I do, and nothing delights a childish intelligence so much as the music of a merry-go-round on a spring day. . . .

As ever,
John

400 East 59th Street,
Friday [April of 1948]

Dear Polly and Winter,

. . . Mary goes to the doctor's today. Even Sue is getting impatient and says that if the baby doesn't come soon, she doesn't want it. . . .

Yesterday at noon the doorbell rang and I found a ruddy, white-haired old gentleman standing in the hall. He said that his name was James

Cheever and that he came from Princeton, Mass., and that whenever he visited a strange city he always called on the other Cheevers to see what they looked like. He seemed disappointed in my looks. he said there were some colored Cheevers in Augusta, but I don't think this troubled him so much as some Irish Catholic Cheevers he uncovered in Saint Louis. He said that the name was Norman, a fact that delights Mary since the name is obviously a corruption of Chevres the Norman word for goat.

As ever,
John

400 East 59th

May 18th

Dear Pete and Lib,

On May 4th, which was Mary's birthday, she spent the afternoon pricing bathrobes at Bendel's, and in the evening went up to Harkness and had a seven and one-half pound son whose name is Benjamin Hale Cheever which I made up myself. Naturally this made us both very happy. We think he's handsome, intelligent, wirey, and strong; and actually he's very unlike Sue. Sue is in New Haven and hasn't seen him yet, but I'm going down to get her tomorrow. Mary came home from the hospital on Saturday in the company of a nurse who costs eighty-four dollars a week and who is nearly worth it, considering our earlier experience, and all is well.

Best,
John

Trygve Lie was then secretary general of the United Nations.

Friday [1948]

Dear Josie,

I've wanted to write you much sooner than this about the Partisan Review piece which I liked a great deal and about Mary. . . . the piece, unlike much of the stuff in Partisan Review, was written by someone with creative experience as well as with creative ambition. I wish you'd do more of them. It's a unique magazine God knows, but it seems to have the effect of parching those springs that are its only excuse for existence. Issue for issue I've never read more discouraging and repulsive criticism. People who love literature as well as covet it, should write for them. They seem to be sitting on the whore house steps.

On Mary's birthday, May 4th, she went up to Harkness and an hour after her arrival had a son. His name is Benjamin Hale Cheever which is the fanciest name I could think up. He has a silver porringer with his name engraved on it in cemetery script and the Ettlingers gave him an early edition of Madame Bovary. He's a fine looking dark-eyed lively boy, very different from Susie even now. Mary came through it well and this time we have a good nurse. Then the day before the nurse left Mary came down with a complication in her breasts and she's been in bed for the last week. However she gave Ben his bath yesterday and will again today and if she gets plenty of rest she ought to be allright in another week. She's crazy about Ben and talks to him as if he were Trygvee Lie. He's fine.

John

Just back from Treetops.

400 East 59th Street,

September 19th [1948]

Dear Polly and Winter,

. . . New York was humid and overcast when we pulled in on Wednesday morning and so ended one of the best summers we've ever had, and we cannot possibly thank you both for your perfect generosity and your patient kindness.

Mary has never felt so well and so rested. She is very pleased with the apartment and enchanted with her maid. This maid has a gray uniform with an apron which she wishes to wear and if either of you can pay us a call we would be very grateful. She wears funny glasses and is no great shakes as a cook but at noon we all cram ourselves into the vestibule, ring a little bell and she brings in a plate of deviled ham sandwiches and trails after her a rich blend of patchouli and Nuit D'Armour. On the three days that we've had her she's been willing and pleasant. Naturally we're all so polite it would give you a headache and nobody goes around barefooted anymore.

As ever,
John

Mary Wickes starred in the adaptation of the Town House stories.

Friday
Dear Josie,
Mary and I went down from New Hampshire to Boston, holed up at the Ritz and got stinking. In Boston the show was a sentimental and moderately funny piece of bunk and with Mary's family and my family in the orchestra and the balcony full of former maids and cleaning-women it was a smash-hit. Max Gordon waltzed Kay Brown around the lobby and said they were going to sell it to pictures for a million dollars. Then George Kaufman began to shine it up. He got so many gags in it that it sounded like a recitation from a joke book and he wouldn't listen to anybody he was so sure he had a money-maker. Whenever I said anything he would tell me to go and write a short story. The set was wonderful and we had a wonderful actress—Mary Wickes—playing the Esther part and in general Mary and I had a fine time. I made fifty-four dollars and it cost Max Gordon and his friends a hundred thousand dollars. I'd like to do it every year but Max says he can't afford it.

Everything's the same here now. Ben is a wonderful fellow—even tempered and merry and Sue is studying carpentry at the Brearley School and we hope to get her a Union Card in another year. I don't work on the novel because I haven't any money. However I've been working very well and if I can keep it up I ought to be able to pay the bills by Christmas and write a chapter or two.

Best,
John

400 East 59th Street,
Sunday [Sept. 1948]
Dear Polly and Winter,
Sue went off to a birthday party yesterday afternoon, dressed in her navy blue knit wear, looking like a French Princess; a fat Princess, but

a Princess au fond. She's been on a diet ever since we reached New York and hasn't seen a cake, candy, cookie, or piece of white bread in that time but yesterday when I picked her up at the party there was frosting in her ears, several pieces of candy in her mouth, and when she came away from the party she was carrying several small baskets and parcels of candy so that I'm afraid all of our hard work has been undone.

The play closed on Saturday night, but this did not surprise us. I don't quite know who to blame, with the exception of myself, but it is a consolation to realize that none of the seventy-five thousand dollars belonged to us. I feel very sorry for Mary Wickes who finds it difficult to get a good part, and now and then I feel sorry for myself because I had such wonderful ideas for spreading the money around, but it's a speculative business and I'm glad we confined our speculation to day-dreaming. We did have a wonderful time in Boston and I'd like to write a play this winter so that we could have another opening in September and do it all over again. The amazing thing is that Gordon, and Kaufman, two of the oldest hands in show-business, were so sure of themselves that they put their own money into it. It just wasn't good enough and in a way I'm glad that the theatre is this discriminating.

As ever,
John

400 East 59th Street,

Election Day [November 1948]

Dear Polly and Winter,

... The social climate that surrounds Brearley sometimes makes me uneasy. I took Sue up to school a few mornings ago and as we entered one little kindergartner was saying to another: "My farther went to Harrvard and so did both of my bruthers."

But Sue loves the school and they seem to accomplish miracles of patience and tact there. Sue recently made herself a costume of a soiled apron, a torn scarf, several yards of twine and two card-board wings. It takes her twenty minutes to tie herself into the contraption. . . . Well, this morning she wanted to take the damned thing to school. I tried to disuade her, I offered her bribes, but she wouldn't compromise and off she went with her costume in a paper bag. She got out of the taxi at noon decked in the torn apron, the soiled scarf and with the wings tied

to her ample stomach; but her self-esteem was unimpaired and I don't
see how the teachers did it.

As ever,
John


400 East 59th Street

November 25th [1948]

Dear Polly and Winter,
. . . Mary went up to Brearley one day last week to check on Susie's
progress and everything there is happy and industrious. Apparently
one of the things money can buy is a good primary education. There
are no problem children in her group—the teachers says—and the
classes are sunny and loving. One the Sunday before Christmas Sue is
going to be an angel on the alter at Saint Thomases, wearing genuine
high-church episcopal wings. I hope they don't expect us to repay them
with a stained glass window, but I know that they do. . . .

As ever,
John


Polly and Winter had given my parents the below-mentioned gifts.


400 East 59th Street,

Wednesday

Dear Polly,
. . . When the children had been put to bed we arranged the books in
the shelves and Mary then wrapped herself up in the Chinese shawl
and did a dance while I looked up Cranmer, Chares Edward Stuart and
Luther in the encyclopedia. Then Mary examined the table clothes,
which are beautiful and began to plan a terrifying dinner party at which
there will be as many people as there are napkins. While she worried
about this I looked at the pictures in the History of the Ancient World.
It is a wonderful history in which the prose is decorous and en-
lightened while the illustrations dwell entirely on carnage and lust.
While the text concerns itself loftily with advances in constitutional
government the illustrations interpret history as a series of busty and

naked women running away from the lecherous Goth and the horny Hun. It is my favorite history.

As ever,
John

My father had been trout fishing at Gus Lobrano's wilderness camp on Cranberry Lake.

400 East 59th Street
New York 22, N.Y.

May 29th [1949]

Dear Polly and Winter,

Mary and Sue leave tomorrow for three days in Pennsylvania—a bargain that was agreed upon when I went to Cranberry Lake. I'm to stay home and take care of Benjamin but I've booked baby-sitters for the mornings and afternoons and I may book baby-sitters for the evenings. Benjamin has gotten to a point where there is almost nothing in the house that he can't break, tip-over, unravel, or eat and while he still can't walk he makes up for this with stealth and speed.

Sue's school closed on Thursday and we went up to B. for the final assembly. Sue's class sang: Hark! The little cow-slip bell in the breeze is ringing, etc. Then they skipped around the stage for a few minutes and received storms of applause. There were a lot of younger brothers and sisters in the audience who kept hooting at the performers. Most of the music and the dancing that followed was equally quaint and simple, the costumes were self-made and it was fascinating to watch the little girls and observe with what cruel inequality the gifts of grace and felicity are distributed among the fair sex. For every three perfectly formed and gracious little children there was one dog-toothed fat-girl, sweating and puffing and wearied to death of being compared to her pretty betters. The only thing about the ceremony that worried me was that you could pick out the scholarship pupils with your eyes shut. They just don't look the same, somehow. After the ceremony the parents retired to the hall to shake hands with one another and I've never seen more well-groomed and weary women, more preternaturally shabby Harvard men, more imperious grandmothers with walking

sticks, less jewelry, less perfume, and a more intense atmosphere of
genteel comfort. It was just like a funeral in Framingham. I'm afraid
we may have to change our ways. Poor Sue can't be expected to adapt
to this sort of thing so long as I go on eating peanut butter out of the
jar.

As ever,

John

400 East 59th Street,

October 13th [1949]

Dear Polly and Winter,

Susie stopped sucking her thumb when we got back to New York
and demanded the dog she'd been promised. I took her out to Westbury on the train where all the rich dogs live and we looked at a litter
of dark brown standard poodles. We picked a bitch named Caprice,
which was a very good name at the price and a week later Caprice was
delivered to us in a new station wagon. Five minutes later Sue's eyes
got enflamed and she began to cough, sneeze, and wheeze. The doctor
told us to get rid of Caprice and on the following afternoon Mary took
Susie to the corner dug-store for an ice-cream soda and I took Caprice
back to Westbury. The parting, of course was loud and tearful, but
she still doesn't suck her thumb and I doubt that her heart is
broken.

As ever,

John

400 East 59th Street

[Nov. 1949]

Dear Josie,

We'd like very much to have you here for Thanksgiving dinner. If
you should feel like coming in we can put you up, not too comfortably,
on one of the beds in Susie's room or still better, engage a sumptuous
hotel room for you, an offer I make humbly but that you know I
wouldn't make if I couldn't well afford it. The maid is going to stay to
wash the dishes so that we can sip chartreuse and smoke cigars.

There is another writer in this building. I've had my eye on him for about six months now. I often see him in the elevator. He emerges at around four o'clock in the afternoon with the mark of the pillow on his cheek, his eyes enflamed from a catnap and his arms full of rental library books that he has glanced at, not because he enjoys them but because he wants to see what kind of trash they're buying nowadays. Once a month he appears in the lobby with a brief case under his arm, obviously on his way down to Colliers or Cosmopolitan to discuss an idea for an article about dirty restaurants or the abortion racket. Like many writers he is not precisely sure of his place in time and he dresses like a secondary school freshman in a tweed jacket with leather elbow patches and gray flannel pants that are mussed from his many naps. Yesterday as I was descending in an elevator car with many fancy ladies and gents the writer joined us. He was carrying Mary and the Egyptian, the whole left side of his face was red, his eyes were bloodshot, and his fly was open from top to bottom. I didn't tell him that his fly was open and the only reason I'm telling you this is to illustrate how profound the schisms are in the literary world today, how little there is left that one writer will freely tell another.

Best,
John

Josie had written this note at the top of the letter below: "From Cheever after letter from me saying Scribners had phoned in alarm to find out if I was alive. Coffee had phoned them saying he had heard from Peggy Cowley I was dead in Paris." Katherine Anne was Katherine Anne Porter, Josie's old and not-so-good friend. Frederick Lewis Allen was then an editor at Harper's.

Dec 10, 1949

Saturday

Dear Josie,

The way I heard it, Katherine Anne is the one who's dead. Not in Paris but it Pottsville, Pa., where she was overtaken by fish poisoning on her way east to attend a testimonial dinner given by Sommerset Maugham for Glenway Wescott, both of whom have been reported dead. Irwin Shaw said that somebody told him that Leonard Erlich was dead, but Mary saw Leonard at the dentists a few days later, more dead than alive, to be sure, but who are we to judge? Leonard said that Irwin was dead. The man in the liquor store said that his wife said that she had heard a radio announcer say that Mayor O'Dwyer was dead and we had a baby-sitter sometime ago who came in with a long face and said that Frank Sinatra was dead. Peggy Cowley is an old hand at this and I tell people that she's dead. She told me that Bob Coates was dead. On the other hand Fulton Lewis says that Franklin Roosevelt, Lenin, Ivar Kruger, Stavisky and Kautsky are alive. Your publisher is nicer than my publisher. The last time I went to Random House Bob Linscott walked to the door with me, wringing his hands, his eyes ablaze with the reflected glitter of an insurance policy, he said: "Whatever you do, John, don't hang yourself."

. . . Do you remember a story of mine called Vega? Harpers ran it this month with a little note in the front of the magazine saying that the story interested them because it was about people who lived apart from society and that the political histories involved were of no consequence; they did everything, in short, but run a footnote saying that the story was run by mistake. So far as I'm concerned, Frederick Lewis Allen is dead.

Best,<br>John

400 East 59th Street,

Saturday [1949]

Dear Winter,

. . . Ben gets bigger, redder, and more opinionated every day. For a day or two he could wave goodbye (bye-bye) when he was asked, but Mary forced things by teaching him patty-cake too soon after this and now when he's asked to wave goodbye he flails his arms around in the air, wets his pants and slaps himself on the stomach. Sue is the same dish of tea; now bitter; now sweet.

As ever,<br>John

William Faulkner won the Nobel Prize in literature in 1949. Hemingway didn't win it until 1954.

400 East 59th St.,

Monday [1949]

Dear Josie,

On Suday night I had a dream about a letter Hemingway might have written to The New York Times. This is the way the letter went. "I think it's fine that Bill Faulkner got the Nobel Prize. I think the judges did a fine thing. The Nobel Prize is like that purse they give in Verona for the shot who bags the most sitting ducks on a clear day. There are other kinds of shooting, but they don't give prizes for it. There is the kind of shooting that you get in the Abruzzi in the May snows and underwater shooting and the kind of lonely shooting that you have when you take your sights in a pocket-mirror and bring down a grizzley over your left shoulder but they don't give prizes for that kind of shooting. Mr. Thomas Hardy and Mr. Herman Melville did that kind of shooting but they never got any prizes. I think it was fine they gave Bill Faulkner the Nobel Prize before he was dead."

It's a slender comfort, but anytime that you want to sleep on our sofa, you're welcome to it. . . . Susie went to the ballet on Saturday and has since spent all her time trying to do entrechats. She keeps falling down, trying all the time to keep on her face the imbecilic smile of a ballerina. Ben has a cold and a hoarse, deep voice, but he will recover.

As ever,
John

Ross was Harold Ross. Gibbs would be The New Yorker writer and editor Wolcott Gibbs. The party was to celebrate the twenty-fifth anniversary of The New Yorker.

400 East 59th Street,

March 6th

Dear Polly and Winter,

There are a few reverberations from the New Yorker party. The hotel management sent Ross a note saying that they had never seen such a well behaved crowd. Gibbs said:"That party proved one thing. It proved that lady writers don't die. I danced with Harriet Beecher Stowe twice."

As ever,
John

400 East 59th Street,

March 22nd

Dear Polly and Winter,

I'm reporting on the New Yorker party while my memories are still
more or less fresh. Mary wore a short black dress and long white gloves
and looked very chic and distinguished. I wore a short tuxedo and no
gloves and thought that I looked very distinguished. We got to the Ritz
at a quarter to ten where a barrier of secretaries and plain-clothes men
were screening the guests. In the confusion I got in but Mary got left
outside and very nearly went home in a huff with Colburn Gilman who
was trying, unsuccessfully, to crash the party. Finally Mary and I were
reunited and we climbed the stairs. The hotel management had made
Ross rent both the Oval Room and the ballroom because, as they said,
there were bound to be a lot of elderly people at a twenty-fifth anniversary and elderly people have to sit down. The mayor was expected and
he hadn't come and this made Ross nervous. He had stationed E.B.
White, John McNulty and Phil Hamburger on the stairs to greet his
honor when he did arrive but the reception commmittee got impatient
and tipsey and when the mayor did arrive they were somewhere else.
There was a disorderly supper at one o'clock and at two o'clock the
management began blinking the lights in the Oval Room but this only
whetted the guests love of pleasure. At half-past three Mary and I and
some others went down to the Shaws with Irwin to say hello to Marion
who has been in bed for five months. She was pleasant, considering
the hour. Then we decided to go back to the Ritz but the shrewd
managment had blocked the ballroom doors with potted palms and so
we had to go home. We got undressed a few minutes before the children woke up and I spent this morning on the merry-go-round in
Central Park with Susie and Ben. They enjoyed it more than I.

Mary and Sue are in Greenwich today and tomorrow Ben goes to the
hospital for his operation.

As ever,

John

My only recollection of this operation is that I wouldn't go into a super-
market for several years. This was because the men who worked in super-
markets wore white jackets, and I assumed they were doctors and would
hurt me.

400 East 59th Street
New York City

March 24th

Dear Polly and Winter,

The bottle from the Maison came a little before dark as it has on every one of our anniversaries and it was the closest to a celebration that we had. It was very kind of you to remember and our most sincere thanks. We have been drinking a scotch that is manufactured, I believe, in Bloomingdale's basement and this was a wonderful change. It also picked up Mary's spirits and enabled her to forget the Great Operation for an hour.

We were told to get Ben to the hospital at twenty minutes to nine yesterday, which we did. . . . when a doctor finally tried to examine him at ten o'clock, he put up a terrible fight. "Well it's going to be traumatic anyhow," the doctor said, "give him to me." "I will not," his mother said. She stretched him out on the table with her own hands. He was returned to us about an hour later, swathed in elastic bandage with one red and suspicious eye showing. We took him home early in the afternoon and for the rest of the day he was an object of hushed and tearful pity, but in the middle of the night his elastic bandage fell off, leaving only a small dressing over the scar, and he's been in wonderful spirits since then. I think they take the dressing off tomorrow and there will be no scar. There will be no scar on Ben's face, that is: there will be a deep wound in our purse.

As ever,
John

400 East 59th Street

Tuesday

Dear Polly and Winter,

. . . Easter went off well. Susie and Ben woke up at five. Susie locked Ben in the bedroom and then began to hunt for treats in the living room. I released Ben who went downstairs and ate two hard-boiled eggs with the shells on. Sue was given a very pretty purple dress which she put on. Ben was given a serge coat and a cap with a visor which he would not put on. We haven't been able to get him into it yet.

As ever,
John

400 East 59th Street

April 19th

Dear Josie

... A few nights ago we were invited to watch Bennet Cerf on a radio program that is looking for sponsors. We were invited, I think, because my laughter is thought to carry. It was a terrible program and half the audience walked out in the middle of it. I can remember when publishers used to stay home at night and smoke merschaum pipes.

John

A variation on the Treetops cook mentioned below appears in "Goodbye, My Brother."

The cook we had that year was a Polish woman named Anna Ostrovick, a summer cook. She was first-rate—a big, fat, hearty, industrious woman who took her work seriously. She liked to cook and to have the food she cooked appreciated and eaten, and whenever we saw her, she always urged us to eat. She cooked hot bread—crescents and brioches—for breakfast two or three times a week, and she would bring these into the dining room herself and say, "Eat, eat, eat!" When the maid took the serving dishes back into the pantry, we could sometimes hear Anna, who was standing there, say, "Good! They eat." She fed the garbage man, the milkman, and the gardener. "Eat!" she told them. "Eat, eat!" On Thursday afternoons, she went to the movies with the maid, but she didn't enjoy the movies, because the actors were all so thin. She would sit in the dark theatre for an hour and a half watching the screen anxiously for the appearance of someone who had enjoyed his food. ... In the evenings, after she had gorged all of us, and washed the pots and pans, she would collect the table scraps and go out to feed the creation. We had a few chickens that year, and although they would have roosted by then, she would dump food into their troughs and urge the sleeping fowl to eat. She fed the songbirds in the orchard and the chipmunks in the yard. Her appearance at the edge of the garden and her urgent voice—we could hear her calling "Eat, eat, eat"—had become, like the sunset gun at the boat club and the passage of light from Cape Heron, attached to that hour. "Eat, eat, eat," we could hear Anna say. "Eat, eat . . ." Then it would be dark.

Tree Tops,
Bristol, New Hampshire

July 18th, 1950

Dear Josie,

We leave here at the end of this month for Martha's Vineyard and we will write you as soon as we get settled there with the hope that you will come and visit us. I don't know how long we've been up here but it seems like a week. Susie is brown and fat and happy and at night she plays Slap-Jack with Marie de Grasse the Old Domestic. Ben is brown and fat and Mary is brown. I have been struggling to work every day since we arrived but there have been a lot of interruptions. The pump has broken down three times and yesterday the wells went dry. These are small problems but the truth is that I would rather help the plumber than write.

The gardener's Stalanism has been refreshed by the war and he's rooting for the North Koreans. . . . Marie De Grasse hides the cigarets in the washing machine and sleeps at night with a hatchet under her pillow. The cook is a crazy Pole who likes animals. At night when the dishes are done she butters a loaf of bread and goes out to feed the chipmunks, porcupines, birds, and fishes. "Eat, eat, eat," she shouts at them. Mary reads Dreiser in a dark room and I fly kites.

Best,
John

Martha's Vineyard.
Seven Gates Farm,
Vineyard Haven, Mass.

Sunday [1950]

Dear Josie,

We got down here about a week ago. The house has a big ice-box with a special compartment to keep the butter soft and hot and cold running water in all four (4) toilets and is much fancier than what we're used to but so is the rent. . . . we have two good maids rooms available and if you don't like maids' rooms I'll put Susie in a maid's room and let you have her quarters. . . .

I wish I could give you some idea of what it's like. The place was established at about the same time as Yaddo, I guess, and I think of

Yaddo whenever I smell mouse-shit, but that's about the only connection. There is two miles of beach and a lot of land in which eight or ten houses are hidden. There are all kinds of people. There is a big red-faced Irish Lawyer from Washington named Shay. His wife reads Stendhal. Everybody reads Stendhal. There is a nice fellow and his wife named Dreier who was at Black Mountain for sixteen years. There is a very handsome and spirited woman named Margot Morrow who appears to be both comforted and saddened by the fact that there are always a couple of pansies at her feet. However our house is remote, the beaches are long and empty and I've been working every day from eight until five, trying to pry a saleable story out of my head.

Mary sends you her best and hopes you'll come down.

as ever,
John

The house in Scarborough, New York, was small, but it was not a garage. It never had been a garage. In fact, it had a garage of its own.

400 East 59th Street,
New York City

January 28th, 1951

Dear Malcolm,

Thanks a great deal for the essay you sent along to the Guggenheims. It's very generous. I'm not sanguine about getting a fellowship. After having asked you for a reference it occured to me that I didn't have a chance in a million and that I shouldn't have asked you or anyone else to suppose such a doubtful entry. I am very grateful to you for your support. . . .

In the spring Mary and I are moving into a garage in Westchester. A lot of people in Westchester live in garages. Our garage is in Scarborough. Once we get into this garage I expect that we will be out of touch and I hope we'll see you and Muriel here before we move.

As ever,
John

He got a grant of $2,000 to work on longer stories.

400 East 59th Street,

March 30th,1951

Dear Malcolm,

I got the word from the Guggenheims this morning. I am very pleased. It seems to put the excellence of the stories squarely up to me now and there hasn't been a time in my life when I'd rather have had it this way. My sincere thanks for your help in this.

We move out to Scarborough in May and I hope that you will come to see us there, or that we can drive up to Sherman.

My love to Muriel,

As ever,
John

Katharine White was *The New Yorker's* fiction editor. She bought the first two pieces my father sold to that magazine. She and Polly both went to the Miss Windsor's school in Boston. This had been on Beacon Street. The Vanderlips owned the estate in Scarborough, New York, on which my family was to rent a house when we moved from 59th Street.

400 East 59th,

April 30th [1951]

Dear Polly and Winter,

On Friday I had lunch with the celebrated Katherine Angell White who said that her maiden name was pronounced Sergent and that her daugther-in-law is "part Windsor". She said that she was in the last class to graduate from Beacon Street. We went on Saturday to Scarborough and had a picnic on one of the lawns that we will share with Mrs. Vanderlip. Mary seems pleased at the thought of moving and we will discover life in the suburbs soon enough.

As ever,
John

# TO THE SUBURBS

* * *

O n May 28, 1951 the family moved from 59th Street to a small house on the estate of Frank A. Vanderlip in Scarborough, New York. The house had previously been occupied by my father's friend and colleague, E. J. Kahn, Jr. It backed up against the high brick wall that girded the estate. Through the wall we could hear the heavy trucks on Route 9. These rattled the dishes, and sometimes cracked plaster, but inside the wall our world had been laid out with a good deal of thought and money. I grew up loving to play outdoors and thinking that the wilderness was a series of slate paths bordered by giant rhododendron bushes. Aside from the magnificent swimming pool there were numerous gardens, and a working farm. There was also, on the property, a school that Vanderlip had designed and constructed for the education of his children. Susan, Fred and I all attended the Scarborough Country Day School. Its main building had an auditorium constructed on the model of the Little Theatre in London. The inscriptions above its two doorways were: "Life Is for Service" and "Manners Maketh Man." Frank A. Vanderlip's estate has become the Beechwood Condominiums.

I was just three years old when we moved to the wilds of Westchester. Family legend has it that I was playing on the slates in front of the house when the Memorial Day Parade came booming down Route 9, and I flew inside shrieking "Indians! Indians!"

400 East 59th

[May 22 1951]

Dear Mrs. Josie

We move on the 28th—a week from yesterday and from now on in, I guess, unreality takes over. We have a pleasant, Hungarian moving man who keeps asking:"Who knows what brings the future?" . . . We count on you to come and visit us.

We saw Eleanor Clark a few nights ago, and she looked about as Roman as you can get to look. I mean this to be a serious compliment.

She spoke very affectionately about you and wondered how to get in touch with you. Her hair is gray and fair, her features seem more massive than ever and she moves with a kind of heavy, pre-Christian grace. I like Eleanor very much; or at least I like the very little I know about her. . . .

John

Scarborough, New York

June 8th

Dear Josie,

Here we are and you'd better come out and take a look at us. I overdrew the bank account the day we arrived here, and at about the same time the swimming pool overflowed. The swimming pool is curbed with Italian marble, luscent and shining like loaves of fine sugar. The trees are huge and beautiful and now and then a vast herd of sheep moves around the park, frightening Benjamin. I have a light, quiet room to work in and Mary is very pleased with her living-room. She keeps standing in a corner pretending that she just strayed in by chance. We haven't forgotten our beginings, and from the dining-room table we look squarely into Mrs. Vanderlip's garbage pail. It's a good house for us and if I can lay down some kind of a temperate routine I think I can work more easily here than I did in New York. It's not far from the city. It's less than an hour on a good train and less than that in the car. We want very much to see you and I'll leave your coming up to you. If you don't take the initiative, we'll try to extort some dates. There's a pleasant room here where you can spend the night, the food and drink are plentiful. Our telephone number is Briarcliffe 6-0075.

We saw Katherine Anne at a party last week. She was sitting on a sofa talking with a countess. She was describing, in a very brittle way, the minimum conditions in which she finds life bearable. "I must," she was saying, "live in a world capital. Rome, Berlin, Paris, New York . . ." Mary joined the conversation at this point and asked: "What about the four years you spent in Los Angeles?" That was the end of that.

Best,
John

The West mentioned here was the writer Nathanael West. I don't know if Josie was touched by my father's flattery, but it's interesting to note that he found occasion to express admiration for the letter-writing skills of just about everybody who wrote him. There are letters to Don Ettlinger about what a great letter writer he is. There are letters to Phil Boyer about his brilliant letters. There are letters to John Weaver about people pulling out letters from him and reading them in public. There are even letters to my grandfather, Milton Charles Winternitz, praising him for the writing in something called The Bulletin, a compendium of family news that he regularly circulated through the mail, a compendium that his own daughter recalls as deadly dull. Doubtless many of the people my father corresponded with were superb writers, but my father's talent for admiration must in some cases have exceeded the talents of those whom he was flattering. *Nothing Is Sacred* was Josie's first novel. It was published by Coward-McCann in 1928.

[1951]

Dear Josie,

I talked recently with a man named Bob MacGregor from New Directions who said that in going over West's correspondence he found the letters from you to be head and shoulders above all the rest and who wanted to know about you. He said that he would read Nothing Sacred with an eye to reprinting it and that he wondered if you would be interested in editing some of West's papers. "We don't pay anything," he said; but I guess he meant that they don't pay much. They must pay something. If you haven't heard from him and if you're interested I'll write and give him your address.

Everything is quiet here and unexceptional. I gave Random House a hundred pages of the novel on Friday and now I wait nervously for the telephone to ring; but it will probably never ring and if they should call the conversation can't come as a surprise since I've planned it exhaustively. "We like some of it," they say, or, "We like the way you've handled the material, but we don't like the material," or "One of our editors took the manuscript home to Westport with him and left it on the train," or "we wish that you could write a little more like James Jones." I think that the material is exceptional but I base my opinion on the fact that it is unlike anything that Random House has printed in the last couple of years. Anyrate, I like it.

Everybody sends their love,
John

Josie had sent me a valentine and some toy monkeys. When asked about the work of other competent writers of prose, my father was in the habit of saying that "writing is not a competitive sport." But he could be wicked to the competition. He was probably particularly wicked in 1952, because he was having "such a lugubrious time" with his own novel. Nathan Asch was an old friend, and my father hadn't even seen the book on which publishers were turning such a gelid eye.

[February 1952]

Dear Josie,

Benjamin loved his valentine and will be happy to be your valentine. He has no other feminine attachments although he still thinks he is Billy the Kid and you'll have to consider this. The monkeys delighted him and started a long series of questions. Do monkeys live in barrells. Do monkeys bite. Do monkeys do ka-ka on the floor. Do monkeys make Susie sneeze. Can I have a monkey for a friend? Why can't I have a monkey for a friend. Mary once had a monkey at Sarah Lawrence and the burden of answering these questions falls on her. Such are the rewards of a classical education.

I'm sorry to hear that Nathan's having such a lugubrious time and I hope that his books are good and that the publishers are fools although I can't help but feel that the opposite may be true. I've spent so little time in California that when people settle there they seem to drop, not only out of my life, but beyond the scope of my imagination: I can never imagine people in California eating a meal or walking to a bus-stop. Poor Nathan. I can remember him saying in Washington: It's all running through my mind like quicksilver! What a book I will be able to write! And in this connection Josie, be kind to your deluded colleagues. I often think of them. To each of them comes a month, sometimes a year, when they feel that at last they have hit the purest spring of creativity. What rapture! What transports! With their eyes inflamed and their pants unbuttoned, they come out of the basement or the coat closet at dusk, convinced that they have the world by the tail. It does not really matter that the manuscripts they leave behind them will be nothing but a sore and a humiliation to their descendents.

Speaking of Hemingway there is a painter in the neighborhood (Reggie Rowe) who is having a show of Cuban landscapes for which the old man wrote a puff. "The Light in Cuba," he beings, "is the light of

the Sudan, although in lattitude Cuba is south of Karachi, India." It
goes on like this.

                                                            Best,
                                                            John


My parents had ring-necked doves. A pair of these doves appeared on
the cover of *Time* with my father in 1964. Josie had been persuaded to take
in a bird of her own. The Philip Boyers were friends who lived in Westchester and kept a variety of animals, including doves, Labrador retrievers
and a pair of toucans.


                                                        [April 1952]
Dear Josie,

I think you'd better get a female for your dove. He may seem happy,
but as you well know, he doesn't know what he's missing. The Boyers
have a young dove and as soon as it does something indicative like
laying an egg or cleaning up the seedtray, I'll write you and maybe
you'll like her. Our dove had big problems of adjustment when the
female first went into the cage. He bowed and cooed for two days but
she just looked sicker and sicker. Her eyes looked glassy, her feathers
lost their gleam, and she wouldn't eat or drink. Then—fwung—she
dropped an egg. Then—fwung—she dropped another. Mary put them
into the lining of an old hat and a few days later the dove waddled over
and sat on them. At first the male scolded and walked up and down on
her back but now he brings her things to eat and feeds her with his
bill. They seem very happy.

When we spoke to you about the story it was not with the idea that
you would change anything or that you should change anything and
the only reason that we tempered our enthusiasm was because so much
cheek-kissing goes on today among writers and friends that everyone
seems to be wandering around in the dark. If we all behaved like
Glenway Wescott and Katherine Anne God knows where we'd be.

Poor Ben has the trots and has lost a lot of weight but before he got
sick he went boldly off to school every morning and the world seems
to suit him from top to bottom. The Boyers had a big Easter egg hunt
and poor Ben began by replacing tenderly every egg he found with an

egg from his basket. Someone discouraged this sentimentalilty and in the end he won the prize.

If you're still on a two-day dentist schedule call us up and come out again.

Best
John

Random House didn't like my father's book, and this was a difficult time for him professionally. He'd been trying to publish a novel for more than twenty years. In his journal my father wrote: "Still no word from Linscott. This seems to imply no enthusiasim, and if the work I've sent him is bad I have made some grave mistakes. My eyes are wrong, my heart is wrong, and I have been mistaken in listening for all these years to the rain. . . ."

Another entry at about the same time expressed his disappointment and bewilderment: "Thinking again, in the dentist's chair, that I am like a prisoner who is trying to escape from jail by the wrong route. For all one knows that door may stand open although I continue to dig a tunnel with a teaspoon. Oh, I think, if I could only taste a little success."

The Warrens were in Grosseto, Italy. They were staying in a vast stone fortress called La Rocca, which we rented in the summer of 1957 when we were in Italy. Dancing classes were being given at the main house on the Vanderlip Estate.

Scarborough, New York

July 3rd [1952]

Dear Eleanor,

It did seem to me, when we came in town to say goodbye to you, that Red Warren was sitting on a boil, but maybe it was my fault. It usually is. . . . I think of you in Grossetto with a great deal of intense feeling. I have never so much wanted to shake the dust of Westchester from my heels. Even the children seem to be infected. On the last day of school Susie arose and announced:"In the autumn I am going to sail to Europe and go to school there." Her teacher called excitedly to say that in her opinion Susie should not be taken abroad next year because her adjustment to this neighborhood has been so rich and deep. "Susie has roots here and there is nothing remote or shy about her," the teacher said, giving me a fishy look. One of the drawbacks about this way of life is that everyone is supposed to be rooted. Ben is rooted. Susie is rooted. People keep asking me: "How do you feel, now that you've put some roots down." I often think of you as I play miniature golf at the Wee Bonney Brae on the Old Boston Post Road under a flood of insect-repellent lights. Low man buys frozen custard—27 flavors—for the foursome. Farther down the road, near the Harmon train yards, you can eat Mrs. Kronberg's Chinese Egg Roll while you watch Quo Vadis. I keep writing a story that begins: "We lived in Westchester for six months." I think we'll be here for years.

God knows its a long way from Grosseto and there's never much to report. Beechwood remains bizarre, but that's all pretty obvious. Mrs. Vanderlip's ancient poodle, Baby, dines at the table where Herbert Hoover used to dine and the cook and the social secretary sometimes have such rows that we can hear them in our kitchen. The last of the Beechwood Dancing Classes is on Saturday but I still haven't gone up to see them because who wants to watch a bunch of old people dancing the Samba. I do, I guess, but it seems unfortunate and even the trees on Marlborough Road enjoin me to look away from grotesqueness into light and softball. After a year of observation it is astonishing to find how many of the people in this neighborhood are precisely what they appear to be. Of course if you look hard enough—and I do—you can find a drunken woman lying on a terrace, but she never seems to count for much anymore. One warm night last week I walked down these shady streets and saw, through a window, a man in his shirt sleeves rehearsing a business speech to his wife who was knitting. I often long for the windows of New York where foxglove sometimes grow and where women iron in their underwear. I have been riding and it turns out that there are miles and miles of wonderful trail in the neighborhood and all that part of it—the country and the swimming has been great.

Mary sends her best. Susie told the maid that she has a friend who lives in a castle in Italy. On our map of Italy Grosseto is marked with a church, a boar, a hare and a gull.

As ever,
John

The summer place in New Hampshire from which this letter was written had a stone house, in which my grandparents lived, and a series of smaller wooden cabins without cooking facilities. The latter were named after evergreens: Pine, Hemlock, Balsam, Spruce. The cabin used as a sort of dormitory for the older boys was called Bushes; the laundry, Birch. The main building, which had a kitchen and dining room, was called Apple. I don't know why I'm referring to these places in the past tense, since Treetops still exists, and some of my grandfather's descendants still go there in the summer. In 1952 Susan was spending her first year away at camp.

Treetops

Dear Bill,

I was of course very pleased and surprised that you liked the story. On the drive up here on Wednesday it seemed to me that every large maple and every old house reminded me of how differently the story should have been done. "It should have been longer," said an old house in Windsor Locks,"it should have been more discursive," said all the trees in Deerfield. . . .

. . . The Stone House still smells wonderfully of fires and carnations, etc. We are in a house that we have never stayed in before; matchwood, hornets in the rafters, books that no one ever wanted, a lithograph of Windsor Castle. . . .

The cook this year is a very old lady named Anna. She is much too old to work. The waitress was a country girl named Alice who kept a Boston terrier named Bittey Baby tied to a chair leg in the kitchen and held it on her lap between courses. She chewed gum, came to the table with her hair in pins, opened peapods with her teeth and resigned last night at dusk, after a fracas. We get mixed reports from Susie—most of them doleful—but I think she will live. It is very hard to work here —very hard even to think of working because the air seems so mild and clear and empty. I want to take a long climb or walk next week, visit Susie, and return to New York.

As ever,
John

Famous for his dislike of cats, my father was making a point to the cat-loving Maxwells about how well Goldfarb was being treated. My sister, Susan, says that there was no second visit to her at Camp Kaora, no "Green Grow the Rushes, Oh," no Justine Eliot. He must have made the whole scene up and added it to please Bill and to please himself.

Tree Tops, [1952]

Wednesday

Dear Bill

As I write this Goldfarb—who has lost his belled collar—is rolling and stretching on the rug at my feet. If it's any comfort to you, he came to us from the SPCA and excepting the day when I slammed the door on his tail, he has not known a moment of insecurity. He was happy in Scarborough and although the mountain air made him sleepy for a day or two he quickly adjusted. He lives now on a diet of plump field mice, runs with an old battered Tom cat who lives in an abandoned barn on the mountain and he is missed passionately by Susie. If there is anything dark in Goldfarb's life since leaving the SPCA, it is that he is unworthy.

As for Susie she wrote us some sad and forceful letters to say that she was perishing of home-sickness. From her counselor and from the directoress there were conflicting letters to say what a cheerful Kaiorian she had become. We drove up to see her on Friday. Her smile was broad and forced. She kept seizing my hand and saying: "I'm participating in everything, Daddy." She was shrill. "I can undress under water, swim a quarter of a mile, I sing in the choir and participate in all games." We watched her swim, stuff a balsam pillow, row a boat, play box-hockey and plunge into a game of kick ball in which she was the only enthusiastic participant (several of the players hid under the lodge) and the last member of the team—when it began to rain—to give up. "Rainy Day schedule," shouted the counselor, blowing on his whistle. "Square Dancing!" Susie steamed into the lodge for the Virginia Reel. After this we walked with her through the rain to the riding ring where we watched her walk, trot, and canter. The riding mistress took me aside to say that Susie was not herself; and she did seem exhausted. As she was getting off her horse I said that we were leaving. "Wait just a minute," she sighed, "oh wait just a minute." I said that we might be late for dinner and that we had to stop in Plymouth and get the cook's shoes. So did Mary. "We have to get the cook's shoes, dear," she said. We stood on a dirt road, saying goodbye and talking about the cook's shoes. Then Susie called after me and I went back. She was not crying but her eyes were full of tears. "You understand Daddy, don't you," she said "that I am homesick every minute of the day." I said that I did. She walked away and we drove off slowly, looking back to see where she went. She went into the woods. "She is too young to walk away from her parents and hide her tears," Mary said. I felt very guilty because the camp had looked as bleak and characterless to me as an army camp, the food had seemed tasteless, the games dull, and many of the children lonely. On Saturday Susie was to be in a play so we returned to see this. She smiled at us from the stage, sang Green Grow the Rushes Oh with the choir, kissed us lightly and ran off with a little girl named Justine Eliot. I've never seen her so happy.

There is no one here now but Polly and Winter, Mary and me and so I will stay until Friday when the Griswolds begin to arrive. I don't seem to do any work. The landscape has finally taken up a place in my mind so that when I point out the mountains to strangers I realize that they see something different. It is two places—the green shire to which old Dartmouth graduates who are in the blanket business would like to retreat and raise apples, beef-cattle, chickens—they're never sure—but it would be a simple life, swept by the mountain winds and lighted by open fires. It is the subtlety of the landscape that makes the post-card manufacturers paint snow on the mountains where there is never any snow. There are the pitiful ruins of the town of Cheever which is a little to the north of here and there is the view from the terrace which is mostly the country of chagrin. The awning is torn so that on these nights when the light is like October, at six and like February by nine we can hear, as we sit by the fire playing Scrabble, a noise of wings. . . .

John

Scarborough,

November 4th

Dear Eleanor,

After a wonderful summer, Westchester seems dim. We had just settled ,this fall, when we were embroiled in the kind of strife that does so much to reflect the general mental emptiness of my friends and neighbors. An lagoesque nuisance in the next village, who has never met me, told someone that I was living here in order to collect material for a libelous chronicle of the Vanderlip family. This developed until I was writing a book, implicating the late F. A. Vanderlip in the Teapot Dome oil scandal. The family was galvanized. People were telephoned to ask about my character, letters and copies of letters were sent here and there, and I was finally told the secret. I demanded apologies, and got none; but things have quieted down. Mrs. Vanderlip is teaching Susie to do the Lindy Hop. Susie goes up to Beechwood and the two of them shag and truck up and down the library; but I'm not writing any book about it.

I dream about the custom-shed in Genoa but I seem to understand that a man whose children lose their shoes as often as mine do, will not travel much. We would love to see you, and if there is a chance of your coming over to dinner, it would please us both. Our best to Red.

As ever,<br>John

Discouraged by the reception of his novel, my father thought of publishing a second collection of stories.

Scarborough, New York<br>December 29th [1952]

Dear Malcolm,

I am writing to ask a favor. Of the stories I have printed since the end of the war, fourteen seem readable to me. Cerf wouldn't print them —not even when an English publisher offered to split the production costs. Funk and Wagnalls, who are looking around desperately for the beginings of a trade list, are going to bring them out in February. I would like to know what you think of them and I wondered if you would have time to look at the galleys. That you might not be interested in looking at them seems very likely to me and I would not be surprised or offended if you said so. The stories are all about what you used to call Palefaces and they all appeared in The New Yorker. I think they're all right, but I'm not the man to say so.

As ever,<br>John

The galleys mentioned were for The Enormous Radio and Other Stories. The apologetic note is interesting here, since later in life my father saw "Goodbye, My Brother" as one of his best stories. This may have been what maturity gave him. It's also quite possible that he grew to like it because Malcolm had so many questions about it. He used often to read "The Death of Justina" when asked to appear in public, and he liked to tell his audience that the story had been turned down by *The New Yorker*. "They thought of it as an art story," he would say, before presenting it to the Rotarians, the Chamber of Commerce, the University of Ishkabibble, whatever group had invited him to speak. Rob is Malcolm's son. Rob married my sister in 1967.

Scarborough

February 8th [1953]

Dear Malcolm,

Many thanks for going through the galleys, and for the note to the publisher. All your remarks were helpful and God knows I need advice and counsel. It seems hard to find. I would have written much sooner but we all—all four—have been in bed with influenza and this is my first day up. Mary and the children are still down and our other-directed neighbors are still coming to the door with custards.

Another friend who saw the galleys had more or less what you had to say about the Goodbye Brother Story and this troubles me—or it seems to be a good point on which to center my troubles. In writing short stores I've tried to work at several levels. This may all seem, in the end, to be arch and idle. The brother story, in its bare outline, was the story of one man. There was no brother; there was no Lawrence. (In the finished story he speaks only a few lines and the bulk of his opinions are given to him by the narrator.) I tried to bury this outline then under several others so that the story would unfold like an un-cooked onion. I had hoped that the women—dark head and gold—coming out of the sea, would clear away any ambiguity. I seem to have failed and what troubles me is that I seem to have failed not in execution, but in feeling.

We had planned to go abroad last April for a year, but I couldn't clear the passage money. I will try again this fall. Hardly a day passes in which the collapse of the hot-water heater or the collector from Consolidated Edison does not inhibit my literary ambitions, but the heater and the collector are real enough and it seems only sensible to include them in our plans. I am really not yet tired of the suburbs. . . . I would like, before leaving Westchester, to feel saturated; I would like to feel that I had taken something and lost something here. . . .

I got the stories in page-proof last week and they looked better—at least they looked better to me in this form. It seems to be one step further away from the magazine. Now and then the prose seems wrong and Mary, who is critical of the whole operation, pointed out one whopping set-piece about a thunderstorm; but I keep telling her that its always good to have that kind of thing behind you. But I seem to miss the Big Things, the Big Shapes; I miss them in this letter. I almost always miss them by a mile and since I can't get off the ground my only recourse seems, at times, to go underground. I think I could write a set of long stories to be called A Chamber of Horrors and I think I could master the gooseflesh, the smell of burnt hair and the face in the window but it seems on the other hand that there have been too many good times, too many good days, to settle for this form.

And many thanks for having read the stories and for having described them so generously for the publisher. I would like very much to read what Rob is doing. My love to Muriel and Mary sends her best wishes to you both.

As ever,
John

The Enormous Radio and Other Stories was 237 pages long, had fourteen stories and cost $3.50. Arthur Mizener in the May 25, 1953, issue of The New Republic wrote: "Mr. Cheever is not a writer of any great talent, but the stories in his book are all skillfully worked out and loaded with carefully observed manners. Congreve, who might, for a while at least, have been a great success in The New Yorker, once remarked that he selected a moral and then designed a fable to fit it. . . . It is the glaring fault of Mr. Cheever's stories that they all appear to have been produced in that way."

Scarborough
Thursday

Dear Malcolm,

Funk & Wagnalls have used the good words you put down about the stories in a couple of advertisements. They look very well and I don't know whether or not I ever adequately thanked you for them. As it turned out the reviews weren't bad; there just weren't any reviews.

I liked your piece in Harper's a great deal. You seem to be one of the few, if not the only critic writing today who can point out the cracks in the ceiling and preserve an affectionate regard for the well-being of literature. Most of them seem to aim to plow it under.

I think a good deal about your advice to go abroad and if I can swing it I will try to take the family over in the fall. Perhaps I do waste my time writing up indictments of these harmless neighbors. The fact that no one found the story collection worth while reviewing has reaffirmed the importance of writing a novel, but I still seem to come at it with deeply mixed feelings. The form seems bankrupt. I don't seem to be able to get away from that feeling; but maybe I will.

Mary sends her best regards and joins in love to Muriel and in thanking you again for your words.

As Ever,
John

My parents had become friendly with Phil and Mimi Boyer, who lived in a house on Teatown Road in Ossining. The Boyers had a pond for skating in the winter, a copious supply of alcohol and a great many large dogs. They raised Labrador retrievers, and in 1952 we made our first attempt at dog adoption since the unfortunate poodle, Caprice. The dog was a black bitch named Cassie, short for Cassiopeia, the black queen, the wife of Cepheus and the mother of Andromeda. We all adored Cassie. She did not make my sister wheeze, but this was just about the only troublesome thing she didn't do. My father put great stock in the intelligence of Labrador retrievers. He once said that when he died he expected to be judged by a panel of them. If this was the case, I'm certain that he came off well.

One of the most outlandish of Cassie's indiscretions occurred when the entire family had taken a picnic to a tidal pool on Nantucket. We took off our clothes, left them on a dune, and spent the day swimming and digging clams. When we climbed back to the sand dune that afternoon there was nothing there but one shoe. This was Cassie's work. My father had to slink back to the house naked, and then return with clothes for the rest of us.

In her middle years Cassie stopped being a dog and became a "formerly dog." She was said to be a dowager in reduced circumstances. She was supposed to be the founder of Dogs for Goldwater in northern Westchester. She was said to be a deposed member of the Russian nobility, and to possess a large fortune in rubles. Cassie was the first of the formerly dogs. Daddy spoke to all our dogs, and I suspect that they all spoke back to him. One Christmas my sister bought a tape recorder and he made up a number of stories and poems for it including one that began like this

Easter is really rotten for dogs
Christmas is worser yet.
They hang the halls with mistletoe
But nobody kisses a pet.

Easter is really rotten for dogs
Christmas is worser yet.
They put our food out in the snow
So our feet get cold and wet.

This letter was supposed to have been written by Cassie to Phil and Mimi Boyer. The Boyers still owned Cassie's mother.

1954

Treetops, bristol, n.h.

Dear aunt mimi and uncle philip,

I drove up here in the back seat of that bangedup and crumbly little dodge that the cheevers drive around in and it was very hot and disgusting for a retriever who is the great grand daughter of a field trials champion and also it wasn't too safe because the old man had been booze-fighting since practially before dawn. he was cleaning out the liquor cabinet not to tempt burglars etc and I personally saw him drain a gin bottle and on top of this the ride was very uncomfortable and I won't go into what i suffered in the way of bladder trouble. in the cool of the evening we reached massachusetts where i was able to relieve myself but my troubles were far from over. in the morning we started north again and about 10 a.m. or even earlier the old man and his wife and the children began to argue about where they would stop to have their stuffing lunch. naturally this was a matter of utter indifference to me since i don't get any lunch, but i couldn't sleep because it was too crowded and hot and anyhow their voices gave me a terrible headache. the old man wanted to stop in a chinese restaurant but as you can well imagine he wasn't stopping there for the chowmein or any of that but because he happened to know that this chinese restaurant has a bar which sells martinis which is not so easy to find in new hampshire as it is in say new jersey. well she wants to stop in a place where they have lobsters and from the outcries and lamentations which this aroused in the old man i could guess that this lobster place has no bar. the 2 children have their minds set on something called horrid johnsons, also with no bar, and the old man keeps telling the children how delicious chinese food is although you could tell by the way he was licking his chops that it was no suey. well we go into this place which is icy cold, smells of gin and is run by enemy aliens. . . . The manager takes one look at me says solly solly no dog. the family was naturally indignant about this and you can imagine how he carried on with the martini practically in his hands. then we drive along to a place called ye marston manse. also no dogs. the same thing happens at ye copperbowl and the sign of the wigge and finally they get the sense to stop at a railroad diner where i was very welcome and which is where they belonged anyhow. they all had the ipswich clams and both the old man and the children being sloppy feeders i got enough to keep body & soul together. well i'm in the mountains now enjoying the horsemeat, open fires & swimming.

give my love to mother.

bow-wow
Cassie

According to Emmy and Bill Maxwell, the rug featured below was a very ordinary piece of carpeting, which they had borrowed for five years. They had many cats, so they had had it cleaned before it was returned. Niles Spencer was a painter and a drinking companion of my father's.

Scarborough

Tuesday [1954]

Dear Bill,

The Tale of the Rug, so far, goes like this. We left here at six (to hear Leonard Rose) putting our children in the hands of an elderly widow named Mrs. Coutances who cannot liberate herself from the conviction that she will someday be raped. When the doorbell rang at half-past-six—so Susie tells me—all hell broke lose. Ben was comissioned to draw the curtains, Susie turned up the radio and Mrs. Coutances disappeared into the closet. The poor delivery man called to say that he had come to deliver a rug. His voice—Susie tells me—sounded very rough and perhaps drunken and only deepened the general anxiety.

He kept ringing the doorbell and there was a conference in the closet. The upshot of this was that Ben was comissioned to go to the front door and shout loudly: "Give the rug to Mrs. Vanderlip." He did this several times without any results. After another conference Susie went to the door and asked for credentials. The poor man shouted the name Maxwell as well as Cheever several times and then slipped the map you had drawn for him under the door. This satisfied Susie and the rug was delivered, although Mrs. Coutances remained in the closet and was still very uneasy when I took her home at midnight.

The rug is in such a wonderful state of preservation that my natural proneness to guilt is enflamed. I can remember clearly the edges used to snap up and trip people but now they lay flat; and the old cigaret burn that Niles Spencer made the first year we were married (Mary cried after he had gone) seems cleansed and purified. I have never seen a rug show such improvement and we are grateful and happy.

Best,
John

He'd been visiting his mother in Quincy.

Scarborough

Friday

Dear Bill,

Many thanks for the check. It found me more alive than dead; but tired. My departure was the stormiest yet. By the time that I carried the dishes out to the car the hurricane had already sunk it's teeth into southern New England. "You can't go," Mother said. "It's an emergency." the lights flickered and went out. A large metal sign advertising Jenney Gasoline sailed through the air like a kite. "I must go," I said. "You'll be killed," Mother said. "I have to go," I said. "Come back," she said. Down came the rock maple in front of the Congregational Church. "Goodbye," I said.

There is some suspense here now. On Wednesday someone called from the University of Iowa, asking if I would teach this year. I said I would. It seemed sensible to get out of Westchester, even if I were traveling in the wrong direction. Now from Iowa City there is a perfect silence. I expect to get a letter on Monday saying that Winifred

Grapeshot, whose wealth of teaching experience and whose many publications on the theory of beauty give her precedence, has bagged the job. I am going to write a short story about a short story writer who drove a 1950 Dodge through a hurricane and who was mistakenly offered a job teaching creative writing in Iowa.

Best,
John

Scarborough

Tuesday

Dear Bill,

I am fine, but I am not prolific. However something will come along. I never know how to cultivate these roses. I've been getting to bed early and walking to and from Ossining but on Wednesday I stayed up late, drank a pint of bourbon and worked like a streak on Thursday. I hope it has nothing to do with the degeneration of the tissues.

Best,
John

Scarborough

Tuesday

Dear Josie,

Someone called from the University of Iowa and asked me if I wouldn't like to go out and teach. I said I would. My acceptance was followed by a big embarassing silence, and presently a note arrived saying that the job was filled. Mary thinks that the University called the New Yorker and asked for Jean Stafford's telephone number and got mine by mistake. Here I sit, peering out of a dirty window, waiting for the leaves to fall.

John

Scarborough,

Wednesday

Dear Bill,

Any lapses of taste in the piece I'm enclosing, any shoddiness of thought and style, the horrendous spelling and the yellow paper can all be blamed on the fuchsia. I spray it twice a day with a rich mixture of Pear's soap and nicotine sulphate. I spend hours standing over it, waiting for the parturition of the White Fly. The only results so far have been that the White Fly has spread from the plant to me. At least I scratch a good deal more than I used to.

When I was shinning my shoes on Monday night a letter from you feel out of the box in which we store the polish and the brushes. It was three years old and it said that I should learn to be less intense. I will; I will.

John

"Your villa" referred to Eleanor's *Rome and a Villa*. He had joined the Episcopal Church.

Wauwinet,
Nantucket Island,
Massachusetts

June 24th [1955]

Dear Eleanor,

. . . I am very sorry that you can't all come and I console myself with thinking that we will rent this house next year for the full season and then you and Red and the two children can pay us a visit. There doesn't seem to be any place I would rather be. Even today when it's rainy and the roof leaks and Ben weeps and I drink whiskey and Susie makes a mess in the kitchen baking cookies it seems fine. The beaches are grander than anything on the cape. There is no one else on them and to reach them we only have to walk through the clothes-yard. We've found a seapond that is full of blue crabs, cherry-stones, white-shelled clams and oysters. In the evening I read the work of Henry Cheever. Poor Henry thought of all Polynesia as a challenge to our piety and saw in his mind all it's golden-skinned women, rank upon rank, dressed in Mother Hubards with the badge of the Temperance League pinned to their fronts.

I don't get the Kenyon Review and I don't have their address and if you could send me a copy I would appreciate it very much. I will send it back in good order and I'm very anxious to read anything you write.

I did read the Youcenar book in this connection, and what crap. Then I went back to your villa and found it full of vitality and intelligence.

As for happiness I think I know in part what you mean, for having lived much of my life like an odd mixture of man and cockroach I found, not so long ago, that the cockroach had left me and I am still now and then bewildered by the strenuousness of my pleasure. I am mostly bewildered because I do not understand why everyone else should not be in on the game. I cannot say, as you do, that we were meant for this, and so I became a communicant. I keep telling the rector that I did not reenter the church because I travail and am heavy-laden, but because I was happy; but he shakes his head. The clergy is lachrymose. The cockroach returns now and then and I despair and shudder at the sights of my life; but not for long.

Mary joins me in saying how sorry we are you can't come here. It is a new place, of course, but it is a place and we can see light houses out of the windows of these matchboard rooms and hear the surf most of the time. . . . I'll be in New York in August and I'll telephone to see if you have a son or a daughter. And I want the Kenyon Review. And everyone sends their best wishes.

John

The *Topaze* is the ship sailed by Leander, the father in *The Wapshot Chronicle*. In *The Chronicle* the rudder chain broke and the ship went down. The book wasn't published until 1957, but early versions of some sections had been published in *The New Yorker*. "The Housebreaker of Shady Hill" was published in the April, 14, 1956, issue of *The New Yorker*.

Wauwinet,

Thursday [July 21, 1955]

Dear Bill,

I'm enclosing the first Housebreaker; and many thanks for the checks. By way of celebration I took Mary to Hyannis on an excursion boat. This was also research, the boat being unseaworthy and rather like the Topaze. I walked around the decks, thinking about the wreck, and right in midpassage the damned helm broke. They rigged up an emergency helm but the sailor who took it was so frightened that you could see his heart beating under his shirt and I sat down with a can of beer and began to think up something about the rescue of the Topaze. . . .

I hope the story doesn't give you too much trouble. I wanted it to be lively and sometimes I feel lively and then just as often I feel dull and I think some of the dullishness comes through---the droning sounds I make when I've been drinking.

As ever,<br>John

Another letter from Cassie, the black Labrador.
Ouida was a pen name for Louise de la Ramée whose books included *Under Two Flags* (1867) and *The Nassarenes* (1897).

July 1955

wauwinet, nantucket Island, mass.
dear aunt mimi and uncle philp,
    Summertime again and dogs writing letters but i thought you'd like to know whether or not i was dead. early on wednesday morning he rolled me over unceremoniously to see if i was en rut and then we made a hurried start, one step ahead of the county trust co. and the collection agency for rabin's bootery inc. it was the usual guttapercha —don't put your head out of the window cassie, don't bark at the lady cassie, be a gude dog cassie, etcsteta. we had dinner with a very old lady in quincy and then we drove on to wood's hole where pinch-penny shacked the family up in a motel to save a buck. This was an arrangement of several bedrooms along a single porch and in the dead of night himself got his signals mixed and wondered into a bedroom where a jewelry salesman and a waitress from the green hornet dough-nut shop were passing the time. They could have thought that he was a private eye except that he wasn't wearing anything but a wristwatch. pandemonium.
    In the morning we took the steamer which was nothing for dogs. himself spent practically the whole voyage looking behind newspapers and under hat brims to see if there wasn't anybody he knew. then we

came to this quaint old-fashioned village where he tried to kite a check. the only reason he ever came to nantucket being that he figured they wouldn't hear his checks bounce this far out to sea. no soap. well then we came to this place called wauwinet where i was able to relieve myself for the first time in 36 hours. here we are.

In the morning it's everybody out to dig clams. in the afternoon it's everybody out to get oysters. in the gloaming it's everybody out to catch butterfish and all the time he sits up in his rooms, pretending to be ouida. She's very lonely and wishes you would come to visit her. the telephone has only rung once and that was whiting's milk co. when the mail man comes she runs out with a pitcher of limeade and a plate of cookies but he's already full of doughnuts. I've come in for a lot of criticism because I rescue strange children and try to board strange boats but how they love to see me dive into a high surf and ride back on a comber with a piece of driftwood in my teeth and a silly grin on my face. how they squeal. give my love to mother. she is never far from my thoughts.

yr. XXX obedient chg.
Cassie

Jingo was the Boyer Lab they planned to breed Cassie with.

Wauwinet
Wednesday, 1955

Dear Phil and Mimi,

We're sorry that you can't come down. It is wonderful here but the journey is long and expensive and this part of the summer is nearly over. Mary is beginning to wash bedspreads and sweep sand out of closets. . . .

The dog news is that Cassie is in the throes of rut. She chases little male dogs up and down the beach. I think that we've saved her for Jingo. It's been difficult. This house has no cellar and several dogs have shacked up underneath the kitchen. If there should be a knot-hole that I haven't plugged up, we are lost. . . .

As ever,
John

By now he was well established as a writer for *The New Yorker* (ultimately he would publish 120 stories in that magazine). Jack Kahn was and still is a *New Yorker* writer, and I guess everybody knows who William Shawn is. This is from a letter written to John Weaver.

Dear John,

. . . William Shawn, the number 1 editor came out last week to have lunch with the Kahns. Jack telephoned and ordered me to hurry over and say hello to the boss. I put on my best pants and went over and when the conversation flagged Jack suggested that we play some touch football. Shawn was on my team and on the third play I threw a wobbly pass in his direction. he tried to catch it, slipped and went down, crashing and tinkling like a tray of dishes. I don't know whether he's out of the hospital yet or not and I haven't dared telephone to find out.

This letter was written from a hospital room. The Maxwells have a country house in Yorktown.

Room 204

Wednesday

Dear Bill,

You take very good care of me—no one has ever done as well; and I would have called you on Saturday when I was incarcerated but the thought of you writing a novel in Yorktown and editing a magazine on 43rd street, traveling on off-hour trains, caring for a cold and sheltering under your wing a multitude of unstable, ragged and wayward men women and children of all nationalities made my lot seem so much lighter than yours that I let the telephone rest. Everything is well now and I may go home tomorrow. There was a stir about Tuberculosis and I think the doctor shared with me a feeling that I would be transformed into the spit and image of Robert Louis Stevenson and would have better table manners and a more graceful social presence but the spot on my lung cleared up at once and I think the doctor was disappointed in not having transformed a boiled potato into a tubercular intellectual.

No old lady in an almshouse, forgotten by the world, could have taken more pleasure in your roses than I. I sniff them, I smell them, I snort noisely over each bloom like a terrier. It is a perfume that mystifies and pleases me. It doesn't seem to be heart or nostalgia—it isn't grandmother's jam-pot—and what it is, I suppose is the possibility that someone of great beauty might walk onto the scene. That's the way they smell this morning. They are the only flowers I have excepting a pair of whiskery orchids. . . . One of the nurses said: "Jaysus, look at the jackinthepulpits." I told her they were called orchids. "Well," she said, "I don't know what they call them now but when I was a girl we used to walk in the woods and pick them and they used to call them Jackinthepulpits."

I have some exrays today and if the spot is cleared I'll come home and probably go on up to Yaddo and try and finish the stories I've been sniveling over for the last month. I feel very guilty about disassociating myself from the confusion of the household but if there's a room at Yaddo I think I'll go for two weeks. I'll call you today and I hope I'll see you before I go.

Best,
John

Yaddo
Saratoga Springs
Friday

Dear Bill,
. . . This is an excellent place for working—I don't know anything like it and you might try it someday—but there isn't quite enough conversation. I eat breakfast alone at eight and work until one when I nibble a sandwich from my lunchbox and drink a thermos of tea. There is a hint of indecency about eating alone in a bedroom. I feel as if I had stolen the food. Then I write until four when I put on my skiis and coast down the front lawn for an hour admiring the sky and every day the sight of a big red dog-fox who seems to me a piece of luck. Then I retire to my room, hide in my closet, pour whisky into a tooth-brush glass and toss it off, knocking my head against the coat-hangers. I do this several times and go to the dinner table fairly tipsy. There are three other writers here, they all wear buckskin desert boots and they are all speechless. I talk all through dinner and then retire to my room to catch up on my reading—Nostromo, for instance—but at about half-past nine I begin to talk loudly to myself. I tell myself old stories of my

interesting childhood, relive thirty-year-old love affairs, describe my tragic Aunt Florence and chuckle over my recollections of the time Uncle Ralph set fire to the sofa. I can see my mind wandering away from me like a fool but I cannot call it back. I go to bed at ten. . . .

Bill has a daughter named Kate.

Scarborough

Tuesday

Dear Bill,

Mary—who eavesdrops—said that when I asked you Does it hold together? she has never heard a more oily or disgusting tone of voice and that you should have told me to go stick my head in a bucket of water; but I had enjoyed writing the story and had spent the day hanging around the telephone trying to think up reasons to call you such as:Has Kate's cold improved—or—would you like to invest with me in the cultivation of hot house roses? Nothing to do with the story of course. I should have some TV money coming in and if no one likes the story it wouldn't really matter—and there I go—oily again.

Best,
John

"The Bus to St. James's" ran in The New Yorker in the January 14, 1956, issue.

Scarborough

Wednesday

Dear Bill,

This on Mary's typewriter, Mary's bedtray and in bed—not to say a bed of pain—but I went to the hospital on Thanksgiving to have my hindquarters rebushed. It passed off allright. The old man who came to shave me at dusk said that the river used to freeze over when he was a boy. The doctor who came to relieve my bladder at dawn was a middle-aged German woman with much eyeshade and mascara. The surgeon who operated came with a nearly empty kit. "What's become of all my knives," he exclaimed. I had one bad night and one-half bad day and then I seemed to rally. Yesterday morning there was such a long line in front of the toilet that I called Mary and asked her to bring me home. I see the doctor again on Thursday and as soon as I can sit down again on a chair I'll call you. I'd like to go over the Bus.

So much money from you and so little work from me seems all wrong but perhaps I can straighten it out with some decent stories; I am very grateful. But today I don't seem able to write a letter.

As ever,
John

Cowley had been urging my father to go to Europe.

Scarborough

All Saints Day

Dear Malcolm,

. . . I stopped in Quincy to see my mother—whose vigor is unimparied at 82—and saw her for what she is for the first time in my life. To come back to a house where every stick of furniture was, until recently, swamped in agony—to sleep in those rooms without dreaming of bogs,hell-fire and the smell of burning hair—is a great joy.

. . . I have come to agree with you on the relative unimportance of northern Westchester. I was delighted when we first came here to be asked to so many parties (I have always been afraid of being left alone) ---delighted to find myself in the thick of such a rich, powerful and unselfconscious community. But I seem to have been mistaken in my estimation of their power. I seem to have been wrong in assuming that because they are rich—because they give an illusion of timeliness ---their deterioration is significant. And I seem to have been mistaken in assuming that a kind of rock-bottom irritability was poetry and truth. I am on civil defense here and a few days ago we had a meeting in the church chapel to discuss The Disaster. They were all there---the rayon blanket tycoon, the vice president of the Life insurance company,etc. The chapel smells of old rooming houses. The autumn sun gleams through a glass face of the lamb of God. So we sat in the bad smell and the colored light, discussing the end of the world, but what

struck me was the utter triviality, the lack of true apprehension and
suspense in the gathering and that the foremost thought on my mind
was to get out and play some touch football and that this was right.
What I mean to say is that a kind of pessimism and it's company, seems
to have been vitiated. We seem to have exhausted at least one phase of
anxiety. I don't mean the stupid good-cheer of people like William
Barrett and Anthony West who seem to feel that literature should be
recast in order to describe their particular, sluggish,conjugal bliss; and
I don't underestimate the murderous conformism here. But some new
proportion seems to have been given to the picture. We seem, in our
forties, to have come of age. The letters that I get from friends—
sometimes from people I haven't seen in ten years---all mention the
fact that they are stirring themselves to get out of the gloom.

You wrote last spring that my stories must get better. I sometimes
wake up at three or four in the morning, saying:Better, BETTER—but
I think they do. I have always wanted to let some light in among my
characters and I seem able to now; and I have so many bags, boxes,
orange-crates and trunks filled with descriptions of physical and spiritual anguish that I can always draw on these to keep myself from
seeming too cheerful.

I hope someday that you will find yourself on route 9—two miles
north of Tarrytown where we are. My love to Muriel, and Mary sends
her love to you both.

As ever,
John

Scarborough

Dear Josie,
. . . Mother died on Wednesday. She meant to; and although she was
afraid of many things in her life—crowds, confinement, deep water—
she seemed to face with death completely unafraid. Then yesterday
morning Gus Lobrano died. He was an excellent man and a true one
and he taught me how to fish and I will miss him. I seem to understand;
but why then should I feel as if I had been hit over the head with a
baseball bat. I'm going to Yaddo on Tuesday for three days. If anything
interesting happens I'll report.

Best,
John

# MOVIE MONEY

* * *

Early in 1956 Dore Schary of M-G-M bought the film rights to "The Housebreaker of Shady Hill" for $40,000. *The New Yorker* had paid $2,075 for the story, which ran in the issue of April 14, 1956. Henry Lewis was my father's West Coast contact. The movie was never made. The next two letters are to John Weaver.

Scarborough

Thursday [May 3, 1956]

Dear John,

It was very good, it was wonderful to get your wire this morning and it brought the first real note of reality into the proceedings. Mary doesn't believe that the story's been bought for that much money and she keeps buying cheap meat-cuts such as tongue and shoulder-steak. But you know how things are in Hollywood, she says. Susie seems to believe me but she's not much interested except in who's going to be in the movie. The dog seems to believe me but she has eight puppies who live in this little room where I am supposed to work and who are now old enough to unlace my shoes and bite me in the ankles. The reason I told the dog about it was because when Henry Lewis called there was no one here but Ben and me and the dog. Mary and Susie had gone to see a movie called The little Kidnappers. I don't believe that children Ben's age should be told about money and so that left me with the dog. After I had told the dog Ben wanted me to read him a chapter from Winnie the Pooh and so I read him the chapter called How Piglet Meets a Heffalump. . . . Then I came downstairs and drank a pint of whisky. . . . Then Mary came home, received the news sniffily, and went upstairs to sleep. This made me cross so I drank more whisky and sat broodily on the sofa thinking how with this money I could have prostitutes of all kinds, dancing to my whip. Now that we have your wire we all feel better.

It couldn't have come at a nicer time. I think I can see the end of a book, I don't have a short story in my head and there's nothing in the bank. In this way I can finish the book and perhaps in the fall we can go abroad for a year. However Mary says she won't go abroad if she's pregnant which she may well be and as I say, she goes on buying shoulder- steaks.

Love,<br>John

[May 7, 1956]

Dear John,

Your letter helped a great deal and tonight we are having roast beef for dinner, although I think she plans to stretch it over three meals. I have bought an electric egg-beater, a quart of Jack Daniels and the children had frozen custard for dessert at lunch. It seems that we might go to Rome in the fall. . . . But the most important thing is for me to finish this book which is called The Wapshot Chronicle. I've laid so many eggs that I can't be sure I won't drop another.

Best,<br>John

Michael Bessie met my father at a lunch party. Some time after this, my father wrote that Random House had paid $2,400 for a Cheever novel, but that this relationship was exhausted. "These old bones are up for sale," my father wrote in a letter that seems to have been lost or misplaced. He went on to say that many people thought he would never write a novel, and that these people might be right, but that if he did ever write such a book the contract for it could be had from Random House for $2,400. "I called him up," Bessie recalls, "and said, 'Where do I send the check?' "

Michael Bessie became the editor for the not-yet-completed *Wapshot Chronicle* under one condition: that he never ask how the book was going. For years my father had been running into Bennett Cerf at parties and publishing functions, and every time this happened, he could see Cerf searching clumsily through his mental files. "Oh, you're Cheever," he'd say. "How's that novel going?" So Bessie swore not to do the same, and he admits now that it wasn't easy always to think of something else to say. But he never brought the book up unless his author-to-be brought it up first.

When the book did come in, it required no editing, according to Bessie, although he does recall having to ask for one change. *The Wapshot Chronicle* had been accepted by the Book-of-the-Month Club, which meant a great deal to its success. The club wanted one word deleted. When Moses Wapshot married the beautiful Melissa Scaddon, her interest in sex fell off precipitously. The scene in question began when he ran her to ground in the bedroom. Here she put him off one more time, pinning up her hair in an unattractive style, and taking a long bath.

. . . Then she opened the bathroom door and came out—not naked but dressed in a full, heavy nightgown and busily running a piece of dental floss between her teeth. "Oh, Melissa," he said.

"I doubt that you love me," she said. It was the thin, dispassionate voice of the spinster and it reminded him of thin things: smoke and dust. "I sometimes think you don't love me at all," she said, "and of course you put too much emphasis on sex, oh much too much. . . . "

"But I love you," he said hopefully.

"Some men bring work home from the office," she said. "Most men do. Most of the men that I know." Her voice seemed to dry as he listened to it, to lose its deeper notes as her feelings narrowed. "And most men in business," she went on thinly, "have to do a lot of traveling. They're away from their wives a lot of the time. They have other outlets than sex. Most healthy men do. They play squash."

"I play squash."

"You've never played squash since I've known you."

"I used to play."

"Of course," she said, "if it's absolutely necessary for you to make love to me I'll do it, but I think that you ought to understand that it's not as crucial as you make it."

"You've just talked yourself out of a fuck," he said bleakly.

Did it have to be "fuck?" the Book-of-the-Month Club wanted to know. The story from which this part of the novel evolved had run in *The New Yorker* without the word. Aside from the probability of increased sales, the deal with the club involved a substantial amount of money. But my father was adamant. *The New Yorker* had supported him, published him since he was in his twenties, and for *The New Yorker* he would do most anything. But this was his book and the word was exactly the right word. Bessie agreed, and he went back to the bargaining table. He was successful in these negotiations, and that's how Book-of-the-Month Club members got "fuck" for the first time ever.

When Bill Maxwell read the finished manuscript he sent my father a telegram that said simply: "*WELL ROARED, LION.*" When asked why a man who had written so many and such fine short stories should have waited so long to write a novel, my father told people that he hadn't wanted to publish the book until his mother died. It is possible that my grandmother's death in 1956 gave him freedom to finish the book, but it is also true that he had submitted an earlier version to Random House in 1952, when his mother was in splendid health, and had been working on and submitting other novels throughout most of his professional life. The explanation had a ring to it, though, and was repeated frequently thereafter in the press. In fact it was received with such enthusiasm that on at least one occasion it was reported that he had delayed the publication of his first novel until after the death of his father. Frederick Lincoln Cheever died in 1946, a full ten years before *The Chronicle*, but then a good lie is worth amplification.

In the summer of 1956 the family rented the Friendship, Maine, house of Arthur Spear, an old friend.

Friendship, Maine

June 26th

Dear Eleanor,

I've signed the M-G-M contract and so I guess I'll get the money. I expect I can pay as much as $175 for an apartment. I think we'll sail in October. . . . I'm very excited at the thought of seeing you in Rome and pleased to say that I've finished a novel. At least it looks like a novel. It doesn't look like a short story, anyhow. It's much heavier and costs more postage.

. . . This—Friendship—is a lobster village with a little out-cropping of Bostonians. The coast is lovely, but our neighbors throw their garbage into the sea. "There are so few of us," they say. We get our sail boat on the weekend and things ought to pick up. I'll be here until the first of August when my best address will be c/o The New Yorker, 25 West 43rd St. Please Forward, etc.

I seem fairly competent at describing stray pets and dull dances but the windfall, the book and the thought of seeing you in Rome are outside my range. Eureka!

Best,
John

Friendship,Maine

June 26

Dear Josie,

I wrote you a long, silly letter about a month ago, establishing some kind of foundation and meaning to send you a check. (small) I tore up the letter and now I send you the check which should be spent on gin, shoes, and rose-bushes or anything else.

I finished the book on Thursday and we drove up here on Friday. . . . I've rented this house (The Spruces) from a friend—a fire-department member—and what the picture seems to be is a lobster fishing village with a small point, where we are, stuffed with the relations of three or four New England families. The coast, as you must remember, is lovely and when the weather is fair it seems like the top of the world; but the weather is capricious. We would love to see you here and if you flew to Rockland I could meet you there, but it's only fair to tell you that the house is full of children, other than my own. I sometimes think of a quieter place myself.

As ever,

John

Another letter from our black Labrador bitch, Cassie, to the people who bred her. Son was one of Cassie's puppies. He was named Ezekiel, after Ezekiel Cheever, the first Cheever in this country. Zeke stayed with the Boyers when we went to Italy. Afterward, we let them keep him. He was an extremely handsome dog, and Phil was once offered $2,000 for him. A bust of his head still sits in the library of my parents' house in Ossining. Zeke was hit by a car and killed when trying to get home after one of his sittings at the sculptor's house.

Friendship, Maine

10 July, 1956

dear uncle philip and aunt mimi,

The swimming is very good here for dogs. it is too cold for people. we take some motor trips but mostly to the liquor store in rockland where son woofled up the skirts of a salvation army lassie. you should have heard her tambourine rattle. the old man thinks now that he will settle in rome italy and he has bought those gramophone records that guarantee to teach him to speak italian like a native in about 3 minutes. he sits by the gramophone with his bottle of gin and the gramophone says che chosa desidera and he says un po di pane, per favore. he does not know the words for gin or whiskey yet. she is very patient about all this ishkibble but there isn't much she can do.

son has chewed up 3 prs shoes. 2 sweaters. 1 purse, 1 fielders mitt, 1 bat and has hidden 3 shoes, 1 pr eyeglasses and 1 rudder-pin. i am teaching him to run away with the bailing can while the old man is floundering around in the boat.

> yr affectionate & devoted niece,
> Cassie

My father was forty-four when *The Chronicle* came out. He'd been working on one novel or another since he was eighteen. When I was in college I memorized the closing lines of the book, and as I read them, I can still hear his voice.

Leander, a suicide, had left a note in the family copy of Shakespeare.

. . . "Advice to my sons," it read. "Never put whisky into hot water bottle crossing borders of dry states or countries. Rubber will spoil taste. Never make love with pants on. Beer on whisky, very risky. whisky on beer, never fear. Never eat apples, peaches, pears, etc. while drinking whisky except long French-style dinners, terminating with fruit. Other viands have mollifying effect. Never sleep in moonlight. Known by scientists to induce madness. Should bed stand beside window on clear night draw shades before retiring. Never hold cigar at right-angles to fingers. Hayseed. Hold cigar at diagnonal. Remove band or not as you prefer. Never wear red necktie. Provide light snorts for ladies if entertaining. Effects of harder stuff on frail sex sometimes disastrous. Bathe in cold water every morning. Painful but exhilarating. Also reduces horniness. Have haircut once a week. Wear dark clothes after 6 P.M. Eat fresh fish for breakfast when available. Avoid kneeling in unheated stone churches. Ecclesiastical dampness causes prematurely gray hair. Fear tastes like a rusty knife and do not let her into your house. Courage tastes of blood. Stand up straight. Admire the world. Relish the love of a gentle woman. Trust in the Lord."

Friendship, Maine

July 26th

Dear Malcolm,

. . . The reason I haven't written was because I was in the running-down-hill section of a novel which I think is done. As you can imagine, this is quite a triumph for me. I made so many bargains with the devil about the completion of a book that when I had put down the last word I took a bath, put on clean underwear, and went to the doctor to see if anything was damaged or missing.

We will be up here—or down here—for about a month and then I think I will spend some of August in a New York hotel. I'll call you then and maybe I can see you and Muriel. The book hasn't gone to the publishers yet and a lot depends on their reaction. Random House told me to pay up and get out last year and Harpers bought up my contract at a reduced rate. If the book is passing I think we will go to Europe in the fall for a year.

As ever,
John

Friendship, Maine

Thursday [1956]

Dear Bill,

I wait for this place to unfold. All the summer houses we rent fill up at once with children other than our own. I think it's the groceries. First they creep through the garden and ask if they may use the hammock and the porch furniture. Then they ask for a glass of water (very politely) and settle on the sofa. Then they say that it will be all right with their mothers (who have all gone to Portland) if they remain for lunch. Then they penetrate to the bedrooms where they play sardines which is what they are doing now. It is very foggy and to look out of the windows is like looking at a stone. Tuesday was lovely and I have never seen such an evening light anywhere.

As ever,
John

By "the Wapshots," he meant the manuscript of the novel. This was to be sent back from Harper's with comments. Cass Canfield was Michael Bessie's superior at Harper.

Friendship

The Sabbath [1956]

Dear Bill,

This place still doesn't seem to unfold, perhaps because I spend so much time trotting to and from the post office, waiting for the Wapshots to arrive, which they don't. I feel poorly and spend much time waiting for my noon martini and my five o'clock whisky and write myself, in this spare bedroom, congratulatory letters about the book (dazzling!) and also letters of discouragement. (Mr. Canfield has gone to Illinois with Adlai Stevenson but he left word that you should write this off as experience, put it behind you and make a fresh start.) The coast is lovely, strung with spruce islands, but we see none of it from this house. Yesterday I rowed Mary and Ben out to an island for a picnic and this was the most fun we've had. In the evening there was a ceremonial clam bake. The men went out to the island at three to lay the stones, light the fire and drink beer. At six the ladies were transported to the island in a launch and this—the lonely island, the roaring fire and the approaching boat-load of wives—was quite a sight; but it took hours to cook the lobsters and clams, we didn't eat until after ten and everyone got very drunk including a fat lady from Boothbay with a toy poodle who kept saying: Juss call me Sis. I got very drunk and kept diving into the sea.

It would be wrong to say that this is the kind of community where on Sunday morning, people sit in their clothes-yards drinking martinis out of jelly glasses, but it would be at least half the truth. In detail we have on the lawn, a white tin table with a red umbrella and two pink canvas chairs, one of them labeled Gov and the other Queenie. Beside this is a flag-pole flying a pennant with the house name THE SPRUCES. You might be interested in the fire-places in the community. Ours was built by a one-eyed Greek who took the name of Murphy— a local joke. It is made of egg-shaped, grey stones that Murphy picked up on the far islands in a barge. The stones protrude and they frame, above the cement mantle, a French clock. There is a rubber mouse on top of this clock. Arthur Little, across the street is a retired minister and his fireplace is made of stones that were given to him by members of his parish. There are stones from Yosemite and stones from the valley of the Jordan, stones from Greece and stones from San Francisco. The Pratt's fireplace, up the street, is made of stones and iron bars from the Old Bailey gaol. Grandfather Pratt was in England when they remodeled the old dungeon and he thought how nice the stones would look in his parlor. His descendents seem depressed. The houses in the village are all white trimmed with wooden lace, all very apart and plain and when you stand with your back to the sea it looks like a lonely prairie town. Women push baby carriages up and down the main street. Wash is hanging out everywhere. Lupin grows wild in the fields but there is not a rose in the town limits. The lilac is just going and the peony buds are green and as big as filberts. Tulips are still in bloom. When I said goodmorning to the lady across the street she said: "In Friendship we don't say good morning; we say Hi!" She comes into our house once a day calling: "Yoo, hoo, Yoo, hoo, Yoo, hoo, etc." The people are all very nice but conspicously disinterested in anything, I think, that does not concern Boston or Newton. I've seen one book: Sloan Wilson. "We used to subscribe to Life," Quincy Wales said, discussing literature, "but I found that we didn't read it."

The only purpose of all this, of course, is that I find myself happiest and most tranquil when I am sitting at the typewriter. I hope to be able to move out into the sun and stop telling myself stories for a day or two. I have the Hollywood money in my suitcase and I think we will go to Rome. A high school girl arrives to help Mary on Tuesday and I think, as always, of going to New York and resting in a hotel. I think I will feel better when the Wapshots come.

As ever,
John

In his journal he wrote: I would like to write a story but I seem to have none to write. And I think I will be out of money, before we leave. By the time I've paid boat passage, bought a car, trunks and clothing and paid the income tax, we won't have much left.

# GOING ABROAD

* * *

We crossed the Atlantic on an Italian liner called the *Conte Bianca-mano*.

Conte Biancamano

October 30th

Dear Josie,

... We nosed out of New York harbor straight into a six-day blow with medicine bottles and bon-voyage baskets flying this way and that. After seven days at sea we reached Portugal. ... We got to Barcelona at noon on Sunday and took the children to the zoo. Only three people boarded the ship at Barcelona but hundreds of people came down to see us off and waved and shouted as if we were their only children. Cannes the next day at sunrise—very cold with snow on the mountains—and Genoa at five were we went ashore for dinner. ... it has been a trolley car for the last week with people embarking and disembarking, weeping, laughing and at every stop throngs of visitors come aboard, admire the art works in the lounge and use the water-closets.

I keep forgetting that I'm not the first person since the dawn of history to travel in this direction but I think you should come while you can.

As ever,
John

I was eight when we took the boat, and completely ignorant of my father's growing fame. I met a young woman at one of the ship's bars, and she bought me ginger ales. When she heard my name—and it's possible that she already knew my name and this explained the ginger ales—she wanted to know if my father was "John Cheever, the writer." I didn't think so.

"Does he sell short stories to *The New Yorker*?"

I wasn't sure. He had a typewriter, I knew that.

Well, she said, Cheever is an unusual name, if he has a typewriter and he lives in New York, he must be John Cheever "the famous writer."

"Oh, no," I said. "It couldn't be."

When we were in Italy, Phil Boyer sent his letters to the family over the signature of our black Labrador Ezekiel.

Via del Plebiscito 107 Roma. 11/17/56

Dear Phil and Mimi

Zeke can certainly write. Not, I think, since Mark Twain, has such a star risen on the literary sky. The children read the letter and laughed uproariously for about half an hour and then burst into tears and bawled for the rest of the night, crying: We want Zeke, we want Zeke. In the morning Susie took the letter down to one of the parlors in the pensione—many bad paintings and a stock tea service that was never used—and read it to herself laughing and weeping so noisily that the manager asked her what was the matter. "It's a letter from our youngest dog", said Susie and we moved that afternoon.

We are in the Piano Nobile of the Palazzo Doria—the 17th century wing—and it was all built for giants. There is only one chair in the salon where I can sit and have my feet touch the floor and there are two chairs where my feet don't even hang over the edge. Sometimes it seems like a joke. Sometimes it seems like a terrible mistake. Sometimes it seems beautiful. Mary likes it, of course, and stretches out in long chairs and sighs and may be planning to write her autobiography. It is Saturday noon and I miss you all. I will go to the broom-closet—away from the Popes and Cardinals who hang on the walls—and drink a snifter of Roman gin.

As ever,<br>John

France, England and Israel were at war with Egypt over the Suez Canal. The Hungarian revolution was being put down by Soviet tanks and troops. He's talking about the American Academy in Rome.

Via del Plebiscito 107
Rome, Italy

November 24th

Dear Josie

We are settled in Rome at last and write me your news. So much has happened on the trip that I still can't make much sense of it. I can write on set and limited topics such as roses: war: gin:Atlantic gales: sex: musical chairs:ruins, etc but any general picture is beyond my powers. I think about war much when it rains and at nightfull and of course to the Romans, Hungary seems very close. Many of the papers have run maps showing how Russia could sweep over Europe in a month and the facts of evacuation, occupation and imprisonment are so familiar to most of the people here that their concern may be hysterical but it is natural and deep. The papers are pessimistic and terrible; the people are handsome and gay; and maybe I should have picked roses as my topic.

Roses are still blooming in the Forum and there is a rose tree in bloom on the slope between Santa Maria Arecoeli and the steps up to the Campidole. They are the last though, and it is autumn here, quite cold and rainy with skies no lighter than the skies over New York in December. There is a large American colony here divided in to parts: Academy and unAcademy. Both parts contain some excellent people and also some duds and I am very intolerant about the duds. It cost so much money to get over here and get settled that when I hear some plain-spoken fool start to tell a story about last summer on Cape Cod I feel as if I'd been sold a ticket to the wrong stop and get very cross. However, I will relax, and in the meantime write me your news.

Best,
John

La Rocca is a stone fortress in Port'Ercole.

Via del Plebiscito 107

November 24th

Dear Bill,

I was determined not to write you a letter until I had written a story, but now I write you anyhow, all the tightness in my life never having

been very rewarding. . . . I miss you. I miss your person and your
advice. I was very pleased to have your letter and read it, like any other
American, on the Corso. All Americans here wear berets and read their
mail in the streets.

There is no one I would rather write to than you and yet it still seems
difficult to write a decent letter. As for facts: Ben has a friend named
Ronald Aung Din. I think the Aung Din's like Ben because of his
coloring. They are Burmese and they all keep pinching and patting
him. Ben had Thanksgiving dinner with them; rice, raw fish, brandy
and wine. He loved it. The rest of us ate salami sandwiches in the
kitchen and Susie cried. . . . Then I decided to buy a turkey, which
made everybody happy. Then yesterday I drove to Grosetto again
through the rain with the Warrens, under the walls of Tarquinia but
through a very dreary landscape. Everything changed when we got
onto the penninsula where the Rocca stands. It was lovely and most
like what I think I have come to see. An old woman cooked us some
meat on a brasier and told us about King Farouk's visit to Port'Ercole.
The first chamberpot that he sat on crumbled under his weight. Then
a call went out through the village for chamberpots. Many were produced and tried, but none was adequate. Then a great iron fishpot was
brought up from the port, emblazoned with the royal arms and carried
by the people through the streets to the king's hotel. Much laughter
and tears. I walked around the Rocca. The ghosts seemed more substantial than the ghosts in the Forum. Buggle-calls, the changing of the
guard, the squealing of the whores at Mi-careme, etc. Then we climbed
to La Stella, another fortress and drove back to Rome through hail and
rain.

My love to Emmy and your daughters and I hope you have some
rest now.

As ever,
John

Via del Plebiscito 107
Roma,etc.

November 25th

Dear Malcolm,

We are settled here now in the mediterranean cold which is as dire
as you had told me it would be. It is splendid when the sun shines but

when the sun does not shine the sky is as dark as the skies over the Grand Concourse and the wind is like the wind on Riverside Drive. I cough and sneeze my way down the Sacra Via. . . .

Harpers tells me that the galleys of the book will be out next week and I've asked them to send you a set. If you like it of course I will be very pleased and if you don't like it I'm sure you'll have good reasons and in any case I'll be very grateful to you for looking at it. I liked it when it was done,but that was a long time ago.

This coming to Rome was the best thing we've ever done although it is expensive. The children were homesick, but are over this now. Susie is a day student at a convent where they work the nose off her and Ben goes to an international-type school where he gets along mostly with Burmese. There is much talk about war and there are evacuees from Cairo and refugees from Budapest in the city now but my knowledge of Italian is so sketchy that I can't figure out what is going on.

My love to Muriel.

As ever,
John

Via del Plebiscito 107

Dear Phil and Mimi,

Nothing pleases us so much as hearing from you and Zeke and this time nobody bawled. . . . I still cook breakfast in my underwear in this Palace of Justice or Haunted Public Library and at nightfall the combination of dim-lamps and Roman gin makes me feel very peculiar. The gin is terrible. They make it in Torino. The city seems mercurial and while it is lovely in the sun with the fountains sparkling it looks, in the rain, like that old movie-shot: European Capital On Eve Of War. Everyone carries a wet umbrella, there are anxious crowds around every newstand, the consulate ante-rooms are full of Egyptian evacues asking for news or mail, and the atmosphere of anxiety and gloom is dense. Then the sun comes out and everything seems fine.

This place isn't much good for entertaining because you can't HEAR anybody or else they echo. I pretend to work in the mornings and visit ruins in the afternoon. Castel San Angelo is my favorite but I like the Forum which is very near here. It's a good time of year for sight-seeing because we seem to be the only tourists left. Now and then you run into a cluster of determined Germans but they are infrequent and seem autumnal and a little sad like the honking of geese. The art galleries are empty and so dark that you can walk for a mile without picking out the shape of a foot.

As ever,
John

Barbara Frietchie was a white mouse of mine. She knew how to climb up a light chain, and once performed in a small and extremely progressive circus in Connecticut. She also made an appearance—with a piece of cheese —on a hat and won me second prize in the hat contest on the boat in which we made the Atlantic crossing. She was named after the character who confronts Stonewall Jackson in the John Greenleaf Whittier poem that bears her name. She comes to a window as Confederate troops are marching by and waves the Union flag.

"Shoot, if you must, this old gray head,
But spare your country's flag," she said.

It wasn't until years later that my father told me that he'd been so embarrassed by the prospect of being caught digging a grave with a spoon in the Villa Borghese gardens that he'd dumped Barbara's tiny casket into a trash bin.

December 2nd [1956]

Via del Plebiscito 107

Dear Josie,

It is still much easier to write letters than anything else; and so I fire back at you the minute your good letter has slipped from my fingers. The children are fine and I have never enjoyed them so much. Susie is very useful in the customs offices. She offers them one of her bags to open and, finding it full of old shoes, soiled clothes, sea-shells and broken china, they let the rest of the bags pass. For the first two weeks we were in a pensione with all the celebrated dreariness of such places and Mary and I went out nearly every evening. I have read so many bad books in which there are some children who live in a pensione in Rome and whose parents come into the dining room each night to kiss them good-bye, that I had expected the children to be sad. Not at all. They hardly looked up from their spaghetti. Then there was the day that Barbara Frietchie, after a triumphant crossing (the Captain had her on the bridge) and a sensational entry into Naples, kicked the bucket. Mary bought violets in the Piazza di Spagna, Barbara was laid out in a candy box and I was commissioned to bury her in the Borghese gardens but the ground was hard and she got a sordid resting place. Then the children cried and cried and asked to be taken home; but since then they've been very good. Susie goes to a convent where she has to curtsey, pray and work hard and she's risen to the whole thing handsomely. Ben manfully boards his school-bus at the Piazza Venezia. When things have been difficult—and travel, as you know, has its abysses—they have been excellent. All of this to express the fact that I am inclined to underestimate the resiliance of everyone.

I'm very anxious to know what you think about the book but I don't know when you'll get it. March, I guess, although I'm not sure of the publication date. They offered me all the galleys I wanted last summer but as soon as I crossed the Atlantic they changed their minds. I'll try and get some galleys for you. I haven't seen them myself. No publisher is so happy as a publisher with an author across the sea.

As ever,
John

The collection *Time* was supposed to have pasted was titled *Stories*. Farrar, Straus & Giroux brought it out in December of 1956 and it included work by Bill Maxwell, Danny Fuchs and Jean Stafford as well as my father. J. D. Salinger had been asked to be part of this book, but he declined and suggested Bill.

Via del Plebiscito 107
Roma

December 7th [1956]

Dear Bill,
. . . I think the sala is about as big as anything in the Century Club. Our bedroom is also very big with a fine ceiling, but that's about the end of it. There is a long interior hall behind the sala and a large reception room with a staircase and mirror. The children's rooms are small and there is a tangle of dark corridors leading in the kitchen. We

have not had any help which means that Mary or I sweep the sala, let in the milk man, make the beds and cook diminutive meals in the dimly lighted kitchen. However a maid came yesterday and can now be seen raising great Biblical clouds of dust in the middle of the sala. Mary's Italian is splendid—so good that she can keep secrets from me. I go to something called La Societa Nazionale Dante Alighieri and study. The teacher is a heavy, grey-haired woman in a suit with a large amythest brooch and a bum leg. Before the class is half-over she is covered from top to bottom with chalk dust. To call for silence she goes psssst.

Mary loves the palazzo and has no morning sickness. My feelings about the place are still mixed. The place discourages any mildly humorous descriptions of its vastness and its inconveniences. People are impressed when they come in—which I enjoy—but mostly I don't seem to notice it. In a letter from Philadelphia yesterday a lady—a stranger—said that Time had pasted my stories and if this is so I hope no one else in the collection suffered. I walked to the Piazza esedra and bought a copy of Time, but it was the wrong issue and so I will never know. The city is changeable. Yesterday the wind was from the mountains—a bitter fog and I would have been happy to pack my bags and go home. Today the sun is out and it is lovely. It is like May and all the windows are open. I ought to have a story done in a day or two; and now I will get back to work.

As ever,<br>John

This letter was written to Mary Dirks. John and Mary Dirks are longtime friends of the family. John's father created the cartoon strip "The Katzenjammer Kids" and John continued it until it was retired. John is also a sculptor, and was one of the group of men with whom my father used regularly to lunch. This group was known as the Friday Club. Mary Dirks and my mother taught together at Briarcliff College.

Via del Plebiscito 107<br>Roma<br>December 17th

Dear Mary,

That was a fine letter and made us all feel happy here which is what letters are supposed to do. We are usually happy enough but it isn't

like Scarborough and I will try to tell you the little I know about social
life in Old Rome. To begin with there is an awful lot of it and I'm not
sure of the quality but it may be that I'm such a downbeat type that I'm
not fit to comment on anything, but I'll try. Yesterday for instance. A
Christmas party given by some people we will call Snodgrass who live
in a fifteenth Century palace which we will call Palazzo Snodgrass.
These Snodgrasses are from Chicago and they are loaded. The party
was for parents and children. Ben's mice had been asked to perform so
I took Ben over early. They live around the corner from our palazzo
and in order to get there you pass the ruins of a temple. This for color.
Anyhow we got there at four and found the hostess and her best friends
rehearsing the lines for a commedia del arte puppet show with Venitian
puppets. There is no describing these palazzos. All the rooms are a
mile long and all the ceilings have pictures on them. To drink there
was a weak champagne punch. As the hostess pointed out, Italian
butlers don't pass drinks. You have to walk over to the bowl yourself.
Then a hired pianist came in and began to play cocktail music. This is
the same stuff in Rome as it is in the east fifties. I took up a firm
position by the punch bowl and the other guests began to drift in.
Every child was given a fur cap and an ice-cream cone. Almost all the
ladies are divorced. Dresses are very tight here this year and just the
elasticity in the girdles in one sala would have had the force of an
atomic explosion. If you dropped a thousand dollars on the floor there
wasn't a lady there who could bend over and pick it up. At about six
the commedia began—in Italian,of course. Then Ben's mice performed
and then the curtains closed jerkily—like all puppet curtains—and
flew open on a snow scene with an angel and we all stood and sang
Silent Night and Jinglebells. This was good and wild and sad—all the
creaky American voices raised under the golden rafters in Jinglebells.
A few divorcees cried. Then the lights went on and the party, so to
speak, began but I was bored and went home. We stopped in a bakery
to buy some cornetti for breakfast. The baker took one of Ben's mice
out of the cage and frightened his wife with it. She was a very fat
woman—not really frightened at all—but a great performance of
shrieking and hiding under the counters that tickled everyone and
brought quite a few people in from the street. That, with its ups and
downs is a typical night around the via del Plebiscito.

A very happy New Year. The Boyers is where we would be and our
love all around and think of us kindly when the clock strikes.

                                                                                    John

Peter and Ebie Blume were friends of the Cowleys and the Cheevers. Peter is a painter.

Via del Plebiscito 107

January 7th

Dear Malcolm,

Those are very generous letters and I am very grateful. There were a lot of unanswered questions in the book and the reason for this is because I'm such a pig-headed fool. The questions had been raised, politely enough, but I refused to answer them feeling that for once I was on my own and would not change or explain a word. . . . Twenty-seven is much too old for Melissa and maybe I can catch this in page-proof. I enjoyed writing the book and I can't tell you how pleased I am that you liked reading it. It was a long push and you've been interested and helpful all along the way.

We see the Blumes who seem to be about as clear, sweet and blue-sky as any people I have ever known. We talk a good deal about your coming over with Muriel. You would like it so much and do a great deal to liven up the academy. . . .

This is a palace, vast, drafty and handsome with a long sala and a golden ceiling, but I don't seem to be able to describe either the palace or Rome. Having lived for so long in a world where a touch football game or a scrap of gossip made the day I am floored by the events of the last two months. Walking back from school this morning (I study Italian at a foundation for strangers) I came into the piazza in front of the Pantheon which was full of sunlight, people and water and then stepped into an alley, as cold as sin where there was one, large marble foot—the remains of a collosus—and a powerful smell of hot bread. Yesterday was Capodanno with elephants in the Piazza Venezia and after kissing Susie goodnight I looked out of her window and saw the Principessa Doria in the courtyard, shaking hands with a procession of Dutch nuns. The principessa was anti-fascist and spent the occupation hiding in a cellar in Trastevere. It is a long story, but nothing like the long stories in Scarborough.

Our love to Muriel. Mary is very tranquil and worries about nothing. The children are fine.

As ever,
John

Via del Plebiscito 107

February 25

Dear Bill,

And why shouldn't I tell you a story about Irwin Shaw's command of languages? It was told to me by a young Roman lady who had drinks with him at the Excelsior before going on to dinner. As they left the hotel Irwin stopped at the desk and asked for his mail in Italian. He spoke such gibberish that the young lady offered to interpret for him but he said that wouldn't be necessary. The governess of his son, he explained, was Italian and that was why he spoke so fluently. Irwin got his mail—a large bundle of it—and they went out to the chauffer-driven car that Irwin always has in Rome. "I'll ask the Chauffer to hold my mail," he explained and then made another assault on the bella lingua. "Si, si," the chauffer said when Irwin had finished,"si signore." Then, as Irwin climbed contentedly into the back seat of the car the chauffer trotted down the street and stuffed Irwin's letters into a mailbox.

I hear from Irwin who very kindly asks me to Klosters but I can't leave Mary at this point. First the doctor said she had toxemia; then a hidden edema. Then he put her on a diet of spinach—nothing but spinach—with pills. . . . She seems fine now, but she's very close to the end and I can't go away. I did go down to Naples to say goodbye to the Warrens and I also took Susie to Florence for a weekend but I go nowhere now until the baby comes. The Minstery of Finance Bank performed Beethoven's 7th yesterday in the Forum. I thought this might precipitate the baby: but no. Neither that nor the selections from Lucia De Lammore that followed.

Work is the only thing I worry about but suppose I did begin to work wonderfully, then where would we be? We would never be able to come home, Susie would end up drinking gin in Port Said and I would die in Rapallo. I don't do as much as I should here, mostly because the ceiling is too far from the top of my head. My thoughts either bound upwards and beat against the gold carving or else they fly downwards: never an even keel. But it is, as the invalids say, like learning how to walk again. After all I've never had to describe anything before like a bishop falling down the stairs at Assisi during a thunder-storm. And then there is the baby, the book and my struggles with the Italian language; but mostly the book I think. I haven't written anything much since that was done and I will feel much better when that goose is cooked.

Love,
John

Via del Plebiscito 107
Rome

February 26th

Dear Malcolm

Mary still hasn't had Il Baby and we mostly wait for that. It is due any minute and I wish to hell she would stay out of Roman trolley cars. So do the Roman trolley-car conductors. But she has a fine time and hasn't seen the working end of a dishpan since December. . . .

I've asked Harpers to send you a bound copy of the book. They've done a very good job on it in every way. I got my copy yesterday and seem done with it now that I've seen it in print. And it's high time. It was done seven months ago and I've done very little since then but sit on the toilet and receive imaginary compliments.

My love to Muriel and Mary sends her love to you both and I will write as soon as we have Il Baby. It would be great fun to see you here.

As ever,
John

Via del Plebiscito 107

March 22nd

Dear Bill,

Federico which is now his name is registered as a roman citizen in the books of the Comune di Roma. We wanted to call him Frederick but there is of course no K in the alphabet here and I gave up after an hour or two. Cheever is impossible and I have to spell it out every time. Che aca a ancora a vue a ire. The offices of the Comune which handle the affairs of two million people, do not contain a typewriter or a filing cabinet. It is like Gogol. There are thousands and thousands of clerks with signet rings and dirty linen who write all day long. Records are kept either in immense books or in bundles tied with twine. This charming system does not work at all. It has taken me four days to authenticate poor Federico—but he is a fine boy, very handsome with a clear, well shaped head and he gives us almost no trouble.

Mary was in the delivery room about half an hour. The nuns, with their white habits and gentle voices were very satisfactory. She had a room with a balcony overlooking the Villa Sciarra (nightingales and peacocks) and beyond this the squash-colored or golden city, depending on the light. The whole thing cost much less than it would have cost at Home. It's been so long since we've had a baby around that I'd forgotten what fun it is. He looks very clean and is usually fragrant and seems to enjoy the ceilings. The children love him and cart him around although poor Ben sometimes looks as if he sensed a terrifying change in the wind and his great solace—the countryside—is not here.

I should be working, but now I wait for reviews. I not only wait for them: I write them. I've written them all, even the Albany Times-union. If the New Yorker reviews it could Tom airmail me a clipping. But this foolishness will soon be over. I think I will buy a car and take Eleanor's Rocca for the summer. . . . Irwin blew in long enough to pick up an Alpha-R and give a dinner party. Now I will go and buy Mary a present and study my irregular verbs. I will also send you a Roman door-plate.

As ever.

John

In 1957, he wrote a paragraph in his journal about the paintings in a villa at Caparola. His conjecture of how these artists might have felt about their work says a lot about how he felt about his own: "The painting, like most of the painting in the villa, is distinguished by its charm and abundance. There was so much to be painted—it would never all be done— and how delighted the painters must have been to portray themselves, their wives and mistresses and children as saints, apostles and members of the courts of France and Spain. It must have been great fun."

Saul Bellow had just had a son named Adam. Adam is also a writer.

Via del Plebiscito 107
Roma

March 28th [1957]

Dear Saul,

Mike Bessie sent on your letter and I'm very pleased that you got through the book and liked it; pleased and grateful. Good Conduct is right. You get the prize for the man with the most talent and the best conduct in exploring it.

And congratulations on your son. We had one at about the same time and perhaps they can pool their forces when they grow up. Bellow & Cheever. A livery stable. A ship chandler. A liquor store. No anthologies.

Gratefully and Sincerely,
John

When my father received Saul's letter he wrote this in his journal:

A copy of the book arrives and also a generous letter from SB and I am intoxicated or at least upset—mostly because I may commit the sin of pride; find humility difficult to arrive at. But if the book is any good it is plain luck and there is no point in my assuming that it is a product of industry; passionate application, etceterra etc. But dizzy with excitment I went out to buy cigarettes and the pretty girl at the cafe, quite a flirt, gave me a look of pure disinterestedness and so I am crushed and feel like myself again. . . .

The operation mentioned below was Fred's circumcision. When he was in Italy, my father had trouble writing short stories.

Tuesday [1957]

del Plebiscito

Dear Bill,

I have bought a new typewriter ribbon, but the right end of my typewriter seems to be falling away; but this, like Fred's operation, will have to wait until we get home. I know that my adjustment to Rome is lacking in many ways but I am never more sensible to the nature of this failure than I am when I see my friend, Ned Chandler who is a Fullbright (research) who lives in a pensione and who I just made up. To put it crudely Ned is a moralist—a crude one—and he wastes his time in Italy trying to smell out the moral nature of things. I see him often, I know many of his mistakes but I will just touch briefly this afternoon on his friendship with Maitland Rush who is known to almost everyone in the English-speaking colony in Rome. Maitland is a millionaire which is not unusual in Italy. They are thick, all the way from Florence down to the Sorrento penninsula—mostly the sons of vigorous, original, self-made men. They have not been able to live up to their parents' exacting and sometimes ridiculous expectations and so they have retreated to Italy to write, paint, collect furniture and spend their money. If you asked what Maitland did—a question that is almost never asked in Rome—you would be told that he was a violinist. He didn't perform in public. He didn't have to, people said. That he was an industrious violinist was well-known to everyone. He went to his studio at nine every morning and could not be reached until five when he returned to his palace for tea. He could not even be reached in cases of emergency such as when his son fell down a staircase and broke his neck. He lived with his children and his pleasant—but very fat wife— in fifteen or twenty rooms of a splendid palace. His social life was limited because of his industriousness. He never went out to lunch and went out to dinner only once or twice a week, explaining that too much social activity interfered with his music. But poor Ned had even begun to question these simple facts. What kind of instrumentalist is he, he would ask, who refuses to perform in public. What kind of a man is it who has dedicated ten or twenty years of his life to perfecting a violin technique that has never been heard. Ned should have left the subject alone. Maitland had an excellent chef and excellent wines and Ned liked to go there for dinner although it did irritate him when Maitland rang for the chef at the end of each meal and complained, in Italian, about the salt in the soup. But he should have let his irritability grow in this direction and left his host's career alone. It was none of his business.

But the question had been raised—it must have been raised by someone closer to Maitland than Ned—and Maitland decided to give a recital in his palace. He sent out a hundred invitations, rented eighty golden chairs, and when Ned went there that evening he found fifteen or twenty people sitting in the front rows although it was already late. The great room, lit with hundreds of candles, the famous ceiling mural (Alexander taming Bucephalus) and the quantities of roses only deepened Ned's anxieties and suspicions. Presently Maitland and his accompanist appeared—in white tie—and the concert began. It was terrible. The rest of us would have said as much, admired the ceiling mural and waited patiently for the buffet and drinks. Not Ned. He suffered through every minute of it like an animal in a steel trap. He squirmed in his chair as if he was the violin that was being scraped at. The sweat dripped off his forehead. This is my buttocks that has gone to sleep, he thought, this is my tuxedo that binds at the crotch, this is a unique night in my unique life that is being paid out in excruciating misery. He gave his host a wicked look, thinking about the fraud of his industriousness and how he must have spent twenty years in a musical studio, taking naps, reading detective stories, swatting flies. Maitland could not play—he knew it himself and at one point he gave up—shrugged his shoulders and snickered—but the accompanist commanded him to go on and he tried. His problem was a difficult one. Without talent or enthusiasm of any sort, and with a million dollars to spend he had tried to give his life an aspect of order and discipline and it was probably not his fault that he had put such a pretentious name on his idleness. When the piece ended and there was an intermission Ned's clothes were so soaked with sweat that it was uncomfortable to move. He looked at the people in the seats around him and seemed to be surrounded by homosexuals—not the dead-eyed type—but very flighty young men who began to discuss cooking and to plan a trip to the campagna to get wild flower cuttings from the garden of the house where they all seemed to live. When Ned spoke to them they began to praise the music—hadn't it been divine—but with an open insincerity that seemed to cost them nothing. Ned headed then for the punch bowl which turned out to be full of watery Frascati that tasted like carrot water. he had tasted this when he saw his hostess approaching him and he bolted. He knocked over a chair bumped into a stranger and without an apology or a goodnight or any other trace of manners ( and leaving his hat behind him) ran out into the street. The buffet was excellent, if he had stayed, and so was the wine but instead of this he wandered angrily and miserably around Rome. You can see what a fool he is and I hope I can see as much myself very soon.

As ever,
John

Vittoria and Iole were both maids. This was Archibald MacLeish, the poet. The Dorias owned the building in which we rented our apartment.

Via del Plebiscito 107
March 28th

Dear Eleanor,
I didn't answer you a presto because I wanted to make up my mind about the Rocca which I just did a minute ago. We would like it;

and please tell me if this is too much trouble or if I've taken too long to make up my mind; and here endeth the business end of the letter.

What happened before the baby came was that on Thursday and Friday Mary seemed very absent-minded and strange and confessed to such things as that she had never paid the tailor who made Susie's coat. Then on Saturday morning she had mild labor pains but refused to call the doctor and asked Ronald Ang-dingh to come here and play with Ben. The pains went on and at noon I called the doctor over her protests and he said for her to come to the hospital for an examination. This was at four. She dragged her feet all the way; refused to take a suitcase and told Vittoria she would return for dinner. I left her at the hospital where she confesed that she had not paid for her plaid skirt and took Ronald home. He lives way the hell off and gone. When I got back to the hospital Mary was alone in her room in great pain but I had only been there a minute or two when a nun took her away and returned to tell me, fifteen or twenty minutes later, that I had a son. Then the Blumes came up with whisky and Chesterfields. He's a very good-looking boy. At least I think he's very good looking. When Iole first saw him she cried: IL Duce, IL Duce! Now she holds him in her arms and crows Piccolo, piccolopiccolo Mussolini.

It is hot here now and the streets smell like the sea. All the sandal-wearing fratti have thrown away their socks. . . . I've seen the Pope in his Sedia Gestatoris and also had tea with the Dorias. A nightingale lives in a rainpipe (or tree) in the Palazzo Venezia and sings all night long. . . . And then there was the night when the Macleishs forgot their portoni key at the Caetani, and I assured them that I could get the Secura to open the gate. Drunk and speaking a terrible mishmosh of Italian I led the poor M's over hill and dale for a couple of hours. They finally escaped me and took a cab to the academy where they seem to have found a bed. . . . I'm so glad you liked the first of the book and I hope you'll like the last. Everyone sends their best and we miss you all.

As ever,
John


Helen Puner is a neighbor and friend of the family. She had just read *The Wapshot Chronicle*, and had written to say that she liked it.

Via del Plebiscito 107

March 29th

Dear Helen,

You are very kind and do I love it. Wipe that disgusting smile off your face says Mary when I put down your letter but now I've retired to the galeria and am smiling and smiling in private and grinning and chuckling. I think I've been very lucky on reviews and I hope it sells. I'm going out and buy a car this morning; I'm going out and try to buy a car. Then I will try to drive it for the traffic here is really murderous. When you first arrive and Fiats keep ripping the buttons off your suitcoat you think Ah yes, but no one ever gets killed. Then you see an old lady bowled over by a Vespa and rolled the breadth of the Piazza Rotounda like a beer keg and you begin to wonder. Then you're shown statistics and realize that more people are run over in a year than were ever killed in the gladitorial combats as you poke along the corso you think up moral judgements about life in Rome.

Mary is very well and what began as Frederick and is now Federico is a fine boy and also very well but today is gloomy and cold, although the wisteria is all out, and I seem to miss the country and so do the children. The only information I seem to have today deals with poor Princess Doria. She is lovely, willowy, witty and the last of a line that began with Numa Pompilius but she cannot get along with men. An owl has come to nest in the tower here (above a family from Philadelphia) and hoots a song about the end of the family all night long. Dukes and earls are fetched from England to take her to dances but she does not like them. You might suggest that she go to an analyst until you realize that a princess cannot lie down on a couch. So, as Ben says, we all have our troubles.

Best,
John

My father sold only one story to *The New Yorker* during the year we were abroad. This may have had something to do with his having completed *The Chronicle*, but it may also have had to do with the strangeness of his surroundings.

Via del Plebiscito
Roma

June 14th [1957]

Dear Malcolm

Ben's school closes today and we are supposed to leave very soon for the Rocca but Mary keeps putting it off. And I have to get a passport for Federico which will take another ten days. We sail on the second of September but the months in the country will go very quickly as they always do and Mary has already begun to try and put off the sailing date. She says it would be so much easier for her to pack if she could pack in the spring, but I am anxious to get home. You get out of touch. The three and five year expatriates sit around talking about what a terrible country the U.S. is. The food is all frozen, you know, they say and everyone has a tv set right in the living room. And you have to do your own shopping, etc. God knows we'll miss the maids. They do everything but shave me and lace my shoes. They help me into my coat and used to brush my hat before I lost it. But I find it hard to work and think it might have been easier if we had settled in the country. We've been going out to Anticoli for weekends and as soon as I get there my head is full of ideas but when we get back to Rome they seem to be extinguished by the noise of trolley-cars. Maybe I'll do better when we got to the Rocca.

As ever,
John

La Rocca is a vast stone fortress that overlooks the Mediterranean in the now-fashionable Italian community of Port'Ercole. It has now been restored, but when we stayed there it was a magnificent ruin. The dungeons were littered with rusted tin cups and discarded shoes. There were even some bones, although it wasn't at all clear if they were human. We shared the inner court with a goat that was losing its hair, a couple of chickens and a score of famished cats. A bucket of water was needed to flush the toilet. My father gave a description and some of his feelings about a place that sounds a good deal like La Rocca in the opening of the story "The Golden Age," which ran in The New Yorker in September of 1959.

Our ideas of castles, formed in childhood, are inflexible, and why try to reform them? Why point out that in a real castle thistles grow in the courtyard, and the threshold of the ruined throne room is guarded by a nest of green adders? Here are the keep, the drawbridge, the battlements and towers that we took with our lead soldiers when we were down with the chicken pox. The first castle was English, and this one was built by the King of Spain during an occupation of Tuscany, but the sense of imaginative supremacy—the heightened mystery of nobility—is the same. Nothing is inconsequential here. It is thrilling to drink Martinis on the battlements, it is thrilling to bathe in the fountain, it is even thrilling to climb down the stairs into the village after supper and buy a box of matches. . . .

When I read the letter below I was astonished to find that my father had actually tried to fire Iole Felici, the cook. Iole had come to work for us in Rome. Unmarried at the time, and childless, she fell completely in love with my brother, Fred. She still likes to tell us how Fred preferred the food she prepared him to his mother's milk. Iole returned to the States with us in the fall of 1957 and has remained an active force in all of our lives.

My father is supposed to have tried to fire her before we went to La Rocca because Eleanor Clark had warned him that Ernesta, the woman who ran the place, would almost certainly fight with Iole. Sure enough, they detested each other. La Signorina owned the castle.

La Rocca
Porto Ercole
(pr di Grosetto)

July sixth (I think)

Dear Bill,

We came out here on Friday for the summer, presumably. (I have cut my right hand with a sickle and so the typing is wilder than ever) I drove back into Rome on Monday to get the rest of the bags (windup toys and evening dresses) and will go back into Rome next Monday again to finish up some business and where I hope to find a letter from you. We fired the cook but she came along anyhow and so now we have three maids (Ernesta, Iole and Vitoria) and very sketchy arrangements for washing ourselves and going to the bathroom. The hygienic arrangements are on a par with the darkest provinces of India but the sea is a deep purple and gin is a wonderful curative, I think. La Bella Lingua goes on and I will now take lessons from La Signorina. Eleanor told everyone about her unhappy love for a Prince of the Church but she never told me that the old lady is only three feet tall, has the eyes of a tit-mouse and is such a miser that she makes her supper on a crust of bread. Everything blooms in this heat: boys, girls, figs, palms and eccentrics and when Porto Ercole was bombed and the people ran up here for shelter in the ramparts the old lady stood at the drawbridge, trying to charge admission. The fort is renascience in that at its most vulnerable points—those places where the turks were expected to swarm up the walls—there is a good deal of fine, architectural detail. I do wish the beach was cleaner but if the beach was cleaner I suppose there would be regulations about bathing suits and people would begin to worry about modesty, virtue, impotence, indigestion and constipation and the purple would fade out of the sea. They do worry about their livers. They all worry about their livers.

It is very hot, it is African between twelve and five and everyone takes the siesta. Even the asses stop braying. But from five on it is lovely and the sun rises at four am. So does Frederick. Iole keeps trying to pry little birds out of the stonework to cook for our lunch, but the birds get away. Eleanor tells me that Iole and Ernesta will quarrel; and who cares. . . .

Auguri,<br>John

La Rocca<br>Porto Ercole<br>Pridi Grosetto

Saturday

Dear Bill,

The people are beautiful, and remain so I think because there are so few stranieri. They mean to be beautiful and I don't think you can get away with this in the modern world. I have never seen such a blaze of vanity and perfect innocence. The boys wear brightly colored codpieces and the girls are very modestly covered and they take hands and make a circle in the sand to play a game our children call fill-in-the-gap but that seems to be as old as the sea. I sit on a rock, watching them, dressed in my long Brooks Brothers bathing drawers, which have drawers within drawers in order to avoid any embarrassing suggestion of the facts. I thought I might buy something sportier but there were howls from everyone—Iole and Susie the loudest. My drawers are not only baggy but when I dive they fill up with air like a balloon. But the people here are not built like americans which was apparent a few days

ago when a nice American boy strode onto the beach. Someone seemed
to have blundered.

John

John Becker was a writer and magazine publisher.

Via del Plebiscito 107

Monday

Dear Bill,

I should figure out some new way of writing letters to you—graphs
or water-colors or codes. One of the first things it says in my journal
here is: stop trying to write Bill a coherent letter, but I still try. Sitting
in the little look-out at La Rocca, sitting on the terrace of the Becker's
villa at Anticoli, setting in a box at the opera, sitting in the bath-tub
drinking martinis, sitting in the villa at Caparolla, sitting in the Fiat,
sitting on many mossy rocks all over Lazio, sitting on the throne-chair
here, sitting on the beach at Porto Ercole, sitting up in bed at three in
the morning (waked by a nightingale who seems to live in a drainpipe
in the Palazza Venezia) sitting in buses and trains and gondolas and
churches I think: now I will write Bill a coherent letter, but I never
will. It's neck and neck with what happens and my journal and roses,
for instance, a subject I haven't touched on, would take a book.

What happens is that the Beckers have loaned us their villa for weekends where the roses grow up to the bedroom balcony. We alternate
this with the Rocca which is wild and lovely. A friend was robbed of
six hundred dollars and her passport in the lobby of the Excelsior and
the cook, Iole, says she will die if she cannot stay with Federico. I love
Federico. . . . Ben had his birthday party here. I go to see Otello for the
second time tomorrow night. And having planned to begin a letter on
one subject I end up with nothing but remain,

As ever,
John

Palazza Doria
Via del Plebiscito 107

August 10th

Dear Bill,

This is a change of address, there having been a blowup at the Rocca yesterday. Things with Ernesta, Eleanor's cook, have been touchy ever since we came back from Siena. . . . Anyhow the sirocco began to blow on Wednesday. Mary and I went swimming on Thursday, but it was dangerous. A shark was seen on the sand bar. Friday morning the lighthouse keeper invited the children to pick some figs from a tree near the lighthouse. When Ernesta saw them she began to scream. Iole was on the terrace with Federico. It was his festa, he was five months old and had on his white golf, his red pants, high socks, suede shoes and a cap with a viser and strap per fare il polo. Ernesta got the figs away from the children and Iole shouted vada al'inferno, strega. Vada al' diavolo, shouted Ernesta. Then a great deal was said that I couldn't understand and Ernesta got hysterical and stood among the thistles and old boots in the cortile, stamping her right foot and screaming kakakakaka. I went down to intervene and so did Mary who was doing a water-color of the old tower. Then Fosco, Ernesta's husband joined us, braying like an ass and an hour later I drove the family to Orbetello and put them on the train to Rome. Susie and I drove back to the Rocca and got the bags. Then I paid Ernesta a full month's wages, told her I did not ever want to see her again and we drove down the via aurelia for what I guess is the last time this years. Iole had taken everything out of the kitchen at the rocca—salt, pepper, sugar, etc. and had an excellent dinner on the table here by eight o'clock. It seemed like home.

Best,
John

# BACK IN AMERICA

* * *

In the fall of 1957 we returned to Scarborough.

Scarborough

22nd

Dear Josie,

It was very good to hear from you and I haven't answered you sooner because our house is so full of men, women and children—also dogs —that I haven't been able to find a table on which I could put the typewriter. I'm writing this from an office in Ossining which is not altogether satisfactory. We sailed from Naples early in September, bringing Iole home with us. She is wonderful and we all go on speaking Italian and eating pasta and have no reason to long for Italy. All except Susie who, having bellyached about Italy all year now gets a faraway look in her eyes and says she wishes she was back in the convent.

But I am really very glad to be home. I like the autumn here, I like being able to understand what I overhear and I hope to get back to work. My hopes are at least more vigorous than they were in Italy where I did nothing. I want to return—like Susie—but not until I have a decent piece of work behind me. I haven't done anything decent since the book was finished. I went up to Yaddo for a couple of weeks and found that it was much easier to work without a dog in my lap and a baby in my arms, but I seem to have contracted for these distractions and I am lost without them.

As ever,

John

My father was elected to the National Institute of Arts and Letters in 1957. "Ah root tee toot/Ah root tee toot/Oh we're the boys of the Institute/ Oh we're not rough/And we're not tough/We're cultivated and that's enough." He began to recite this to his children shortly after his election, but he warned us not to repeat the verse in public. There was a limit to his irreverence. One of his first acts as a member was to nominate Saul Bellow. Felicia Geffen had the title of Executive Secretary to the National Institute of Arts and Letters and the American Academy of Arts and Letters, whose members were drawn from the Institute. She also had my father's admiration.

Scarborough, New York

October 9th 1957

Dear Miss Geffen,

Thank you so much for having been patient with the nomination of Saul Bellow. There were no members of the Institute in Rome but Mr. Ciardi, Peter Blume and myself when we made the nomination. Mr. Blume had never read a novel of Mr. Bellow's and so refused to second the nomination. This accounts for the fact that we lacked a signature. I did not write a citation when you first wrote since it seemed to me that someone else surely would have nominated Mr. Bellow. I hope the citation I'm enclosing is suitable.

Sincerely,
John Cheever

[Enclosure]

John Cheever

Saul Bellow's first published novel THE DANGLING MAN appeared in 1944. The book was thought by many reputable critics to introduce a most original writer. In the novels that have followed—THE VICTIM and THE ADVENTURES OF AUGIE MARCH Mr. Bellow has developed his considerable gifts with such energy and adventurousness that he stands today as the most original writer in America. No one has done so much to display, creatively, the versatility of life and speech in this country.

This was a letter to John Weaver in March of 1958. The award was for *The Wapshot Chronicle*. When I read this letter, I assumed he had made up the part about the judges. I don't know if he had three friends, but the judges for fiction for the National Book Award that year were Van Wyck

Brooks, Albert Guérard, Elisabeth Ann McMurray Johnson, William Maxwell and Francis Steegmuller. Both Bill and Francis were good friends. Clifton Fadiman is the writer and critic. Robert Penn Warren won the poetry award for *Promises: Poems 1954–1956* and Catherine Drinker Bowen won the non-fiction award for a biography of Sir Edward Coke titled *The Lion and the Throne*. Randall Jarrell, the guest speaker, was a consultant in poetry to the Library of Congress. The chimpanzee was J. Fred Muggs. He appeared regularly on the Dave Garroway show. According to John Weaver, Jean Stratton Porter is a misspelling of Gene Stratton Porter, the popular writer whose works included *A Girl of the Limberlost* and *Birds of the Bible*.

Scarborough

Saturday

Dear John,

Just in case you should ever want to get a National Book Award I think I can give you some advice. First you have to have at least three good friends among the judges and then you have to have strong nerves, a commodious bladder and a good supply of bourbon. On Monday I made six whattheycall tapes. You go into these hot little studios where there is a man with small eyes and a big voice, a card table, two folding chairs, a dusty piano and a bullfiddle. Then the sound engineer comes out from behind the glass partition and tells you about his stomach. They always do this. Then they give you a time signal, your tongue swells up to twice its normal size and the man with the little eyes asks you in a booming voice what you think about the American reading public. After six of these I was so tired that I couldn't sleep at all and on Tuesday morning I sneaked a little bourbon at about half-past ten. Then Mary revealed to me that she had bought a new dress which cost one hundred dollars. She said it was cheaper to buy a new dress where she didn't have to wear a hat than to buy a hat to wear with her other new dress. We drove into New York and I went to Parlor B, Mezzanine C at the Commodore where there were quite a lot of people penned in by velvet ropes. . . . Then Clifton Fadiman said he was going to give us a plaque and a thousand dollars but all he gave us was a plaque. Then they took this away from us. Then Fadiman gave us the plaque again and they took it away again. Then we pretended to autograph books . . . and Fadiman gave us the plaque again and took it away again. Then I went to the bathroom. Then we went down stairs where there were more people. It cost ten dollars to get in. Fadiman gave the plaque and a check to Red Warren. Then Red made a ten minute speech about the poem as structure and structure as the poem and sat down in a chair with a sign on it saying POETRY WINNER. Then Katherine Bowen made a speech but I didn't listen to this because I was afraid I would forget my own speech. Then I made a speech and sat down in a chair that said FICTION WINNER and Randall Jarell, who had just washed his beard, made a long speech the gist of which was that Bennet Cerf is a shit, that South Pacific is shitty and that people who look at the sixty-four thousand dollar question are virtual cocksuckers. This went on for forty-four minutes and the Random House contingent coughed all the way through it. Then some screens were removed and there was one of those bars made of a trestle table covered with a bedsheet and a couple of hundred highball glasses each containing two ice-cubes and a teaspoon of whiskey. . . . Then we went to Toots Shors where there was one of those buffets they had for movie previews. Smoked butt, baked beans and one old turkey. All the publishers got drunk and sang Down by The Old Millstream. Then we went back to the hotel where there were some friends drinking my bourbon. They did this until about two. Then early in the morning I went to the Dave Garroway studio which is really a store window on fifty-second street and outside there were about four hundred women milling around and holding up signs saying:HELLO MAMA. DORIS. SEND MONEY. GLADYS. HELP. IDA. I was asked to wait in a green room where there was a chimpanzee drinking coffee, a man with a long beard and a lady in Arab costume practising a song. She said the song was in Arabic and that it was about how the little raindrops fill up the big well. Then she went up and sang her song and then they said it was time for me to go up but it took two strong men pushing and pulling to get me into the studio and everybody on the street shouted: It's Gary Moore. I sat down at a baize-covered table and quivered like a bowlfull of chicken fat for fifteen minutes and then I drove Mary home. Mary took the check away from me and Ben hung the plaque up in his clubhouse which is in the woods and is made of two packing crates so I may not be any richer but I sure am a hell of a lot more nervous.

Love,
Jean Stratton Porter

Scarborough

March 17th

Dear Josie,

As you must know Red and I were given a thousand bucks on Tuesday after a good deal of hard work. The breaking point nearly came on Wednesday morning when, suffering from a hangover, I had breakfast with a chimpanzee.

Everyone is well except that Mary wants to buy a house and is quite difficult on this score. I can't afford to tie myself down with a big mortgage at this point. Mary has been collecting money for the Briarcliff Library and it seems that all my rich neighbors (in the advertising business to a man) consider themselves to be the peers of Milton. Sitting on their red leather chairs in their 17-room houses they say: "Oh if I only had all the free time your husband has I would have written many novels."

The baby is wonderful. He walks, speaks Italian and dances the way Ben used to. He has a wonderful disposition. Everyone sends their best.

As ever,
John

Crows Nest [1958]
Wauwinet
Nantucket Island, Mass

Thursday

Dear Bill,

This is on Mary's Olivetti which doesn't respond to my touch. Your house is bigger than our house. Our house is very small and Susie has a guest named Pinni. They lie in bed in the mornings and giggle and say vraiment and think up names for the cottage like "What's Nest". Their room is separated from the seat or throne of the household by a thin sheet of matchboard and to go to the bathroom is like sitting down on a pot in the middle of the Vassar commencement. It is disconcerting. Pinni was planning to leave on the morning plane but now the air is very dark and growing darker.

I walk on the beach every day, thinking mostly foolish things. . . . I also read books for the Grants committee and what is that old man doing at twelve o'clock noon? He is pouring himself a glass of gin.

What does he hold in his hand? He is holding a sensitive novel by a young man who wants to go to Rome. How can a drunken old man judge the merits of a sensitive novel? He cannot. What a cruel world it is where the destinies of the young lie in such shaken hands! What is the old man going to do now? He is going to pour himself another glass of gin.

As ever,
John

John Foster Dulles was Secretary of State under Eisenhower. He wrote that "the ability to get to the verge without getting into the war is the necessary art. . . ." Elizabeth Ames was the director at Yaddo, and she signed her notes E.A.

Scarborough

Wednesday

Dear Josie,

Sid Perelman doesn't speak to me either but I think it's because he's gotten far-sighted or jumpier than ever. He has his troubles. You seem to have more than your share now. . . . But it seems to me now that the world may be disintergrating although this could be a reflection on my sanity. I think it has to do with the bomb. But how can anyone who has watched the sky deny that in the last six months this has changed; and I don't like it. Yesterday at around four in the afternoon it seemed to me that Dulles had plainly pushed the wrong button. An unearthly green light was beating out of the west. Overhead there was a mackerel sky, mares tails and dark brown cumulus. Either I am nutty or something has gone very wrong upstairs and I don't mean my personal upstairs.

The big children have gone off to camp. We have very funny letters from Ben and nothing from Susie who was sent,quite by accident,to a Jewish camp. Federico is with us and also his Italian nursemaid who doesn't ever want to return to Italy. It's been very interesting to watch her opinions change. She liked nothing here in the begining and had some very sensible observations to make but the charms of hot water, abundant electricity and a tax-free radio have seduced her. . . . I took a walk with Saul Bellow after the Yaddo corp meeting and he spoke affectionately of you in Chicago. . . . Elizabeth blooms and blooms. Dorothy Parker is at Yaddo and receiving,I expect, little notes such as:Please do not put your banana peels in the waste-basket. E.A. Please try and return your lunch-box more punctually. E.A. Please do not practise the Jewsharp before four-thirty. There are other studios nearby. E.A.

In spite of the fact that this seems to me to be very nearly the end of the world I am able to work and have a fairly good collection of stories coming out in the fall. The novel, in spite of all its good luck,did not net enough cash to keep a family of five in shoe-leather and I'm damned if I know how I can finance another. And for some reason I feel fed up with the short story. I can write them without too much trouble but it seems like short-selling. The kind of writing I do least of all these days is letter-writing. I seem to have lost the taste. It may be all that green light outside the window.

We drove Ben to his camp and stopped off to see Mary's parents who are still, in their middle seventies,carrying on their eccentric love affair. "She wakes me up at two in the morning," he said,"to tell me that her left foot feels squashy. Then she wakes me at three in the morning to tell me that all the feeling has gone out of her left foot. What can you do with an embicile like that." "Has he gone to pieces again?" she asks. "Has he gone to pieces again? If he's gone to pieces again I'm going to have another drink." Day and night. Now I'm going into town and get a Geiger counter and some lead underwear.

Best,

J

[October 10, 1958]
Scarborough

Friday

Dear Josie,

. . . David Selznick was rumored to be determined to have me write the screenplay of Tender is The Night. All I had to do was sit beside the telephone and graciously accept his invitation to lunch when it was issued. I sat beside the telephone for two and one half weeks but the only person who called was a little Chinese boy who wanted to invite Ben to his birthday party. I think Ben Hecht got the job. I hope he did.

Iole, the Italian so-called nursemaid sailed for home about two weeks ago and I'm back in an apron again after nearly two years. The baby is marvelous, but he does not like to hear English. This is a fact. Our noble tongue grates on his ears—he cries when he hears it. He is very lively and great fun to take walks with and I explain everything to him as I did with the other children at this age: the inutility of a smooth prose style, the problems of sex, the slippery greatness of Virginia Woolf. It is a fine season here, the best we have in this valley.

John

He means Edward Teller, father of the hydrogen bomb.

[December 1958]

Dear Josie,

We are all well. Mary sings The Creation on Saturday with a bunch of electricians,plumbers, station-crossing attendents, and bar-maids. She enjoys herself. She can't read a note of music but she has a strenuous trill. I gave a lecture at Princeton to a group of such elegantly and expensively dressed young men that I felt like a newsboy or some other kind of stray ragamuffin and I think the only impression they took away from my remarks was the fact that I wasn't wearing garters. I saw O'Hara and Carlos Baker and coming home on the train I heard a very croupy and vastly cultivated voice at my back talking about the little, little towns near Toulouse. It was Mary Macarthy. I break my arse writing stories in order to have a clear summer but it doesn't look that way now.

Iole is back from Italy and the poor baby is all screwed up on his languages once more. he was just beginning to speak a little English but now all of that has gone out the window. We have hyacinths, Russian violets,snowdrops and thousands of songbirds,mostly cardinals but the days cloud over early and stay overcast until dusk and I blame all of this on Dulles and Teller. The baby has just discovered that if you stand on the bridge and throw a stick into the brook it will reappear on the other side of the bridge and I blissfully spend hours doing just this with him.

Best,
John

He was sending John Weaver copies of *The Housebreaker of Shady Hill* (Harper & Row).

[December 8, 1958]
Scarborough

Monday

Dear John,

Thursday

The books went off on Monday, all suitably inscribed, and I'm very sorry to have been so slow about this but I haven't been in town since I last saw you. No one in town asked me to come in and I kept thinking that if I stayed at home I might get something done. What I got done was a rotten headcold. It's been the first I've had in years and I think it's very interesting but Mary's love of me does not seem to include my infirmities. She seems lost in some race-memory where primitive men, once they began to sniffle, stripped themselves naked, lay down in the snow and let themselves be eaten by crows.

As ever,
John

"Clementina" ran in *The New Yorker* on May 7 of 1960. The Fred mentioned here is my father's brother. Fred had helped out my father when they were young, and my father helped out Fred when they got older.

Scarborough

Friday

Dear Bill,

I keep meaning to send in the contract but I find that I've always left it in my desk at the house. I did want to thank you for the check which has saved my life. Fred now has a job and I think things will be easier. I keep watching Iole with the hope that she will reveal an ending for Clementina but she seems to be reverting, not to her past in Rome, but to her life in Capronica. On Monday, when the storm set in, she wanted a fire. She got a hatchet, cut an armful of hemlock branches for the fireplace, ignited a newspaper at the kitchen stove and raced through the living-room with this mighty torch, damned near entorching (if there is such a word) herself and the rest of us, but carrying fire from one place to another as she did in Capronica. Later, the baby spilled his pasta on the table and she wiped it off the table onto the rug. "I am not a baron," I said, "but it gives me fastidiousness to see you wipe food onto the rug." "It is nothing signore," she said, "I did it only for the dog." Then she went into the kitchen and broke some plates. Mrs. Stone (no connection) said to me: "I have the most marvelous story for you. You can write it up for the New Yorker and buy Mary a mink coat for Easter. Old Mrs. Fullerton has a shrunken head on her mantlepiece and I asked her to tell me about it and she said 'My dear, I'm so glad you noticed him. I think he's so beautiful and in all these years you're the first person to ever mention him.' Isn't that simply marvelous?"

Love,
John

Dear Bill,

I'm so glad you think Clementina can be fixed. That cheered me up. I think the enclosed needs something—the family isn't quite right— but I seem to have written it with the end of my nose and I want to get it off.

I gave Susie the Salinger stories yesterday and she said "Why he writes just like Jane Austen." Let's take a walk or have lunch or something.

Best,
John

Cassie was our black Labrador. Picci was a diminutive for my brother, Fred. "The book" was Bill Maxwell's novel *The Château*. Bluebell was another Boyer Labrador that lived with the Maxwells for a time.

Surfside [1959]
Nantucket Island, Mass.

Saturday

Dear Bill,

They've fixed up Providence but that long run from Greenwich to the borders of Rhode Island seems to be an affront to the dignity of man. It was a bright day and with the exception of two bridges there is not a shadow on the road and who, at seventy miles an hour, can see the color of the sky. We spent the night at bizarre motel in Hyannis.

The toilet seat, drinking glasses, and bureau drawers were sealed for our sanitary protection and when you opened the frosted glass louvers you looked out at the back door of a restaurant and a row of garbage pails. The furniture was of no discernable period or inspiration and I think if you studied the dressing-table long enough you might go insane. The padrona had dyed straw-colored hair and insisted that Cassie sleep in the car. We crossed over in the morning on the Siasconset which seems to be made of card-board and which was crowded with people like ourselves who would head for the sea-islands in the last of June, even if the islands had sunk. The strike is over today and the first steamer is expected at noon. It will be met by women in old-fashioned costumes but a northeaster is howling on the heath, sounding whole octaves of sharps and flats in the corners of this cottage and it's not very good weather for hoop-skirts. The weather has not been bad and we have all busily,industriously, sometimes furtively, been exposing ourselves to the sun expecting to be turned from white into gold, to have all our imperfections cured, and to become wildly attractive to one another.

We have no car and I'm not going to bring it over. Ben and I bicycle into the village two and sometimes three times a day. We both enjoy this very much and feel healthy and muscular. I have a little seat on my bike for Picci but he likes to pretend that he is a bird,waves his arms around wildly and we've had two terrible spills giving me a bruise in the withers and a sprained thumb. I've not been able to do much work because I have to keep bicycling into the village. It's an ideal arrangement.

I do hope you're feeling more rested and that the affairs of the book are settled. I want very much to read it. Why is it that when publishers die they leave estates of millions while our dear children must clean out bathtubs, which is precisely what Susie is doing in Wauwinet. Last summer she cleaned out the bath of the duchess de Tallyrand. It was ringed with dyes. My best to Bluebell.

Love,
John

Nantucket

Saturday night

Dear Bill,

Operator summer-cottage checking in. This is the Yates-Shepard cottage in Surfside, a place I've never been to before. Mr. Yates gave the cottage to Betty as a wedding present and the sense of the wedding and the present is still in the air. They would have been married at Trinity—the stump-towered Episcopal church in the village—and had a reception at the Yacht Club. God knows when they were divorced but the sense of the miscarriage is stated clearly by the rooms although the reason is withheld. There is no trace of a man's ever having been in the place. In what rooms did the quarrel take place? What time of day was it when he packed his suit-case and left? She is a water-colorist and her childishness is displayed in the pictures that hang on every wall. The forms of naked men and women, landscapes and whales are all contained within the roundness of a young lady's penmanship. Did he reflect on her gifts as a painter, I wonder. Did she accuse him of having burdened her with children and wrecked her career as a painter. I sense his presence with passion. I somehow think he admired her gifts as a painter. I sense his presence in the back room, a slim good-looking young man, much paler than the rest of the family since he's just arrived from New York. They go surf-casting together, they lie in one another's arms but they cannot overcome the bare facts of incompatability. I think he has not remarried and lives with his oldest sister in a garden apartment in Hastings and she goes on rendering sunsets and storms at sea in the same round caligraphy with which she sends out invitations and regrets. There are no wedding presents around; no bulky lamps, Italian dinner plates and massive canape trays. Do you suppose his father was a railroad conductor or his mother a gymnastics instructor in Iowa. What else could account for the absence of wedding presents? There is, of course, a seashell collection, more ambitious than most. Sets of shells are glued to boxtops, neatly labeled and hung like pictures on the wall. Poor Henry seems to have been the least success-ful. Most of his shells have come unglued, his printing is terrible and I can hear them asking: "Can't you do better than that Henry?" I feel for little Henry, I am little Henry, sitting on the floor with a collection of shells that have lost their lustre and a box-top. "Don't spill the glue, Henry, will you?" they ask but as soon as they leave I shall.

Love,
John

Surfside

Friday

Dear Bill,

You have much more, of course than my indulgence; you have my admiration and my love. The book seemed to me an impossible task—especially when your father lay dying—and it was a great pleasure to see you ride through all the changes and obstructions. You had everything to cope with but a major fire. I think there may be some connection between writing straightaway and those glands that refresh our courage. I am much less afraid of burglars when I am busy. It is very nice to know that Bluebell is loved. Tell her that Ezekiel, her handsome brother, has been bred to Bridie, the yellow bitch Phil bought in Scotland. Ezekiel is the most beautiful and foolish of the lot. He has a heart of sweet butter and carries himself like a princely lion. When Bridie came into heat Ezekiel went on playing baseball and chasing butterflies. We were all terribly embarrassed. Jingles, the father, was then called in to romance Bridie. Ezekiel watched this performance with amazement. Jingles commerce didn't take and Ezekiel was given another chance. He then did what he had seen done with great gentleness and strength and we all feel better.

As ever,
John

My father's extremely close friendship with his father-in-law had ended, and he refused to visit the old man on his deathbed.

[Sept. 1959]
Scarborough

Tuesday

Dear Josie,

We are all well excepting for Mary's father who has been at pain of death for the last month. This means that Mary has had to speed up to New Hampshire whenever the doctors announce that he is dying. Then he rallies to everyone's astonishment, some people's embarrassment and a few cases of indignation and Mary speeds home to me; but in the meantime I seem to do an awful lot of house work and spend most of the time with Federico who is stunning but about as tractable as a cockroach. I throw in the sponge at around three or three thirty, set him down in front of the television set to watch a gun-fight and drink a little straight gin. However Mary got back last night from what may have been her last trip.

Best,
John

In 1959 Josie told my father that she was saving his letters. He never kept carbons, and was quite surprised when he found out years later that Josie had sold his letters to Yale for a good deal of money. Joe Schrank was a mutual friend. He was not thought to be particularly discerning.

Scarborough

Friday

Dear Josie,

I'm tickled to know that the letters still serve, although I always throw the damned things away myself. Yesterday's roses, yesterday's kisses, yesteryear's snows. I'm embarrassed to find out that Joe Schrank thinks I'm on the way to getting famous but I think that's what it amounts to: Joe Schrank. If I am famous why should I have a hole in the seat of my pants and not enough money for last month's bills. I needn't have a hole in the seat of my pants because I have just inherited my father-in-laws wardrobe but he is ashes, but he is ashes and I can't bring myself to open the package and try on the pants so my underwear shows which is perhaps what I am famous for.

I think It's an awfully good idea to move into town and I'm glad you're doing this. And I do hope the book moves along. I work all the time and am happy at this. . . . Ralph Ellison stopped by to say that Saul's baby is toilet-trained. My baby is not but as Mary points out this keeps our sense of analty refreshed and it was the loss of this sense, as Freud pointed out, that was the scourge of western culture. Not me. Not us.

Best,
John

Iole had married Sam Masullo, an older man who worked on the Vanderlip estate. Angelo was Sam's supervisor. Iole was the inspiration for a story titled "Clementina."

Scarborough

Friday [November 1959]

Dear Bill,

We had a storm over the week-end. Sam and Iole had a dustup on Saturday night which flared up again on Sunday. He beat her and she fled the house in a wrapper. I found her with a friend on Monday without (as she said) clothes, money or documents. Sam was jealous, she said, of our milkman. (Mary thinks the milkman is in love with her.) Iole did not dare return to her apartment because she was afraid Sam would murder her. I then checked with Angelo who said that if I thought Iole was in a bad way I should see Sam. His left ear was mutilated and he had two black eyes. The fight had begun it seems, when Iole had taunted Sam with an obscenity that translated literally,means "cabbage stalk." Angelo's wife then joined the conversation to say that, being married herself to a man of fifty-seven, she had been able to warn Iole about what to expect from a man of sixty-two. Angelo snorted and said that women had to be kept in their place. You had to show them who was boss. Victor Mazzacone was married fifty years and his wife bossed him all the time. Whenever he sat down to drink a beer or look at TV she always found some work for him to do. Last summer she made him dig a big hole in the back yard and he had a stroke and won't ever be able to work again. If you don't keep them in their place they'll kill you. I was supposed to call Iole back but I did not and when I tried to get her in the morning she had vanished into the city. Sam is back raking Mrs. Vanderlip's leaves as he has raked her leaves for the last forty-six years.

Best,
John

My father had enclosed some not-completed work. Freddie Packard was a *New Yorker* checker of notable refinement.

Scarborough

Saturday [November 17, 1959]

Dear Bill,

Yard goods and I'm afraid they're too disjointed.

Iole, Clementina, La Tata came back. First Sam came down here on Wednesday and shouted Mr. Cheeve,Mr. Cheeve under my window. I went down. It seems that she wanted two documents. In one he was to promise never to be jealous. In the other he was to give her half of all his worldly goods. He was on his way to see a lawyer and asked me to come along as interpreter. I did. "Where you from?" the lawyer asked me. "Massachusetts," I said. "I know," he said,"but where in Italy?" Do you think Freddie Packard was ever taken for a frog? Anyhow Sam was intractable and seemed a little drunk. He wanted the lawyer to bring her back altho;ugh the lawyer had no idea of where she was. On Thursday at noon Mary announced that she was off to a lunch party. The baby's food was on the back of the stove and the diapers were in the laundry. Ta ta. Off she went. I ranted so angrily and loudly at the walls and pictures that the baby got frightened and asked to be put to bed with a bottle. I did this and went over the monthly bills until dusk when Mary blew in, smelling of French cooking. I thought I was very courteous—Chesterfieldian—but I must have seemed a little sarcastic because Ben, who was practising the piano, burst into tears. Mary accused me of nagging Ben and I then began,very loudly, a dictionary of my complaints, but I had just begun when Angelo stepped in with an armful of red,white, and yellow crysanthemums. I knew he had brought the flowers as an excuse to bring some news. She's a come back, he said, she'sa come back. Mary arranged the flowers and I gave Angelo a drink and Ben went back to the Ode to Joy.

Love,<br>John

This answered a February 1960 letter from the National Institute of Arts and Letters asking for citations for Philip Roth and Norman Mailer. It was sent to Felicia Geffen, Executive Secretary.

Scarborough

The Day Before the Deadline

Dear Felicia,

To Norman Mailer, born (I don't know where) for his fine sense of the literary crises and for the nearly singular gift of substantiating his challenge to tradition (Nihilism?) with a vigerous talent.

To Philip Roth, born in Newark New Jersey, (I think). Mr. Roth has done so much to make the landscapes and the populations of his part of the world interesting and human that it is now possible to travel through Newark and the Oranges without pain. Goodbye Columbus and the other stories in his collection mark (Oh God!) the arrival of a brilliant, penetrating and undiscourageable young man.

Could I do better, dear heart, better is what I would do.

I'll say the 16th for the Grant Committee meeting. I do want to get away.

> Best,
> John

Milton Greenstein was legal counsel at *The New Yorker*. According to Bill Maxwell, Greenstein once said that no free-lance writer should own property. "I tactlessly repeated this remark to your father," said Bill, "and it rankled."

Dear Bill,

We are in the process ( I think) of buying a house and I suppose you ought to be the first to know. I've told the Knickerbocker Mortgage Company & Bank to call the magazine and I hope Milton won't wash his hands of me. There were two houses up for consideration. One was a very small house in the slums of Sparta for eighteen thousand, occupied by two retired English servants. The lady had fine grey eyes, her hair dressed with a barrett, much as it must have been dressed in the midlands fifty years ago. She was in a wheel-chair. Her husband had a red face and rather loose false teeth. In the first year we bought this house—he said—I struck my head on a beam and was in bed with brain fever for two years, Mother got a boil on her spine and lost the use of her legs and the baby died of meningitis. Do you think I should have bought that house? I suppose Milton would. The second costs thirty-seven thousand and belongs to an exploded public relations man. It has some fine trees, a brook, a stately living-room and enough bedrooms for us but not enough for Mary's sister to come and stay. I shall buy it.

The decision was quite difficult to make. Should we ally ourselves with the retired servant class or the ruins of a career in public relations. But the slums of Sparta will only get slummier and poor Picci is just begining his life. I was so worried on Saturday night that I had a fever and the following dreams. In the first the Duchess of Devonshire was reading her verse to a group of Princeton undergraduates at the Ivy Club. She had a fine fresh skin, light brown hair but her right eye was alas, much smaller than her left. Her poetry was awful and one of the young men, to avoid saying so, asked her grace to tell them about her part in the war. "The war," she said, "was dreadful. Breakfast was terribly early and there was never any bacon. Lunch was a farce. There was so little for tea that I seldom bothered to go down and dinner was invariably a disappointment." The second dream involved the commencement of an enormous archeological expedition, launched on barges. The first three barges held friends of mine and the fourth the public address system said: "And now last, but not least, that sterling young man who, but for an accident of birth would today be President of the United States. THE KING OF SWEDEN." The king of Sweden appeared, wearing spectacles and carrying a placcard that said:"Tea with lemon free for people over fifty." I woke Mary and told her we would buy the house.

Love,
John

Scarborough
Monday

Dear Josie,

. . . We are trying to buy a house which seems a long chance to take but I may as well take it. The house is near here but has a peculiar power over us both,partly I think because it resembles your place. It is stone, not terribly big, built against the side of a hill with a brook and some weeping willows below the front porch. I am working on the novel,a play, five stories and a speech to be delivered in San Francisco on the 20th but much of the time I just sit in front of the typewriter and count the cigaret butts in the ash tray.

. . . I am rereading Agee's book on the sharecroppers for the first time since 41. Jim and I were friends but never very good friends but the fact that I can't anylonger anticipate hearing his voice gives the book a radiance and a velocity that I never found there before. I think it's terrific. I went up to Yaddo for the annual meeting. . . . It is all the same—the fine air, the broad views, the shadowy figures of poets and painters crashing into the underbrush at the sound of a strange footstep. Elizabeth has aged not at all and looked quite handsome. I only stayed the day and came home Sunday morning.

Mary joins in sending our affectionate best,

As ever,
John

Scarborough

September 16th [1960]

Dear Malcolm,

I would of course be happy to sponsor you for a Guggenheim. I would be honored if the word didn't seem too heavy to use with an old friend.

Our big news, our only news is that we are buying a house and how strange it seems. Mary has been looking at houses for five years. She has seemed possessed and driven. She reads the real estate news every night. At least three afternoons a week she tosses the baby into the car and goes off to poke through some manor or cottage that the owners can no longer afford to maintain. Three weeks ago she found a stone house in a valley behind Ossining that she claims to have seen in her dreams. It is a beautiful house with a brook and large trees. I went to the bank for a mortgage but the bankers were sulky, suspicious, disrespectful and rude. Then one of our rich neighbors offered to underwrite the folly and all I have to do now is to write a short story a week for the next twenty years and turn out plays and novels in the evenings; and having been exposed all my life to the possibility of emotional disaster I now find myself exposed to the possibility of financial catastrophe. But it is exciting to think of having a place of our own. Neither of us sleep much these days. I scythe the orchard—at three in the morning—and Mary tosses and turns as she rearranges the furniture.

You sound tired in your lettter and I do hope you'll feel better and stronger. I go out to San Francisco on the 20th for Esquire and will speak on The Death of The Short Story and model sports coats. I am continuously on view until the 23rd when I think I will be ready to come home. Harpers brings out SOME PEOPLE PLACES AND THINGS THAT WILL NOT APPEAR IN MY NEXT NOVEL in March and the novel itself goes on. It's never quite what I want but there are

always two or three days in the week when I think I can bring it off
and that's a pleasant feeling. My best love to Muriel.

As ever,
John

A description of his room at Yaddo.

Yaddo [1960]

Monday
3 pm

Dear Bill,

Catalogue of room #6. 20 windows. (13 leaded). Pink velvet rug.
Much mended but pretty. Overhead one ecclisiastical vigil light, un-
lighted. On the window-sill two vases marked IHS. On the bookshelf
one marble vase of Bacchus with grapes in a bronze stand of goat's feet
with the pine cone as a syumbol of immortality. On the next shelf
Minerva in marble with a staff, serpent and helmet. Next a photograph
of Queen Elizabeth of Rumania. She is in deep mourning and stands in
a forest. She has written: "My trees whisper to me of all those I have
loved." Next a gilt statue called Le Jour Naissant. Le Jour is a nude
male holding a torch and a lyre. Next les Champs Elysees, I think.
Anyhow Homer, Sappho, Orpheus, Dante et all. They all wear laurel
and seem happy. Next a Sienese panel of the Annunciation. Next a prie
Dieu and a vast chair ornamented with the cross. Then one marble
putto under a Hudson River landscape of four cows hock-deep in a
mountain pool. One upright piano. Some Merry Andrew has completed
the iconography by hanging a horseshoe over one of the pink tiffany
lamps of which there are 7.

The cast: 1 Hungarian chemist turned novelist. Astrid and Bob
Coates. 1 young poet from Cambridge who has the dazed and disheveled look of someone recently fired from a cannon. Ruth X, a novelist
who wears black shoes, leotards, a black shirt and sweater. This is all
covered with lint. She keeps her hair behind her ears. Also old Elizabeth Sparhawk-Jones who wears a shakko to dinner and JC who, considering how his heart leaps at the thought of his sons seems unable to
convert this energy to the work at hand. The light is much finer than
the light in the valley; the blues at this hour an octave deeper.

Best,
John

Leonard Field was a friend my father and John Weaver shared from the Signal Corps. I recall Brendan Behan as hugely jolly and hugely fat. He was wearing swimming trunks when I met him and had a cigar in his mouth and a navel that seemed almost as black and stuck out almost as far as the cigar. When I read *Borstal Boy*, I was particularly struck with the scene in which the lean, young Behan looks down at his slim torso and wonders idly what it would be like to be overweight. Leonard Field was producing a play by Behan. Vincent owns Sardi's; Leonard Lyons was a gossip columnist. Ginny was Lennie Field's wife, and Mrs. Vanderlip was the woman who owned the house we rented.

Scarborough

Some Tuesday

Dear John,

I saw Lennie last week for the first time I think since spring and he is fine. We had lunch with Behan and I'm sure the show will be a great sucess because why otherwise should Vincent come to the table practically on his hands and knees and why should Lennie Lyons embrace me? Also Behan had canneloni (What the fuck, he asked, is this fucking canneloni) and they gave him a special one, full of minced chicken, much better than anything we got. On Saturday Ginny brought Behan out for a swim. Now that I'm off the sauce—he said—I'm much more interested in farney. What is farney—asked Mrs. Vanderlip. Farney, Mam,said Behan, is an abbreviation for farnacation. I like him tremendously and I'm sure the play will be a great success. Lennie's sterling qualities were never so apparent. He is as kind, unhurried and pleasant as ever.

Mary and I are trying to buy a house which is a source of tension and also very embarrassing because no bank will give me a mortgage. The reasons are that I am self-employed or unemployed and also that I am old. The house is beautiful, the price is modest but the banks are cruel . . . .

John

My father went to Hollywood for a couple of brief stints and he did some writing for Twentieth Century–Fox. Jerry Wald was his contact out there. One of his projects was an adaptation of the D. H. Lawrence novel *The Lost*

*Girl*. John Weaver and his wife, Harriet, were the chief port of call when my father went to Los Angeles.

Twentieth Century-Fox [1960]
Beverly Hills, california

Dear Bill,

Here I am and feeling quite shook-up. I have a hotel apartment with a broad view of Los Angeles, a well-furnished living room with a water-cooler in the corner. Last night I walked up to the Weavers and was tremendously moved by the noise Harriet made opening a bureau and flushing the toilet. I am somewhat homesick. . . . My office is not at all luxurious. It is like an old bath-house at the edge of the lot. There are three telephones with a complicated system of push-buttons that I do not understand and this makes it almost impossible for anyone to reach me. Also there is no men's room in the office so that when people do get to me they find me quite jumpy. My secretary has just arrived wearing a reddish sack with beads. She is very genteel and I can think of nothing for her to do but I suppose she can answer the telephone. I don't seem to have anything to do myself.

It all seems to have been put down somewhere; the magnification of all our vices, most of our infirmities and some of our vitality. There is a revolving ten foot papier-mache nude outside my bedroom window and beyond her an enormous image of a man offering me a glass of beer. In the room next to mine there seems to be a recluse, a woman I trust, who plays a music box in the evenings. It can be heard quite clearly through the wall. The weather is sunny but quite cool and roses are in bloom. I have rented a white car and drive around in this; and God willing I shall be home by Christmas.

John

We bought the house on Cedar Lane in Ossining for $37,500. We moved in at the beginning of 1961. His fourth collection of stories, *Some People, Places and Things That Will Not Appear in My Next Novel* (Harper & Row), was published in March of that year. He'd been unhappy with the fact that he'd had to sell early versions of parts of *The Wapshot Chronicle* as stories in order to stay afloat financially. Part of the reason for this unhappiness doubtless had to do with the fact that when he had sold parts of a book as stories, it became much easier for the critics to say that the novel didn't hold together.

JOHN CHEEVER<br>Cedar Lane<br>Ossining, New York

Tuesday

Dear Bill,

. . . If I don't see you before I leave there are some deletions I would like made in Marito. One is the description of his wife adressing fund-raising literature. I seem to have ground this axe too often. I think it's mentioned twice but it comes out easily. The other is to simplify the lines spoken by his mistress. She simply says: "I never wear perfume when I'm going to make love." No more. And then:"Someday I'm going to write everything I know about men on a piece of paper and burn it in the fireplace." Then he says you don't have a fireplace.

Susie is home from college and the world appears to be at her feet. It's a marvelous thing to see. However this leaves me with no place to work and I've bought a small tent where this is being written. It's quite dark but for a soft green light, the color of artificial lime-drink. Everything gets wet during the night. Only Mary and I are going to Italy and our address will be c/o Alan Moorehead, Porto Ercole, Provinncia di Grossetto. . . .

Best,
John

The C's were the Cass Canfields. Cass Canfield was Chairman of the Board at Harper & Row. Sally Swope is an old friend of the family. We rented her house in Wauwinet on Nantucket.

Monday

Dear Bill,

The roses were beautiful; still are. Mrs. C, bending her long neck to sniff them asked:"And these too (chew, she said) No, I said. They come from Bill Maxwell's. It all passed pleasantly although we wished you and Emmy had been here and I'm still wondering how I could have persuaded you to return. I took them(as I had planned) up the outside stairs to the library. They exchanged several they've-bitten-off-more-than-they-can-chew looks. Susie curtseyed deeply to Mrs. C. Mrs. C positively beamed. the dinner was excellent but Iole took all the coffee upstairs so the gentlemen had no chance to pump ship. Halfway through the evening this plainly began to prey on Sally Swope's mind. Her old father has been visiting and I think this may have had something to do with her behavior. Anyhow she said that Mr. C. must see our dressing room. She infected me with her anxiety and both of us, feeling that he must be about to burst, got him out of his comfortable chair and rushed him towards the toilet. He admired the dressing room and then slipped out of Sally's hands and quick-stepped back into the library. A pleasant rain fell throughout.

I'm enclosing the galleys with two deletions and two ammendments. Please come and see us again.

Best,<br>John

The same dinner party was also reported to the Boyers in a letter written over Cassie's signature.

Dear Zeke,
    It was very good to hear from you. you will never know how much yr letters mean to me now that i am nearing the end of my journey. oh i know you will say no mother dere, no, no, no, but the truth is yr old mother has got so weak in these last months that she can no longer raise herself up to the lid of an average-sized garbage pail. uncle cabot is very lame and cousin delilah has mange.
    daisy maxwell came to visit. She is yellow all over and comitted several discourtieses that i do not choose to describe. the old fool got smeared on tuesday and invited his publisher to dinner. this publisher is a rich old man who is named cassio and so naturally there were a lot of mix-ups such as when the old fool would shout: cassio, get your face out of the cracker dish or cassio, shut up. mrs. swope was there and she giggled. they had pasta to eat and some kind of meat with sauce that did not agree with me. pfffrrt, pffrt all night long. i simply didn't shut my eyes once.

please try to enjoy yourself and try not to let the thought of your lonely impoverished and enfeebled old mother come between yourself and your happiness. look away from the body into truth and light.

yr loving
Mother

The next two letters record the first real dispute my father had with Bill Maxwell. He'd submitted "The Brigadier and the Golf Widow." Bill told me that the story had two endings. He said he tried a cut to see how that worked. My father was in the city that day, visiting the offices of *The New Yorker,* and he saw the truncated story on a desk and assumed that it had been drastically changed without his permission. At first my father thought that he could go along with the change, but he phoned Bill in a fury that night and the story was run at full length. The first letter below was written to John Weaver several weeks after the second letter below. I've reversed the order because the version he gave Weaver was so much more complete.

[December 5, 1961]

Dear John,

I'm very glad you liked the story and there was a story within the story. When I went in to correct galleys I found that the story had been cut in half and was told that Mr. Shawn wanted it this way. I saw trouble ahead and told Bill I'm meet him at the club in half an hour and had a couple of drinks. I kept the conversation,during lunch, on the subject of his wife and children but when we said goodbye he asked about the cut. "Do anything you want," I said and walked over to the station where I bought a copy of Life in which J. D. Salinger was compared to William Blake, Ludwig von Beethoven and William Shakespeare. I went into a slow burn which didn't erupt until nine that evening when I telephoned Bill who happened to be entertaining Elizabeth Bowen and Eudora Welty. "You cut that story," I yelled,"and I'll never write another story for your or anybody else. You can get that Godamned sixth-rate Salinger to write your Godamned short stories but don't expect anything more out of me. If you want to slam a door on somebody's genitals find yourself another victim. Etc." Anyhow the

magazine had gone to press and they had to remake the whole back of
the book and stay up all night but they ran it without the cut.

Best,
John


Monday

Dear Bill,

I had your letter after seeing you and perhaps I should explain my
reference or whatever to Salinger. It was merely the coincidence, prov-
idential as I see it now, of reading a piece in which Salinger was
compared to Blake, Beethoven and Shakespeare a half hour after my
own judgements and gifts had been seriously challenged. I admire
Salinger, of course, and I think I know where his giftedness lies and
how rare it is. Another reason for my irritability is the fact that I am
never content with my own work; that it never quite comes up to the
world as I see it. This is not to say that I despair of succeeding; I think
I may—but I am touchy.

Best,
John


This is Bill Maxwell's recollection. "I thought the story had two endings,
one on top of the other, like the coda of a Beethoven symphony. I often put
a story in working proof, which meant that it didn't go to Mr. Shawn or the
proofreader until something had been fixed. That's what happened with
"The Brigadier and the Golf Widow." I left off the second ending so that
your father could see how it would read in print (which often looks different from the manuscript). It wasn't about to go to press. It wasn't scheduled.
It was a working proof, for him to consider. When he saw it he got excited
and I had Hell's own time calming him down. In fact I didn't, it would
appear from the correspondence. I don't remember that he ever called me
up about it. At different times Elizabeth Bowen and Eudora Welty have
been in our house in Yorktown, but never together. The story was run as
he wanted it."


My father used to give people money. He gave it to the members of his
family, of course, but he also gave it to friends. When he knew of a young
writer in need, or an old writer in need, and he had the money to give, he
gave it. Josie was often in real need, and had asked for some money and

gotten it. One of the many extraordinarily impressive things about Josie was that she just kept on writing. She had some successes but also a great many disappointments, and so found herself as a middle-aged woman without the money to pay her electric bill. But she kept on writing.

Cedar Lane

Friday

Dear Josie,

Don't give it a thought. I'm glad you asked and having some experience in this field I know how difficult it is. I am very generous between three and four in the morning. I plan to set up my brother in an advertising agency in Denver, install a vast bathroom in your house and send the local music teacher through Juillard and buy a pipe-organ for Yaddo. But at seven when my feet hit the floor I get very miserly and squeal like a pig at the thought of parting with a nickle.

The money of course is pleasant and having been near-broke for most of my life it involves a change of pace but nothing serious. I haven't been taxed yet and I don't know what will be left but there will be enough for me to write a novel without having to publish a word in advance.

Best,

John

My father was eager to have Josie see the house in Ossining. She'd visited us soon after we'd moved into the rental in Scarborough, and he explained to me that while he adored Josie, "It is my considered opinion that she has some of the powers of a witch." If she spent the night, he thought, and burned something in the oven, any unhappy spirits inhabiting our new house would be persuaded to leave.

Josie said she'd love to come, but that she had this wonderful cat, and for some reason she couldn't keep him, and maybe we could keep. Josie came. She brought a coal-black cat, and left.

The cat had been living with Josie and her friend Elizabeth Pollet for some time. Elizabeth Pollet had been married to the poet Delmore Schwartz, so my father named the cat Delmore. He would claim afterward that Delmore had been described as a kitten. I don't know if this is true, but he was definitely not a kitten, in fact there was some question as to whether he ever had *been* a kitten. He was then a fully grown male with bald patches between his ears and his eyes. He hid under a bureau in my sister's room for a few days, and then he came out and began to squirt the walls. A veterinarian was consulted, and it was suggested that Delmore be "fixed." "If the knife should slip," my father told the vet, "there would be no harsh recriminations."

Delmore Schwartz stopped squirting the walls, but he still didn't fit in. There was so much ill feeling about the treatment of Josie's darling that she stopped speaking to my father, and he stopped speaking to her. When the correspondence was revived a couple of years later, my father reported that Delmore had voted for Goldwater. Josie said that the cat she knew would never have voted for Goldwater, that the cat she knew would have his balls cut off before he voted for Goldwater. She won that argument because Delmore had had his balls cut off.

[December 6, 1963; Josie's date]

Cedar Lane

Ossining

Some Friday

Dear Josie,

It's been years since we had anything but the most sketchy communication. . . . I've long since owed you an account of the destiny of your cat and here we go.

The cat, after your leaving him, seemed not certain of his character or his place and we changed his name to Delmore which immediately made him more vivid. The first sign of his vividness came when he dumped a load in a Kleenex box while I was suffering from a cold. During a paroxysim of sneezing I grabbed for some kleenex. I shall not overlook my own failures in this tale but when I got the cat shit off my face and the ceiling I took Delmore to the kitchen door and drop-kicked him into the clothesyard. This was an intolerable cruelty and I have not yet been forgiven. He is not a forgiving cat. Indeed he is proud. Spring came on then and as I was about to remove the clear glass storm window from Fred's room, Delmore, thinking the window to be open, hurled himself against the glass. This hurt his nose and his psyche badly. Mary and the children then went to the Mountains and I spent a reasonably happy summer cooking for Delmore. The next eventfulness came on Thanksgiving. When the family had gathered for dinner and I was about to carve the turkey there came a strangling noise from the bathroom. I ran there and found Delmore sitting in the toilet, neck-deep in cold water and very sore. I got him out and dried him with towels but there was no forgiveness. Shortly after Christmas a Hollywood writer and his wife came to lunch. My usual salutation to Delmore is: Up your's, and when the lady heard me say this she scorned me and gathered Delmore to her breasts. Delmore, in a flash, started to unscrew her right eyeball and the lady, trying to separate herself from Delmore lost a big piece of an Italian dress she was wearing which Mary said cost $250.00. This was not held against Delmore and a few days later when we had a skating party I urged Delmore to come to the pond with us. He seemed pleased and frisked along like a family-loving cat but at that moment a little wind came from the northeast and spilled the snow off a hemlock onto Delmore. he gave me a dirty look, went back to the house and dumped another load int the kleenex box. This time he got the cleaning-woman and they remain unfriendly.

This is not meant at all to be a rancorous account and I think Delmore enjoys himself. I have been accused of cruelty and a woman named Ruth Hershberger keeps writing Elizabeth Pollet, telling her to take the cat away from me, but Delmore contributes a dynamic to all our relationships. People who dislike me go directly to his side and he is, thus, a peace-maker. He loves to play with toilet paper. He does not like catnip mice. He does not kill song birds. In the spring the rabbits chase him around the lawn but they leave after the lettuce has been eaten and he has the terrace pretty much to himself. He is very fat these days and his step, Carl Sandburg not withstanding, sounds more like that of a barefoot middle-aged man on his way to the toilet than the settling in of a winter fog but he has his role and we all respect it and here endeth my report on Delmore the cat.

I hope all is well with you. Mary teaches, I write, the children go to various schools and all is well.

Best,
John

In late 1963 he sent Malcolm a copy of *The Wapshot Scandal*. Malcolm's pinewoods were famous for their tidiness.

Cedar Lane [1963]

Ossining

Friday

Dear Malcolm,

It was very good of you to call and it was because you have always been so magnanimous that I worried. I was afraid you wouldn't like the book and would find it embarrassing to say so. Also my pine copse is in terrible shape and I felt that I had failed all down the line.

My love to Muriel,

As ever,

John

Cedar Lane

Saturday

Dear Malcolm,

I was very sorry to hear that you've been under the weather; but this doesn't seem to have eclipsed your generosity and I am very grateful to you. How I wish the book had been massive and redoubtable. Anyhow it's behind me and I hope I can go on to something better. I have never suffered so galling and prolonged a lack of self-confidence over any piece of work; and I seem, in the last three years, to have been faced with a series of interruptions and tasks from which I've been slow to rally. These interruptions are never more grave, for example, than the morning Ben knocked lightly on my door and said:"I'm sorry to bother you,Daddy,but my cock is stuck in a zipper." I have been lucky,I think, in leading a life that has arranged itself around me eventfully but when I've removed the zipper I can't always get back to work.

My love to Muriel and I hope to see you both soon. If you're ever free for lunch in town I'd love to come in. You've been very helpful over all these years.

As ever,

John

I came home from school one afternoon to find a tall, slender Australian in a suit and vest attempting cartwheels on the lower lawn. My father was standing off to one side watching. While himself full of what reviewers liked to call "a childlike sense of wonder," my father was often harsh when other men violated his own curious sense of decorum, and I remember thinking, "Daddy isn't going to like this guy." But when Alwyn Lee left, there was no critique, and I was astounded. Alwyn wrote the *Time* cover story that ran in March of 1964.

In this letter to Malcolm Cowley, Alwyn was identified simply as editor A. Actually, we knew that Alwyn was going to accompany us to Stowe, and I believe *Time* paid for the trip. I don't think there was anything sinister or self-serving about this deception; it just made for a better letter.

The collection he mentioned was *The Brigadier and the Golf Widow* (Harper & Row, 1964).

> John Cheever [1964]
> Cedar Lane
> Ossining, New York
>
> Tuesday

Dear Malcolm,

I wouldn't have had much of a career without you and any such as it's been would have been intolerable without your common sense and your magnaminity. The first I knew of TIME was when a painter called from Pittsburgh to say that he was flying east to do my portrait. Ben and I took the next train to Stowe. Aboard the train was a TIME editor and a research girl. They followed me up and down the mountains asking how tall my mother was. When I returned from Stowe a second editor was waiting here and the painter was working on the picture of an old shirt of mine, draped over a chair back. Now it appears that editor A—who is the senior—plans to do a serious and a charitable account. Editor B wants to poleaxe me. Editor A has a bad pancreas and should his wits or his organs fail him the job and the story will go to editor B. Editor B has been asking indecent questions and I told him to leave the house. It was raining. He got very wet going from the door to his car. He was vindicitive. I keep telling myself that they can do me no good and they can do me no harm and it's better this way than hiding in the bathroom like Salinger who never seemed to find his way out.

All is well here although I'm finding it difficult to get back to work. A collection of stories will come out in the fall and I like these better

than the novel. I hope to take Mary to California in April and if the
TIME story is ever published I will go back to Italy until this blows
over. My love to you both.

John


John Cheever [1964]
Cedar Lane
Ossining, New York

Dear Malcolm,

The TIME grilling has been unfunny but there was one funny story.
Sally Ziegler, a small-town Georgian who lives in the cottage on the
hill, has been preparing herself for the TIME interview for a month.
On Friday the doorbell rang and she let the man in. "I don't approve
of this kind of sneaky journalism," she said, "but the truth is that I
know a lot about him because I can see him from my windows. I mean
to say that I know he's a very heavy drinker and I often see him out
there at twelve o'clock noon with a martini cocktail in his hand. And
he sometimes chases his wife through the orchard in full view of my
children. And he almost never wears his bathing-suit when he goes
swimming and I've always thought there was something peculiar about
men who go swimming without their bathing-suits. But as I say I don't
approve of this kind of gossip and if you'll ask me some suitable questions about his habits I'll try to answer them to the best of my ability."
Then the man said:"Lady, I'm your Fuller Brush representative."

As ever,
John


The *Time* story, titled "Ovid in Ossining," was not unflattering. Nor—
and I think my father would have been more sensitive on this point—was
it uninteresting. In it Alwyn made much of the moral foundation of the
work. "The first Cheever in America," he wrote, "was a Puritan schoolmaster
who was eulogized by Cotton Mather for 'his untiring abjuration of the
devil' and who believed that 'man is full of misery and all earthly beauty is
lustful and corrupt.' " While making it clear that John Cheever's vision of
the world was more elastic and more cheerful, Alwyn also wrote that "the
easygoing realism that accepts wife-swapping or any impiety of evaded
obligation with a sociological shrug enrages him, for at bottom he is a New
England moralist."

Under a subhead that described my father as "The Monogamist," *Time* went on to report that "the Cheever marriage is a subject of more than ordinary interest to their friends, seeing that the bulk of Cheever's work concerns somehow a vexation or a crisis in relations between husband and wife. The heart of the matter is probably best deduced from the fact that John Cheever, almost alone in the field of modern fiction, is one who celebrates the glories and delights of monogamy." Of course his fiction also celebrated the glories and delights of adultery, but I wouldn't have dared to bring that up in 1964 either.

The piece ended on a note that sounds as true to me today as it did then.

Ultimately Cheever tries to "celebrate a world that lies spread out around us like a bewildering and stupendous dream." Says he: "One has an impulse to bring glad tidings to someone. My sense of literature is a sense of giving not diminishment. I know almost no pleasure greater than having a piece of fiction draw together disparate incidents so that they relate to one another and confirm that feeling that life itself is a creative process, that one thing is put purposefully upon another, that what is lost in one encounter is replenished in the next, and that we possess some power to make sense of what takes place."

# RUSSIA

* * *

In the fall of 1964 my father went to Russia for just over a month as part of a cultural exchange program. For a part of that time he traveled with John and Mary Updike. He met and came to admire the Russian poet Yevtushenko. In Russia he also met his translator, Tanya Litvinov. Tanya's father, Maksim Litvinov, was Stalin's foreign minister before World War II. Litvinov was the man who staked his reputation on an anti-Nazi alliance joining Russia and the Western world. He was replaced by Vyacheslav Molotov. Molotov helped negotiate the infamous nonaggression pact between Stalin and Hitler. Tanya's mother, Ivy, wrote stories for *The New Yorker*. My father's friendship with Tanya lasted the rest of his life.

John Cheever
Cedar Lane [1964]
Ossining, New York

November16th

Dear Tanya,

The names of my children are Susan Liley Cheever, Benjamin Hale Cheever and Federico who was born in Rome. The black dog is named Casseopea and the yellow bitch is scotch and named Flora MacDonald. It will surely be much less than four years before I return to Russia. The pleasure and relief a luxury-loving Westerner is supposed to experience upon leaving Moscow for Amsterdam, missed me completely. I sat very glumly in the elegant airport there, drinking gin and tonic and wishing I was back in Moscow. I love your country and I love your people. . . .

I found Berlin depressing and flew home from there. Mary looked lovely and was indeed lovely and Ben was home from school for the weekend. The Russian trip was so swift and of such emotional power that I still feel suspended between two worlds. . . . I am convinced that I will someday see you running up the garden stairs. Nothing untoward has happened excepting in church on Sunday where I went for Holy Communion. After the Agnus Dei I had a paroxysim of coughing and was unable to take the sacrament. "He's been to Russia," someone said, and so I have.

Love,
John

This is a talk he gave later about his trip to Russia. He spoke at the National Institute of Arts and Letters.

My reading knowledge of Russian is confined to restaurant menus, my conversational vocabulary in Russia contains less than a hundred words, and my travels in Russia lasted a little over a month, so I am no more competent to speak of that vast nation and its people than any other foot-sore tourist.

I was briefed for my trip by the State Department at a time when anti-communism seemed learned by rote and to have no relationship to change or the force of events. I was told that my liberty would be in danger, that my possessions would be rifled, my conversations bugged, and my walks shadowed. Nothing of the sort happened. A delegation of writers met me at the airport and I have never seen such affectionate, candid, and impetuous people. There was no unpleasantness of any sort and only once did I apprehend any. This was in Tibilisi late one night, when a Ukranian with whom I was traveling came to my hotel room on what he said was an unpleasant mission. "I am sorry to have to be the one to tell you this," he said,"but you need a haircut."

On our last day in Moscow—I was traveling with John and Mary Updike—Yevtushenko called and asked if he could come to the hotel at two. I said yes, not knowing whether or not he expected lunch since the Russians seem not to have worked out any discernable schedule for eating. He came in his best suit, wearing a salt and pepper topcoat that he must have bought abroad.

"I have come to give you a present,"he said.

"Yevgeney," I said, "I don't want a present. I leave for West Berlin tomorrow morning. I'm packing my suitcase. I have four fur hats, two ikons, and I've had to throw out all the Georgian drinking horns."

He said,"No, no, this is nothing you take with you. This is something special."

We got into his car and drove out of Moscow through the housing developments into a sort of slum and ran up some stairs in a tenement, an old-fashioned brick tenement where I was introduced to an old lady and a young man and his wife and children and taken into a small living room that was used as a studio. There were then presented twelve of what struck me as very good paintings,very independent paintings and I said the polite and awkward things one says on seeing paintings, but I thought it very good painting—brilliant,progressive, and heretical. We then left the flat and ran down the stairs. Yevgeney is a great runner. Then he exclaimed—throwing out his right hand as he does on-stage: "So! He cannot show his painting. He cannot sell his painting. He cannot discuss his painting. My present to you is the invincibility of his painting."

December 14 [1964]

Dear Josie,

I went to Russia. The Soviet writers invited me and off I went. I expect the people have not changed greatly since you were there and it is the people I remember most clearly and cannot in fact forget. It is difficult to fall in love with a population of over two hundred million and it is very embarrassing for the State Department but that's what I seem to have done.

Best,
John

This was my father's response when Helen Puner, a neighbor and friend, wrote to congratulate him on the Howells Medal. Lewis Mumford is the sociologist and critic. Saul is Saul Bellow. Katherine Anne is Katherine Anne Porter.

John Cheever
Cedar Lane
Ossining, N.Y.

Friday

Dear Helen,

It seems inconclusive. Mine says 14k on the edge and I was told it would raise four hundred at any pawn shop but it weighs a pound and shouldn't a pound of gold bring more? It is nicely engraved with a portrait of Howells on one side and palms and laurels on the reverse. If it should be dross it would be suitable. Firstly I got The Letter, The Black Spot from Mumford. I drafted a letter, oh very gracefully, regretting the honor and showed this to Mary. She said I had to take it. I asked Art Spear. He said I had to take it. Then I had lunch with Ralph Ellison and asked him if he knew what sonofabitch had put me up for it. He said angrily, that it was he and that it had been uphill work. Louis Kronenberger abstained. Everybody else wanted to give it to Saul except Glenway Wescott who had promised it to Katherine Anne. She wanted it. She's crazy about jewelry. The reason Ralph insisted that I get it was because when Ralph and Saul lived together in Tivoli Saul, stepping out onto his terrace one morning, slipped and fell into a pile of dogshit. He asked Ralph if he couldn't train his dog. Ralph said that Saul didn't understand. The only dogs Saul had ever owned were mongrels. Ralph's dog was a chien du race and it was their custom to shit on terraces. A bitter quarrel ensued. Saul's tongue is longer and sharper than Ralph's and Ralph evened things up by getting me the medal. I keep it in the piano bench.

Best,
John

Elephant is Tanya's husband. Kornei Chukovsky helped introduce my father's writing to the Russian public. He was a distinguished literary figure in Russia, and when my father visited they met and took an immediate liking to each other.

May first

Dear Tanya,

John Hersey did write A Bell for Adano and Hiroshima; and He has a long Lincolnesque neck and long arms. He is, in the best sense, a most acutely conscientious man, raised in China, the son of a missionary and one of a few American writers who extends his responsibilities beyond literature. He was married for years to a wealthy woman who appeared to be beautiful until she turned thirty whereupon it developed that she was a shrew. He then married Barbara Adams who is lovely, pure-hearted and lithe. They have a young child and Barbara can't travel.

We have a long, vehement and marvelous spring here; the trees full of colored song birds, the brook full of water, the garden of flowers and the rivers (sometimes) with fish. There is a large white magnolia in front of the house which is the first to bloom followed by plums, apples, cherries and a pre-Cambrian tree called Dogwood of which we have a forest. In this part of the world we go in heavily for the preservation and encouragement of song-birds and they make a great din.

. . . We are all wet. We visited Ben at his school last weekend and saw a LaCrosse game. This is a marvelous sport invented by the Indians. The school is small, a little like one of the English public schools, a definite rear-guard action on the part of the American upper-class but the playing fields are green, the trees are massive, the voices of the ladies are musical the food is ghastly and the boys are privileged and while it may be a scene from the past, it is a charming scene. Ben, I'm happy to say, does not take it seriously. Susie, at the other end of things, will teach at a Negro University in Alabama this summer. My best to Elephant and Kornei.

Luv,
John


Frederick Exley and my father began a correspondence in the 1960s. The dog-raising Boyers owned the place on Whiskey Island. My father admired Exley's writing.

John Cheever
Cedar Lane
Ossining, N.Y.

June first [1965]

Dear Mr. Exley,

That was a very pleasant letter and if you're ever in the neighborhood please call. I would be happy to give you several drinks. The literary kingdom is not as peaceable as one would hope. I claim fatuously, to be an innocent, concerned only with the General Welfare and in fact my admiration for Saul's work is genuine; but Updike,whom I know to be a brilliant man,traveled with me in Russia last autumn and I would go to considerable expense and inconvenience to avoid his company. I think his magnaminity specious and his work seems motivated by covetousness,exhibitionism and a stony heart. I put all this down to show how truly innocent and generous I am. Bellow's mind is, of course, erudite, bellicose and agile and as a companion I find him one of the most difficult of men to part with.

I spend a few weekends each year on an island called Whisky off the town of Clayton and I do know the river. My difficulty on Whisky is that I don't play tennis and I find it extremely painful to overhear the sounds and voices of a game I cannot play. I feel like some damp-souled child, remanded to the edges of the playing field and I detest the feeling. My host, who does not understand, keeps giving me a bottle of whisky and a novel by Louis Auchencloss and urging me to enjoy myself while he cleans up the men's doubles. . . .

With every good wish to you,
John Cheever

Bibber is the sick little boy who is left alone in the house while his mother testifies before the highway commission in "An Educated American Woman," *The New Yorker*, November 2, 1963. He comes down with pneumonia and dies.

June second [1965]

Dear Tanya,

No one likes Bibber's demise but that was the way it was written and I think that's the way it should stay. I couldn't possibly cope with her emotions on remembering her only son and so I moved the scene to Florence. It comes down, I guess, to an autobiographical grudge. When I was eleven I was attacked by a virulent strain of tuberculosis. A few days after the crisis my mother covered me with a blanket, gave me a pile of clean rags in which I might bleed and went off to chairman some committee for the General Welfare. As a healthy man I expect I should be grateful to be alive and to have had so conscientious a parent; but what I would like to forget is the empty house and the fear of death.

. . . The President of the United States has invited me to dine with him on Tuesday. I'm utterly bewildered by this. Susie thinks it's all a terrible mistake. I expect I'll find the Updikes there. He has some assinine poems on Russian cities in the last New Yorker. It rains and rains and this makes me very happy.

Love,
John

John Cheever
Cedar Lane
Ossining, N.Y.

Monday [June 1965]

Dear Mr. Exley,

Russia I'll talk about; in fact I can't be stopped. It begins with a rainy night in Moscow, sweeps down through the Crimea and includes a fifteen minute impersonation of Yevtushenko. Updike and I spend most of our time back-biting one another. I find him very arrogant but my daughter tells me that I'm arrogant. We dined together at the White

House last Tuesday and I did everything short of putting a cherry bomb in his bug juice. It made me feel great. I'll talk about Russia but I don't seem able to talk about the books without intense discomfort. As I tried to explain to my wife last night the image of the runner, the swimmer is my best sense of things. I am conspicuously disinterested in where I've been and feel that a hint of self-consciousness about the work would bring it down in a heap. There are no books of mine in this house. This is not modesty; it is commonsense.

. . . Auchincloss is rather a spinster and knows as much. It is a most unfortunate attitude. He was also at the White House. So was O'Hara and Jim Bradley and Stan Musial and Marianne Moore. We had plenty of cocktails but bug juice with the buffet supper. Coming in late last night I opened the ice-box and grabbed a piece of cold meat, swallowing a false tooth which included a plastic backside and two sharp hooks. Neither the doctor nor the dentist (A Watertown boy) are expected in their offices until tomorrow, but noon is approaching and I seem to be experiencing no more than the customary anguish of an overcast Monday. I keep telling myself that I am rich, beloved by many passionate and exceptionally beautiful women, the owner of an 18th century stone house and a brace of faithful Labrador retrievers, the father of three comely and brilliant children and a frequent guest at the White House. How could such a paragon be felled by a false tooth?

                                                                    Yours,
                                                                    John Cheever

It is Tuesday; and I live.


                                                                    John Cheever
                                                                    Cedar Lane
                                                                    Ossining, N.Y.

                                                                    Monday

Dear Mr. Exley,

It was the Watertown-born dentist who, in the end, seemed to suffer most. Having got me bibbed and tuckered he asked what part of the bridge had I swallowed. When I said that I had swallowed it all he got white. I said cheerfully that I thought I had passed it. He said, in a hoarse voice, that I couldn't have passed it without medical assistance. "Not" he said, "with those hooks." I wished to hell he would shutup; but he seems to have been wrong. It is true that when I fart these days it sounds like a police whistle but I suffer little pain and it's very easy for me to get cabs.

updike and I were not asked to the Festival. We were asked to an earlier dinner with Stan Musial, John Glenn, etc., but in the light of your revery I must point out that I'm quite able to fend for myself. Our troubles began at the Embassy in Moscow when he came on exclaiming:"What are you looking so great about? I thought you'd be dead." He then began distributing paper-back copies of the Centaur while I distributed hard-cover copies of The Brigadier. The score was eight to six, my favor. When we went to Spasso House the next day he forgot to bring any books and I dumped six. On the train up to Leningrad he tried to throw my books out of the window but his lovely wife Mary intervened. She not only saved the books; she read one. She had to hide it under her bedpillow and claim to be sick. She said he would kill her if he knew. At the University of Leningrad he tried to upstage me by reciting some of his nonsense verse but I set fire to the contents of an ashtray and upset the water carafe. But when I pointed out to President and Mrs. Johnson that the bulkiness of his appearance was not underwear—it was autographed copies of The Centaur—he seemed deeply wounded. I've invited them to stay with us in Wellfleet but there's been no reply.

Best,
John Cheever

Tanya had a dog named Trika.

John Cheever
Cedar Lane
Ossining, N.Y.

June 15th

Dear Tanya,

. . . To carry on my idle account of the minutae of American life I found a snapping turtle on the lawn Sunday morning. He was three and one half feet long with a spiked tail and a jaw that could break a man's leg. It was very exciting to find this prehistoric brute in so decorous a landscape. I put ten shot-gun shells into his head. We drove to Providence for Susie's convocation and graduation. The university was founded in 1760 and a great many rites and arcane ceremonies have accumulated over the years. Bells rang, maces were carried from here to there, laurels were presented, there were orations in Latin and speeches in English and interminable processions and Susie was finally given her diploma on Monday afternoon. On Tuesday I took the plane to Washington for the White House party. As you may know there has been a great deal of dispute about whether or not American intellectuals should accept the invitations of a President whose foreign policy they detest. I accepted. We were about sixty guests including astronauts, ball-players, poets, novelists, physicist, doctors and one actor. It was great fun. The President looked weary but Mrs. Johnson was gracious. The Updikes were there and I did everything short of kicking him in the trousers. This made me feel better. I flew home on Wednesday and on Thursday took Susie to the plane for Alabama where she will teach in a negro university. Ben, who is my favorite, returned on Friday. Tell Trika that the yellow bitch was bred on Wednesday and is expected to throw a litter in themiddle of August. Pow, as the children say. This is current slang. Pow means good. Zilch means bad.

Pow,
John

John Cheever
Cedar Lane
Ossining, N.Y. 10562

16th

Dear Exley,

Although I've never met you or your wife (and I'm convinced that you and I would destroy one another) I'm very pleased to hear that she's back with you. It seems to me that, for a writer, separation and divorce can be a massive waste of energy. When you write that you have never lied to her about what she might expect, I think you exaggerate. Neither you nor I nor anyone else can describe the volcanic landscapes a poor girl strays into when she marries a literary man. I couldn't tell my wife what to expect in the next twenty-four hours. Writers wives are not allowed to correspond. That would be treachery.

They are seldom allowed to meet and when they do they exchange very soulful glances. One more thing. When you find a good room to work in you will sure as hell be evicted by child-birth, a litter of puppies, visiting relations or if necessary fire. At least that's my experience. I have a nice square room here now with a door onto a terrace but Mary announced last night that she had invited a troubled student to come and live in it. So off one goes again to find some spare room, tool shed, office, loft, or garage.

Best,
John

Cedar Lane, Ossining
etc.

June 25th

Dear Tanya,

I finally got the Housebreaker off, registered airmail. I hope it reaches you before the snow. It's a poor copy on cheap paper but the only one I have here. When you come to visit us, as I'm sure you will, I'll see that you have a decent copy.

My very good friend Arthur Spear and his wife Stella are going to Moscow in the middle of August on some sort of International Amity Excursion. Arthur is a fishing and drinking companion, he votes the conservative ticket, goes to church twice on Sundays and is an impacted member of our traditional middle class but I find him excellent company. His wife Stella is the daughter of a Bishop and I won't attempt to describe her beyond saying that she plays the viola. I think you would enjoy Arthur and if I may I will give him your telephone number. I shan't without your permission. I love the Russian people as you well know and I will be very interested to see how my conservative friends react.

To ask a woman if she is happy is merely a secondary male characteristic. The male is always asking the female if she is happy and the female always retorts that the question is obtuse and unanswerable. It has been going on since the dawn of humanity.

Happy?
John

I have today a letter from John Hersey whose opposition to our foreign policy is so strenous that he has cancelled his trip to Russia.

John Cheever
Cedar Lane
Ossining, N.Y.

[July 21, 1965]
Wellfleet

massachusetts

dear tanya,

   This is on a broken typewriter in a rented house by the sea. i gave the typewriter to my son ben for christmas and can now reflect on what a truly ungenerous man i am. we are all here. susie returned from alabama on the weekend, very excited about her brush with racial strife. she was spat on by white segregationistsand finds us all thoughtless and conservative creatures of habit. ben wears his hair down over his brow. he chases girls. fred collects shells, stones and dead crabs for his marine museum. this is on the dinner table. the old dog, my true love, is failing and will not leave my side. the yellow bitch is approaching her whelping hour; and i do shamefully little. i think i will leave next week.

   this is cape code, a stretch of morraine pushed into the sea by th glacier. it forms a stupendous beach about a hundred and fifty miles long. it is the easternmost point of the continent. the surf is thunderous. the shallows are green. the deep water is purple. it is splendid. the long beach is part of the national park but there are some stuborn and curious class distinctions. the sheltered bay beaches where the water is tepid and still are patronized by people whose grammar is questionable and whose clothing is cheap. it is on the wild and clamorous open shore that one hears the unmistakable bray of the upper classes. the beaches are never crowded. our house is old—1820—and stands in a grove of poplars. one hears the surf all night. but i do no work.

                                                          as ever,
                                                          John

The story was "The Geometry of Love." SEP is *The Saturday Evening Post.*

John Cheever
Cedar Lane
Ossining, N.Y.

October fourth 1965

Dear Exley,

I wrote a short story, a couple of weeks ago, the first in over a year, and sent it to the New Yorker. Silence. At dusk on Saturday a fiction editor appeared here, looked at me sadly, patted me gently,said that the story was a ghastly failure and implied that I had lost my marbles. The story went to the SEP on Monday who; took exactly ten minutes to pick it up for three thousand. This cheered me.

Yours,
John

Rust Hills was then at *The Saturday Evening Post.*

John Cheever
Cedar Lane
Ossining, N.Y.

Saturday

Dear Exley,

Of course I wasn't worried about the New Yorker. The story seemed to belong to the others although it does have a controversial scene in which a woman, who has been drinking,describes in detail how her husband dropped the kitten into the Waring Mixer. Bill Maxwell came over one afternoon to tell me the story had failed. it was getting dark. I was drinking gin and romping with the dogs. I have ten dogs. Bill's face was very long and he seemed to suggest that the story had not only failed but that the failure was, in some subtle way, profound and irreversible. I could not,with a skinful and surrounded by so many loving animals, take him seriously and I reminded him, cruelly, of all the other stories they had rejected and of all the editorial crap I've put up with over the years. That was Saturday. On Monday the Post bought the story for three thousand and threw in a hymn of praise from Rust Hills in case I should be feeling lonely and insecure. Maxwell not only said that I was a story machine; he said that I was *his* story machine.

No diminishment was intended. The original comparison was to a tomato plant.

Best,
Cheever

John Cheever
Cedar Lane
Ossining, N.Y.

July 13th

Dear Tanya,

They are making The Swimmer in Westport now—a town near here —and I think they're doing a splendid job. They're using thirteen pools and Burt Lancaster is Ned. he is fifty-two, lithe, comely and somewhat disfigured by surgical incisions and he looks both young and old, masterful and tearful. I've taken Art Spear down to see the production and he drinks quantities of gin and kisses all the actresses. Eleanor Perry, who wrote the screen play has added a couple of scenes but she's followed the line and sense of the story precisely. There are no flashbacks, no explanations for his mysterious journey and it ends in an empty house in a thunder storm. It will be finished in September and maybe you can see it at the embassy. Mary and I are going to walk through one of the scenes.

It is very hot here now and we mostly sit around and say so; and I will now join Susie on the terrace and discuss the heat.

Best,
John

Bill Maxwell also grew to adore Tanya on a trip to Russia.

John Cheever
Cedar Lane
Ossining, N. Y.

Monday

Dear Bill,

Tanya would be thrilled to have a copy of your novel and why don't you write her a note. . . .

She proudly sent Susie a new Russian gadget. It is made of pink plastic and is about the size and shape of a male member. You glue it to the bathroom wall with vile-smelling Russian glue. On the underside of the tip is a magnet. There is a second magnet with prongs which you press into a cake of soap. Thus by putting the two magnets together your soap is suspended in air and is kept from getting sticky. "It is," she wrote, "very phallic but isn't everything excepting rugs and wall-paper."

Best,
John

He wrote the following entries in his journal.

I dream that I wrestle a spry negress in the library apartment at the academy in Rome. P is in the next bed trying to make out with someone I don't recognize who keeps saying:You're just wasting your time. At dusk Ben and I cut the playing field at the Children's Center. Father and Son engaged in charitable acts. I agree to take M and F to Romeand interview Loren but M does not seem cheered. They go off to the movies and I wander through the house saying loudly:how happy I am to be alone,how happy,happy,happy I am to be alone. I drink on the terrace,wish on the evening star,chat with the dogs. The doctor calls. I think of him as a young man with an uncommonly round face, round eyes and an enthusiasim for medical science that does not include any knowledge or respect for the force of pain. He seems to possess some vision of a rosey future in which there will be pills to cure cloresterol and melancholy, pills for sloth, lust,homosexuality,anger,anxiety and averice. Try this red one for your fear of planes,he says enthusiastically. Try the yellow one for your fear of heights. Take the white one when you have the blues. Pills,pills,what beautiful pills they have these days. They're working on an elixir of youth but they haven't quite got the bugs out of it. I'm confident they'll have it next year.

The healthiest man in Ossining has gas pains at ten and takes a Miltown without much success. I mumble on about the maze, the labarynth,the mirrors which might work. At noon I take some gin and a massive intestinal tranquilizer that anaestheitizes my gut but that leaves me with a lingering and unpleasant loss of sensibility. I read a short novel that follows the classical unities without much success. I regret to say that I am pissy at dinner. In the evening I suffer from chest pains,loose bowels, a sore throat,a seizures of sweatiness. At nine

I knock myself out with Nembutal. Wake at dawn, not in any great sorrow, but all the color seems leached from my reveries. I see a three year old child clumsily kicking a soccer ball and I protest vehemently. If my imagination is going to produce a soccer game I want to see a professional Italian team.

John Cheever
Cedar Lane
Ossining, N.Y.

August third

Dear Tanya,

Naples seems to have done it; Naples and Rome. I remember your saying that Elephant loved Italy and so do I. On American planes these days they show movies and we (Mary and Fred) sat in a dark cabin watching a tedious movie while the sun rose over the English chanal, Mont Blanc and the Matterhorn. I think I speak Italian fluently and get off the plane gabbling like a turkey. We had a car and a chauffer and drove from Rome to a Saracen fishing village called Sperlonga. This is all white-washed staircases leading to the sea and at six in the morning, American time, we were eating tomatos and mozzarella and sporting in the waves. A cold rain had been falling in New York and none of this made much sense.

My job was to interview Sophia Loren and we went down to Naples for this on Monday. She is a great beauty—intelligent and capable—but so anxious not to appear controversial that it is difficult to give her much dimension. However I've done the story. We went to Positano, Amalfi, etc. and then returned to Rome. Rome seemed more beautiful than ever. We boarded the plane on Wednesday noon and watched another terrible movie as we sailed over Mont Blanc and the Matterhorn. I seemed to have dropped my bete noir into the Atlantic.

All is well here. Everyone goes to the mountains on Monday and I'll get back to work on the book.

As ever,
John

My sister, Susan, was teaching near Aspen. Flora was a yellow Lab that had once been mine, and she got quite fat with grief when I went away to boarding school.

John Cheever
Cedar Lane
Ossining, N.Y.

Wednesday

Dear Ben,

I am snowed in again and this is on your Mother's typewriter on which I make many mistakes. Susie telephoned to say that she is coming home for vacation so I guess you don't get to go to Aspen. Maybe you can go together to Stowe. She said she felt isolated. So does Flora and when no boy-dogs show up she goes up and down Cedar Lane and brings them in. We watched the Westminister Dog Show on tv last night and were shocked to find that only one Labrador had been entered and that the judge didn't even glance at him. you could see him in the background , waving his tail, but no one cared. The so-called sporting dogs all had long coats that dragged along the ground. Tick traps.

All is well and uneventful here. I took Fred bowling and he was awful. I kept shouting at him: "You're not even looking in the direction of the pins." He doesn't seem to mind. Everyone sends their best.

Best,
Father

Art is Arthur Spear.

Dear Tanya,

I've seen a good deal of Art and we frequently turn to one another and exclaim: "Oh if Tanya could only see that." Driving into New York one winter afternoon,just as the lights of the city were going on, Art exclaimed:"Oh if Tanya could only see that." Mary and I were guests at a debutante cotillion which was indescribably lavish and vulgar and Mary could be heard exclaiming above the music:"Oh if Tanya could only see this." Susie would like you to see the mountains of Colorado and Stella would like you to meet her daughters. It seems that you must either visit us here or we must return to Moscow. The distances involved—the North Atlantic and the land-mass of Western Europe— seem to have an inhibitive affect on the amiable sport of letter writing.

Writing to Moscow seems, to me, very different from writing to friends in this country or Italy. When I try to express my feelings for you, your people and your country my prose style goes straight into humbug. I don't know why this is. I wrote Igor Petrovich a few days ago recalling Kiev, the autumn leaves, etc and while my memories are vivid and feelings genuine by prose was portentous rubbish. It may be that the common minutae of life—the raw material of most good letters—seems too trifling to be flown across the stormy Atlantic.

Everything goes well here. The book moves nicely. My marriage—which has it's stormy passages—seems idylic. The children appear to be happy (I'm enclosing a picture of Ben with a phoney beam of light across his hair) and in The afternoon I walk the dogs through the snowy woods. The old black insists upon coming although when she returns to the house she isn't able to move for the rest of the day. We had a heavy snow over the weekend. Our house is quite remote, the cars were all buried in snow and we were confined from Saturday through Monday but it all passed pleasantly. I will lunch with Art and at some point during the meal he will exclaim:"Oh if Tanya could only see that." If you only could. Mary is shouting from the next room to send you her love.

Luv,<br>John

In May of 1967 my sister, Susan, married Rob Cowley, the son of Malcolm Cowley.

May 9th [67]

Dear Tanya,

The wedding was practically Tolstoyian and I wish you'd been there. The church is 18th century and remarkably handsome. Susie wore a short lace dress and a veil. When I was a very young man and first heard the Purcell trumpet voluntary I decided to marry and have a daughter and lead her up the aisle to these triumphal strains and so that was the music. Susie was frightened. I think I've seen her frightened once before. That was when, at the age of five, she first saw the skeleton of the Brontosaraus Rex in the Museum of Natural History. When the trumpet sounded I was delighted to give her my arm. I think I've never felt so requited as a Father. The service was the original Cranmer including the vow:"I do thee with my body worship". After the bridal couple Ben, walking like a gorilla, took his Mother out and I took out the Mother of the groom who is a very possessive woman and was not expected to live through the service. It was a cold and rainy day but we had an immense pavillion raised in the church garden, filled with tables, flowers, waiters and rivers of champagne and every one of the two hundred guests struck me as radiant, comely, intelligent and affectionate. Everyone acted in character. Mary's unstable sister seized two vases of flowers and carried them out to her car. Her husband—a shy man—retired to a nearby saloon and got drunk at his own expense. Mary—very chic—upstaged Susie and nearly ran off with the groom. Fred, attended by his Italian, ate six pieces of cake and I kissed eighty-three women and drank a pint of bourbon. My old friend Mrs. Zagreb raked the male guests and, pointing to a painter named Peter Blume said hoarsely:"That's what I want next."

Everything is in bloom here now. We had a thunderstorm last night and, waked by the noise I thought:"The dark, the night is a mansion with many rooms through which I walk easily." For some reason this contented me.

As ever,
John


The man with the horn was Ted Ziegler, Sally's husband.


John Cheever [1967]
Cedar Lane
Ossining, New York 10562

Dear Tanya,

Ben graduates at the end of the week and Susie and her husband are thinking of moving to London to escape his possessive parents. They keep calling to ask why the children don't come and visit them. Mary and I are nearly as bad and the children have the good sense to spend their weekends at the sea. . . . In the house nearest us lives a young man who practises the French horn. He flats and sharps every note and makes a particularly brutal assault on the Mozart Concerto. Last night I marched up the hill, announced that I have perfect pitch (a lie) and that if he persisted in abusing the Mozart I would fire off my shotgun at intervals of five minutes. He went on playing and I clapped my hands over my ears and retired. Mary thought it all very funny.

As ever,
John

In *Bullet Park* Hammer's bête noire also followed him, and like my father's own depression it also missed connections.

The cafard followed me throughout that trip but it followed me without much guile either because it was lazy or because it was an assassin so confident of its prey that it had no need to exert itself. On Saturday morning I woke, feeling cheerful and randy. I was just as cheerful on Sunday but on Monday I woke in a melancholy so profound that I had to drag myself out of bed and stumble, step by step, into the shower. On Tuesday we took a train to Fondi and a cab through the mountains to Sperlonga, where we stayed with friends. I had two good days there but the bête noire caught up with me on the third. . . .

Malcolm Cowley and his wife, Muriel, live in Sherman, Connecticut. Elizabeth is Elizabeth Ames.

John Cheever
Cedar Lane
Ossining, New York 10562

Wednesday

Dear Josie,

Mary and I were both delighted to hear from you. New bread and fresh fish will cure almost anything. Mary and the various children are well. Dear Ben is at Antioch. Late one Friday afternoon in December a friend called to say that he was locked up in the Cincinnati workhouse. Bail was nine hundred dollars and the charge was disturbing the peace during an anti-war demonstration. I got Western Union here to stay open until I had raised the money and he was sprung in the morning and will be tried in FebruaryHe was home for Christmas—very much himself—although he looks at me a little distantly since I've never served time in a work house. He is now a newspaper reporter in the little town of Vandalia and has a blonde.

I seem to have come into or to be passing through a curious time of life. I began, about a year ago to suffer from severe melancholy. In July Mary,Fred and I went to Naples. The cafarde seems to miss the plane but it did catch up with me when we got to Rome. Then in September I blew a fuse in my privates. This was disconcerting and expensive and the doctors seemed confused. I wrote Tanya Litvinov in Moscow and asked her to pray for me at St. Basils. She did and this healed but I still have the cafarde five days out of seven. This does not seem to have had any effect on my ability to work and I knocked off a piece of the novel last week that is as good as anything I've done. I think(today) that the book is off the ground and when it is finished I will take my arse to some gleaming beach and spend a summer throwing skimmers.

Susie and Rob are happy in the best possible way. It is rather like a fable in that Muriel—and Malcolm at times—have behaved like the most wicked king and queen. They want the young prince back home in his bed and they seemed to sit on their thrones in Sherman, weaving nets and wearing crooked crowns. It is a strange story and Mary and I were unprepared but the children are invincibly happy, diplomatic and sage and the evil king and queen have taken their bag of tricks to Mexico for the winter. I had a note from Elizabeth at Christmas and I believe she is,at the moment,blind, but determined to recover. The power she wields over that place has not lessened with her illness and I have a feeling that when she goes she will take it all with her—the fir trees, the lakes and the mansion. Poof. This comes with all our love.

John

January 30th [1968]

Dear Tanya,

I have written you several times since my recovery and the letters may be going astray but my letters at this time of year seem to consist mostly of dull weather reports so all the thief will have learned is that it snowed or that it didn't snow. My health thanks to you, has improved but I am having a terrible time with alcohol and if you would be good enough to mutter a few incantations about this problem I would appreciate it. I try not to drink until noon but I am not always successful. Ben called last night to say that he was let off with a small fine. He was, in case you didn't get my earlier letters, arrested in a peace demonstration. . . . Last night was also the Academy meeting to discuss Russian literature. Babette Deutch (Yarmolinksy) made the best speech. The audience is very venerable, distinguished and deaf and I don't think they heard what was said. Bill sat in the back rown and winked at me. I find Kennan's mind quite dry. Lillian Hellman and Kunitz also spoke. It seems that we all love Russian literature and the Russian people although we're not quite sure why. The Pirosmani came and is hanging on the wall.

The old dog is dead. (This is the sort of news that will galvanize the mail-thief.) She lost the use of her legs on Sunday and her wits on Monday and I had the vet kill her yesterday afternoon. She was a wonderful companion and I loved her dearly but I shed very few tears. Fred cried for about an hour. We had her for fifteen years and she led a very active and useful life but when I last took her for a walk she fell in the deep snow and had to be carried home. Some years ago I went to a psychiatrist who told me I was obcessed with my Mother. When I told him that I liked to swim he said: Mother. When I told him that I liked the rain he said: Mother. When I told him that I drank too much he said: Mother. This was all rubbish but sitting here with Cassie one evening I saw her raise her head exactly as Mother used to and give me a pained, sweet, fleeting smile that was unnerving.

Love,
John

Cedar Lane
Ossining

February 26th

Dear Tanya,

I perused most of James when I was eighteen and was intoxicated by the inuendoes, the cirumlocutions, the pools of light and the high-flown speeches delivered at dusk. Five years ago I bought the complete works and settled down to read it again. It was appalling. I remember your saying that you detested "stuffs" and James seemed to be just that. I could not imagine why he had spent so much time rigging the scenery, arranging the flowers and brewing the tea. I could hear his heavy breathing behind the walls of all those so wonderfully beautiful rooms. I felt as if I were caught at some unsuitable occupation such as embroidery. (My sort of novelist walks boldly onstage, belches, picks his teeth with a match stick and sneaks a drink of whisky from the bottle hidden in the fireplace.) But the work seemed to me to have so little moral urgency, so little ardor that I gave up with volume five. This is still heresy here and if I said as much at my club I would be dropped.

The book is my waking and my sleeping and the only news I have is what I see from my window. A leafless tree. A dog with a bone. A cloud shaped like a cloud. . . .

Best,
John

The Styron book would have been *The Confessions of Nat Turner* (Random House, 1967). Polly was Elizabeth's assistant at Yaddo.

# DEMON RUM

* * *

Monday [May 1968]

Dear Josie,

That was a very encouraging letter and many thanks. Some stormy night I'll put the cafarde out with the cat. Allied to my melancholy is my struggle with Demon rum. There is a terrible sameness to the euphoria of alcohol and the euphoria of metaphor—the sense that the imagination is boundless—and I sometimes substitute or extend one with the other. My performance is sometimes comical. I leave my typewriter at quarter after ten and wander down stairs to the pantry where the bottles are. I do not touch the bottles. I do not even look at the bottles and I congratulate myself fatuously on my will-power. At eleven I make another trip to the pantry and congratulate myself once more but at twelve when the bull-hord blows I fly down the stairs and pour out a scoop. The same thing happens in the afternoon. I take long walks, split wood, paint trim and shovel snow and while I exclaim loudly over the beauty of the winter light there lurks at the back of my mind the image of a bottle of sour-mash. It seems to be, most of the time, an equal struggle.

Ben got off with a $150 fine and banishment from Cincinnati for life. This simply means that he takes the plane from Dayton. He seems very pleased with everything and is a most gratifying son. I had thought Elizabeth was gravely ill because she dictates her letters (which are dispirited) and has forbidden Polly to write me. I'm delighted to know that she's well. The Styron book seemed to me astonishing. I had no faith in his ability to bring it off; and I thought he did. I've read almost everything published this year and I don't know of anything equal to it. I also think he a very good man. There is no bluff in his work at all. When I was an NBA judge I got stoned before the meeting and then talked uninterruptedly for three quarters of an hour. It worked.

Now I'll make my eleven o'clock trip to the pantry. What discipline! What will power!

Best,
John

May 22nd

Dear Tanya,

The Swimmer—which is not first-rate—was fairly well received here and seems to be doing good business. John's new novel (Couples) has made him a millionaire. Would you like me to send it on? It is obsessively venereal but the descriptions of undressed women are splendid. Great advances have been made here recently in writing about venereal sport. The pure, correct and ancient vocabulary is used freely, the techniques of masturbation are discussed and the sense is of freedom, discovery and newness. Phil Roth leads the group. While all my friends are describing orgasims I still dwell on the beauty of the evening star.

My malaise continued until Easter when suddenly the megrims, the bet noir, the cafarde, the melancholy and the infection all packed their considerable baggage and went away. The weather may have routed them since this is the most beautiful spring within memory. The river valley is a wall of green, the clouds are like mountains and almost every night some rain falls. It's one of the reasons I don't want to go to Leningrad; I didn't really want to go anywhere but perhaps I'll do it in the fall.

As ever,
John

John Cheever
Cedar Lane
Ossining, New York

Alan Pakula is a director whose films include *All the President's Men*. He was married to the actress Hope Lange.

June twenty-eight [1968?]

Dear Tanya,

I'm getting along with the french horn but not well enough, I think, to discuss spit. I sometimes think he means to needle me. This morning, for example (brilliant and sunny) he began to play Greensleaves at quarter to seven. This, for someone with an overly sensitive musical memory, can ruin a day. I'm glad you liked the Bostonians. I think they are our best and I've been hearing them for longer than one might imagine. Shortly after I was conceived my Mother, casting around for some way of improving the destiny of an unwanted child, subscribed to the Boston Symphony and attended every concert, letting the peaceful sounds of music waft into my rudimentary ears. It may have worked since I was reported to have been a happy child. I don't really think you're very much like _____. He is supposed to be here now and I rather dread picking up the telephone and hearing that sepulchral voice. Homosexuality seems to be a commonplace in nature and if this is so why should he seem, spiritually, to be so ungainly. Procreative nature is surely not that exacting and vindictive. I would like to live in a world in which there are no homosexuals but I suppose Paradise is thronged with them.

My very good friends Hope and Alan Pakula are coming over for the film festival on (I think) the fifteenth of July. I'll tell you their hotel as soon as I know it. He is a very amiable young man and I once fell in love with her. I mooned, swooned and walked in rainy woods. I think you'll like her and I know that Elephant will. There is a chance now that I may go to Italy for a week in July. I think that I've never felt worse in my life. I am attacked by all sorts of absurd anxieties, my sleep is troubled, my work goes slowly, my palms sweat, my ears ring, my heart pounds and I think that if I'm going to crack up I may as well crack up in the Holy See. Maybe the Boston concerts didn't work.

Love,
John


John Cheever
Cedar Lane
Ossining, N.Y.

July 16th, 1968

Dear Tanya,

I finished Bullet Park at noon on Friday and put it into the mail. . . . I didn't tell anyone I'd finished the book and there were no celebrations. On Sunday I was waked with a toothache. I had the fang plucked on Monday morning and suffered the most profound melanchoy on losing this much of myself. At noon the agent called to say that the book was magnificent but I couldn't reply because my mouth was full of cotton wool. I decided to celebrate last night and we went out to dinner but for reasons that I can't recall the evening ended in a bitter quarrel with Mary. I suppose it all means something but I miss the tooth more than I miss the book.

Ben was home for two weeks with an asortment of his generation. There was a runaway waife from the East Village, a black who wore jewelry and burned incense and a barefoot young man with hair down to his shoulders. Ben ditched his blonde and took up with a brunette who arrived here one day at dawn, climbed into Ben's bed and remained there pretty much for the next week. Now and then they would come down for dinner. Last night I gave your address to my former publisher—Cass Canfield—who was taking the night plane to Moscow. I keep thinking that I'll go to Moscow tomorrow or the day after that but I have to wait until my jaw heals and anyhow I'm tired and I get discouraged when I think of the Chicken Kiev at the Ukraine. So toothless,bookless,I remain,

Yours,
John

My father admired Exley's *A Fan's Notes* (Random House, 1968).

Cedar Lane

July 21st

Dear Fred,

That was a friendly and a helpful letter and my sincere thanks. I've never intended to be patronizing. As a child I was told to remember, at all times, that I was a CHEEVAH. I thought this bullshit had cured me. I am at times reserved because of the speed with which I become involved with people. I danced with a stranger at a wedding for five minutes and was gone for six months. I am a sort of roundheels. I have never dumped on A Fan's Notes. I still remember the enthusiasim with which Mary and I read the book. It has a prominent place on the shelves here and I am delighted by the number of people—mostly young—who single it out. I do not belong to any New Yorker group and I have never considered myself important.

Some of my difficulties with Time may have been inheirited. My brother had three alcoholic breakdowns in his fifties and Time for my father was a tragedy. At one point he was thought to have killed himself. I went to claim the body and found him instead, dead drunk, riding the roller-coaster. A large crowd had gathered to watch the old gentleman. It is nine-thirty. The maid is cleaning the carpet. She stands directly between me and the gin bottle in the pantry but if I ask her to empty the ashtrays in the living room I will be able to sneak into the pantry. Will John Cheever hit the bottle or the Librium or both? Stay tuned.

Yours,
John

John Cheever
Cedar Lane
Ossining, N.Y. 10562

August 21st [1968]

Dear Josie,

I finished the novel and we went to Ireland and I thought I'd keep you posted. After I finished the book I had a terrible toothace. The tooth was extracted and then I got drunk. This seemed pointless so Mary, Fred and I got a plane to Shannon and drove south to County Kerry. Nothing in the world, I guess, is like anything else in the world but Ireland is a most unlikely place. It is, in the pleasantest sense, haunted. The mountains are blue and green, there are chains of lakes, salt estuaries and salmon streams in whose pools are reflected ruined castles with trees growing out of the highest tower and bumble bees in the great hall.

I'm not at all sure of the quality of the book but the agent and the publisher are excited. The book is very, very clean. There is not a cock or an arsehole in it and the word fuck does not appear once. While all my friends are playing stinkfinger and grabarse I admire the beauty of the evening star. I hope it works. And I hope this finds you well. Mary and Fred went to New Hampshire as soon as we returned and I am alone here now and idle but I trust I'll get back to work.

                                                              Best,
                                                              John


                                           John Cheever
                                           Cedar Lane
                                           Ossining, N.Y. 10562

                                           Curacoa

                                           December 20th [1968]

Dear Exley,

We go off to the Antilles next week. Rich, rich, rich. My oldest son is not only embarrassed about the trip; he anticipates being embarrassed by a January tan. He dislikes people who are brown in January. He can put his head in an expensive bag. My sincere, affectionate, best wishes to you and your wife.

                                                              Yours,
                                                              Cheever


Bullet Park came out in April of 1969 and received mixed reviews. It sold 33,000 copies in hard cover. The notice that ran on the front page of The New York Times Book Review on April 27 was written by Benjamin DeMott.

For half of its length John Cheever's new novel is a collection of sketches of a suburban nuclear family names Nailles; the detached narrator's focus shifts from mother to father to son, with an occasional glance at some Bullet Park neighbors. In mid-course these people vanish and a new storyteller appears—an unappetizing melancholic named Paul Hammer, bastard son of an Indiana klepto and a socialist millionaire, who offers autobiographical-picaresque rumination. The parts are wedded at the end, when Hammer arrives in the suburb determined, for no intelligent reason, to commit an act of violence against the Nailles's son.

... this third novel can't fairly be described as a first-rate addition to the man's oeuvre. There's the structure problem to begin with—the book is broken-backed, parts tacked together as flimsily as the Hammer-Nailles ploy suggests.

John Cheever's short stories are and will remain lovely birds—dense in inexplicables and beautifully trim. But in the gluey atmosphere of "Bullet Park" no birds sing. ...

The impact of this wounding review was heightened by the fact that my father was drinking heavily at the time. "The manuscript was received enthusiastically everywhere," he reported in a *Paris Review* interview," but when Benjamin DeMott dumped on it in the *Times*, everybody picked up their marbles and went home. I ruined my left leg in a skiing accident and ended up so broke that I took out working papers for my youngest son."

DeMott wonders what connection there can be between the dutiful, home-loving Tony Nailles and the debauched and self-indulgent Paul Hammer. It's an easy mistake to make. I made it myself at the time the book came out. I can remember sitting on a rooftop in Cambridge, Massachusetts, eating Chinese food out of paper cartons and reading the passage about Nailles's home-loving cock to a girl I planned to marry. I presented my father as the lone proponent of monogamy in an adulterous world. I wanted to believe in Nailles, and so, I suppose, did he. But there couldn't be a Tony Nailles without a Paul Hammer, and they are the same person. Nailles is too good to be anyone you ever met, and Hammer is too bad.

By and large his letters convey the sociable, lovable side of John Cheever, but the careful reader will see another figure lurking in the background, the vain, ungenerous, ruthless and self-indulgent Paul Hammer. It's like the wolf seen at the edge of an Alpine forest a moment before nightfall. Without that wolf there would have been no sleeping children, no thatched cottage, no village at all.

John Cheever
Cedar Lane
Ossining, N.Y. 10562

Tuesday [1969]

Dear Exley,

I've done nothing since I finished the book, I've not even kept a journal. My only, only brother showed up yesterday on his way to England. After twenty-five years of acute alcoholism, paranoia and marital mayhem he appears at sixty-two, handsome, intelligent, sober and well-dressed. His wife, however, is in the abyss these days and I wondered (sneakily) if this had anything to do with his well-being. We sat up late, the Good Brother and the Bad Brother. The Good Brother (me) drank nearly a quart of bourbon while the Bad Brother sipped a gingerale. At breakfast the Bad Brother was all charm and composure. The Good Brother was one fucking mess.

Best,
John

Drinking had always been part of the family culture. When I was a teenager, home for the weekend, I went out barhopping one night in our station wagon. I woke up at 5 A.M. with a splitting headache, and the vivid memory of an accident. I was in boarding school at the time, and the dormitories were full of stories about students who had been sent off to military academies after scratching the fenders on the family Pontiac. I lay in bed, relishing my headache, and dreading what I expected would be a drastically altered future. Finally, at about 6 A.M., I got up and went down to the driveway to have a look at the car. Our station wagon was so badly banged up at that time that you couldn't distinguish my accident from anybody else's.

So the merry, heavy-drinking attitude of my father was not without advantages for a teenage son. But it became clear as the 1960s drew to a close that the tragicomedy of our lives was swiftly becoming solid tragedy.

John Cheever
Cedar Lane
Ossining, N.Y. 10562

March sixth

Dear Bill,

I can't write you a story. I can't write anyone a story. I know that Bullet Park is not that massive but six months later I still feel pole-axed. Twice I seem to have had a donnee but I don't seem to have any motive for following through. I think I'll have to start all over again. Also the stuntiness of Barthelme disconcerts me. One can always begin: "Mr. Frobisher,returning from a year in Europe,opened his trunk for the customs officer and found there, instead of his clothing and souvenirs, the mutliated and naked body of an Italian sailor." Blooey. It's like the last act in vaudeville and anyhow it seems to me that I did it fifteen years ago. There's the rub. I start on a story and realize that I've already written it.

Not working is terribly painful and I'm still having a fight with the booze. I've enlisted the help of a doctor but it's touch and go. A day for me; a day for the hootch. A beautiful, blonde,intelligent and responsive movie actress whom I adore announced to her husband that she had to spend three hours alone with me. He sullenly agreed. I took her skating.

Best,
John

I recall Hope Lange and her husband, Alan Pakula, coming up the stone steps to the house on Cedar Lane. I think Hope called me "dear," and she may even have kissed me. I was in my early teens at the time, and I complained about it later to my father. "I never met her before. She doesn't know if I'm a dear or not." He said that was the way people were in Hollywood, and that it didn't mean anything.

After one trip to Hollywood, my father had boasted to me about dates with Peggy Lee. He told how they'd driven around together in a convertible, and he'd "bussed" her. We'd sit around the house and listen to Peggy Lee albums. I thought they were pretty good. So there was public discussion of other women. Susan and I used to joke about "the stacks of satisfied starlets" he'd left on the beach in California. But still I didn't get it. I must've thought he just kissed them. But when Hope and her husband actually showed up at our house on Cedar Lane, I began to suspect something more serious than kissing was going on. My father's on-again, off-again relationship with Hope continued until his death.

Toward the end of his life he invited me to come into the city to meet her. He and I and Hope ate together at a steak house. We all did a lot more smiling than talking. It was like an installment of a not very good family television show, the one titled "Father Introduces Eldest Son to Mistress."

I still don't know exactly how a son is supposed to react to his father's adultery. It's tricky, because I loved my father, but I love my mother too. When Biff finds out about Willy's indiscretions in *Death of a Salesman*, he completely loses faith in the man. I don't know how this went over when that play first opened, but the reaction looks a little antique today.

After my father died, I had lunch with Hope, and she gave me copies of the letters he'd sent her. She told me that there was never any question of my father's leaving my mother. "He would never say anything bad about your mother to me," Hope said. In any case, my parents did stay together, and I, for one, am glad of it. Their relationship was troubled, and it often gave them both pain, but it was also extremely fruitful.

I asked Hope when she learned that my father was bisexual.

"After reading the later books," she said.

"But you didn't suspect at first?"

"No," she said. "He had me fooled. He was one of the horniest men I've ever known."

John Cheever
Cedar Lane
Ossining, N.Y. 10562

Tuesday

Dear Hope,

I love you. I haven't written sooner because I had a small skiing accident. Swooping (or so I thought) among the trees in the orchard I went down like a tray of dishes and tore all the ligaments in my left knee. It isn't serious or painful and I go to the hospital tomorrow for a plaster cast. When this is better I'll come to the coast. I won't get a job or anything; I'll just stay with the Weavers and hide behind palm trees and watch you get in and out of your car. I do wish I had a picture of you but this seems corney and anyhow I know how you look. My feelings seem completely uncomplicated. I am not broody, moody, jealous, anguished or anxious. I love you.

Love<br>John

Iole, the Italian maid who raised Fred from birth, was still closely involved with our family.

April third

Darling,

I am really in a bind here and this is only to say, in my unworthy way, that I love you. The cast goes from my hip to my foot and I can barely reach the typewriter. Mary and Iole have been terribly nice. I thought that instead of getting a job on the coast I woulddo an interview of you for Esquire. Would you like to be interviewed for Esquire? The doctor will see me on Friday and I'll know more about my future mobility then.

love,<br>John

The book was *Bullet Park*. He was fifty-seven.

Friday

Darling,

I'll be in the cast for another three weeks. It's immense. People come to see it, bringing me flowers and picture puzzles. I have dozens of picture puzzles. For awhile I thought the cast might signify the beginning of a new sober and industrious way of life but it hasn't worked out that way. Iole brings up the ice and bottles at eleven. The book comes out in a week or so and I've spent most of my time posing for publicity pictures and I must have posed about fifteen times. I don't much like this. After an hour or two I get a phoney, bland and seraphic look and gaze into the lense like a hound dog. The publicity on the book is so exhaustive that I begin to feel as if I had not written a book but produced a line of cooking utensils—rust-proof, light-weight, etc. .

I think of you all the time and wish that I had a photograph. I saw you on tv Saturday night but it wasn't much help. Here comes another photographer followed by Iole with the bottles.

> Love
> John

That's his old friend Lennie Field. Rutuola is the guru in *Bullet Park*.

> John Cheever [1969]
> Cedar Lane
> Ossining, N.Y. 10562
>
> May 8th

Dear Tanya,

Lennie's wife is named Virginia and she is called Ginny and sometimes (alas) Gin. His daughter is named Katherine and called Kathy. I'm so pleased that you got the leit-motif. A reviewer here said that the book didn't hang together. I thought this wrong since the book is so closely constructed that it can be read backwards.

I too could use Rutuola but he went back to Baltimore. I am sure of few things; but I am sure that when I die and you (many years later) die we will meet at once and have a very stimulating eternity. The cast is off but the leg remains swollen and painful and the night is not my house. All of this will pass.

> Love,
> John

I'm enclosing the TIME review because it fits into the envelope.

> John Cheever
> Cedar Lane
> Ossining, N.Y. 10562
>
> May fourteenth [1969]

Dear Exley,

Good luck with the Rockefellers and I will praise your voice. It's hard to know what choice they'll make. The Ford Foundation asked me if I would like a grant to write a play. I accepted their kind invitation. They then wrote to say than an unexpected number of people had accepted the invitation and that they wouldn't decide until August. In August they wrote to say that my work wasn't up to scratch. They gave the grant to William Goyen. Gass is the sort of thing they like. They're very impressed by people who can't write.

I'm out of the cast but not quite out of the woods. The book is a best-seller,my wife is loving, my children are comely, my gardens are in bloom but I seem stuck in a morass of alcohol and melancholy. This will pass.

Best,
Cheever

July 8th

Darling,

I got stoned last night and wanted terribly to call you but I couldn't find your number and I guess its just as well. I should at least be sober. I miss you but this isn't at all gloomy. You have a kind of brightness that seems to exclude nostalgia,soft music and greenish yearnings. I have a long bill of particulars about how unworthy I am and that its best not to see you because when I do see you I don't see anything else for quite sometime. I imagine you going to work in the morning and eating Chinese food. I always seem to be hiding behind a palm tree.

The big dinner dance kept us busy and it seems to have come off. Susie and her husband go to Majorca next week and we follow them on the twenty-second. Mary then goes to Rome but I think I'll stay on the beach. The book is not the bestseller Knopf had anticipated but about four hundred people buy it each week and how I love those four hundred. I think they wear sneakers.

Love,
John

Christine Keeler was the party girl with whom Britain's Secretary for War, John Profumo, was guilty of an "impropriety." Profumo resigned when it was revealed that Keeler was also on extremely friendly terms with a Soviet official suspected of being an intelligence officer.

John Cheever
Cedar Lane
Ossining, N.Y. 10562

[Sept. 10, 1969]

Darling,

It was very good to hear from you. I've been rooting around in the mailbox hoping for a letter from you but all I found were wedding announcements and free razor blades. I thought I had bored you and I tried to telephone. Information produced a David Albert Lang and I called him. He sounded sleepy and cross. He said that he'd seen you on tv but that he didn't know your telephone number. I think of you a great deal.

Travel notes: Susie and Rob met us in Palma and we then drove over the mountains to the other coast. Deya is a cluster of stone houses between the sea and a steep range of mountains. The prices are incredible. Wine is nine cents a bottle and a full pension is less than three dollars a day. Mary, disconcerted by these circumstances, took off for the Madrid Ritz and then the Hassler. I remained in Deya. In the morning I worked and then walked a mile or so through olive and lemon groves to the sea. The coast is rocky and the water is as transparent as air. Above the sea is a small cafe in a cave where you can play chess and drink gin and tonic. In the afternoon I walked to a second cove where you climb down a long ladder into the sea. After dinner everybody goes to the cafe. This is a mixed bag of Europeans and American expatriates. One man is famous for having spent five nights with Christine Keeler. I felt great and returned happily but things are dim here and I go off to the St. Lawrence river tomorrow.

Family notes: Susie and Rob leave Deya this week for London where they will spend the winter. Ben announced on Tuesday that he would be married on Thursday and he was. She is intelligent, witty and pretty, but her father is security chief for IBM and the family had another sort of union in mind. They came out of shock in time for the wedding. When the knot was tied I skinned across the chancel and rang the bell. I rang it very loud. They took off for their honeymoon on a new motorcycle. After an hour in the saddle they agreed that they were terrified and uncomfortable and stopped at the first motel. They finished the trip in a car.

Please write from time to time. I don't mean long letters but notes saying that you're well and so forth.

Love,
John


September [1969]
22nd

Darling,

I see your lovely face looking out of so many newspaper advertisements and television sets that I'm beginning to feel that you're a national possession like the Grand Canyon. Sometimes you look very beautiful, sometimes you look very earnest and I suppose you're both. I once saw a woman on an elevator carrying a book of mine. She held the book backwards so I could see myself peering over her elbow. I found looking at myself very disconcerting and when she had left the elevator I had a terrible feeling that she was taking my face away with her, leaving me nothing to shave in the morning. I hope you don't have any trouble like this.

I don't have anything to say really and I carry on only because it's a little like talking with you which I would like to do. I went to the St. Lawrence river to work and catch some fish. I did some work and caught some bass. We fished for Muskies which weigh fifty pounds and have mouths like steam-shovels. You brain them over the head with a baseball bat and I kept wondering what would happen if I caught one; but I didn't.

Ben keeps taking me for rides on his motorcycle. I don't like riding on his motorcycle but I haven't said so. It is autumn here now and quite cold. I still go swimming every day which leaves me shivering and magnanimous. I don't know what I'll do to sweeten my disposition when the water gets too cold. I don't know what the winter will bring.

Love,
John

John Cheever
Cedar Lane
Ossining, N.Y. 10562

October third

Dear Tanya,

I guess this finds you at the sea. The only Russian coast I know is the Black sea at Yalta where I used to swim. . . . When the world is more peaceable you must come and see the beaches here. There is a stretch of white sand that runs from Maine to Cape Hatteras. Gulls scream, the waves rumble, and the crowned beach is resiliant and wonderful to walk on. We used to summer on one of the sea islands and I would walk miles up the beach to a seapond and fill a sack with clams. Mary would then make a clam soup that smelled of the sea with onions. So, (I invent a gentle rain) one went to bed.

Bullet Park was not as successful here as the publisher had expected although I think it sold a hundred thousand copies. There was a hostile review in the Times and the publisher stopped all advertising. I may have made a mistake in using a suburb as a social metaphor. One would sooner read about fornicating in mountain passes and storms at sea. The reviews were mostly respectable but strangely diagnostic as if I had been mistaken for a philospher. Several critics have urged me to return to St. Botolphs but how can I. It never existed.

Love,
John

The letter below gives a glimpse of what became "The Fourth Alarm." Also Cedar Lane, Oct. 20, 1969.

October 20th

Darling,

. . . New York particularly theatrical New York mystifies me. If I went to the theatre and were asked to undress I wouldn't mind terribly but what would I do with my wallet,wrist-watch and car keys. I mean I wouldn't look like much in a naked love-pile clutching my valuables. Let go of my wallet,etc. In this connection you might be interested in your neighbor Mrs. Burns. She has a husband,two young children and until very recently taught 8th and 9th grade English in the High School. Either bored or curious she tried out for a part in Oh Calcutta and got one. Now she appears on the stage eight times a week jay-naked. She is the happiest of women. No lawyer will take her husband's divorce suit because there is no precedent for simulated copulation in public as grounds for divorce. I don't know what the moral is for this.

We had a heavy frost last night and now an old man named Vincent is raking up the last of the leaves.

Love,
John

Ivy was Tanya's mother, Vera is one of Tanya's daughters. Ivy wrote stories for *The New Yorker*.

John Cheever
Cedar Lane
Ossining, N.Y. 10562

January 13th

Dear Tanya,

John Swope sent on some wonderful photographs he took of your, Vera and Ivy. It's been so long since I've seen you that I had forgotten your eyes. Spear tried to steal the picture of you with the wine glasses but I got it away from him. He did steal the picture of you in Georgia. I find the three generations—Ivy with a reading glass, you with a wine glass and Vera with a cigaret—very exciting and I spend a lot of time look at them.

The ground is covered with snow and it is very cold. I still lunch with Spear on Friday but he has given up skating. I've decided that I don't like Bullet Park. I don't quite know what went wrong but I think something misfired. However I'm in love again and that usually helps things.

Love,
John

John Cheever [1970]
Cedar Lane
Ossining, N.Y. 10562

February 20th

Dear Tanya,

As for Ben I thought I'd written to you. He did marry. He announced on Tuesday that he would be married on Thursday. She is beautiful and witty. She is an only child. Her Father in in charge of security at IBM. This means the enforcement of the most conservative satorial and intellectual customs. He is a pleasant, slender man with a thin and absolutely permenant smile. It would be uncharitable of me to say that if you put his hand into fire the smile would not change; but I am not uncharitable. She must have been quite a pretty woman. They neither drink nor smoke nor do they read. They were shocked by the marriage until it was a fact whereupon they became happier (I've been told) then they've ever been. They have a son.

They were married in church because Ben likes the book of Common Prayer as do I. Ben wore a suit that fitted him the way suits fit bears and chimpanzees in the circus. The bride was beautiful. When the benediction was over I looped across the chancel and rang the bell. I think loud bell ringing is very important. I was worried about champagne but her Father produced a little. Then Ben and his bride mounted a motorcycle and rode off in the dusk. You would like Ben. he is immensely gentle, thoughtful and strong but he's one of those men whose clothing never fits. I've taken him to the most expensive tailors but he still looks like a bear.

Love,
John

I am no longer on speaking terms with my former in-laws, but I must point out in their defense that they each used to smoke a package of Salems every day. He's right about the suit.

There was always a competitive element to the friendship between my father and John Updike—and my father could be quite nasty about John behind his back—but there was also genuine admiration and affection.

John Cheever
Cedar Lane
Ossining, N.Y. 10562

April 24th [1970]

Dear John,

It seems that we will meet in Seoul and this will be very pleasant. I've been thinking of taking Mary and my thirteen year old son and going on from Tokio to Leningrad. This is madness. We will be stoned in Seoul, robbed in Tokio and jailed in Leningrad.

I think we've not met since the cape which was a year ago and I look forward very much to seeing you both again. My love to Mary.

Yours,
John

This is John Weaver.

John Cheever
Cedar Lane
Ossining, New York 10562

Seventeenth

Dear John,

It was very good to hear from you and I'm delighted to know that you have a book coming out. I've enjoyed your letters so much over the years that I've missed them but my own letter-writing proclivities seem eclipsed. Who cares that it is raining or not raining or might rain? Whenever I start a story these days I discover that I've written it. I went up to Saratoga last month and walking the three miles down Union Avenue I saw exactly twenty-seven details that I had used in stories—a wooden tower, old parimutuel tickets, a three legged dog, an iron deer, a dying elm, etc. I go on Monday for a change of landscape to Tokio and Seoul but I go with John Updike who is very grabby about the mise-en-scene. He walks a little behind me and hogs all my sensitive observations. Mary and Fred are coming along and I will be a PEN delegate in Korea.

Hope and Alan are getting a divorce but I seem, through some sleight of hand, to have ended up with Alan. Hope has found what she calls an "uncreative" man. Susie and Rob, who are living in Londan spent a month here and that was pleasant. Ben and his bride are living in New York. The swimming pool situation here is very critical. Most of the pools I use—and their attendants—have grown old. Pools that used to be open in May are not yet painted. I am studying Japanese and can say Good Morning (Ohiyoh) and where is the men's room (Oh-toh-koh noh behn-joh wah doh-koh dehes hah.)

Saranoya,<br>
John

This letter was written in Ossining on paper that must have been distributed at the P.E.N. Congress in Korea.

XXXVII INTERNATIONAL P.E.N. CONGRESS
SEOUL—1970
Chosun Hotel

Cedar Lane<br>
Ossining<br><br>
Thursday

Dear Bill,

Oddly enough we did come back quite well and happy. The flight was long—seventeen hours—and in Fairbanks (Esquimos, trappers, etc.) we were joined by thirty-six members of the Akron University Faculty with their wives. They all had their name, street address and zip code sewn to their clothing and the women still wore the dead or dying flowers that had been given to them when they departed. They were on their way around the world via Tokio, Singpore, Tashkent, etc. and many of them carried bottles of water from Akron. There is, as you must know, nothing like Akron water. Tokio and her mountain were lost in smog when we arrived and families, taking their evening walk, all wore surgical masks. We stayed in a deluxe hotel and I kept waking up in the morning shouting kharma, kharma. In Seoul John's paper was brilliant and so was John. We went to a great many receptions in palaces with curved eaves. The reception rooms had mirrors and chandaliers and were the sort of rooms where people sign treaties. There was a marvelous party in a Geisha house where I was washed, examined, kissed, and fed by hand and not only did my Geisha prostrate herself when she buckled my shoes, she took my hand and led me through the rain to a taxi. She was beautiful and wore blue and her name was Saw.

Seoul is surronded by mountains and the enemy live in the mountains. The president is surrounded by body guards and when he drives down the street you are ordered to close your windows and draw the curtains. There is a curfew at midnight. They gave us silks and chests and flowers and scrolls and a three volume edition of the President's speeches. When we returned to Tokio we didn't go to Expo. We saw some shrines and Cedar forests and waterfalls and I kept shouting Karma, Kharma.

John

He remembered the same trip in his journals:

What then do I remember vividly. The fishbone pines in Fairbanks. This outpost. The light in the sky is grey but there has been no diminishment in its brillance forfifteen hours. The faculty wives from Akron,wearing dead flowers and carrying bottles of home-town water. What a waste of time to ridicule them. They are out to see the world and what is wrong with that. They will have some excitement,pleasure,a dossier of colored photographs and dihorrea,athletes foot, anti-american riots and the peril and fear of sudden death in the Berring sea. The smog in Tokio obscures the city and its mountain. The cab driver wears a surgical mask. Made in Japan was a watchword of my youth. Almost everything for sale in that paradise—the five and ten cent store—was made in Japan. Gold fish, toys, screw-drivers, can openers,beads—were all made in Japan. That city bombed and fire-stormed, is long gne but on the street corners you sometimes see an old house with surved eaves that was made in Japan.

In the following letter, Fred is my brother. Coverly is one of the two brothers in the Wapshot books. My mother taught at Briarcliff College for ten years. Toward the end of her time there, the administration changed, and most of the people she liked and admired left or were fired. Sandra Hochman was a friend of my mother's. Sandra's novel Walking Papers (Viking) was a best-seller in 1971. The old Kress estate was near my parents' home on Cedar Lane, and it had a pond that you could swim in if you were very hot, or very drunk. Otherwise you'd notice the mud. Art is Arthur Spear, a longtime drinking, walking and fishing companion from whom we rented the house in Friendship, Maine, in 1956.

My father's teaching experiences at Sing Sing would help provide the backdrop for *Falconer*, although in the *Newsweek* interview that ran in March of 1977, he told my sister, "I didn't go to Sing Sing to gather material any more than I got married and had children to gather material."

Here's a letter written in April of 1974 to the writer Allan Gurganus about my father's continuing relationship with Donald Lang. Lang had been a student of my father's at Sing Sing. After Lang got out they remained friends.

On Monday night Lang went to a terrible black saloon called the Orchid Lounge. He was picked up by a blonde dude. They got into a fight. Lang chose a cro-bar for his weapon. The dude ended up in the hospital and Lang in jail. Lang called me from jail early Tuesday morning and I spent three hours (in my very best suit) talking to the backs of black and white police officers. It was tiring. Lang is merely a friend but his freedom is very dear to me. At around noon I got to a judge, who set bail. I got the cash and out came Lang, unshaven,unwashed and carrying his shoe-laces. I wondered what your reaction would be, he said. Say thank you, said I. Thank you, said he, and we, for the second time, stepped out of jail into the sun. . . .

Monday [May 9, 1971, for sure]

Dear Ben,

FLASH. Fred is five foot seven. He is taller than me. Speaking of height an admirer called not long ago at three-thirty A.M. I'm only five foot five, he said. I'm five foot six and one half, I said. You don't sound like John Cheever, he said. I said I was Covery Wapshot and terribly sleepy. His name is Woiwode. All of my admirers telphone at three thirty in the morning and have names like Exley, Ohno, Mukenfuss and Woodcock. My favorite—Popescue—lives in Bucharest at 16 Julius Fuck Street. They all seem either drunk or mad and I have a terrible nightmare in which they all pile int the dining-room.

It is pleasant here now. The cherry tree is in bloom and Mary is writing poetry which makes her happy. Things at her college get sadder and sadder. Sex education has been added to the ciruculum but it says in the catalogue that There Will Be No Demonstrations. All the faculty who have been fired are going to march in the Commencement Procession, weeping. Sandra Hochman arrived on Saturday with a new stud. He described himself as a "gymnast". He's better looking than the other one. They were followed by Susie and Rob who made a frontal assault on a roast of beef. It vanished like snow but they seem happy. I went swimming at Kress on Friday and damn near froze. As a consequence my brocnial tubes sound like the Cleveland Symphony. Art, and I and the dogs walked to the dam on Saturday where we were invited to join some pleasant young people who were reading Martin Buber and drinking wine. Walking over the Kress Hill yesterday I heard voices from the woods. "Dorothy Parker was highly unreliable," a man said. I joined them and they were pleasant but no wine. Tomorrow I go to Sing-Sing to talk with the warden about giving a course in the short story to convicted drug-pushers, etc. If you don't hear from me you'll know what happened. Clang.

Our love to Linda.

Yours
J.

Wednesday [end of May 1971]

Dear Ben,

The class was great on Thursday. The high point came when a puertorican drug-pusher (age 24) got up and exclaimed: "Oh what a cool motherfucker was that Machiavelli." It isn't always that good. Yesterday Fred and I took three boxes of books over for the prison Library. As soon as we put the books into the processing room they locked us up. We would have to wait until a proper authority had examined the books. I wasn't as bad as I might have been. I mean I didn't go around saying:"Will you *kindly* give me your name, etc. When I asked if I could go out to the car and get a cigaret the guard made a face at me and I damned near hit him which would have made everything dandy. We were in for about a half an hour but the warden called this morning to apologize.

Mary's classes are over but she seems quite happy with her poetry. A film company is making a sex-horror movie in Beechwood and I went over yesterday to see the shooting. Everything is shabby and broken and the ballroom is full of actors dressed as ghouls. Cha Cha. I've finished a long piece which makes me happy and all is well. Everyone sends their love to Linda.

Yrs,
J.

My sister was working at the *Tarrytown Daily News*.

Friday [June 4, 1971, I'm sure]

Dear Ben,

I've lost black Pat Boyle, the fellow who held up Korvettes. They transferred him to Auburn on Tuesday. They moved out about two hundred men and I seem to have lost the Machivelli fellow as well. A new bunch moved in yesterday. They are about as straight-looking a group of men as I've ever seen but I suppose they strangled old women in dark alleys. I'll never know. They don't like to talk about their mistakes.

The New Yorker turned down my new story. Esquire wants to buy it but they'll only pay fifteen hundred. Considering the length of time it took, this is less than Susie makes on the Tarrytown paper. Harpers is out and the Atlantic still doesn't know about orgasims and that's that.

Mary seems very well and happy. She and Fred plan to go to Colorado and they think I'm going with them; but I'm not. One, I don't want to go. Two, I really can't afford to go. I'll tell them my decision some day soon. It's been pleasantly rainy and the lawns are very green. Fred is on a diet which seems to involve eating everything in sight excepting spinach. Love to Linda.

Yrs,

J.

This is to John Updike. The book was *Rabbit Redux* (Knopf). Zhenya is Yevtushenko.

John Cheever
Cedar Lane
Ossining, N.Y. 10562

December third [1971]

Dear John,

I read the book and thought it great; a term that is not often used on the north or the south shore. Thinking that I might have deceived myself I read it again and came to the same conclusion.

Zhenya was preposterous but I find him exciting. He pointed out that I was wearing the same clothes I'd worn seven years ago. He was wearing a full-length coat of sea otter skins, trimmed with mink. Peter, wearing Updike gifts, is a nice boy who giggles when he's tickled. It snowed a lot and I was presented to the President of the Supreme Soviet Union. He has a shoeshine machine in his office.

My love to Mary
Yours,
John

F. is a Russian official who had also accompanied the Updikes on their Russian trip.

Cedar Lane
Ossining

December 28th, [1971?]

Dear John and Mary,

I missed you both in Moscow. They mentioned Bech and I snapped at them. Redux doesn't seem to have reached them but they clearly know how important you are and greatly admire you,your work,your wife, your children, your house, your etc. I took my youngest son. [F____] was with us throughout and there was only one scene. "Now is being time for resting," said [F____], "and in ten minutes will be peeping into house of Pushkin." That's when I made the scene. The Writers Union invited me to celebrate the Dostoivsky jubilee but when we got there [F____] said:"Is being in Riga the jubilee so shall we be peeping into Tblisi?" That's what we did. I was taken to Fyodor's grave in Leningrad but it was closed. The sign said: Jour de repos.

Oh the Ukraine, the Ukraine. Now snow and ice. The enormous revolving doors let in a bitter cold. The lobby smells of wet wool and rabbit fur. Under the concave mural of The Peaceable Kingdom outer-Mongolians sit in imitation leather chairs. The chairs are patched with friction table. The right elevator bank is a Rugby Scrum. The smell of a million empty bureau drawers---I *think* that's it—is positively heady. It's all there, the stopped clocks, the dusk in the corridors, the miles of carpet, the dead-end sitting rooms with ferns and paintings, the hint of life imprisonment. In Leningrad we stayed at the Europe again. There was Ganymede,Apollo and the unmoored stair carpets. The Winter

Palace badly needs a coat of paint. I saw almost everyone and everyone spoke fondly of you both.

Fondly,
John

Tanya's daughter, Vera, was coming to visit.

Cedar Lane
Ossining,New York

January 15th

Dear Tanya,

It's just that my muse remains in Portugal and I seem to have no inspiration for letters or for work. All I can do is wait for the jade to return. She has strayed before. Nothing seems very acute or significant. The day is overcast. It looks like snow. John Updike has gone to Africa. My marriage is in the dumps. I drink vodka for breakfast. There is skating and in this I find absolute forgetfulness. The ice froze suddenly and but for the air bubbles is black and transparent. I can see schools of carp scatter under my shadow. On Saturday I took part in an anti-war demonstration. I walked around and around. It seemed penitential. Mary was assailed by a reactionary but no one bothered me. Mary, who is quite beautiful and vain does not like to carry a picket sign because it conceals her face. I spend some time and much energy at prison. My newest student—a young black—is in for twenty-six years. I get along wonderfully with murderers.

. . . We wait for Vera; I wait for my muse. I have always been the lover —never the beloved---and I have spent much of my life waiting for trains, planes, boats, footsteps, doorbells, letters, telephones, snow, rain, thunder etc.

Love,
John

He had been to Russia again.

February 18th

Cedar Lane

Dear Tanya,

I've been expecting to hear from you and since I haven't I wonder if I was offensive or boring on that snowy night at the Ukraine. You looked tired. I was tired and disconcerted by the loss of your tooth. I am absurdly concerned with cosmetics. I was tired and am tired today. I am tired of drinking scotch for breakfast, tired of worrying about money this late in life, tired of making love in motels to men and women I'll never see again, tired of these winter skies. . . .

Playboy has taken three stories. I like one of them. It is the story of a man as told by his abdomen. I've stopped working on a long piece because it seemed more like an essay than a story and I am not an essayist. . . . Yevtushenko is still here but I've seen him only once. He is galvanizing audiences all over the place and it's gotten to seem like such a circus that I think I would not like to see him again. One of my students at the prison was released after twelve years. I went down to see him out and it was very exciting to see the way he looked at the sky. John and Mary Updike were at Yevtushenko's party John has a broken leg. Mary is as enchanting as ever. I hope this finds you well and toothsome.

Yours,
John

In the fall of 1972, my father visited the Writers Workshop at the University of Iowa and gave a reading. Fred Exley, who was at the university, had encouraged him to do so.

Cedar Lane

Dear Fred,

That was great fun although I do worry about all the tabs you picked up. We seem to have something basically in common, something more lambent, I hope, than hootch and cunt. I flew from Chicago with a Panam stewardess. At the end of the flight she embraced me ardently and said:"You are one of the most charming and interesting men I have ever met and by far the craziest." She wore a red cape.

On Yaddo you should write Curtis Harnack Executive Director. As soon as you've written I will write. I think Elliott and Roth will be there in February but I'm not sure. I look forward to seeing you here.

Yours,
John

In November of 1972, John "Jack" Leggett, the Workshop director, invited my father to come back and teach.

Cedar Lane
Ossining, New York

Dear Jack,

Firstly it was very pleasant to see you and to meet your charming wife whose person, whose pasta and whose bread I remember vividly. I was greatly taken with Iowa. I thought the community serene and the students responsible. There are some imponderables. I don't know what to do about this house,my marriage is in the annual dumps and on Tuesday my daughter-in-law had a large son. Do you think grandfathers should be allowed to teach literature to the young? I'm not sure.

In any case nothing seems pressing and I expect this might find you in the alps. I do appreciate your kind invitation.

Yours,
John

Once, in the 1950s, my father had been invited to teach at Iowa, and the invitation had been withdrawn. I still think an astonishing modesty was shown by the fact that he wondered if Jack might have second thoughts. His lack of self-assurance was also an indication of a growing desperation.

Cedar Lane
Ossining, New York
January 15th [1973]

Dear Jack,

Firstly this is not my typewriter—it is and Olympia that belongs to my son—and I am not responsible for errors.

I do hope your skiing trip was a great success. I miss skiing very much. I am seriously interested in your kind invitation to come to Iowa. I would sooner teach one semester than two if this would be possible. I'm bound to miss the east. The imponderables here are settled. My son will go to boarding school and my wife will remain here. I think I'm a competent instructor in writing although I will have to change my Sing-Sing voice. My newest student is a former editor of SCREW and is in for twenty-six years.

It all seems remote in time if you have any doubts, second-thoughts or questions I would be happy to have them.

My best to your wife.

Yours,
John

Bourjaily is the writer Vance Bourjaily. The school my brother Fred "settled on" was Andover.

Cedar Lane
Ossining, New York

January 23rd [1973]

Dear Jack,

I would be delighted to come to Iowa for the first semester and your terms are very generous. Perhaps I should make another visit in the late winter or spring to learn more about the university. All I seem to remember is the snow, your wife's lasagna and the Bourjaily's livestock.

My son hasn't settled on a school but he makes a tour next month and I'm sure he'll find something he likes. If you are in the east I would be happy to come in town for lunch. I do hope you have good snow.

Yours,
John

John Cheever
Cedar Lane
Ossining, N.Y. 10562

February 7th

Dear Jack,

I wrote you a week or so ago to say how happy I would be to teach the fall semester. There's been no reply and I trust nothing has gone wrong.

Yours,
John

John Cheever
Cedar Lane
Ossining, N.Y. 10562

Dear Jack,

I shall apply for a parking permet and I would like to live at Iowa House. I must tell you that I had a massive heart attack two weeks ago and will be in the hospital until the middle of June. My recovery is described as Beautiful. I've not mentioned Ioaw to the doctor and I see no reason why I should. I have an accelerated heart beat and an injured but not damaged muscle. I'll write in a few days.

Yours,
John

March 22nd [1973]
Cedar Lane, Ossining

Dear Fred,

I'm not really uptight about Iowa but thankw for the help and I'll look up the Foxes and the barman. I guess Vance will be around to recommend a heart specialist. Clothes seem to be a problem. I've lost a lot of weight, nothing fits and I got some great pants at the Army & Navy. They fit but the zippers don't work and when I piss I have to take my pants off, stretch them on the floor and reunite them link by link. By the time I'm dressed the lights are out and everyone's gone home.

I hope things square off with you and the book. Twenty-two thousand seems allright to me but I guess the agent would know. I'm very anxious to read it. I work slowly and clumsily and I hope that a change of rivers will help. Keep me posted.

Yours,
John

Despite the breezy tone of these letters, the recovery was not speedy, or certain. I recall a terrible afternoon in intensive care with my father in mid-May. One of the only times I remember him being a boorish snob was when he was going through delirium tremens during the forced withdrawl from alcohol that followed his heart attack. He'd been extremely high-handed with the hosptial staff. My sister—who had taken over the management of his recovery at this point—felt that if a family member wasn't by the bedside the staff might handle him with a roughness that could be fatal to his weakened heart. I was deeply involved in a troubled and isolating marriage, but was still drafted for the afternoon shift. I remember that my father was in the hospital on May 15th, because my wife was annoyed that it interfered with her birthday. I was very much afraid of my wife's displeasure at that time in my life, but I was also afraid of my sister, and my sister insisted that I take my turn in intensive care—and for this I am deeply grateful. The scene with the son at the father's bedside, the heart monitor and the oxygen tubes has become a TV and movie cliché, but it retains a certain horrid originality in real life.

Daddy was lying on his back whispering to himself in some sort of delirium and searching the sheets for a cigarette. I'd been alone with him for a while when he caught sight of the lights on the intensive-care ward's control panel. These he took to be the lights of a tavern. When he was irritated he'd become highly aristocratic, his accent would deepen, and he'd sound haughty and crisp. He was very high-toned that afternoon despite his hospital gown and the somewhat less than elegant surroundings.

I don't suppose the conversation that follows is exact to the word, but it comes back to me with a force of memory that indicates a high degree of accuracy.

"Ben," he said," could you step around to that bar and buy me a package of Marlboros and a martini? If they don't have Marlboros, Winstons will do. And why don't you make that martini a double." He'd had a heart attack; he had oxygen tubes in his nose. It seemed likely that the gin would stop his heart and a cigarette would blow us both up.

"That's not a bar, Daddy," I said. "You're in the hospital. You're in the intensive-care unit. That's the nurses' station you see."

"Are you completely without imagination and initiative?" he asked. "If that is not a bar, then why don't you go out and find one? And when you've found one, if you're capable of finding a bar in a state that is crammed with them, then why don't you buy that pack of cigarettes for me and a double martini?"

"I don't think I should, Daddy."

"Well, then, I'll just get up and do it myself," he said.

"I don't think you should either," I said.

"Isn't that for me to decide?" he said.

"It could kill you," I said.

Then he started to get up. This excited the heart monitor, and I was afraid of what the oxygen tubes would do to his nose, so I grabbed the rails of the bed and made a barrier of myself. First he struggled, then he lay back down. Then he hit me in the chest with his forearm. It didn't hurt, but it did surprise me. He was furious. "You've always been a disappointment as a son," he said.

In any case, my father's illness wasn't a minor incident. He used to drink a fifth a day. In an attempt to cut back on his use of alcohol, his doctors had prescribed tranquilizers, which he took along with his gin. He was killing himself, and he not only knew it, he said it. My younger brother, Fred, was still living at home during the worst of this period, and he found himself in the god-awful position of being his father's caretaker. There were lots of trips to the hospital, and they were often preceded by a period of days in which it was clear that something was dreadfully wrong.

My father loved all his children, and he loved us all in different ways, but he loved Fred best. I think he would have loved Fred best no matter what. Fred was born the year that Daddy published his first novel. Fred was named for his beloved brother. Fred also seems to have come into the world with a character that elicits love. Iole, our Italian maid, for instance, altered her life, changed her citizenship, because of Fred. So Fred may have fallen into the apparently enviable position of being most loved, but he certainly earned it once there. Fred was the boy who took care of the wayward man. Fred was the one who picked Daddy up when he fell down, and Daddy usually said something cutting to whoever assumed this role. In a letter to the writer Allan Gurganus, a student of his at Iowa, my father acknowledged that adulthood had been forced on Fred rather early, and that this had altered his character in some fundamental way.

"Both Susie and I grant him [Fred] absolute maturity. We both feel that, in his earlier life, he had a successful but unbrilliant business career, married twice and raised seven children. He has never given me any reason to doubt this." Fred would have been in his twenties when this was written.

I was trying without much success to make a go of my first marriage. Weeks would pass without my visiting my parents' house. My sister never abandoned her responsibilities, but my sister didn't live at home when the things were at their worst. My mother was there, of course, and she also took quantities of abuse, and paid them back with patience and support, but my mother was an adult, and was equipped to bear the wounds to self-esteem that Daddy was in the habit of inflicting on a regular basis. Maybe it was as bad for her as it was for Fred, but it's easiest for me to understand the immensity of Fred's accomplishment, because Fred was Daddy's child and so was I. And Fred not only helped Daddy, he helped the rest of us too.

I recall one ghastly Thanksgiving in particular. Caption it: "What's wrong with this picture?" See the family all dressed up, here's the linen tablecloth. The blessing is asked, the turkey is carved, and then they commence to eat. But why does the man at the head of the table have an open wound on his forehead? Why is his face swollen? He's trying to eat a forkful of peas. His hand is shaking so violently that the peas fall off the fork before he gets it to his mouth. Nobody says anything for a while, and then somebody suggests that the head of the household use a spoon. He puts his fork down. "You have a father who is dying," he says. And Fred, God bless him, says, "We have a father with a taste for melodrama."

This is to John Updike, who apparently had proposed John Barth for the National Institute of Arts and Letters.

John Cheever
Cedar Lane
Ossining, N.Y. 10562

June first [1973]

Dear John,

I don't really like Barth but I'll agree to anything that will bring a new face to that gathering. I met him at some dinner. Jean Stafford embrace me and said:"You're reputation in literature is very shaky but if you'll drive a knife into his heart you'll live forever." I don't feel that strongly.

The crises is over although I still have an unruly ventricle. The important thing is that this makes me feel much closer to The Century Club. I can't for example climb stairs. This will make me a much better clubman.

I miss you both and trust that we will someday walk on a beach.

Yours,
John

# *GATEWAY*
# *TO NEBRASKA*

* * *

The great thing about having a heart attack is that when you're in the hospital they don't give you anything alcoholic to drink, so when Daddy checked out he was dry. I believe he was still dry when he went off to Iowa in the fall of 1973. The Friday Club was the name given the group of men who ate regularly on Fridays at the not particularly distinguished restaurants in and around Ossining, New York. The group included the cartoonist and sculptor John Dirks, Arthur Spear, the folk singer Tom Glazer, Eddie Newhouse, Roger Willson, who now works for the Rockefeller family and associates, and the actor Barrett Clark. There were many guest appearances.

Iowa Memorial Union
Iowa City, Iowa 52240
September 8th [1973]

Dear Arthur,

I do miss the Friday Club but I haven't been able to think of any excuse to bring that great organization out to the middle west. The architecture goes from the 1840's to Abramovitz & Harrison but it is nicely separated by the river and great stands of elmsthat are nursed by the Department of Agriculture. It is in a random way one of the most agreeable villages I have ever seen. The students are respectful,comely,barefoot and carry piles of books. There are spires but no chimes; many orientals, a few Chicanos and American Indians and almost no blacks.

They are restoring the old State House and selling pieces and I thought of buying you a length of cornice but I wouldn't know how to wrap or mail it. The State House is quite pretty but not worth the trip. If you and Tom could work out an act---Troubador and Historian---I'll present it to the administration.

My best to Stella.

Yours,<br>John

John and Mary Dirks are old friends of the family. When my father writes, "I do Justina," he means that he's to give a reading of the story "The Death of Justina."

September 20th [1973]<br>Iowa House

Dear John and Mary,

I thought there might be a harp in this crowd but I followed them out to the stadium for the Michigan game and there wasn't. There was a marching band (150), a lot of acrobats on trampolines, drunken alumini ringing cowbells and shouting advice, a small airplane advertising Big Iowa Insurance and a PA plug for an undergraduate performance of Pinters Old Times. The Iowa team is terrible but everybody stays for the last down andthen you walk home under the elm trees which are numerous. Theatre,film,parachuting,rugger,ceramics, weaving,cricket,bookbinding,soccer and LaCrosse are all swinging and the bumper sticker is WELCOME TO IOWA, THE GATEWAY TO NEBRASKA. There is a tenfoot Paul Bury fountain across the river from my window but it's more of a pool than a fountain. The architecture ranges from the 1840's through brick buildings with Pindar and Aristotle on the cornice to a lot of Abramovitz. The elms and the river help.

I missed the rocking chair contest (80 hrs) and last night the amateur Topless Go-Go Girls contest was delayed beyond my bedtime.

Had I written a few days ago I would have said that the place was genuinely innocent but there do seem to be academic politics. However they don't concern me. My students are brilliant and diverse and when we bring off a seminar it takes three men to get me off the ceiling. I'd never known that particular high. I do Justina in Nebraska next month and I think she'll make North Dakota. It's all almost very,very good. Welcome to Ossining, the gateway to Iowa.

Love,<br>
John

Minnie was Arthur's Labrador. Stella, his wife, is a musician.

Iowa House<br>
Sunday [Fall 1973]

Dear Arthur,

. . . I'm having a great time but I am getting tired and I am having trouble with alcohol again. I rush from the boat races to the Rugby field and from there to a date with a Bengalese beauty who lectures on Wordsworth. I shout myself hoarse at football games, take young women to concerts,dance the Virginia Reel, play football, lecture on the problems of modern fiction and generally splatter myself over this part of the mid-western landscape. The country is beautiful. The campus elms have been saved but the elms in the country are going. There are large stands of oak. The harvest is about half in, the country is hilly and the light and air are pure.

Tell Minnie that the dog situation is poor. There are many so-called labradors with skinny legs, curly tails and floppy ears. I throw sticks for them when I'm lonely. Tell Stella that there are quartets, orchestras,soloists performing almost every night. One the other end of things there is a very active parachute club and one of the undergraduates has an ascention balloon in which he and his girl drift over the campus on Saturday afternoons.

Yours,<br>
John

This is to John Updike.

Iowa House
Iowa City

October first [1973]

Dear John,

I was serious when I spoke of the enthusiasm which which the students here regard your work. The vogue for Barthelme is over and while they do read Kosinski they will not defend him. I am moved, of course, by the pleasure I would take in seeing you here. It would tie in with the White House, the beach in Wellfleet, Moscow and Seoul. I walked around the place—it's really a village—asking the trees, the sky, the buildings, the cast (young women from California who are waiting to be raped by a poet and see their first snow) if it would be worth your while. I'm not sure; but it would be great for me. They'll pay at least a thousand but I will not mention this letter to anyone until I hear from you. The place would go to pieces.

Yours,
John

When my father returned to New York and called me up, I could tell by his voice that he'd been drinking again.

Cedar Lane
Ossining, New York

January 10th, 1974

Dear Tanya,

. . . I think I last wrote you in May or June although I can't remember. It seems that I nearly die every two years but then I always rally with a strapping apetite and one couldn't find a better way to live. In August I went out to Iowa to teach a semester at the university. I felt very sorry for myself—leaving for the loneliness of the prairie towns and the cornfields. I remained there until Christmas and have never had a better time in my life. However I did not work and since writing seems to be my principle usefullness I came home where I am not terribly happy.

... When I left for Iowa Fred left for boarding school in Andover where he studies Russian. He has to memorize a page a day. these are simple matters about opening and closing windows but he works with a tape and has learned to make marvelous,nostalgic Russian noises that remind me of the streets of Moscow. He seems very happy in school. We have had very heavy snows and the sense of being blockaded does not contribute to the kind of serenity one needs to write a novel but the snow must melt and I trust I will get back to work.

Love,
John

This is to Fred Exley.

January 31st [1974]

Dear Fred,

I'm very,very sorry that you've been sick and I am glad to hear that you're going to Lanai. I didn't know about the Houghton Mifflin unbid. Susie and Rob have been having marital problems and I've not seen him for a long time. All of the Cheevers seem to be making a frontal assault on Holy Matrimony. This union seems ended. I've accepted a professorship (yes,yes) at Boston University and will move there at the end of summer. Three suits and two pairs of loafers. Five shirts with frayed collars. Mary is very happy teaching at a progressive school in Nyack. She teaches Naked Lunch. Fred,about whom I had worried,loves Andover. I can see him in Boston. I don't know what to do about the Christmas tree, etc.

Have a great time on the islands.

Yours,
John

Allan Gurganus was a graduate student at Iowa when my father taught there. Daddy helped shepherd a story of Allan's into *The New Yorker*. The piece was titled "Minor Heroism." These letters are the first concrete and irrefutable evidence of bisexuality in this book. My discovery of my father's sexual involvement with men came in stages. First I thought that it began after he dried out in 1975, and that his earlier difficulties with alcohol had resulted at least in part from an attempt to submerge this craving. Then I realized that he'd been involved with men before he gave up the hootch, and I assumed that this began during his heaviest drinking. I now know that he was sexually involved with men in the 1950s, and it seems possible that he had been bisexual almost from day one. At the time this letter was written, I was in perfect ignorance of what my father used to call his "difficult propensities." In public he was an ardent heterosexual, and he told me that homosexuality made men vain, ungenerous, and ultimately ridiculous. If I had discovered that I was a homosexual, I wouldn't have dared to tell him. I would have expected him to throw me out of the house.

Steve is the novelist Stephen Becker. John Irving was at Iowa when my father taught there, and they used to watch Monday-night football together.

Cedar Lane

Dear Allan,

I was very pleased to have your letter and I enjoyed it very much. As you probably know by now, Steve and I are old friends and as you certianly know by now he is an extraordinary man. I am not quite sure where his giftedness lies but given the right environment and the right raw material he can project a spirituality that I find very forceful. When one speaks of his Greco hands one means of course, not elongation but otherness. I did trip on your description of good John Irving as fetching. This might go back to the slightly different points of view we take on male beauty. John has always struck me as having been saddened by the discovery that to have been the captain of the Exeter Wrestling Team was a fleeting honor.

I miss you but I shan't turn green. When anything intense,funny or interesting takes place it would be nice to have you here. . . . My marriage is hideously on the rocks and Mary won't discuss a settlement or anything else. She won't even say good morning. She is playing Cinderella in a transvestite pantomime to raise money for the school. The wicked stepsisters are men, of course, the fairy godmother is a boff,prince charming is a young woman who leads Mary off-stage, dressed in my son's Hackley School athletic shorts. It all makes me terribly sad. I cut apple-wood with the chain saw, walk the dogs over the hill,skate a great deal and endeavor to appear very simple.

. . . I sometimes wondered if you might not ask less from me than women do and God knows they're terrible at ball games and in museums. . . . However, if I stay out of museums I'll be allright.

Love,
John

Cedar Lane

February 21st [1974]

Dear Allan,

I was very pleased to have the stories and I enjoy them as I have. It was good to read them in a different climate, a different light and I liked the third. I gave them to Mary who thinks you very talented. I shall send them to Bill Maxwell who is a discerning and sympathetic man. It will be good to have his opinion and there might be some word before you return. . . .

. . . I think I told you that I've accepted the appointment at Boston and will move there in the fall. This amounts to a separation or a divorce. I think I shall leave this house—grand-mother's breakfast table,etc.—in a very light-hearted mood. I shall take nothing,not a shell,not a stone. I wish I brought more comprehension to these problems and there is some discernable petulance in my wish to shove the heirlooms. All I want is a narrow bed and my old blue shirts. This is plainly childish but perhaps I will grow wiser as the flowers bloom. I love you very much.

Love,
John

Allan had just been to Mardi Gras. I sincerely doubt the part about "the seven-eyed Sybil" and Rod Swope, although it makes a fetching tale.

Cedar Lane

February 24th

Dear Allan,

My letters will pile up like some passage of time in TV. Bill has the manuscript and I will be in touch with you as soon as I hear from him. He might be very enthusiastic and he might send on a note saying Sorry. One waits.

I was pleased to hear that you're having such a marvelous time. I would love to have been there with you, or anywhere,but I would have been very much out of place in my rented tails. I really never have a terribly good time at costume balls. My casque needs oil or the mirrors fall off my mandarine coat. There was a trauma. Mary (the seven-eyed Sybil) went off with Rod Swope (A hussar). I, a chinese acrobat) drove home alone and I've never put on a costume since then. It isn't my style. I don't know what your lovers are like, I've never met one, but I trust they're comely and worth your while.

The closings of your letters disconcert me. We started off with love, and moved into respect,devotion and affection. I feel like a national anthem or a savings bank. I suppose we'll go through sincerely,truly, and end up Dictated but unsigned.

Love,<br>John

Cedar Lane

March fifth

Dear Allan,

The excitement here was indescribable. It was like the seige of Karthoum. Bill called a week ago today to say that the story shouldbe published and that you were an excellent writer. However Shawn does his reading on weekends and there would be no word until Monday. This left me in painful suspense and I kept waking in the middle of the night to rehearse our telephone conversation—Alan? Yes. This is John. They've taken the story.—There was another version. Allan? Yes. This is John. Shawn has refused the story but he wants to see more of your work—. This plunged me into a terrible depression and I would curl up in the sheets like a foetus. Bill came over Saturday afternoon and said 1. that I reminded him of Lord Byron. 2. That I reminded him of a dog. 3. That one of the imponderables in your destiny was that Shawn had never taken a story about a homosexual. These three considerations had me spinning, Bill stayed late and I greeted the guests for dinner without any clothes on. I didn't compose or dress myself until halfway through cocktails. I felt dreadfully on Sunday and wondered how Byron used to feel in Venice. I was not supposed to call you you, but of course I did. On Monday morning I hung around the telephone drinking martinis. I called Bill at noon. There had been no word from

Shawn and we might have to wait another week. This would not have been possible. I went on drinking and walked the dogs over the hill. Then Bill called. "You can call him," he said. I did. When my conversation with you ended I wanted to call you back. It seemed to have been not nearly enough. Not nearly.

I'm delighted that it went through Bill and not through an agent; and for me one of the most excitingthings was the discernment Shawn, Henderson and Bill brought to the story. They not only bought it; they consider you an estimable arrival.

Love,
John

Cedar Lane
Ossining

March 8th

Dearest Allan,

. . . You will have heard from Bill by now and I'm very happy about this. You may not like his work but I think he's the best editor on the scene. Nabokov, Salinger,Roth, etc. He sometimes invents a writer (Brodkey) and when the invention gets out of hand he extinguishes the man. However there is no danger of this with you since you came to him full-grown and self-possessed. I love him; and as for love I think you ought to know the modesty of my demands. All I expect is that you learn to cook,service me sexaully from three to seven times a day, never interrupt me, contradict me or reflect in any way on the beauty of my prose, my intellect or my person. You must also play soccer, hockey and football. I once asked myself (while skating) if Allan and I became lovers would I have to give up scrub hockey? I seemed to have forgotten that I lost my hockey stick five years ago.

John

March fifteenth [1974]

Dearest Allan,

How very pleasant to have your letter and to have talked with you. This is not the groan of an unrequited lover but a voice that seems to me this morning quite clear and serene. I love you so much. It pleases me to know that you exist, even on the banks of the Iowa River. I had planned to write a scene where you spurned me in front of the bison while a chorus of hundreds sang Home on The Range. I shall not. I would like to call you oftener but someone, after spending a night with me at Iowa House called me from New York every night for two weeks and I got very aloof about the whole thing, a position I do not intend to grant you. My claim to always be the lover and never the beloved is quite false. . . .

Love, love
John

My father had been elevated to the American Academy of Arts and Letters.

Cedar Lane

March 28th [1974]

Dearest Allan,

My sexual and epistolary importunities are well-known. I do wish you have been more yielding about the former. When I was twenty-one Walker Evans invited me to spend the night at his apartment. I said yes. I dropped my clothes (Brooks). He hung his (also Brooks) neatly in a closet. When I asked him how to do it he seemed rather put off. He had an enormous cock that showed only the most fleeting signs of life. I was ravening. I came all over the sheets, the Le Corbusier chair, the Matisse Lithograph and hit him under the chin. I gave up at around three, dressed and spent the rest of the night on a park bench near the river. In the morning I drove to Massachusetts, embraced my dear brother and swam in the sea. I might have learned something from this experience. When we lived in the Palazzo Doria letters positively poured out of the portico. Bill bound his in tooled leather. Mike Bessie wrote: It is not possible to correspond with you. I was terribly hurt and went down to the Cafe Castello and held hands with the girl who sold cigarets. Josie Herbst always responded with punctuality and zest and then sold all my letters to Yale. Last year a homosexual in Grand Central offered me twenty dollars for my body but I was late for the train. He was young and probably balmy. I was terribly polite.

You've not told me what Bill paid and I'm nearly as hung up on this as I was on the manuscript. I was, after all, an usher at this wedding—the sort of usher whose rented ascot rides up to his ears. If they take another story you'll be asked to sign a contract and it's great fun for me to imagine you going through the various jumps and hoops that lie ahead: Allan in the Century, Allan in the Institute, Allan in Tout Parish. On the other hand I sometimes think I will never see you again. I cannot think of you as a skinny graduate student since I love you muchly. I know your manifest faults and chose to overlook them as I trust you overlook the faults of the chained dogs you pat. Bill, as you must have gathered, is terribly fastidious. He once called to say that he was coming for tea. Mary went wild and cleaned, waxed, arranged flowers, etc. When he arrived everything seemed in order. Mary poured the tea. The scene was a triumph of decorum until Harmon, an enormous cat, entered the room, carrying a dead goldfish. It seemed to be our relationship in a nutshell. I've finished a long piece which includes my observation that St. Basils is a madness of cocks. The New Yorker will love this. I'm really not difficult (I think) but I doubt that I can take my chair at the academy with any grace. I would sooner be in your arms than in your prayers but the choice was never mine.

Love,
John

Cedar Lane

Saturday

Dearest Allan:

How clever of you to have discerned that the Cheevers are spiritual canines. I was rather slow to realize this myself. The day after Mother died I was sitting in the library here with my old black Labrador—the grandmother of the yellow you saw. She had never lost a rabies tag in her life and had along rope of tags, hanging from her chain collar. It looked like a necklace mother used to wear. I spoke to her. She raised her head very high and spoke to me. The message was quite clear. "John," she asked, "can't you try to be a little neater?" Mother had made the switch in less than twenty-four hours. Shortly after that I dreamed that I was brought before a canine tribunal who would decide whether or not I could become a dog. They decided in my favor. That dog who bites your glove is some part of me.

I've very glad you're putting the Father pieces together. My interest in your destiny as a writer and a man (I'm not sure of the order) is considerable and deep, as you know.... If I don't see you in Iowa I'll see you somewhere else and very soon. In the meantime be kind and loving to dogs.

Love,
John

# BOSTON UNIVERSITY

\* \* \*

I n his journal he wrote:

I am in a very bad or self-destructive routine. M leaves at seven, long before daybreak these days. I stir somewhat later, drink coffee barearse, get sauced and never approach this machine with the clear eye and the clear head that I need. Towards dusk the day begins to take shape very briefly. Am I crepuscular? Work, discipline, self-respect.

The sun is rising. The day is clear. My head is clear enough for work. I think, I pray.

I do get the mail off and trust I botch nothing.

The letters written in the fall of 1974 and early 1975 sketch out my father's final alcoholic collapse. He went alone to Boston University to teach writing. Friends, including his brother, Fred, and John Updike, did what they could do to help. Bill's book *Ancestors* (Knopf) was published in 1971. I was working at a newspaper in Nyack while my father was determinedly drinking himself to death in Boston. Eddie Newhouse, who had seen my father in Boston, phoned me and said that something should be done. But I didn't feel that I could help. After all, I'd had trouble dissuading him from having a smoke in the intensive-care unit. When I read this letter I was deeply hurt. He never gave me this phone number. Of course if he had given it to me, I might not have called.

71 Bay State Road
Boston, Massachusetts

Dear Bill,

I don't have Allan's address and he doesn't have mine so would you inform one or the other of us of our whereabouts. This is a part of Boston with which I am unfamiliar and I keep thinking that I am in Chicago. This is no point in listing the contents of these two rooms. It is much too decorous and efficient although there is dirty clothing on all the chairs. I face a block of brick bow-fronts whose windows are topped with granite tiaras. It's part student, part slum. Classes begin on Tuesday and the students are unloading clothes, pictures, record players and African violets. I feel no petulance at all at having been obliged to begin a new life in another city but I do at times feel terribly, terribly tired. I then remind myself of the immense vitality you bought to Ancestors and take hope. For some foolish reason I had my phone number unlisted and I spend a lot of time waiting for it to ring which it can't. I'm not terribly lonely and don't expect to be but I had not planned to find myself at this time of life in a furnished room at the edge of Boston. I will now go and sit beside the telephone. My number is 617-266-2351. Tell everyone.

Much love,
John

The writer Anne Sexton was also on the faculty that term at Boston University. She took her own life in October of 1974.

71 Bay State Road
Boston, Massachusetts

Dear Bill,

I called Allan on Friday for no particular reason and he said he'd had some marvelous letters from you. I did not reproach him for his lack of production; but he has shown nothing since spring. This experience,so far, has been disconcerting. I have thirty-two students which is too many. The administration has been both evasive and untruthful about this. Boston, which is very beautiful, is also very deracinee. One looks no one in the eye. The students gave a party on Thursday to get to know me better. It was in a basement apartment which you entered by a window. The only furnishings I recall were two matresses and a wagon stolen from some super-market. This served as a sort of coffee table. A young man took off my loafers and socks and cut my toe-nails. I have no true nostalgia for more decorous parties but I get drunk and tired. Tonight the New Faculty is to be presented at a dinner to the old fazculty. I shall miss Ann Sexton. We were really the only professionals on the scene and she always carried a bottle of vodka in her bag. When things got dim she would gracefullyspike my drink. I thought her aggressive and said so but she was my only colleague.

John Updike has taken an apartment down the street. I don't mean to try to understand that marriage. John and I have been to the museum together and will go together to Andover. There is,I think,a conspicuous ego clash between us that makes a merry friendship unlikely. I am often terribly lonely but then I suppose one is meant to be. I have no mistress and I have no Allan. I am eating almost nothing which have provoked in Mary a Vesuvian maternalism and she is speeding down on Friday with groceries.

Love,
John


The Friday Club had sent him a table mat with their combined thoughts. The House Committee was one of the make-believe legislative bodies within the Friday Club.


John Cheever
71 Bay State Road
Boston, Massachusetts 02215

Monday [1975]

Gentlemen;

I do appreciate the table-mat correspondence and I hate to bring a touch of gloom into the Friday Club but this place is straight asshole. The pictures in the museums are great and the globe on the State

House is brilliant but most of it is asshole. This building has been
looted seven times since I've been here. I've lost a watch and fifty
dollars. I now wear my watch and hide my money. The difficulty is
that I can't remember where I hid it. The sight of a man, looking for a
fifty dollar bill hidden in the toe of a boot is perhaps something that
should be brought up before The House Committee. This building has
been stripped repeatedly of every fur coat,hi-fi and fenceable table
silver. A new lock is simply a challenge. They go after them with
crowbars. My principle anxiety is what shall I say to a burglar when I
meet one at work in the hall. The university has just commanded me
to install a Police Lock at $75. The difficulty here is that the locks are
difficult to operate and in case of fire you don't have a chance. The
charming street on which I live is brick bow-front with a luminous
pink sign on every house saying: Apt for Rent. On the south side of
the street they hang plants; I mean jungles. Also cocoanuts that look
like men, souvenirs of foreign travel family photographs and religious
statuary. The rooms must be quite dark. Asshole.

  Walking along the river is nice and I love thumping down Commonwealth Avenue to the Ritz but the administration at the university is
disorganized and sinister and the classes this semester seem sluggish.
. . . I have only one good-looking girl and she had influenza. This is all
very gloomy but you can have another drink and so can I.

Yours,<br>John

# SMITHERS

* * *

My father had always been wary of Alcoholics Anonymous. He referred to its members as "a bunch of Christers." Before he would allow himself to be checked in at the alcohol and drug treatment center where he finally dried out for good, he phoned my sister and asked her to call the place and make absolutely sure that their program had no affiliation with AA. She called the clinic and then phoned him back to say there was no connection. This was a lie, but he would say later that it had saved his life.

April Fourth [1975]

Cedar Lane

Dear Bill,

Boston University was a dreadful mistake. Ann Sexton killed herself on the first week and I never quite got over this. The students were marvelous and the administration was ineffecient to the point of forgetting to pay my wages. I lived in furnished rooms over Kenmore Square which is a decadent part of town. Every house has a sign in luminous pink that says Apt for rent. It seemed quite sinister. The walking was wonderful but my memories of the years when I lived in the city were overwhelming and my drinking worsened. So did my heart condition. My dear brother saw that I was in danger and drove me home. I went to the doctor who sent me to the hospital to be dried out. I then went to a psychiatrist who has signed me into a twenty-eight day clinic for alcoholics. I am allowed out only to go to church on Sundays. This is The Smithers Institute at 54 east 93rd street. Any mail will be welcome.

How dull this all is. I'll live in a dormitory so I won't be able to list the contents of my room. I'm not allowed to return home because I might drink; and Mary will drive me to New York on Wednesday.

I can't recall having written so dreary a letter in my life. I shall
improve.

Love,
John

Daisy and Flora were both dogs.

John Cheever
71 Bay State Road
Boston, Massachusetts 02215

Smithers Clinic
56 East 93rd Street
New York City

The Fourteenth

Dear Bill,

I seem to be showing some improvement. This is not the most
bizarre stop along the way but it is strange. The house is palatial and
not at all shabby. The tenants are forty-two drug addicts and clinical
alcoholics. We are confined. The confinement is voluntary but I will
have to wait twelve days before I can leave these rooms and then for
two hours to attend Morning Worship at The Heavenly Rest.

I just got your letter (al mano) and it cheered me immensley. Especially the dog and Dover. I'm very sorry to hear about Larry and
Brookie; but I've seen how happy Susie is after leaving that exceptional
husband. Tell Daisy that Flora had dreadful trouble with her hindquarters. She went to Granow, the doctor in Briarcliff, who put her on a
costly diet of meat and vegetables. She can now climb stairs and chase
timid delivery men although she claims to miss me. As I sorely miss
the world. Susie took Mary to a party yesterday, after visiting me. She
was presented to this year's three beauties and said quite loudly: "I
rather like the plastic one."

Love,
John

The following letter is to John Updike.

The Smithers Clinic
56 East 93rd Street
New York City

The fourteenth [1975]

Dear John,

I seemed to be dying in Boston, I'm not quite sure why. My sweet brother rented a car and drove me home and the doctors confined me to a palace on 93rd street with a large group of drug addicts and clinical alcoholics. Beyond the fact that my heart was fluttering I don't understand why I should have chosen Bay State Road for a grave.

I couldn't have come further from Crane's Beach. My confinement is for 28 days and I must keep a civil tongue in my head. This may be possible. My love to you all.

Yours,
John

The Smithers Clinic
56 East 93rd Street
New York City

April 19th

Dear Art,

... I have been confined since the 9th but I will be let out tomorrow morning to go to church. Mary will visit me tomorrow afternoon. The indoctrination here is stern,evangelical,protestant and tireless. The cast is around forty former drug addicts and clinical alcoholics. The setting is a mansion from the twenties with rooms from other mansions and or castles. Austrian would be my guess. I share a bedroom and a bath with four other men. 1. is an unsuccessful con man. 2. an unsuccessful German delicatessen owner. 3. an unemployable sailor with a troll's face and faded tatoos, and 4. a leading dancer from American Ballet. Our windows look onto the backyards of 92nd street. There are a few dogs, a baratone, a cat, church bells, no voices other than the baratone.

Half the time I know why I'm here; half the time I don't. The conflict is really painful and when it gets me in the middle of the stairs I nearly faint. My release date is the second week in May. I expect you'll be in Maine but I'll see you during the summer. If I stay dry for three months after leaving here I get a free watch-chain but I don't have a pocket watch which is the way my thinking goes.

Yours,
John


Smithers

April 25th

Dear Bill,

. . . The man on my left crochets another hat and complains about the administration. He says that if he were strong enough to carry his suitcase down the stairs he would leave. I've offered to take his suitcase down but he doesn't answer. The ballet dancer is up to his neck in bubble bath, reading a biography of Piaf. I want to get into the toilet but I can't. It is 8 AM. The delicatessen owner is sound asleep and asking: "Haff you been taken care of?" He will be discharged on Monday. He has lost his wife, his children, his house (with the genuine Karastan rug) his delicatessen, his everything. I call Mary from time to time and she is full of complaints. The bank can't add, the dogs (4) are muddy, the lawns are dry, Susie has followed a worthless man to Chicago, and buy (ineuendo) her husband is in a dryout mansion on east 93rd. On Sunday morning I shall dress for Heavenly Rest, rendezvous with Virginia and Lennie Field on Madison Avenue and ride a bicycle in the park. Gods Knows, God cares; God will understand, God is love and public parks and gardens are his temples.

Love
John


Brookie is one of Bill's daughters. She was enrolled in the Playschool of the Heavenly Rest Church. Wendy Adler Sonnenberg Nash was a friend of my sister's.

John Cheever
71 Bay State Road
Boston, Massachusetts 02215

The Smithers Clinic

Some Monday

Dear Bill,

I went to Heavenly Rest yesterday but Brookie was nowhere. The church struck me as highly artificial, an imitation of a church and I bypassed Dr. Houghton (who had been informed of my whereabouts by the Episcopal underground) and walked in the park with Wendy Adler Sonnenberg Nash. She was soaked with Tea Rose which clung to my clothes for the rest of the day. Mary, Ben and Linda came to visit. Mary, under these circumstances, is very docile and loving. The German Delicatessen owner talked all through the night. "Haff you been taken care of," he asked. "Haff you been waited on?" All through the night.

Yours,
John

This is to Allan Gurganus.

Since you ask I did of course sing your praises for Stanford. I sing them all the time.

Cedar Lane,

May tenth

Dearest Allan,

I should have warned you about this predictable turn of events. Once you show a trace of healthy self-esteem the New Yorker will yank at the rug you stand on. I was hurt the first time around; but never again. Bill, after forty years remains indecipherable. I thought I once understood him. It seemed that he was a man who mistook power for love. If you don't grow and change he baits you; if you do grow and change he baits you cruelly. I once shouted at him:"You may have invented Salinger and Brodkey but you didn't invent me." I intended to dedicate

The Scandal to him but he was murderous about the bookand I
changed the dedication to W.M. He underwent a sea-change and
priased the book but the dedication remained W.M. He loves me and
would love to see me dead. One must be oneself. you are Allan/I am
John/these are the stones we build upon/etc. I thought the story beautiful.

This is my second day out of confinement. I am very verbose in three
languages; a subject I remember laughing over with you whom I love
very much today. This may tomorrow seem lamentable fantasy but it
has given me immense pleasure and very little pain. My only complaint
is that any moustache en brosse—the face doesn't matter—gives me
nostalgia. I am delighted to imagine you at Yaddo. I used to slide down
the bannister, smack Venus (with her defunct light-bulbs) on the ass
and jog barefoot over the yellow rug. I should have given Hermes a
smack now and then but I never did. One of the oldest maids re-
proached me. "Mister John," she said, "You can't slide down the ban-
nisters and go barefoot in a mansion." Thus I became Lord Fauntleroy.

I cannot touch the dry-out tank in a letter. It was a montage of
freaks,cons,Irish policemen. Whores,dismal gays (with macaroni ankles) sand-hogs and seamen pasted against the Corinthian columns of
a Hapsburg ballroom. I taught a sand-hog how to play back-gammon
and cleaned him out of his allowance. With this I paid for my postage
and my laundry. I am twenty pounds lighter and feel twenty years
younger which is more of a dilemma than an advantage. My bearings
are the same—laughter, the heat of the sun around noon, rain of
course and the people I love including muchly you.

                                                              John


                        John Cheever
                        71 Bay State Road
                        Boston, Massachusetts 02215

                                                    Cedar Lane,

                                                    May tenth

Dear Bill,
    I can't keep a journal when I return because I'll return as a labrador
retriever. Didn't you know? I remember writing you years ago when I
was ill. Whenever I lost consciousness it was the barking of a labrador
that brought me back. Last year before I left for Boston I took a maple

out of the woods and planted it on the lawn. It seemed to die, then came to life and I left for the university with the happily conviction that I had left something living on Cedar Lane. Now it is in leaf but all the dogs (4) piss on it. When Mussolini's son was killed in the war he ordered every city, town, village, hamlet and farm to plant a tree. They did, of course, but when the cafe closed at midnight all the man pissed on it. When we summered in Anticoli in the fifties the remains of the tree still stood (with a plaque) and one still pissed on it. Thus goes the cadence of my thinking, three days out of the dry-out clink. I love it, but I think Shawn will not. My last gesture was to teach a sand-hog (also an ornithologist) how to play backgammon. I cleaned him out of his allowance with which I bought my postage and paid for my laundry. He had dug under the East River, Second Avenue, Central Park, dreaming of Magpies. Working under air he got eight hundred dollars a week and the promise of an early death. "Do you know why you dig tunnels?" the bug-eyed psychologist asked him. "Daddy was a sand-hog." "That's not it," she said. "You want to return to your mother's womb." He packed his bags and left with a married alcoholic named Agnes: They were discovered, fucking, under the washing-machine. It was the only private place in the palace. He said goodbye to me fondly and asked if he owed me anymore money. Were were natural friends which reminds me of Kenny Wilson (Readers Digest) who asked me (at The Century) why I sometimes seemed so sans culotte. And of Eddie who came over on Thursday, pursued by knats. "For once," he said, "I envy you your hair." We went indoors. Stay tuned. This is continuous.

Love, John

After he left Smithers, he stayed away from alcohol and attended AA meetings three times a week. The "alcoholic wild-man" was Warren Hinckle, one of the founding editors of *Ramparts*. He recently ran for mayor of San Francisco and is now a columnist there. I don't believe he'd object to the characterization.

[1975]
Cedar Lane,
Ossining, New York

June second

Dear Tanya,

I am not tired at all but it was good of you to think of me. I have concluded ,sententiously, that part of my role is to be buried and arise at fairly frequent intervals. My professorship was sinister and deadly. This was in Boston. My brother, in March, insisted that I resign and I did. My wife insisted that I confine myself to a hospital for clinical alcholics and I did. I came out of this prison 20 pounds lighter and howling with pleasure. That was a month ago and I'm still howling. I howl, write, dance,swim,eat,drink (tea only) and am terribly kind and patient to all dogs and children. . . .

My son Fred (you saw him in the Ukraine) is studying Russian. He can make marvelous, squeaky noises and say things like:"Ivan, will you please close the window nearest to the sewing machine." He returns from boarding school tomorrow. Susie is divorced, in love with an alcoholic wild-man and very happy and successful. Ben remains very Mishkin.

John

This "darling" is Hope Lange. Patty is Hope's daughter.

Saratoga Springs

March second [1976]

Darling,

Here I am at the famous Artist's Colony of Yaddo, founded by the late Mrs. Spencer Trask who left her millions to artists, writers and composers because they were the most charming of her guests. Some think that these bums were the only ones to accept her invitations but these are very negative people with whom you and I would have nothing to do. I came up yesterday on the train. I enjoy this train. It slows down at every grade crossing and blows it's whistle. I rented a Red Pinto at the station and drove around the village, thinking of Patty. It is the sort of small race-track town that has a great many fires towards the end of January when the new fire insurance policies are in force. There are two newly burned buildings on the main street. There are Boutiques, Coffee Houses and Health Food stores for the college but I don't think Patty would like it. I think it's charming but it's really quite squalid.

But meanwhile back at The Famous Artist's Colony they were getting ready for dinner. I was given a very small room with an enormous and drafty bath. The tub is the sort of thing bankers used to buy in the last century. It is ten feet long and stands on a dias. I bathed, dressed in some artistic clothing and walked to the dinningroom. There are nine other guests and I think I shall quarrel with no one. We dined by the light of three candles. The dinner was working-class meat, noodles, spinach and a piece of pastry containing preserved fruit or jam. Then I came back here, wrote a hilarious parody of Marquez (my son and I think he's terrible) and got into bed. I will skip my erotic fantasies but I think you should know that I am the sort of man who cries at track meets and gets a hard-on during thunder storms. Anyhow, when I woke the place was knee-deep in snow. I had a nice day and pushed around the place on cross-country skiis. Do spend me a photograph. There goes the thunder again.

Love,
John

Cedar Lane,
Yaddo on Monday

March 12th [1976]

Darling,

I do want my photograph, my picture, my proof of the fact that there is this terribly pretty woman I kissed under a streetlight in Sherman oaks over a month ago. I won't show it around at the fire department or Alcoholics Anonymous. I just want to carry it around in my pocket while I ski.

It snowed like blazes during the train-trip down on Tuesday and this I love. Westchester was buried. I drove Mary to a pre-dawn plane on Wednesday at the Armonk airport. This is a great cracker-barrell airport with mostly private planes and a very mixed bag of customers. She went down to Boston to celebrate the 100th anniversary of the invention of the telephone. T.A. Watson was her grandfather. Fred came down from Andover to reenact this great moment with a great granddaughter of Alexander Graham Bell's. UP carried the story and Fred is tickled at being in all the papers. He comes home from school this afternoon. Right at the heart of the festivities in Boston Mary's crazy aunt—Esther Watson Tipple—kicked the bucket and released one million. It must have been a great party.

Back I go to Yaddo on Sunday. It's marvelous for work and not terribly good for anything else. I ski in the afternoons and play ping-pong after dinner with a couple of Oriental painters who skin me every game. It goes 6-21,0-21. I'll get them to go bowling. There are also two very gloomy poets and one unyoung poet who is very unyoung. I love the working hours but when bedtime comes around I have a definite and painful feeling of incompletion. Anyhow I've got to do the book and since Paramount owns a piece of it I'll have every excuse to come west if you don't come east.

                                                                    Love,
                                                                    John


Tanya had left Russia and moved to England, where she still lives.


                                                            Cedar Lane,
                                                            Ossining, New York

Dearest Tanya,

To address you in Hove instead of Moscow A-47 gives me a keen sense of physical dislocation, something sympathetic, I guess, since I like to think that our sympathies transcend oceans. I imagine you to have crossed the chanel in a row-boat, followed by friendly but curious gulls. Now you are near the sea, the English sea that smells so unlike the Baltic or the Black sea. . . . Your mother's joy at seeing you is vast but controlled. You have dinner in a small French restaurant. . . . I can't imagine what happens after this and so I depend on you to write me. This is to welcome you to England—and since I am not English and can't really do that—it is to say how pleased I am to find you so much closer to Ossining.

All writers suffer terribly from delusions of omnipotence and I am in the throes of this. I feel, at the moment, that if I wanted to go to Hove I would simply have to stand on the sunny terrace here, flap my arms and ascend. I would, of course, break my neck. If the book is done by June I will come to England. However nothing could be more uncertain and my muse is terribly cranky and continues to wear long, soiled sheets. She thinks that I should work longer hours but if I do I will go mad. This is of no importance to her since she went mad when she was working for Wilkie Collins.

Your Mother seems to think that I know nothing about her. I've enjoyed her work, I've heard her described exhaustively I consider her an old friend. In any case do write me as soon as possible. . . .

Love,
John

This was written about his brother's burial. One must remember how terribly important the two men were to each other, that my father's funeral would be held in the church he describes here, and that he would be laid beside the brother to whom he'd spent a lifetime saying goodbye. This is taken from a letter written to Allan Gurganus.

Dearest Allan:

. . . On Thursday I attended my brother's funeral in Hingham. This was in an early 18th century church with such a heady perfume and such vast and splendid windows that we seemed to be in the fields on that summer afternoon. The organ was loud and true and augmented by a brilliant trumpet. Yes, yes, Louisa Hatch did the flowers. The mourners all had sailboat tans, white hair and mannered wives. This is the world into whose umbrella stands my brother used to piss. The text was Tillich, Cummings and Eliot and not a tear was shed. It was spendid.

Love,
John

When *Falconer* came out a year later, Tom Glazer, the folk singer who was a member of the Friday Club, had written to say he liked it. In that book the protagonist has killed his brother.

Cedar Lane

February 24th

Dear Tom,

Many thinks for your letter about <u>Falconer.</u> Three will get you seven that you are the only member or the Friday Club who writes.

When I said goodbye to my brother here last May I said that I had killed him in my novel. "That's splendid,Joey," he said,"that's splendid," and on that we parted.

Yours,
John

It was in the middle of the night on June 1, 1976, that my father was phoned and told that John Updike had been killed in a car crash. My father could joke harshly about Updike, but his affection and admiration for the man were genuine and deep. He burst into tears. It was a crank call, and when he learned that his friend was alive, he wrote this note. In it he shows nothing of the grief he had felt.

Cedar Lane

June first

Dear John,

I guess you know the story by now but when they reported your death at four this morning I cried loudly. "Oh, was it personal?" the man asked. "He was," I sobbed,"a colleague."

Yours,
John

Cedar Lane,
[1976]
Ossining, New York 10562

October third

Dearest Tanya,

I can't remember when I last wrote you or when you last wrote me, and this, of course, may not find you in East Sussex at all but losing your teeth in green apples in Russia. The only thing I have to say of importance is that the book will soon be in bound galleys and I will ask the publisher to send you a copy. Jonathan Cape will publish the book in England. I think it's by miles the best thing I've ever done but Paramount regretted an invitation to buy if for a film and The Book of the Month Club regretted a chance to distribute it among their millions of members. None of this comes as a surprise; although I was wounded. I am the sort of iconoclast—and so I think are you—who will ridicule the establishment endlessly and expect to be seated at the head of the table. They sometimes protest.

Luve,
John

Cedar Lane,
Ossining, new York 10562

October 17th

Dearest Tanya,

Since you are an old, old friend you might like to know that the horse, to whom I feed apples, is well and comely and that Flora, our oldest Labrador, died on Wednesday night. She had hoped to outlive me. She was a distinguished dog and had a most distinguished end. A black gardener named Lyndon Facey—a deacon in the Star of Bethel Church—buried her at the end of the terrace. Mary planted the grave with yellow crysanthemums and strawberries.

Luve,
John

Christopher Lehmann-Haupt of The New York Times and his wife, the poet and writer Natalie Robins, were both friends of my father's for many years. Rachel is their daughter. This letter was sent to cheer Natalie up.

Cedar Lane
Ossining,

December 8th 1976

Dearest Natalie,

All I truly have to say is love ; but I will characteristically go into something lighter and something legitimate, it seems, because the last time we met,you and Rachel and I spent some of the afternoon at Barkers. (I still prefer Barkers to Caldor because Caldor,it seems to me,aims at a higher class with the loss of a dimension.) Anyhow I went to Barkers yesterday to buy skates. My skates were lost in the renovation of the kitchen. Mr. Van Tassel, the manager here, has been demoted to Carmel and young Mr. Loeb has taken over. Yesterday the carrousel,the spaceship and the horse on the sidewalk were freshly painted. When I pushed open the IN and NO SMOKING door (only the exits fly open) and saw the clean and gleaming floors and heard the conservative but deep-beat rock music I wanted to seize on the nearest manaquin—she was wearing a pleated nightgown printed with an arial view of the Grand Canyon—and waltz her through the Smoke Shop,passed the bicycle racks to the coupon sale of hockey skates. Much of this excitement is, for a man of my age, nostalgia. The soapy,oriental perfumes in the air remind me of Woolworths in Quincy. There is the Present of course (spark plugs and toilet seats) but what truly thrills me in Barkers is the sense of being in the well-lived interior of an Unidentified Flying Object. This is science fiction made flesh;this is truly a step into the future. Oh how I love it.

There are disappointments,of course;the coupon hockey skates, for example. The skate shoes were made of black plastic, had the high finish of dancing pumps and were embossed with radiator paint. The sizes were all mixed up and I had to sit on the floor and take off my shoes to try and find a pair that fit. I didn't, but while I was trying the music changed to a Thelonious Monk variation on In A Little Spanish Town and at that moment a single dollar bill drifted slowly towards me over the polished floor. I pocketed this,put on my shoes,shop-lifted a love amulet and chose a pair of fur-lined gloves. Then I took my place in my favorite check-out counter—#8—where the steadfast yellow light was burning.

Oh,ho,oh ho. Compared to check-out #8 the Pass at Thermopylae —the Kyber Pass in the 19th Century—were asshole. #8 is The Real Thing. the senses of life as a passage. The woman in front of me had brassy hair and four,snug pairs of underpants,printed with roses, pansises,liley of the valley and jonquils. This was a pushover,but I let it pass. 11 AM. In front of her was a man with a dirty paper-back,four flash-light batteries and some dog-eared coupons. Expired coupons,as you know,slow things up. In front of him was an old Chinese wearing a plush mink coat and pushing a wagon that held twelve curtain rods,a plastic representation of The Holy Family,four cartons of light bulbs and a pair of rubber gloves. We all pay with Carte Blanche which means summoning the assistant managress. She has ash-blonde hair,wears a gray lace dress and an enormous jewel like the order of St. Stanislaus. She has a strong,unfresh smell like old candy and counts on her fingers. So I made the passage, the doors flew open for me,my stolen amulet and my paid-for gloves and I stpped out into the world,a new man. I truly love you and Christopher and Rachel but I really want to get you back into Barkers.

Love,
John

# FALCONER
## (Knopf 1977)

\* \* \*

The letter below was to John Weaver.

Cedar Lane
Ossining, New York 10562

January sixteenth [1977]

Dear John,

The interviews here for the book start on February .... I've been through this before but I am uneasy. I will lunch,for example,with the twelve editors of Newsweek and at the end of lunch they will vote on whether or not to put me on the cover. I don't have any gifts for this sort of thing. ... The outer coat I wear is Mary's Father's 37 year-old vicuna. When I take the coat off myself I can keep the coat and the linning together but when people insist on helping me out of the coat I am left wearing the linning. This does not embarrass me but it does seem to involve a loss of face. . . .

The cold, as you must know, is unusual but my enthusiasim for this sort of thing has diminished. I went skating on Saturday but when I climbed the hill to get the TIMES this morning I was intensely uncomfortable. . . . I know that covetousness is a cardinal sin but I do today covet your pool.

Brrrrr,<br>John

Duane Michals took the *Newsweek* cover photo.

Cedar Lane<br>February 11th, [1977]

Dear John,
. . . For The Lunch I went up to something like the 175th floor of The Newsweek Building where a lot of people were drinking hootch in a big white barny place. Then I sat on a plush sofa beside the editor and the people asked questions. Once, right in the middle of a long answer, I forgot what the hell the question had been. After that we went into a big white barny dinning-room where a waiter passed lamb chops. I only took one chop because I didn't want them to think I was a rube or hungry or in any way dependent upon them for food. This left me with nothing on my plate but a chop bone for nearly an hour. . . . I went with the editor down to his office and then I talked with some other editors about whether or not Avedon should photograph me. They kept looking at me. Then one of them said that with my face on the cover there would be a drastic drop of newsstand sales but then another man said this was true of all serious writers. After this I went out on a local and called Knopf to tell them the news and the PR man said:"I've been successful." . . .

Yours,<br>John

The *Newsweek* story ran in the March 14 issue with the cover title "A Great American Novel: John Cheever's 'Falconer.'" Notice they didn't say,

"The Great American Novel." The piece was written by Walter Clemons and was called "Cheever's Triumph." Not only did Clemons judge *Falconer* a masterpiece, but he savaged the critics who had condemned the earlier work. *Bullet Park*, he said, was "misunderstood and much maligned." The *Newsweek* coverage also included an interview with my father conducted by my sister. This exchange seemed remarkable for intimacy and candor. Susan asked, "Did you ever fall in love with another man? I mean, because of the homosexuality in 'Falconer,' people are certainly going to ask that."

And he said, "The possibility of my falling in love with a man seems to me to exist. Such a thing could happen. That it has not happened is just chance. But I would think twice about giving up the robustness and merriment I have known in the heterosexual world."

Susan persisted. "Well, have you ever had a homosexual experience?"

"My answer to that is, well, I have had many, Susie, all tremendously gratifying, and all between the ages of 9 and 11."

I still don't quite understand what was going on here, but I think it would be wrong to judge it as dishonesty. Literally it was a lie, of course, but in some figurative sense it was true. He never considered himself to be a homosexual. I don't mean to split hairs, or to separate my father from those people who do consider themselves to be homosexual, but only to say that this was a word he would not apply to himself, and words were frightfully important to him.

> Cedar Lane,
> Ossining, New York 10562
>
> Saturday [Feb. 26, 1977]

Dear John,

I'm very happy you liked Falconer and pleased that you wrote to say so. TIME shit on it this week—a month before publication—because Newsweek is running a feature. It was a bad few hours but only a few. The people whose opinion I value seem to like it. There is, of course, the company of sopranos. Phil Roth called, towards midnight to say in his windiest voice:"Thank you for sending me the book and I'll read it when I next take a vacation but the reason I'm calling is to ask for John Updike's new telephone number."

> Yours,
> John

This is John Updike. My father and mother had gone to Boston to Liz Updike's wedding.

Cedar Lane,

March second 1977

Dear John,

I had not read Poorhouse Fair since it was published and I am delighted to have it again and I thought the preface illuminating—and with the mention of Harry Green—nostalgic. One forgets those years. Your giftedness truly delights me and since you are so young I am delighted at the thought of what lies ahead.

We would have gone to Seoul to see Liz married. We are not,God knows, a family but we are a small and singular company who should,I believe,witness one another's vows. It is, for me, a very rewarding familiarity. . . . It is true that there are no cuffs on my pants. I know this is a mistake. I wore the same suit at my brother's funeral and one of the mourners, glancing at my pants said:"He must be a Spanish dancer."

Your good opinion of Falconer means a great deal to me. There is almost no one I would sooner please and you have been very generous since you wrote,years ago, about the hang of Honora's dress.

Yours,

John

"And now we come to the unsavory or homosexual part of our tale and any disinterested reader is encouraged to skip." This passage appears in *The Wapshot Chronicle,* which was published when I was eight years old, and I guess I would have to be considered a disinterested reader. I read the books, I even read the parts I was encouraged to skip, but I avoided the conclusions I might have drawn. I was encouraged to skip and I skipped.

Looking back at my father's life, and at his writing, it must seem difficult to believe that I didn't know about his bisexuality, but I didn't even suspect. I can remember visiting my parents when I was thirty, and after lighting a fire in their dining room I turned to the guest who was enjoying its warmth and joked, "Well, it's going, and Daddy will be pleased. He had two great fears about me. The first was that I would not learn how to lay a proper fire, the second was that I would be a homosexual." This was said with supreme confidence. It wasn't until a couple of years later that I got my first unavoidable clue. A protégé appeared. A young man had left his job to work on his fiction, and to spend time with my father. This man has a deep voice, a firm handshake and a steady eye. He's an excellent mechanic. He's also pleasant and gentle and witty, but I've never considered this sort of thing to be a tip-off. In any case, he and I and my father were on a bicycle ride, and he and I had gotten ahead. We were talking as we rode. I was envious of my companion's gifts as a writer, and was asking him about his journal. We had both kept journals for some time. "Did you ever notice," I said, "that you never know what's important? You write down what you think is important, but when you look back a couple of years later you realize that you've recorded a dispute you were having with a plumber, and haven't mentioned a near-fatal automobile accident." He nodded. "Also, I sometimes use a sort of shorthand," he said. "Once, when I was married, and my wife used to read my journal, I went out and spent a night with a black man I met at a bar. Every time we did it, he'd call me honeychild, and that was all I wrote for that day in my journal, 'honeychild.' "

I was shocked. I was worried. What if my father found out that his friend was homosexual? I'm the sort who lives in fear of confrontation, and it would have been natural for me to tell this guy that it was okay with me, but that he'd better not tell my father because there'd be hell to pay. But I didn't say anything. We just went on pedaling our bicycles.

When I was thirty-one, I left my first wife and lived at my parents' house for several months. During this stay my father invited me to read from his journals. He kept copious journals, and they'd been lying around the house through most of my life, but we, as children, had been under a stern injunction not to peek. Now I was being asked to read them. One evening my father sat beside me in an armchair while I read, and when I looked up I found that he had been crying. I don't recall what I'd been reading, and he couldn't have known, but I suspect now that he thought I might read about his homosexuality, and he wanted me to.

Toward the end of his life my father used often to come to the *Readers Digest* offices where I worked and take me out to lunch. He used to say over and over again that he hoped I would not have his "difficult propensities." I thought that he meant he hoped I wouldn't have his talent, and I was a little hurt by this, but I think now that he was hoping I wouldn't be bisexual. In any case, I used to ask him then, and he was in his late sixties, if he had any real regrets about his life. And he would say no, he didn't have regrets; his life had been satisfactory in the extreme.

"So what do you mean by propensities?" I'd ask. He wouldn't answer.

I can only speculate as to his reasons for so thoroughly disguising his bisexuality. I suspect that while this was done in part because of his inner struggle, it also may have been done because he hoped that his sons would have more conventional appetities.

He didn't make it easy for me as a child. He hated to hear me giggle, and any other sign of girlishness was treated with cold disapproval. I was almost as angry as I was confused when I realized that he had been a practicing member of the subculture, which he pretended to so abhor. On the other hand, looking back, I can see that I didn't make it easy for him either. I often didn't act as he thought a young man should. I fished and liked guns, but I was not the least bit interested in sports and he wanted desperately for me to be a baseball fan. When I was seven years old, he told me that if I picked a team, he would take me to a game, and after that he'd help me follow the standings in the newspaper. He gave me a list of teams. We lived in suburban New York, but I picked the Baltimore Orioles. "Why'd you do that?" he wanted to know. "Because Oriole is such a pretty name," I said.

We didn't make the trip to Baltimore, but he did take me to see the Yankees. I sat politely in my seat with my hands in my lap and waited for the game to be over. After a few innings of this, he bought me a box of Cracker Jacks. The prize was a miniature pair of scissors and I found that I could use these to cut the paper of the Cracker Jack wrapper and spent the rest of the afternoon happily doing so.

When I was fifteen my favorite piece of writing was Edward Albee's play *The Zoo Story,* and I would walk around the house reciting from it:". . . I've never been able to have sex with, or, how is it put? . . . make love to anybody more than once. Once; that's it . . . Oh, wait; for a week and a half, when I was fifteen . . . and I hang my head in shame that puberty was late . . . I was a h-o-m-o-s-e-x-u-a-l. I mean, I was queer . . . *(Very fast)* . . . queer, queer, queer . . . with bells ringing, banners snapping in the wind."

In any case I didn't know much about the passions that are exhibited in the following letters. My father didn't meet this particular young man until the mid-1970s, and my first inclination was to assume that he didn't become bisexual until then. Then I met composer and writer Ned Rorem. Ned's been open all his life about his sexual preferences, and perhaps understandably he felt a little superior to my father. Ned says that he and my father had their first sexual relationship in the 1960s, and that my father had had many liaisons with men before that. I think Ned's right.

Another writer once said to me with some bitterness that my father had always managed to be in love with somebody. This is certainly true. Some of the people he loved were men. My father tried to help this man sell a story to *The New Yorker*. Charles McGrath was fiction editor there.

Cedar Lane, [early March 1977; the *Newsweek* piece ran on March 14]
Saturday morning
Dear ____,

. . . I do think the silence from The New Yorker is pregnant or—as I'll bet you'd say—gravid. McGrath did say he was very interested but when I looked at the new Ann Beattie story about people opening and closing doors and going up and down stairs I wondered where your hero with his crown of pain might fit in. There is also a Barthelme that I thought trifling. Yaddo is also not your plate but certainly something to consider.

It is cold and dark anda light snow is falling. On Saturday mornings the cheese store proprietor brings out from the city hot brioche, crioissants and bread. I take hot brioche up to the house of my my friend Sara (It is in her pool that I swim and will, I hope, with you) and we drink coffee and watch the Grand Union horse-races on TV. However this will have to be cut short this morning because my daughter is coming out for lunch and to interview me for Newsweek. I think this is a little kinkey. On waking this morning I thought: Would Coleridge have been interviewed by his daughter?

Love,
John

My father's protégé was planning to go to Yaddo in the summer.

Cedar Lane
March 30th
Dear ____,

This is just after talking with you and I love you very much. I do not yearn for you, miss you or pine for you but it pleases me to know that you are around. It seems as simple as that. I am also very much interested in your work and think the summer can be great. I do worry about when we will next meet but I don't seem to worry about this too much. This seems not a good day for writing letters. I have to check bank accounts for the IRS and be interviewed by a Chicago paper. I will tell the reporter that I look for success in love and usefulness as I truly do. The book is bringing in a shirtful and the woods are full of Puerto Ricans with chain-saws turning the place into a park. The Puerto Ricans come at twenty dollars and hour. Tomorrow, the painters arrive to do the porch. Yesterday I bought a Raleigh Grand Prix with a ten speed alpine shift. It weights 28 pounds and is a dynamic blue with silver trim. Wow.

I feel close enough to you to say that the heat is really the big news. Yesterday was the kind of day in which my generation used to race around in convertibles and swim bearass in icy ponds. . . . Yesterday afternoon the Times called and asked me to comment on the 100th anniversary of Peter Rabbit. "My money," I said, "has always been on Mr. McGregor." Oh Ho, said the Times. I hope there will be a letter from you this afternoon and I'm pleased to think of what fun it will be when we meet again.

Love,

John

Cedar Lane

March 31st [1977]

Dear ____,

To scrutinize and examine my feeling for you is idle but there is nothing much else I can do with you in _____ All of my speculations may be no more than the thinking of a lecherous old man who hankers after the skin of someone younger but I will throw this out. Any dizzy analyst would declare that you are the ghost of my dead brother come back from the grave to solace the ghost of my long-gone youth. He would also delcare that I am the spectre of your father,gotten richer and more literary. I think this shit. All I seem to know is that on that morning at ____when we waited for ____ , you seemed to lift from my shoulders, an aloneness that I was happy to lose. I can't imagine what your feeling was. My happiness continued through the plane trip and made Palo Alto seem charming. I wanted only that you be there; that if I woke in the night and asked for you I would hear your voice. That it may be my destiny to carry this aloness forever is a possibility and it is surely not your destiny, as a young man to carry my bags.

That is about it for this morning. The singular heat goes on and the botanicals, having no memory-bank, are all coming into bloom. We have all the flowers of spring. The old wander around,lamenting the fact that the hyacinths will soon be withered and buried in snow but they overlook the fact that they hyacinths are very resiliant. So are you and I.

Love,
John

Tuesday

Dear ____,

BBC is on the way and it has occured to me that I am older than Thomas Hardy was when people like Henry James used to cme out and take a look at him. I think the interlocutor will be named Wyatt Earp,that half-way up the front stairs he will give me Xeroxed copies of the citations his show (Musty Bindings) has won and that he will want to set his lights up in my study. This as you know contains one cat bed, one broken carpet sweeper,three dogs and a long gone TV set that is too heavy for me to move. Outside the window you can see a rusted radiator.

Love,
John

Filler appears in "Artemis, the Honest Well Digger," which first ran in *Playboy* and was included in *The World of Apples*.

Cedar Lane
April 9th

Dear ____,

This is the first thing in the morning (7:30) because I am out of sorts and will only get worse. I am harrassed and think I have too much to do which is a shitty point of view. This brings up the fact that you write a good deal about shit. You shit across this great country, you reminesce about loads you have dumped and you have thought of shitting in ice-trays. This brings up a character of mine named J.P. Filler who became wealthy and famous because he wrote a book about shit. I thought this a very good joke until I started getting letters from an associate professor in Chicago who had written such a book. It was about to be published when my story came out. After this no one would touch it unless I wrote a preface or at least an endorsement for the jacket. He sent me the publisher's reports (haunting and poignant) and he, the publisher and the agent all urged me to help. Without publication he would not get tenure, his mortgage would be foreclosed and his wife and children would be thrown into the stews. He wrote every week and I finally took off for the Danube Delta which, as he pointed out angrily, was the very asshole of Europe. I've not heard from him since.

What I have to do is write a piece about Yaddo for the Times, write my speech for Boston on Tuesday (1,500 seats have been sold) shave, buy a rib-roast, dye and hide Easter eggs for my Grandson, go out for lunch, take Holy Communion, go out for dinner, and of course tie my tie so that the grease spot doesn't show. . . . So now I'll write my speech.

Love,
John

Garson Kanin is the screenwriter and novelist who was for many years married to the actress Ruth Gordon.

Cedar Lane,

Aprilfourteenth

Dear ____,

When we came in from Boston last night there was a vast pile of mail on the table and your two letters, of course, were the ones that mattered. The Boston trip was a lark but the fact that I made it as a public person, without gin and a stiff prick, seemed like racing without a mainsail. I may have to get used to this. The Ritz there is one of the best hotels in the world. I tipped the head-waiter twenty and his mignons forty for the two dinner parties we gave and the service was great. I traveled around in a preposterous limousine and did TV, radio and newspaper interviews. There were seven hundred people at the Book @ Author lunch and it seems that you were supposed to plug your title. When I came off the platform, Garson Kanin said: "You shit.

You didn't mention your novel. You didn't even mention the fact that you write." That was true but at the autographing spree after the speeches "Falconer" was the only book that sold out. Mary tells me that Henry Cabot Lodge stood grinning for an hour by a tower of unsold books. I keep asking her to tell me about how Henry Cabot Lodge didn't sell any books.

Today is splendid with everything blooming and I am very serene. The length of time before we meet again doesn't seem terribly important and if you plug the woman from Missoula I only hope it's a great hump. I might point out, as an older man, that cunts that old lose some of their grip. However, you have a much bigger and younger cock than I. The fact that you are around still seems to please me more than anything else. I can't imagine where or when we will have our long conversation but I know that it will be gratifying and splendid and humorous and lengthy and I seem able to wait.

Love,<br>John

Edgar was a golden retriever. I'd owned her, and am embarrassed to admit that I named her Tara. When my first son was born, I found that the child and dog were too much for our small apartment and "lent" the dog to my parents in much the same way I used to "borrow" money from them at that time of life. My father got to like Tara, but he quickly changed her name and sex, calling her Shithead, and then Edgar. Bella Akhmadulina is a Russian poet.

Cedar Lane,<br>April 25th

Dear ____,

What I seem mostly to do these days is to write letters to you and why not? Who else cares that my scalp itches and that Edgar seems to have stolen both socks. One is customary. I am dreadful at five A.M. but I am also bad between twelve and one when I am under the impression that I have been over-burdened. Then I am shit. Yesterday,after 7:30 church, I cooked breakfast, carved the boned lamb, shaved, jerked-off, multched the Cottoneaster, offered (crossly) to clean the rugs, answered six letters, met guests at the 12:30 train, said

Grace at lunch and felt myself terribly burdened. At half-past four I
was driven to Queens College where I watched, from the wings, the
last act of The Magic Flute. This had it's charms. The heavily rouged
king was tying up the loose plot-lines in a nice baratone while two
highly questionable characters in black tank-suits crowned the two
princesses. Finale. Curtain. Applause. Then when that crowd had gone
in came the poetry lovers. BellaAkmoudalina is tres chic. Hair dyed
light, light brown, and wearing a corderoy suit cut in Paris with gleaming knee-high boots. When the Workers & Peasants go in for chic
there's nothing better. She read (with translators) for two hours. I
welcomed her to the USA and then retired behind the curtains of a box
where I chain-smoked, thought about you and listened to a heavy rain
on the ventilators. Then there was a reception at which there was
nothing to eat but peanuts. I was very hungry and everytime anyone
came up to shake my hand they found it full of peanuts.

                                                            Love,
                                                            John


                                                    Cedar Lane,
                                                    May 12th

Dear ____,
  Brooding, as I must, about homosexuality, I stepped out of the post-
office yesterday morning and saw Them. This was in the parking-lot
that serves the post-office, the super market, the cut-rate drugstore,
liquor store and dry-cleaner. They arrived in a Mercedes 300, beautifully washed and polished. "You wash the car,Michael, I'll wash the
sweaters." They were young & old, a very distinguished couple, distinguished in my eyes by their utter distaste for the merriment in the
parking lot. They sneered at the old lady, looping towards the liquor
store with her stolen four dollars, they sneered at the abandoned shopping carts, they sneered in fact at me. The old one was very skinny
with a few strands of hair,dyed a marvelous yellow. The youth had all
his hair and everything else, I guess, and he might have seemed quite
beautiful if he didn't have a mouth like an asshole. The old one would
be seen to walk as if his asshole were a mouth. In the back seat was an
obligatory Mastaff, a massive, ornamental, brainless dog named after
some international cocksucker. "He'll keep me company when I am
abandoned by Michael," the old fairy will tell his guests. Having judged

their environment to be loathsome they removed themselves from the Mercedez. Then they took from the back seat a large, beautifully wrapped box containing, I'll bet, a lamp base, thrown by the old one (a potter) on his favorite wheel to be mailed on consignment to a former Golden Gloves runner-up who had just opened an antique shop in Savanah Georgia. The message seemed to be that if you take it up the ass once too often you lose the blessedness of locomotion.

I'm delighted to think of you shuffling Falconer around and buying both Apples and a cook book. Apples did very well because (the publisher thought) people mistook it for a cook book. I'll go north tomorrow and spend much time on the telephone trying to straighten out the plane tickets. I have to deal with the embassy, Lufthansa, KLM and Sofia and in the end I'll fly Bulgar Wingski. I seem already to be somewhere between Yaddo, Sofia and Amsterdam and you. I'll write as soon as I get to Yaddo.

Much Love,
John

Cedar Lane

Ascension Sunday [1977?]

Dear ____,

I expect you've lived with enough women to know that many of them get orgasim mixed up with punctuality in meeting common carriers. You can blow them,fuck them, bite them and suck them but you may not discover,until it's too late that the only way you can get them to board the train is to beat them around the ears with the 11 the edition of the Encyclopedia. Mary's flight for Amsterdam was 7 P.M. Since this was booked in Bulgaria and confirmed in Holland it wouldn't be easy to duplicate. At three,Mary lost her passport. It was found at four-fifteen. At four-eighteen she began to feed the cats & dogs and water the plants. It was just like a wedding night. At four thirty Ben and I bagged her and got her struggling,into the car. It was a summer,Friday night on the outskirts of the seventh largest city in the world. Everyone was on the road. We got into the vicinity of the airport at quarter to seven. At four minutes to seven we could see the KLM sign and I urged Ben to go through a yellow light. He was arrested at once by a policeman who wouldn't speak English. I grabbed the bags and started to run. A fat woman said we had missed the plane but then she telephoned the gate and urged us to run some more. I kissed her goodbye as they extinguished the boarding lights. The man who took her ticket asked:"But why are you leaving him?" I've been cheerful ever since.

Bulgaria seems quite dark. The Russians called yesterday to ask exactly what my position will be. I keep saying that Mr. and Mrs. Cheever have accepted with pleasure the cordial invitation of the Bulgarian government and look forward very much to meeting the charming people of this friendly country and to admiring their celebrated landscapes. Amnesty International,of course,is at my ass with long lists of Eastern European writers who have just been dragged off to jail. I will talk with you during the week. I will call you now.

Love,
John

Cedar Lane,
May 24th

Dear _____,

I'm truly sorry to hear about your father and I'm much too old to have anything fresh or useful to say. I felt that I must strike some peace with my own father although we both tried to kill one another. I made him into Leander and struck a useful peace after his death. I think you must do something of the sort; you must try to understand the man. I've told my own sons that when they find me lacking they can continue to love me and find other men who will wear underwear,pitch no-hitters and invent the telephone. It seems to work. I think I've known no man who has not accomplished this.

God knews when I'll meet but I'll call soon or call me. Call me collect and when the operator asks if I'll accept the charges on a call from _____I'll say yes,yes,yes,yes.

Love,
John

Cedar Lane,
May 25th

Dear _____,

As I wrote yesterday I am truly conerned with your response to what your father said because the greatest and the most bitter mystery in my life was my father. It seemed, from adolesence, that we must learn to love one another. Anything less, it seemed, would wreak some basic damage to my spiritual balance. This problem appears in all the books and stories. It was he who invited an abortionist for dinner. It was he who was discovered drunken, debauched and naked but for a string of champagne corks. He was the drunken old man in the rollercoaster when I thought he had drowned himself and he was the old man reading Shakespere sonnets to the cat. I have finessed these scenes but when he failed me, as he did a thousand, thousand times, I found my cock and balls in a wringer. I was determined not to lose that sense of locus that I would have lost if I dismissed him as a tragic clown. I perservered, I may have done no more, but it is all some part of the chain of being and when you have sons, as you will, it will be easier to comprehend.

On lighter matters I think of you at Yaddo and the people you will meet. What remains of the old staff are very dear friends. This is Nellie, the head cook at the Mansion, and George, the retired superintend who lives with his wife in the south end of the garage and Beverly who, on weekdays, will ask you how you want your eggs. Beverly came to the place at least twenty years ago and when I tried to date her she said she had four children. She is still a sweetheart. Among the guest I have already menioned Raphael. I am sure we will see eye to eye on the Harnaks and we can discuss them when we are together. There will be a fellow named Bob Chibka who was in my classes in Iowa. He was distinguished mostly by his industriousness and his intelligent enthusiasim for Kafka. In August there will be a former male beauty named Ned Rorem. Years and years ago he sucked my cock three times a day for three days. I can't remember what it was like but it must have been good because I wouldn't have kept coming. We've met, subsequently, but merely to shake hands. When I first enetered the mansion I was twenty-two. I decided that Mrs. Trask's tastes were no concern of mine and over the years I've observed very little of the place. Above the serving table in the dining-room is a painting that looks genuine. It is not. Among the carved dining room chairs is one that depicts a beheading. On the right of the big staircase is a brass mermaid with a commodius navel and on the newel post of the stairway to the third floor is a lamp with two charming female stayrs. On my way to breakfast I used to slide down the banister and smack Venus on the ass. On the sideboard in West House, concealed by a vase is a representation of St.

George being conquered by the dragon. I know we will see eye to eye
on the trees and the water and the mountains and I know we will walk
there together.

Love,
John

He'd already written to Ned about his protégé's plans to go to Yaddo.
The memorial was for Elizabeth Ames.

John Cheever
Cedar Lane
Ossining, New York 10562

Dear Ned,

I am so glad you liked "Falconer" and many thanks for writing to
say so. The memorial for Elizabeth was suitable, the weather was marvelous and De Tredici, planning to play Schubert ended up with
Brahms. I don't think Elizabeth had anything to do with this but I was
pleased.

_____ _____, a very good friend of mine will be at Yaddo in August and
the first two weeks in September. I hope we'll meet there.

Yours,
John

Cedar Lane,
Monday [1977]

Dear _____,

Of course everything will end up happily and I think your tower
room is the best in the mansion. There are some priest-holes in that
pile. Gurganus had the room last year and got sore as hell when I called
him Rapunzel. His hair was very long. Gurganus is brilliant but he
suffers acutely from the loss of gravity that seems to follow having a
cock up your ass or down your throat once to often. . . .

Cedar Lane

August 28th

Dear ____,

Your description of your love for ____ pleased me deeply since it refreshed my sense of that genuiness of heart I so admire in you and made clear the fact that for both of us the love of a woman is without parellel. . . .

I do from time to time apprehend the hostility of the world, but this is mostly apprehension. Innocence much concerns us and so this morning,because my letters have lacked any literary merit,I will discourse on the Madonna of Konigsgovrod in a little town in southwestern Russia, not for from the contemporary Turkish border. Like so much else, she is almost never shown to tourists. She is the Byzantine Queen of Heaven,quite fair in this case, richly enthroned and,holding on her knees the Prince of Peace. Her throne stands high in a flowering meadow, surrounded by a circle of dancing nymphs and satyrs. Since this is Byzantine we find the nearly geometrical lines of Greece in the dilineation of muscles and draperies but the smiles of the Virgin and The Prince and the celebrants anticipate a much later period in the history of painting.

It will not be until the late renaisience that we will again find such wisdom,charm and lewdness. The breasts and buttocks of the nymphs have a fulness, a beauty and a whiteness that is unprecedented this early in the history of painting. The satyrs are dark-skinned and their legs and buttocks are hairy. They have the hooves of goats and their smiles are intelligent and lewd. Several of them support enormous, hard cocks with clumps of hair growing out of the crevice. Their happiness seems to enchant The Virgin and her child but this peaceable kingdom where the fires of the flesh and the spirit are one is never shown to tourists. It has never been shown to anyone since I made it all up and attributed it to St. Pelagius who was burned at the stake in the fifth century.

The Holiday Inn is full and I've taken a room at the Gideon Putnam where they have room service and a much better menue. I'll talk with you on the telephone long before we meet.

Love, Much love,
John

Yaddo

February 9th

Dear ____,

I will call you tonight or tomorrow and ask you to return for the weekend and when you refuse,as I think you will, I will understand. This seems to be very much a part of my love for you. It all seems quite simple. Neither of us is homosexual and yet neither of us are foolish enough to worry about the matter. If I want your cock or your mouth I know I have only to ask and yet I know there is so much better for you in life than my love that I can think of parting from you without pain. This,of course drives my cock up the wall. It thinks you can hear it in ____. What I want is that which is courageous,intelligent and truthful for us both. One cannot work out a system of true and false in the space of one's life but I can find nothing false in my love for you. Of course it didn't matter that you didn't have an orgasim It wouldn't have mattered had you come sevent times. It's terribly simple. I love you and I love to be near you.

It is late in the afternoon and I will go skiing before the light goes. . . . Goodnight, my love,I would say if we were in bed together and—lumped or unlumped—it would be for me a very good night.

Love,
John


[Early 1978]

Dear ____,
. . . Mary has been sick since her return and I have been doing the shopping and the cooking. My abilities in these fields might,when we live together,concern you. Last night I seved uncooked baked pota-toes,partially thawed frozen peas and burned lamb chops. The kitchen was so filled with smoke that even the dogs,coughing and red-eyed, asked to be let out. I ate my chops out of the broiler. I love you too much to serve you spaghetti at five in the morning. Oh God how I love you and want and need you.

Love,
John


My father wrote an original screenplay for Public Television, which was called *The Shady Hill Kidnapping*. Hope has a brother named David.

Cedar Lane

April 15th, 1978

Darling,

I am not there because all we did was to go to a cocktail party and kiss under a street light and anyhow I'm really working on the WNET show in which you play allthe principle parts. I really want to write a smashing show within the confines of traditional TV and I also want to work with you. I don't really know you at all. I think about you a lot but when I was a kid I used to think a lot about the girl in the Murad cigaret advertisement. I mean she used to stir my little cock but I never got to know what she was really like. WNET is supposed to produce a director within ten days.

What I do know about you is that you knock silver onto the floor in restaurants and that you're not terribly good about keeping secrets and if I ask you not to tell David that I am getting an honorary degree from Harvard you will tell him anyhow. The President and The Fellows and the Directors of the Governing Boards have asked me not to tell anyone. However, now that I've told you I expect, when we meet in May to be treated with a good deal of reverence. Tell me when you're coming back and I'll work on my dignity.

Love,
John
John Cheever DLL

Cedar Lane

Thursday [May of 1978]

Dear ____,

I am miserable,horney,lonely,depressed and unshaven and it all must be because I smoke too much. This is the beginning of the year and I've spaded the garden,brush-hooked the woods and will point some stones this afternoon but I feel like shit. At nightfall I will put on my only suit and drive to Caldors in Bedford Hills where I will be displayed, rather like an egg-beater,somewhere between the Tobacco Shoppe and Household Utensils. Twenty-five books-sellers with shopping bags filled with out of print editions will appear and by the time I have autographed these all the lonely,lonely people who hoped to meet a man as lonely as they will have to go home. I do wish you were around. I thought you were going to spend the summer in ___ but now I don't know where you'll be.

This is the season of accolades and the more I get the crosser Mary becomes. She hasn't spoken for weeks. Saul Bellow tells me that women's literary ambitions are inestimable and his fourth wife is a Romanian mathamatician who can barely read. They seem fairly happy. I am not. I plan to spend one week each month away from here but May is congested and in June I get a Big Prize about which I am not allowed to speak although I would speak to you about it if you were here or I were there or we were together somewhere else.

Love,
John

June sixth [1978]

Dear Hope,

I'll probably call you but anyhow yesterday I saw Paul Bogart who would like to direct the TV show I wrote mostly for you. I can't figure him out. I wonder what you think. Mike Nichols seems bogged down in the show in Philadelphia. Bogart seems highly professional but he wear big shades and isn't exactly driving. Why don't you write or call. I go down to Boston tomorrow to play slap jack with Ephriam Katchalski-Katzir and the President of Bostswana but I'll be home on the weekend.

Love,
John

John Cheever
Cedar Lane
Ossining, New York 10562

June 18th, 1978

Dear Tanya,

. . . Solzhenitsyn was given an honorary degree by Harvard College. He made his speech about the spiritual poverty of the West. He wore two splendid suits, his cheeks were blazing, he has the unyielding eyes of a redemptionist prophet and when I spoke to him about C.'s largesse he said that C. was not truly a large man. I know all of this, of course, because I too was given an honorary degree. Because my name begins with "C" I marched directly behind the Governor of Massachusetts. Aleksandr brought up the rear.

Luv,
John

John Cheever, Doctor
of Letters

Dr. John Cheever Phd.
Cedar Lane.
Ossining, New York 10562

[He'd written in the Dr. and the Phd. in felt-tip pen.]

July 7th, 1978

Dear Tanya,

Do write the Spears. Two months ago Stella was discovered to have cancer of the throat and her throat was removed. She now speaks with a sort of engine, but it was a cruel blow to them both. They both possess extraordinary spiritual robustness and have met this problem with considerable gallantry, and they would love to hear from you.

And I, of course, was pleased to here how happy you are, painting and smoking pot in meadows and bathing in the sea and reading Isherwood. Your soul, of course, is not international nor is the soul of anyone worth their salt. That crowd hangs around the Lido and other such places, proving that without nostalgia one will perish. Since I have been given a Phd I think entirely in the sort of maxims one finds on tombstones.

Luv,
John

Bastille Day [1978]

Dear Hope,

The history of my struggle to get to lunch with you goes on. It was in December that I agreed to do an original for public tv, with the understanding that you would play all the big parts. I did spent January in Russia but soon after I gave them the first outline you sublet your apartment and took off. I then began to plan a trip to the coast so that we could have lunch out there. Paul Bogart didn't thrill me but he was on the coast. Would he go back to All In The Family or would he work with me on the screen play? Yesterday he decided to do both. He will go back to All In The etc. on the first of August but work with me for the rest of this month. I'll leave for the coast tomorrow, said I, and they said: This won't be necessary because Paul is having his deck rebuilt and will come east on Wednesday to work with you here. I only wanted to lunch with you and I'll get to lunch with Paul Bogart who doesn't eat much lunch because he doesn't get up until eleven.

I wonder how your tomatoes are. Mine are half-formed and bright green. I stake my tomatoes lightly because I feel that the tomatoe is basically a vine, disorderly and random. Me too.

Love,
John

August 12th, 1978

Dear Hope,

I somehow think you're in Aspen listening to string music and I really can't remember what you look like. I'll bet you cross your legs when you listen to string music. I was once invited to go to Aspen and to speak with business executives on the 100 Great Books. When I realized that I hadn't read the 100 Great Books I put the invitation into a soup tureen and didn't write them until a year later. They've never asked me again. Of course you may be in Skyewiay with your tomatoes. My crop is vast but slow to ripen because of a wet summer. I have had about a dozen.

I lunch with the Public Television people on Tuesday and I really don't like them. I'm counting on a good director. Bogart is willing to do the show but he is now doing another 26 Archie Bunkers. Nichols is still tentative and a man named Alda is interested. I tell you all this because one of my motives in writing the show was really to have an opportunity to see you. I am terribly lonely. I haven't signed a contract and won't until I'm happy with a director. The crowd I lunch with on Tuesday is now shooting Mourning Becomes Elektra which I think to be the worst play that was ever written in the two thousand year history of the theatre but it would be dumb of me to say so at lunch, wouldn't it?

Love,<br>John

My sister took a leave of absence from *Newsweek* in 1978 and went to France, where she wrote her first novel, *Looking for Work* (Simon and Schuster, 1979). Polly was my mother's stepmother. My mother was planning to visit my sister. The New York City newspapers were on strike.

Cedar Lane,<br>August 24th, 1978

Dear Susie,

Firstly,Polly died yesterday. I loved her very much,of course as perhaps you did,but I will not go down for the funeral. She gave me perhaps a dozen summers that contributed enormously to that optimisim that enables me to be quite contented in a stalled Fiat on a late January afternoon in the slums of Leningrad. It would be pious to say that I fully expect to meet her in the life after death and it would be even more pious to say that I already knew her when we first met in New Haven;but something of the sort seems to have been true. God have mercy on her soul.

Your mother is delighted at the thought of lying on a matress at Cannes and is now doing slimming Yoga. With no Times to read I study the local papers. Item: ____,celebrating her graduation from nursing school,drank 11 ounces of vodka. She then backed her car into a restaurant window,sped up a narrow lawn between two houses,jumped a stone wall,killed a little girl named Alexandra and wrapped her car around an oak tree. Alexandra's parents said:"Our child is dead. We are Episcopalians. We will not press charges." Item: Sparks from a Hibachi grill set fire to the Lamplight Condominiums on Thursday night and destroyed twelve apartments. Eighteen apartments of the Shrade Manor Condominium have been vacated because of an infestation of bats. Eighty tenants of Scarborough Manor,who are paying a thousand a month for single rooms on a four-month lease,held a meeting last night to protest the inoperative elevators and the crumbling walls. Item: The Croton A&P will become a vetrinary hospital,administered by two horse-doctors from the Yonkers track. The tenants of the adjoining store CHICKEN GALORE are not placcated by the assurance that pet chickens will not be treated at the hospital. Item: The Carmel Dam has been declared unsafe and twenty-eight families have been evacuated to the Kent Cliff Armory.

Yours,
John


Mazie was a golden retriever.


Cedar Lane

August 31st

Dear Susie,

The curtain rises on the cloudy glass in the door at The Four Seasons. My train is late and I am late and having run to 52nd street from Grand Central, I am quite winded. I dislike the city,I conclude, because it reminds me of my age. At the head of the stairs I am greeted loudly by one of the Hungarian managers. I am lunching with Paul Gitlin and I recognize a setup. We have a pool-side table,I shake hands with Gitlin,dip my fingers into the water and make the sign of the cross. The manager brings me the guestbook to sign and when Gitlin,who has arranged the whole thing,claims to be astonished at my celebrity I say,very loudly,that is nothing new. My daughter,I explain,is an erstwhile editor at Newsweek and enjoys a twenty-five percent discount at this joint. We meet here for family quarrels,I say,because it's so much cheaper than Cote Basque. The news of a twenty-five percent discount throws absolutely everyone in the restaurant into a suicidal despression. "But I'm their lawyer," says Gitlin "and all I get is twelve." There are tears in his eyes. Several people leave. The manager rushes in to recommend Dover Sole which I order and Gitlin sobs his way through some French Fried shrimp. They look like something you might pick up on route #138 outside Cedar Rapids. We have met as a potential agent and writer but this is obviously not going to work. I thank him for lunch and hook a cab to 89th and Madison where I am to be interviewed by a Russian on the subject of Leo Tolstoy's 150th anniversary. Your mother and I have regretted their invitation to come to Moscow.

Nobody will speak to the Russians these days and my friend is waiting for me in the lobby of an apartment-house that suffers that dreadful twilight Sarinen introduced with the Seagram building. It is 3 P.M. Upstairs his wife, who speaks no English, is in grande tenue and there is enough pastry on the coffee-table to open a shop. As you know, I love the Russians. A dog is barking somewhere and I urge that it be released before we begin the interview. The lady opens the door to a fox-terrier who makes a straight line to my right shin which he bites. There is a great deal of screaming in Russian, the dog is banished and the interviewer explains that the dog is "jealousing". I answer his questions on Tolstoy and then he announces that he will drive me to Grand Central. I protest. It will be much quicker to get a cab. "But you do no understand," he says gently. "You will being giving me a favor. I am not being driving in New York very much and I am needing the practicing." So down Park Avenue we go at about seventy-five miles an hour, swerving wildly from lane to lane, blowing our horn continuously and shouting at the bad-mannered Capitalist drivers. We get a red light at 53rd Street and I get out of the car without saying goodbye and run the rest of the way to Grand Central where the only empty seat in the 3:50 local is in the middle of a large, Chinese family all of whom are reading Star Wars in paper-back. The most interesting story in the local paper—the only paper—is the discovery of a two and one half foot black snake, marked with yellow diamonds, in the parking lot of the Arcadian Gardens shopping center. When the pet store owner refused to recognize the serpent it was taken to the Teatown Reservation and put on display.

Ben and his family came for dinner last night and it couldn't have been pleasanter. Fred's girl comes tomorrow. They will leave presently for Tree Tops and then cross the continent via Canada. Mazie can say Tant pis quite clearly but she plans to destroy the Brancusi rug on the day your mother leaves. Into every life a little rain must fall.

Chin-chin,
John

The meeting with Ginsberg mentioned below was also described in his journals.

And there is Allan Ginzburg I think of M ____ the black and M ____ G ____. It isn't that one is astonished at the number of roles they play;

it is that the roles seem to have an ordained or geometrical progression, that the metamorphoses into opposites seems destined. He fucked himself up the ass with a corncob before a large gathering in Warsaw. He undressed and pulled off his cock in a Princetown lecture hall. Now he is the most immaculate man at the reception. His suit is splendid, his shirt is freshly ironed and his necktie seems more conspicuous than most neckties. He seems a littleshocked at the cigaret burning between my fingers. Burroughs,he tells me, has stopped smoking. That internationally famouscocksucker has extingui9shed his last cigaret. Mary thinks him a very gifted man. It is to Susie whom I will write, I think.

Cedar Lane,

October 19th

Dear Susie,

Notes from the literary world: Doubleday is publishing a new book of verse by Andrei Vozenesensky. His permission to come here was delayed until last week when Senator Kennedy brought some pressure to the situation and Andrei found himself on a plane half-dressed. The New York reading had to be arranged in three days. The Hunter College auditorium was booked,Allan Ginzburg agreed to read the translations and I agreed to do the introduction. Yesterday afternoon two girl graduates appeared—an hour late—in a brokendown Toyota. We started for the city. Twice, in a particularly stormy stretch of the Moshulu Parkway, the hood of the car flew up against the windshield. Anyhow we got there. I had had no dinner and I made a grab at some sandwiches in President Wexler's office but the president told me they were sandwiches from the last reception. Our sandwiches would come after the reading. Andrei appeared and we embraced as Russians will and then on came Ginzburg who I didn't recognize. I find him fascinating. It is not the variety of the roles these people play but the fact that their metamorphosis seem predictable and ordained. I think of ____ 's husband—that militant black who in the end wanted to cut off the hands of the Portugese rebels. There is no violence in Ginzburg but the metamorphosis seems predictable down to the last Cartier cufflink.

One of the last times I saw him he was exhaustively drunk, slovenly and lewd. Last night he was the most immaculate man in the room. Mouthwash,Dial soap, shoepolish, an Academy button and a necktie that was outstanding for its costliness and discretion. We shook hands and chatted. He is now professor of Buddahisim at the Jack Keroak College in Boulder. William Burroughs has just completed his Magnum Opus. All is serene and cleanly in Boulder. We walked down to the auditorium together and it was the look of dismay on his face when I lighted a cigaret that I will most clearly remember. "We have all stopped smoking," he sighed. So we performed. There weren't any sandwiches at the reception. There was nothing but Ryecrisp and cheese. I filled my pockets with this and got the 10:20 to Croton.

Yours,
John

Cedar Lane,

October 22nd

Dear Susie,

Our affectionate and enthusiastic congratulations on having completed your novel. We are all very proud of you. Scything,I think, is the best thing to do when you complete a work of fiction but I don't suppose you could do that in Fayence without causing some talk. I seed lawns,hang storm windows and fell trees. I also pray—no less— for contrition and humility and when I achieve these—always in excess —I go back to scything. I think that to complete a novel is a great accomplishment.

Yours,
John

Cedar Lane

Saturday

Dear ___,

The message here, my love, is that if there is something onerous in your past,never cease to regard this with caution. There seems to have been some critical division in my life between the brooks and meadows where I played and my mother's world of white gloves and dancing pumps. It is a world that seems to possess the authority of an executioner. They do not seem to threaten such green memories as drinking coffee bareass with you; they seem to extreminate such memories. . . .

Love,
John

Susan's then boyfriend, later husband, later ex-husband had also written a book. His name is Calvin Tomkins. He writes for *The New Yorker* and has written a number of books, including a biography of Gerald and Sara Murphy, *Living Well Is the Best Revenge*. Joshua is the name of my first son and my father's first grandchild.

Cedar Lane

November 27th,

It is snowing

Dear Susie,

The news about both of your books is very exciting and I like to think that there is some consternation in the Updike camp. Knopf is giving him a party at the St. Regis on the sixth and while his mother and David will be in the receiving line,David has only published two(2) short stories. On Saturday I gave Joshie a tape-recorder for his birthday and I have urged him to record his most interesting fancies and inventions. When they give you a party at the St. Regis we can perhaps have Joshie,your Mother,Ben Fred and me. No wonder the Updikes are nervous. (A girl in Boston told me that Fred has been studying the past for all of these years in order to write historical romances; and he was reading Sabatini.) . . .

I can't remember when I last wrote you but the most vivid memory of my travels remains the TODAY show in Boston. It was on this show last year that Lauren Hutton said she had fucked her way up the ladder of success. The show was then live. It is now taped and has taken on a Boston Mañana. We were herded into the Green Room for a one o'clock show but nothing was shot until two. You can easily imagine the Boston Green Room. It was,of course,snowing. The buffet consisted of cider and heavily sugared doughnuts. Never eat a heavily sugared doughnut before you go on TV. In one corner of the Green Room were eight little girls dressed as butterflies. Two of them were crying. In the other corner was a five-man combo of gas-pumpers, paralyized with stage-fright. "This is your big chance," the pianist kept telling them. "Think UP, think UP." They were sweating. In the center of the room was a man,surrounded by his life's work. He was,of course,nervous. He had spent his entire life carving birds out of wood and he was surrouned by nearly thirty of these. With him was a man in a dirty sweater who was practising those bird-songs and mating calls he would perform when the decoys hit the screen. On my left was a clean man in a full suit, eating an apple and when I asked him—light heartedly—if he was going on the show to eat an apple his response was choleric. "I am Dr. H.B. Hirshbaum," he said, "and I am going to discuss the Caesarian Experience." I was then thrust into an artificial living-room, blinded by artificial sunlight and—hoary with doughnut sugar—was introduced as "The Grand Old Man of American Letters." Of course the Updikes know enough not to appear on this show. So now, do we. Live and learn.

Yours,
John

# THE STORIES

* * *

*F*alconer's triumph was followed in 1978 with the publication of *The Stories of John Cheever*, and my father's publisher held a dinner honoring him.

Cedar Lane
December 6th [1978]

Dear ——,
. . . Last night was the gala dinner at Leutece and I sat between Lauren Bacall and Maria Tucci and basked in that fragrance of beaver we both so enjoy; but when I went out to take a piss between the 7th and 8th courses I thought deeply of you and of how happy I had been eating French-fried onion rings at Admiral Woolsey's. I was not overwhelmed with sadness but my memory of you was very strong. Very strong.

When I was toasted I told a story and then everybody held hands and sand"For He's A Jolly Good Fellow" and Betty Bacall cried. Everybody got pissed and I chain-smoked. If I were drinking coffee bearass in some kitchen with you this morning you might be surprised to find how angry Iam at the fact that Updike's fourth-rate novel has eighty thousand in print while my printing stopped at seventy. He's a Jolly Good Fellow!

I would be very happy to meet M. but I don't think Hope Wants to meet you. I told her that I loved you profoundly—that's what I said— and she seemed saddened but not disconcerted. Then I told her I loved having breakfast with you at Macdonalds and this drove her wild. Absolutely wild. She chased me around the place with fire-tongs. What can be the meaning of this?

Love,
John

Lynn was Lynda, my first wife. My mother had a new mink. Bathsheba was my sister's golden retriever, but when my sister went to France, Bathsheba boarded with my parents. When we brought the old pets up from the dining room to the bedrooms in the evening, my father would call out "brisky-frisky" in a encouraging way. If this didn't work, he'd push them. If this didn't work, they were carried upstairs.

Cedar Lane

December 6th,1978

Dear Susie,

The most exciting part of the gala dinner came when they brought in the first course. This was a fish quish shaped like an enormous pastry fish and decorated with a pastry frigate in full sail. I had Lauren Bacall on my right and Maria Tucci on my left and very much enjoyed myself. Ben and Lynn were both greatly admired and I was truly proud of them and your mother looked very beautiful. She has a new velvet dress. This is brownish-purple and the velvet has been chewed on by French noblewomen in reduced circumstances. It is very becoming and grand. When I was toasted I told a story and while it wasn't much,Ben observed that everybody sucked air and stared at the ceiling as if they were hearing prophecy. Everyone,that is but your mother,who kept dropping here table silver. Then everybody stood and sang: For He's A Jolly Good Fellow." They only sang the first verse. One verse is all they sang. 1.

If I were the sort of writer I am reputed to be I would write a story about a suburban matron who wakes up in the morning and taps the barometer. Then she checks the weather reports on TV,radio and in The Times. The weather news sometimes exalts her; sometimes leaves her in despair. She is waiting for that disturbance that springs up out of the northeast and is known as "The Mink Coat Wind." The coat is really very handsome and she was the only one in our party last night to have one. Walter Clemmons was there and I told him aboutyour success. He seemed very happy about this. We all remain happy here,although Bathsheba doesn't seem to understand about your success. I think she understands very little. We must comprehend their limitations. Edgar is so near-sighted now that while he insists upon my throwing tennis balls for him he then insists that I put on my glasses and go and find the ball. When bedtime comes your mother and I have to push most of the animals up the stairs. Brisky-frisky!

Love<br>John

This is to John Updike.

John Cheever<br>Cedar Lane<br>Ossining,New York 10562

April second

Dear John,

Since you are the only correspondent I have who works on scrap paper I must explain that this stationary was given to me by a lady who lives down the street and who got tired of receiving letters on Laundry lists. She only gave me one box and I'll soon be back with Woolco Linen Deluxe. This is to say that Mary and I come down to Boston on the eleventh for my freshman appearance at a Book & Author lunch on the twelfth and if you have any free time in Boston we would love to see you.

Yours,<br>John

My father and John Updike were both judges for the Grants Committee of what by amalgamation had now become the American Academy and Institute of Arts and Letters. The Academy is located between Broadway and the Hudson River on 155th Street. This is not quite, but almost the Bronx. John Updike wrote the Maple Stories.

John Cheever
Cedar Lane
Ossining, New York 10562

July 11th, 1979

Dear John,

Thank you for the Malamud support and I've mailed it along to the Bronx. Nominate Emmett Williams by all means. He may be a candidate we won't have to read. In yesterday's mail I was cordially invited to Notre Dame on the strength of the mastery and the penetration of the Maple stories. I think you don't know me well enough to know how vile I can be but in this case I was retiring and pious.

yours,
John

John Cheever
Cedar Lane
Ossining, New York 10562

November 3, 1979

Dear Tanya,

It is a cold, wet, overcast late afternoon in the northeastern United States. Mary is investigating a piece of nearby property that an unscrupulous Italian speculator wishes to have reclassified for an industrial site. My mistress is in Tunisia, playing the wife of Pontius Pilate in a dreadful TV film about our Lord Jesus. She dresses in sheets and says:"You are such an impulsive man. You always regret in the morning what you did last night." I have another lover who is on the Great Lakes. I spent all of last week bicycling in the hills of Vermont and tomorrow I leave for Texas where I will read The Death of Justina and The Swimmer at a university called Southern Methodist. Denis Levertov will represent poetry. Mary thinks her very distinguished; and I will read her poetry this evening.

. . . If Mary were here she would send you her love before she walked the dogs in the rain. Since she is not here I will send you her love and mine and it will be I who will walk the dogs in the rain.

Yours,
John


Wednesday

Dear ——,

I woke this morning with a hard wet cock and it's wet now after talking with you but this isn't all of it; it's talking about the impossibility of teaching and writing and happily eating a New York Steak at a place called the firehouse where the lavish salad bar consists of iceberg heels and pickled chickpeas and laughing and throwing snowballs and you complaining about my tobacco cough and the size of my cock and you driving back to ——with me in the back seat disguised as laundry. I have thought for a year that such love must be perverse, cruel and inverted but I can find no trace of this in my love for you. It seems as natural and easy as passing a football on a fine October day and if fhe game bores you you can toss me the ball and walk off the grass and there will be no forlorness. Both your short life and my long life have been, it seems to me, singular adventures and to hold your nice ass in my hands and feel your cock against mine seems to be a part of this astonishing pilgrimage.

I want your soft balls, I want to take off your glasses, I want your ass, your laughter and your loving mouth.

Love,
John


My father did a Rolex advertisement and was given a watch for himself, one for my mother and one for my brother. He was helping his young friend with his writing,


According to my $6,000.00
Rollex it is Wednesday, the 17th

Dear ——,

I have just talked with you and on the homework I would like to do it on a line by line basis and will. There is no point on my complimenting you on those gifts that seemed so striking to me in ___ long, long ago. I do feel that there has been an appreciable increase of light in the work. You are an intelligent and a loving young man, facts that _____ seemed to challange. My intent in all of this seems to be to goad you into writing a story that Macgrath will publish. This will make P. and your parents very happy, it will give you enough cash to reupholster the back of the Pontiac and put you in a position where you can negotiate an advance with a publisher.

What I don't understand is that you, who are so knowledgable about breathing run five pages without a paragraph. Even a non-smoker will get blue in the face before finishing page one. Here is beauty compromised by a needless density; and you know this well. On page two men and women enter the scene and you introduced the Derbyshires with a good deal of dismay. Since interest is the first canon of aesthetics I think it a mistake to make a character lackadaisical before we know her bust measurements. But here then is the rub; here is the contradiction. The contempt you bring to this cast is very unlike you. You ring the curtain up on a stunning landscape, filled with your extraordinarily keen sense of the world, and then you point out that the characters are full of shit. Nothing could be less like you. Fiction is very like love in that there is something lost and something gained.

                                                                     Love,
                                                                     John

My father and mother came up to Massachusetts to watch me run my first Boston Marathon. I didn't have the telegram in my mouth, but he did find me in the bathtub.

"You finished the marathon?" he said.

I nodded. "And you won the Pulitzer Prize," I said.

                                                                 Cedar Lane

                                                                 Monday

Dear ___,

That's one beautiful story you wrote; and that's mostly what I have to say. Any letter from you delights me but you seem to have written your last letter with a burr well up your asshole. Why write a beautiful story and then complain. . . .

Tonight I graduate from Smokeneders. They'll play Pomp & Circumsances on a stratchy tape and I'll get a fringed diploma with which I'll tickle your balls. Not having smoked for three weeks leaves me, this morning, unable to spell kat. I can usually rally at the sight of The New York Times but I was crushed this morning until I read,towards the end, that Katherine Stark had married Barney Softness becoming Mrs. Barney Stark Softness.

Boston was all winners. We went down in a small plane with props like swizzle-sticks. It flew so low that you could read the titles of the books people were reading in their patios. They were all reading the collected stories of Irwin Shaw. The Boston Ritz is a big winner and after a winning dinner Ben and I walked around the streets. It was like some medieval city on the eve of a pilgrimage. Of the eight thousand runners, most of them were trotting around or doing knee-bends on corners. The morning was 42 degreeswith a light drizzle which is winning weather for runners. My grandson and I took a winning ride in the swan boats and then saw a ceremony commemorating our victory over the Red Coats. Up in Fenway Park the Red Sox were beating the shit out of Cleveland. Susie—that winner—and her award-winning dog and lover showed up for a winning lunch and then we all walked up Commonwealth Avenue to see the race. Ben came in gallantly under three hours which is considered winning and when I returned to the hotel he was sitting in the bath-tub, holding in his teeth a wire from the Pulitzer Prize Committee. Then we all went down—nine Cheevers —to the dining room where the chef produced a Baked Alaska as big as a man, mantled in blazing brandy. The odds are 7 to 3 that he will win this year's baked Alaska prize.

I do very much want to see you and I'll keep calling you.

Love,
John

Despite the men in his life, despite Hope, despite others who have not surfaced in this book, my father and mother continued to be important to each other. There was always humor and vitality in the house. Tom Glazer remembers visiting my father one morning, and having my mother come in. It was clear that she was angry and she walked by her husband without saying hello. My father gave her an exaggerated smile, and Tom remembers that she said, "Wipe that artificial smile off your face." My father replied,

"The only thing artificial about this smile is the teeth." I don't know for sure, but my guess is that my mother laughed.

This last winter my mother bought a new chest of drawers for her bedroom, and so my wife, Janet, and I inherited the one it displaced. In its drawers we found an unopened set of thermal long johns almost certainly bought when my father was dying of cancer and was always cold. These I took. There were also some neckties, and a poem, which my father had written out in longhand to my mother. In 1980 she brought out *The Need for Chocolate & Other Poems*. When it received a bad notice, he bought her a piece of gold jewelry and gave it to her with the poem on the following page.

Janet and I went on our honeymoon in May of 1982. Before I left, my father asked if he could speak with my therapist while I was away. When we returned from our trip, I went eagerly to my first session and found that the woman had not been contacted.

It was on June 6 that he phoned me at work. That was twelve days before he died, and a week or so before he lost the use of his voice. The conversation was brief. He tired easily then. He explained that he hadn't been to see my therapist. This, he said, was "partly because I was busy and partly because I didn't see why I couldn't tell you what I had to face-to-face." He hadn't been busy, he'd been sick, but we both honored this fiction. "What I wanted to tell you," he said, "is that your father has had his cock sucked by quite a few disreputable characters. I thought I'd tell you that, because sooner or later somebody's going to tell you and I'd just as soon it came from me."

"I'd suspected as much," I said.

I have spent a lot of time reliving that exchange. I do keep a journal and once in a while I do write down what matters, although it's difficult. In any case, I recorded that last conversation, and I have referred to my journal more than once in the last six years. But even having referred to it, I distorted what I saw, because I thought I'd said, "That's all right with me, Pop, if it's all right with you." I just looked at the journal again, though, and I wasn't that tough, or that firm. I was forgiving, but mostly I was just bewildered, and I remember now that my reply came almost as a whisper: "I don't mind, Daddy, if you don't mind."

The young protégé moved to New York and continued to be a factor in our lives. Since he was in the neighborhood the letters to him trailed off. Mary McNeil is the girl my brother would marry. Fred was at Stanford in California. Tompkins is Calvin Tomkins, and he was divorcing the wife he

JOHN CHEEVER
CEDAR LANE
OSSINING, NEW YORK 10562

The need for chocolet is much finer

Than the need for gold,

And I have hoped to send you

some of both,

While we have sought the ghost of love

Together — and better yet,

Found something more enduring

Than either gold or chocolet

divorced before he married my sister. Janet is Janet Maslin, the woman to whom this book is dedicated.

March third, 1981

Dear Fred,

Before I received your splendid letter I had written and had not mailed a letter to you saying how pleased I was to know that you are enjoying with Mary (who Susie has described as intelligent, affection, charming and marvelous) so amiable a relationship. The news that you are in love with one another makes me very happy. . . . The geographical distance between us does not disconcert me since my love for you seems quite demanding and is no way inhibited by the breadth of the continent. I would understand if you took Mary to China. We have always enjoyed the freedom to tell one another to fuck off. I would have liked your opinion yesterday when I read some Satre on the unethical nature of history and rallied to declare the history of this country a traditional moral narrative beginning with The Federalist Papers. I have never read The Federalist Papers.

To answer the more serious part of your letter the dogs do not sleep on the sofa because when we go out in the evenings we remove all the cushions. The cats sleep on everything and leave hair balls everywhere. Tompkins is divorced. Janet is going to run in the Maryland Marathon. Ben has taken on his "thin" look if you know what I mean. His face seems very lean and I feel him to be,quite pleasantly, an absolute stranger. Joshie seems fine and they were all here for dinner on Thursday. I find the hairy cat quite difficult although I don't feel free to say so. Your mother is doing a portrait of the hairy cat. I think I have never known your mother to be so contented.

We are both deeply grateful to you for your thoughtful letter.

Yours,<br>John

Philip Schultz was a friend of my father's from Yaddo. Phil used to come out to Ossining and ride bicycles with my father. He also used to join the family on Christmas, Easter and Thanksgiving. An accomplished poet, Phil had always wanted to write fiction. At the time this letter was written, he was completing a novel.

John Cheever
Cedar Lane
Ossining, New York 10562

March 9th,1981

Dear Phil,

The only advice I have to give a young novelist is to fuck a really good agent. Just keep fucking her and if she insistent well then marry her. That seems to be the only way to get ahead. William Faulkner, James Gould Couzzens and even Gay Talese fucked their agents. I am and old man,nearing the end of my journey and if a young talented man should come to me on my deathbed and ask for advice I would whisper: "Fuck a good agent."

I thought the poetry splendid and we'll talk this over when we meet. I am now going to the hospital three times a week for theraupy on my right shoulder but as soon as the days take on a little more length I hope to get back on my bicycle and I hope you will join me.

Yours,
John

The letter below was written to John Updike. He and my father shared duties on the Grants Committee of the American Academy and Insitute of Arts and Letters.

John Cheever
Cedar Lane
Ossining, New York 10562

April 9th, 1981

Dear John,

When I read the few beautiful lines of yours that were quoted in the TIMES yesterday I thought: How splendid is his voice! How inestimable is the contribution he makes to western civilization! This is not to say that you have been forgiven for yielding your chairmanship to Hortense Calisher.

Yours,
John

My mother flew out to California to watch Fred graduate from Stanford with a master's in history. Mrs. Maslin is Lucille Maslin, my mother-in-law. She did come to lunch and nobody was bitten.

June 6th [1981]

Dear Fred,

I remember that in discussing with Mary your very few good attributes and virtues we had agreed on the fact that you had some small gifts as a life-saver. You had, after all, pulled me out from under a falling birch trunk. You seemed last night very much a salvationist in the matter of your commencement. Your mother, evidently, was dying to see you graduate. I very likely would have died had I made the effort. You settled this with the despatch of Bucky Dent fielding a double-play in the 11th inning just as a light rain had begun to make the astro-turf slippery. I thought of you last night when the doctor—a basically insecure supply-sider-pulled the circumcision kit out of his raincoat pocket. I chose to describe what followed as "facial surgery" but I felt like a Calla Liley with my stamen in the Waring Mixer. He kept assuring me that it was a trivial matter but I can this morning barely limp and I am so cranky and distempered that I am afraid that when Mrs. Maslin comes for lunch I will bite her in the neck. Stay tuned.

Yours,
John

This is to John Updike.

Mr. John Cheever. Cedar Lane. Ossining, New York 10562

June 27th,1981

Dear John,

We're delighted to know that we'll see you here and we've done almost nothing since receiving your letter but discuss dates and hours of the day that will best display Mary's beauty and my health. We think that Tuesday the seventh of July would be a splendid date but we can't agree on whether it should be lunch or dinner. Mary looks great in candlelight but I am very robust at mid-day. We will leave the hour up to you but whichever you chose will be a great pleasure for us both.

Yours,
John

Roger Willson was a member of the Friday Club. Dr. Schulman was my father's urologist. Sara Spencer was a neighbor and friend.

Mr. John Cheever. Cedar Lane. Ossining, New York 10562

July 22nd,1981

Dear Arthur,

Your letters are very welcome and I was happy to have your report on the egg situation. I returned from the hospital only yesterday morning and feel exactly like a man who has risen from the dead. Indeed,according to Dr. Schulman,that is what I am. Roger has been very thoughtful but I suspect that he hopes to win large sums from me at backgammon. I steadfastly refuse to play. The first reading of the TV screenplay takes place on the third and they begin filming on the tenth if you would like to play a role in this. You could play opposite that old Bostonian,Tammy Grimes.

Yours,
John

This stationary is given to me by Sara Spencer and can be eaten with sugar and warm milk.

Fred had been disappointed in a try for a summer job. Hamlet was my father's father's brother. He's supposed to have gone to California when the West was young. He was much loved, and my father said that he would write regularly for passage home, and that money would be sent, and then he would write again for money home. He finally did come back east. Mazie, a golden retriever, had belonged to my sister, but had been adopted by my parents when my sister and Rob Cowley went to live in England in 1969. My father had had a series of apparently minor complaints and illnesses. In the spring of 1981 he had one kidney removed. This had a tumor, but I was told that the tumor was benign, and that in any case there was almost no chance of the growth returning. The tumor was not benign.

Ginger Reiman is a neighbor. She and her husband, Don Reiman, the architect, have been friends since the family moved out of Manhattan.

July 24, 1981

Dear Fred,

You will have a job by now, I'm sure and for me to write you a cheering letter on the subject would be ridiculous since I've never looked for a job and I am internationally celebrated as a depressant. My feeling about your job is simply repitition of what I was told about Californians as a child. They have no ability to recognize character or intelligence. That's why they went to California in the first place. If they'd possessed any capabilities they would have remained in Boston and Newburyport. When they do have the good fortune to employ you it will be because some of their eastern merits have survived. Even Uncle Hamlet was unsuccessful in San Francisco. That's going some.

Mazie and I quarrel in the mornings but otherwise things are quite harmonious here. There are blue slip covers in the parlor and a man came this morning to take away the marble table and cut it in two. This is at the suggestion of Ginger Reiman who has studied interior decoration. What is more to the point is the fact that your mother never liked the long stone table. The Hudson Valley is in its midsummer megrims. Everything cultivated and desirable is latent or dying and thorny parasites and lengths of wild grape can be heard advancing during the night. The Cicadas have not yet begun their singing but this is only a matter of hours. I still feel very frail from the defenestration of my kidney and the loss has left me quite sentimental. I sometimes cry when Edgar brings me a tennis ball. Things are bound to look up.

Yours,
John

Wells Fargo had hired a "sixty-year old chronicler of the Korean War" for the job Fred applied for. Tad is Calvin Tomkins. Fred's future in-laws, the McNeils, had made a tape of the Stanford graduation. My father used to listen to this on a Walkman. Piccinino was a diminutive for Picci, which was a diminutive for Fred.

August 4th, 1981

Dear Fred,

We are all pleased to know that you have a desk, we were all pleased with your letter and with the news that you and Mary will be here at the end of the month. It was, of course, only sensible of Wells-Fargo to chose a sixty-year old chronicler of the Korean War for the position. umemployed, he would have been a threat to the welfare of the community and one always has to think of the commonwealth. Mary took off on Tuesday morning for Tree Tops and that, for me, mysterious province. She called last night to say that she was happily alone in the Stone House. Susie and Tad are planning to join her this weekend. . . . —— is here to pick me up when I fall down. He got me on a bicycle the day before yesterday and he thinks he can do this again today but he is greatly mistaken.

Ben was here for dinner last night and is preparing for that damn-fool swim-bicycle-run performance on Sunday. Dear Janet will drive him to the starting line, somewhere in barbarous Rhode Island. The cicades have started their singing. A fellow named Amerigo who was helping with the battle against wild rose and other nomadic parasites was attacked by hornets last Thursday and may never return. This only means that the place may look disheveled when you and Mary arrive but then so may Edgar and I. Mary's parents very generously sent on a tape of your graduation and when your mother exclaimed "Piccininno" I sob freely. The dogs, who feel that the head-phones must be hurting me, come to my side and bark loudly. My love to Mary.

Yours,
John

MR. JOHN CHEEVER. CEDAR LANE. OSSINING, NEW YORK 10562

August 24th,1981

Dear John,

I might write about Mary's beauty and my health but I finished Rabbit Rich last night and I must say that I think it the most important American novel I have read in many years.

Gratefully,
John

MR. JOHN CHEEVER. CEDAR LANE. OSSINING, NEW YORK 10562

September first, 1981

Dear John,

... Mary finds the mastery in Rabbit Rich quite as stunning and important as I. From time to time she put the galleys down to water the garden with me calling after her to say that anyone who could put down such a book to water flowers was idiotic; but in spite of this idiocy she has finished the book and enthusiastically agrees with me on its beauty and power.

Yours,
John

It had been almost forty years since my father had sent a series of letters to John and Harriet Weaver about the glories of the autumn foliage in the Northeast in a semihumorous attempt to convince that couple to give up California and live closer to the Cheevers. Now, as my brother, Fred, began in his turn to sink roots on the West Coast, my father tried the same tack with Fred's future wife, Mary. The results were similar. The Weavers still live in California. My brother has recently moved to Denver, but it is felt here in the East that the first cold breath of winter will send him scurrying back to the Pacific. My brother still has the leaves my father sent him.

September 10th

Dear Fred,

The sumac leaves are the first of hundreds of specimen I will send on to acquaint Mary with the splendors in the northeast that are unknown in California. I saw a scarlet Maple yesterday driving back from New York but the traffic was heavy and it seemed unsafe to to stop and pick a garland. Susie and Tad joined me in the city yesterday for the screening and the production is more than I could have hoped for. They play the commercials very broadly but there is commercial music and art work and I think it ought to be a great success. I think there has never been anything like it on American TV. Everyone around WNET seems excited. Last night your brother called to say that and Janet are happy in a Bar Harbour motel. He said how much he had enjoyed the togetherness that you and Mary enjoy. I think he would like to run across the continent to the wedding and I think Janet would run along with him if the TIMES would let her off.

I have written congressman Ottinger to congratulate him on his pessimism but I did point out that he was one of the first to forsake Carter. I said that there seemed to be, in popular government, some imponderables that Carter failed to master and was thus unable to implement his intelligent and conscientious program. I am writing an article for a magazine called DIAL , saying how great my screen play is. . . . Mary, Mazie, and Edgar join me in speeding our love to you both.

Yours,<br>John

My sister and my wife-to-be had had a falling-out. Lily was a cat.

September 20th, 1981

Dear Fred,

We hope to be in touch with you by telephone before this reaches you but should we miss this is to say that Tad will marry Susie on Thursday afternoon at four in front of the fireplace here. The only guests will be Spencer, Ben and Tad's daughter. Susie has asked you mother to bake a cake. I bought some flowers at Swansons and will get champagne in Pleasantville. After the ceremony Susie and Tad will leave for a little, costly inn in Purdy's. Bathsheba will remain with us for a day or two. . . .

Walking to the dam yesterday with Roger I found only these colored leaves but perhaps some colorful rhetoric will continue to keep ablaze in Mary's mind the glories of autumn in the northeast. I'll go forth on my bicycle after the wedding and see if I can't find something better. Wedding plans seem to occupy us all. lily-Butt is to be locked in the attic, for example. Janet Maslin is not to be asked. The local Justice of the Peace will tie the knot. I am going to ring the bell in the backyard.

Yours,<br>John

September 23rd

Dear Fred,

The leaves are turning slowlybut I'm keeping an eye on them to try and illuminate for Mary the glories of the East. When you were an infant in Italy I was very disconcerted to be told that much of the Italian population had never seen the beauties of the autumn foliage in Vermont and New Hampshire. High in the Abruzzi there are stands of Aspen and Poplar that turn yellow in the fall and they seem to think this adequate. I feel that this explains some of their governmental instability. A people who have never experienced autumn foliage are inclined to be backward. The fact that California has no autumn foliage might have accounted for Reagan's election as Governor.

Your mother has gone to New Hampshire to supervise the installation of a flue for a stove in the Stone House. It is very cold, windy and rainy up there and she reports that she would be quite lost without Mazie although Mazie cannot climb the stairs and barks loudly whenever your mother does. This means that Mary will not be able to take a bath until she returns this weekend. I am with Edgar who presents no problems at all. Ben was here for dinner last night which Edgar and I cooked. It was too cold and rainy to eat on the porch and I had to let Ben into the dinning room. He seems fine. The weather is rather like the first days of winter. The furnace is on and the radiator in the dinning-room goes Whack, Whack. The sky is open and shut, leaves fly in the wind and I will start to put up the storm windows this afternoon. It's too bad that you're missing all of this.

Yours,
John

The cake, champagne and flowers were for my sister's wedding. The shotgun was a 20-gauge. It had been given to me for my thirteenth birthday, and we used it for occasional skeet shooting. We also fired it at the rats that used to pillage the duck food and at snakes. All snakes in my father's world were presumed to be highly poisonous. My most vivid memory of the gun is somewhat unsettling. I had heard that my parents were away and was making an unannounced late-night visit to the house. I was in the dining room when my father appeared at the top of the stairs. He was bare-assed and had the shotgun clutched in both hands. I don't believe it was loaded. He invited me to stay for a drink, but I declined.

September 30th, 1981

Dear Fred,

. . . Your mother has baked a cake with cracked but I have urged her to remember the Liberty Bell and the Venus de Milo. Good champagne is 19$ a bottle and I got six. We've moved the coffee table around so that The Justice of the Peace can tie the knot in front of the fire-place. It was Tad who suggested that a shot gun might be in order but if I bring out the old 16-guage I might be arrested for the possession of an unliscened fire-arm. You mother has arranged flowers very handsomely in all the rooms and I think Susie much happier than I have ever known her to be.

Stanford has sent an invitation, saying that there is no reason why you should be the only Cheever to enjoy "the delights of sunny Palo Alto" and "the pleasures of a California lifestyle." It is very generous of them but with the book being published in April I think I should remain here and send you and Mary examples of spring wild flowers that she will not have encountered in that part of the world.

Yours,
John

Fred's great-grandfather Thomas Watson helped Alexander Graham Bell invent the telephone.

October tenth, 1981

Dear Fred,

It was great to have your letter. Without any reflection on your Great-Grandfather's giftedness I do feel that a correspondence is more elevating than a telephone call. The same goes for television but I will tape a Dick Cavett show on Wednesday in tandem with John Updike that will be shown a few days later. Both you and David Updike will be able to see your dear old fathers on the screen. I have recovered enough strength to bicycle around the block and I try to do this every day now. I think mostly of Mary and the autumn foliage. It is these days in spate. I have tried to photograph this with the polariod I bought for Susie's wedding but one of the glories of the autumn foliage is that it cannot be captured in a picture. It seems to me that it cannot be described. It is, as is everything in the world, most luminous when one is in stimulating company. I am, for example, about to walk to the dam with

Roger and the colors will be less than exalting. But it is—dear Mary—
rather like the phenomenon of fire only it is a retarded fire and its hues
and changes can be observed. You, of course, will come to see this next
year.

. . . Last week I gave Ben galleys of my new book to ask if he wanted a
dedication. He kindly agreed as you did with Falconer. I think Falconer
a better book but in both cases I wished that the books had been more
elevating. I shall persevere.

Yours,
John

Esse Lee, the widow of Alwyn Lee, who did the *Time* cover story on my
father in 1964, had knitted him a necktie. The magazine on whose cover
the necktie appeared was *Dial*. The picture of the necktie and the author is
included in this book.

John Cheever
Cedar Lane
Ossining, New York 10562

October 31st,1981

Dearest Esse,

All the news around here is nectie news. I did a Dick Cavett show
last week,wearing Esse #1. Dick had never seen a tie as beautiful and
voluminous and looked ruefully at his regimental stripe. The necktie
can be seen here on the Cavett show on the tenth of November and if
you don't have the Cavett show it will be shown on a BBC show/where
I am asked for my opinion on John Updike. I wore no vest so that the
tie can be seen in all its splendor. A few days later Richard Avedon
called to ask if he could photograph me for a magazine cover. I wore
Essie #1. He called yesterday to say that the photographs were beautiful,especially the necktie. This cover will be out in late December and
I'll send you a copy. A television original that I wrote was screened last
night for an invited audience. Bathing and dressing I felt quite depressed but at dusk the mailman delivered Essie #2,changing my point
of view and perhaps my life. I put on my best dark suit, a white silk
shirt from Gucci,black shoes and tied the new tie with the crimson
stripe an inch and one half below the knot. The screen play was suc-

cessful but the tie was a sensation. Not only did women and a few men ask to feel its texture but I was obliged to take it off three times to that its construction could be admired. I overheard a conversation at the bar between two strangers. "Which is Cheever," one of them asked and the other said:"The man with the beautiful tie."

Love,
John

John and Mary Updike had been divorced, and he had married Martha. John had asked some questions about Ossining.

Cedar Lane

November 18th

Dear John,

When I asked Knopf to send you galleys of Oh What A Paradise I had meant to include a covering letter to say that I was unenthusiastic about the book and would not expect your good opinion until I had completed another, better book. Your magnaminity is overwhelming. That irascible unpleasantness that distinguishes the truly great seems an attribute that you have been neglecting to cultivate. Martha obviously can't help you in learning to be more ungenerous but there must be some crank in the village who could instruct you. There is no room for such generosity in a man of your stature.

I saw the TV show here alone in the kitchen. Mary and the dogs all went to bed. I thought you comely. I looked exactly like my Uncle James. He used to squint his eyes and speakhesitantly as if he were waiting for some intestinal gas to be freed. He looked rather like a viper who was trying to break wind.

There is an Ossining High School and a beach at Croton Point and it would be my pleasure to inform you on both of these. They are predominantly black.

Yours,
John

# CANCER

\* \* \*

$\mathbf{M}$y father's health had not been good for a couple of years, but all his setbacks had seemed minor, and I had been assured by his doctors that they were minor. He'd given up drinking and smoking, and it was hard to believe that anything wrong could happen at this point. It was at about 2 P.M. on Thursday, December 3, 1981, that my father's doctor called to tell me that the mysterious recent illnesses he had been plagued with were in fact an advanced cancer, "unusually vigorous in a man of his age." The doctor said that the cancer had spread to one of my father's legs, and that the leg looked like a "textbook illustration" of bone cancer. He guessed that my father had about six months to live. Janet and I and my mother were going to a play in New York that evening. Daddy had paid for the tickets. We went. Fred and Mary were to be married in California. The whole family planned to attend.

January 23rd (I think) [1982]

Dear Fred,

... My one-shot try at television got quite high ratings across the country but its highest rating came from San Francisco and I suppose this is because you and Mary rang doorbells and urged people to watch the show. You have been a splendid son. Ben has booked all seven of us onto United Airlines, noon flight from Kennedy to Los Angeles. We depart again at noon on Sunday. We will talk this over on the telephone. Iole has been forbidden to bring many groceries.

The cold and the fall of snow begin to seem unremittent. I think it's not been been below twenty for some weeks. The snow would be marvelous for skiing. My health remains about the same and I see a doctor on Monday and will ask him if progress is usually this slow. I have been on chemotherapy now for nearly a month. Whenever I have felt like myself I go looping around the lawn for a minute and then collapse. I expect I should stay in bed until the flowers come up.

Your mother's love, her thoughtfulness and her practical help have been quite indescribable. Not only does she have to push me around but Mazie has gotten quite infirm and complaining and after she has pushed me up the stairs she hasto start all over again with Mazie.

Love,
John

This is to Bill Maxwell.

John Cheever
Cedar Lane
Ossining, New York 10562

January 31st, 1982

Dear Bill,

I have been ill and I wanted to be the one to tell you, I remember so vividly, over the years, your attention. I am quite beyond visits and flowers but I do distribute The Collected Short Stories among the doctors. They seem in the end to be mostly what I've written---even Honora Wapshot is forgotten—and thank you for your help with them.

Yours,
John

One of the great disappointments brought about by his illness was his being forced to miss Fred's wedding. He'd been at Sloan-Kettering in the city for a while, but toward the end he was treated at a hospital in Mount Kisco.

February71982

Dear Fred and Mary,

This ismy second day home from the ordeal in Mt. Kisco. I still weigh 120 pounds and can barely type. It would be very easy to write a tearsome letter about how I feel about missing the wedding but you all know this and you all well know how deeply I love you. On lighter matters I now have a young doctor named Schneider who, through having glimpsed pictures of me on horseback and glimpses of the house imagines that we live a luxurious life on a vast, well-staffed horse ranch. We are terribly afraid that he will make a housecall to find me dragging the garbage pail up the hill while your mother brings in the groceries from Shoprite. I want to put a sign at the top of the hill that says:"The Cheevers do not live here," or "This is the Cheever's smallest house."

Both Susie and Ben have been wonderfully helpful about the pain and loneliness of this sort of misfortune but Janet and Ben think I ought to have a Betamax and spend my days and nights in bed watching old movies like "What Price Glory". I keep telling them that I don't want to see "What Price Glory" again but Ben pats me on the head and says "But Daddy you won't know how wonderful a Betamax is until you have one." They were going to install one yesterday but mercifully they were invited to a party in Boston. It all goes to show that the unsafe aspects of illness can be quite dangerous.

How idle it seems to send my love to you both since itseems to fill this room. The sensible thing for me to do is to imagine some date when I will be well enough to travel and then to travel to Palo Alto.

Love,<br>John

Mr. John Cheever. Cedar Lane. Ossining, New York 10562

March 9th,1982

Dear Fred,

I'm at the dinning room table, about to answer twenty letters on thet fancy stationary Sara Spencer gives me forChristmas but I did want to tell you how pleased I am that you are thinking again of law school. The quality of your memory and the application of your intelligence to one of our most decadent professions is bound to produce an interesting situation. There is also another piece of good news. The platinum seems to have begun to reduce the size of the tumors. This is the first good news I've had since November. I go back to the hospital on Monday for more platinum.

Love,<br>John

March 21st,1982

Dear Fred,

It's always good to have you letters and you've sent us quite a few. Now that I spend so much time in the bed-pan circuit I have difficulty finding material. Now and then characters stray my way. Across the hall in the hospital was an old man who would tell anyone: "You see my wife has this habit of buying me hearing aids, for presents. These damn things cost around four hundred and fifty dollars. Well she buys me these hearing aids for presents and then she puts then in my pants pocket and she puts my pants in the washing machine. Three times she's done this. Once in the motel in Palm Springs I caught her putting my pants in the laundromat with the hearing aid in the pocket. Three times now, I don't know why she does this."

Last week all of the nurses were good looking and pleasant. My ex-rays haven't been checked on this last one but the doctor said: I think we're rounding a bend. I do hope we can get along without platinum. It is not painful and the nauseau is no worse than seasickness but I don't like having that much heavy metal dripped into my system. They gave me the platinum at two on Thursday. I got an intelligent nurse to see that my door was kept closed from six o'clock on so that I could do my vomiting in private. I got up at half-past five in the morning and packed my bag. A nurse took out my intravenous connections at seven and at eight o'clock Art Spear, bright and cheerful came to take me home.

Your mother's patience with both Mazie and me goes unbroken. Mazie has developed a ghastly yelp which she uses freely. I have my own noises. Last night something I ate gave me ghastly stomach cramps and I spent much of the night on the toilet, wracked with evacuations. However this made me very happy because I felt that I was ridding myself of that unnatural chemical balance I have supported for three months. Towards dawn I felt that I was at long last John CheeverFor all I know, I maybe. I see the doctor tomorrow.

Love
John

Cedar Lane
Ossining, New York 10562

April third

Dear Saul,

With you thinking generously of me in Chicago I am bound to live; but I'm still medically on the ropes and receive infusions of heavy metal and the dregs of the Adriatic. I was told last week—one could have guessed it—that the miracle worker who can cure my cancer is in Bucharest. I can see him watering his dying cyclamens between administering huge doses of horse urine. I do seem to feel better as the days grow longer and at this rate I ought to be myself by summer when all the flowers are in bloom.

Love,
John

My mother was having a studio built for printing.

[April 1982]

Dear Fred,

. . . I decided early on Easter morning that I was bored with cancer and would have it no more and I've felt much better since then . . .

The snow is nearly gone and they're putting up the floor in your mother's studio. It ought to be done in another two weeks. Now that I've thrown cancer out the window I'll have to get back to some kind of work. Maybe your mother will let me use her press.

Yours,
John

Fred was expressing misgivings about getting a law degree. He had been working as a librarian.

April 17th, 1982

Dear Fred,

To search out a career through finding a group of sympathetic colleagues seems to me madness. The tradition of the guilds (and the

Italian schools) ended with the sixteenth century when the recognition of individual talent ended the middle ages. To seek sympathetic colleagues is rather like seeking a guild. You have your own brilliant destiny and as you develop your accomplishments you will, with luck, find yourself in the company of men and women who are similarily accomplished. Can you think of a distinguished man in any field who chose his profession because of the splendor of his colleagues. This is not fatherly advice. The only fatherly advice I have ever given you is not to eat your peas off a knife.

On librarians I do speak with predjudice. The profession in general has always seemed to me like the legitimization and financing of an impulse to collect old socks. It has always seemed to enjoy people who would enjoy handling old socks, smelling old socks and legislating catagories of old socks. But then you know I am terribly predjudiced.

Since the first announcement of Susie's pregnancy the growth and arrival of little Sarah has seem to be the most natural sort of growth and today they take the baby home. Tad is quite as involved in the naturalness as Susie and they both seem to me to be quite lovely people.

Ben and Janet had just left for Boston to run in the marathon. My love to Mary.

Yours,
John

April 25th, 1982

Dear Saul,

Whenever I win any sort of prize I always take out of the middle drawer on my left a yellowed newspaper copy of your beautiful Nobel Prise speech and crib from this. Now I find myself being given a medal on Tuesday and your Nobel Speech has has vanished. The last time I used it the paper seemed very close to disinergration and I packed it neatly between two boards. Now I've opened every drawer here and it isn't to be found. I can't very well say that I'm unable to thank them because I lost Saul Bellow's Novel Prize speech. I have another day.

They've taken me off a medicine that involved letting diluted platinum into my blood and I'm much happier about this. My mainstay now is a pollution that is distilled from the Adriatic. It costs $250 dollars a shot but it makes me feel a great deal better and I'm sure I'll be well by summer when we might meet.

Love,<br>John

This is to Philip Roth. His companion was the actress Claire Bloom.

Cedar Lane,Ossining<br>May tenth [1982]

Dear Phil,

We'd love to see you and we're here most of the time. It would be very exciting to meet Claire. The literary news is mixed. John Updikes' novel seems to me first-rate. My medal wasn't gold but then I don't think my novel was terribly good. I have been attacked by a nuisance of a cancer. My veins are filled, once a week with a Neapolitan carpet-cleaner distilled from the Adriatic and I am as bald as an egg. However I still get around and am mean to cats. We'd love to see you.

Yours,<br>John

Perhaps this is nonsense, but it does seem to me that my father had some ability to predict the future. Besty Logan spiked a bottle of Teriyaki Sauce with "enough ant poison to kill a family" and put the bottle back on the shelf at Buy Brite in *Oh What a Paradise It Seems*. This was long before the first Tylenol poisoning. I don't think that that criminal read my father's book, but I do think that they both sensed the appropriateness of striking out at late-twentieth-century American society in this fashion. It's difficult, of course, to distinguish between a brilliant, sympathetic description and a demonstration of extrasensory perception, but I did always feel that my father was tapped into some deep underground streams.

There are other examples of apparent soothsaying, but the one that comes most cruelly to mind is cancer. My father died of cancer. I can't be absolutely certain, but I believe that the seriousness of his condition was kept from him for some time. It was certainly kept from me. His illness was first diagnosed in 1981, but he'd written about the disease in *The Wapshot Scandal* in 1964.

. . . Cancer was a commonplace but men and women, at its mercy, were told that their pain was some trifling complication while behind their backs their brothers and their sisters, their husbands and wives, would whisper: "All we can hope is that they will go quickly." This cruel and absolute hypocrisy was bound to backfire and in the end no one could tell or count upon being told if that pain in the middle was the knock of death or some trifling case of gas. Most maladies have their mythologies, their populations, their scenery and their grim jokes. The Black Plague had masques, street songs and dances. Tuberculosis in its heyday was like a civilization where a caste of comely, brilliant and doomed men and women fell in love, waltzed and invented privileges for their disease; but here was the grappling hand of death disinfected by a social conspiracy of all its reality. "Why you'll be up and around in no time at all," says the nurse to the dying man. "You want to dance at your daughter's wedding, don't you? Don't you want to see your daughter married? Well, then, we can't expect to get better if we're not more cheerful, can we?"

When my father got sick himself, he encountered the very hypocrisy that he had abhorred in print so many years before. I can recall one terrible scene in which a doctor who had alluded to a good chance of recovery said to another doctor that "anything we do from this point on will be palliative." My father was right there, listening. I presume that the doctor thought my father wouldn't know what palliative meant.

Graham Greene touches on the prophetic powers of fiction in his auto-biographical book *Ways of Escape*. Greene suggests that the dream world from which the author draws is open to the future as well as the past. He wonders if Zola had not written of his own death, "Was Zola, when he wrote of the imprisoned miners dying of poisoned air drawing something from a memory of his own death smothered with fumes from his coke stove. Perhaps it's just as well for an author not to re-read the books he has written, there may be too many hints from an unhappy future."

When I think of my father's death, I go back to the fiction; I think of the last chapter of *Falconer*. I recall that, like my father, Ezekiel Farragut was once in a body bag. My father used to say of fiction that it was an exercise of memory that was imperfectly understood. Was the last chapter of *Falconer* a recollection of the past, or the future? Farragut's cell mate, Chicken Number Two, had died and been zippered into a body bag. Farragut escaped by taking the place of the corpse.

. . . Cunning was needed; cunning and the courage to take his rightful place in things as he saw them. He unzipped the sack. . . . He put Chicken into his own bed and was about to climb into the burial sack when some chance, some luck, some memory led him to take a blade out of his razor before he lay down in the cerements and zipped them up over his face. It was very close in there, but the smell of his grave was no more than the plain smell of canvas; the smell of some tent.

The men who came to get him must have worn rubber soles because he didn't hear them come in and didn't know they were there until he felt himself being lifted up off the floor and carried. His breath had begun to wet the cloth of his shroud and his head had begun to ache. He opened his mouth very wide to breathe, afraid that they would hear the noise he made and more afraid that the stupid animalism of his carcass would panic and that he would convulse and yell and ask to be let out. Now the cloth was wet, the wetness strengthened the stink of rubber and his face was soaked and he was panting. Then the panic passed and he heard the opening and the closing of the first two gates and felt himself being carried down the slope of the tunnel. He had never, that he remembered, been carried before. (His long-dead mother must have carried him from place to place, but he could not remember this.) The sensation of being carried belonged to the past, since it gave him an unlikely feeling of innocence and purity. How strange to be carried so late in life and toward nothing that he truly knew, freed, it seemed, from his erotic crudeness, his facile scorn and his chagrined laugh—not a fact, but a chance, something like the afternoon light on high trees, quite useless and thrilling. How strange to be living and to be grown and to be carried.

[Left alone on the ground he] got the razor blade out of his pocket and began to cut, parallel to the zipper. The blade penetrated the canvas, but slowly. He needed time, but he would not pray for time or pray for anything else. He would settle for the stamina of love, a presence he felt like the beginnings of some stair. The blade fell from his fingers onto his shirt and in a terrified and convulsive and clumsy lurch he let the blade slip into the sack. Then, groping for it wildly, he cut his fingers, his trousers and his thigh. Stroking his thigh, he could feel the wetness of the blood, but this seemed to have happened to someone else. With the wet blade between his fingers, he went on cutting away at his bonds. Once his knees were free he raised them, ducked his head and shoulders from under the crown and stepped out of his grave.

So John Cheever, like Ezekiel Farragut, has escaped us, but never underground.

# INDEX

# THE HISTORY OF VINTAGE

The famous American publisher Alfred A. Knopf (1892–1984) founded Vintage Books in the United States in 1954 as a paperback home for the authors published by his company. Vintage was launched in the United Kingdom in 1990 and works independently from the American imprint although both are part of the international publishing group, Random House.

Vintage in the United Kingdom was initially created to publish paperback editions of books acquired by the prestigious hardback imprints in the Random House Group such as Jonathan Cape, Chatto & Windus, Hutchinson and later William Heinemann, Secker & Warburg and The Harvill Press. There are many Booker and Nobel Prize-winning authors on the Vintage list and the imprint publishes a huge variety of fiction and non-fiction. Over the years Vintage has expanded and the list now includes both great authors of the past – who are published under the Vintage Classics imprint – as well as many of the most influential authors of the present.

For a full list of the books Vintage publishes, please visit our website
www.vintage-books.co.uk

For book details and other information about the classic authors we publish, please visit the Vintage Classics website
www.vintage-classics.info